Political Ideology
in the
Modern World

Political Ideology in the Modern World

Bernard Susser
Bar-Ilan University

Allyn and Bacon
Boston • London • Toronto • Sydney • Tokyo • Singapore

To Shellie and Donna
in the hope that you grow up in a gentler, more humane world

Senior Editor: Steve Hull
Developmental Editor: Carol Alper
Editorial Assistant: Brenda Conaway
Cover Coordinator: Linda Knowles
Editorial-Production Service: Electronic Publishing Services Inc.
Marketing Manager: Lisa Kimball

Copyright © 1995 by Allyn and Bacon
A Simon & Schuster Company
Needham Heights, Massachusetts 02194

Library of Congress Cataloging-in-Publication Data

Susser, Bernard, 1942–
    Political ideology in the modern world / Bernard Susser.
        p.   cm.
    Includes bibliographical references and index.
    ISBN 0-02-418442-X
    1. Political science—History.   2. Right and left (Political science)—History.   3. Ideology—History.   I. Title.
JA83.S778   1994
320.5—dc20   94-21992
                                                             CIP

Printed in the United States of America

10   9   8   7   6   5   4   3   2   1   98   97   96   95   94

All photographs reproduced with permission of The Bettmann Archive.

Contents

Preface   x

Chapter 1: The Nature of Ideological Discourse   1
What Is Modern in Modern Ideology?   1
　　Summary   4
　　Summary   9
Ideology: Definitions in Pursuit of an Elusive Concept   9
　　Summary   14
Ideology: The History of a Concept   15
　　The French Revolution   15
　　De Tracy and the Origins of the Term Ideology   16
　　Marxism and the Concept of Ideology   17
　　From Ideology to the Sociology of Knowledge   19
　　Ideology as Fanaticism: A Restrictive Definition   22
　　Ideology's Positive Role: The Non-Restrictive Definition   23
　　　　Summary   25
Suggestions for Further Reading   27

**Chapter 2: Conservatism: What Conservatives Want
to Conserve and Why   28**
From Traditionalism to Conservatism: Old Wine in New Bottles   28
Conservative Themes   32
　　Precedent and Prescription—Edmund Burke   33
　　　　Summary   38
　　　　Critiques   39
　　Truth is Universal and Unchanging—Leo Strauss   40
　　　　Summary   44
　　　　Critiques   45
　　Human Imperfectability: Saint Augustine, Thomas Hobbes, and
　　　　Sigmund Freud   46
　　　　Summary   49
　　　　Critiques   49
　　The Necessity for Hierarchy: Ortega y Gasset   50
　　　　Summary   53
　　　　Critiques   54
Suggestions for Further Reading   55

Chapter 3: From Liberalism to Social Democracy (1)   57
Modern Liberalism: Dominant and Ambiguous   57

Liberalism's Substance: The History of an Idea 59
Classical Liberalism 59
John Locke 60
Summary 62
Adam Smith 62
Summary 64
The Revision of Classical Liberalism 64
Utilitarianism 67
John Stuart Mill 69
Summary 70
Welfare Liberalism's Practical Program 71
Liberalism: The Enduring Themes 73
Contemporary Liberalism: A House Divided 77
Contemporary Classical Liberalism 77
Friedrich A. Hayek 77
Summary 82
Robert Nozick 82
Summary 86
Suggestions for Further Reading 87

Chapter 4: From Liberalism to Social Democracy (2) **88**
Critiques of Classical Liberalism 88
The Liberalism of John Rawls 95
Pre-Rawlsian Liberalism 95
Rawls's Argument 95
The Original Position 96
What System Would Be Chosen? 97
Determining a Just Distribution of Resources 99
Summary 101
Critiques 103
From Welfare Liberalism to Social Democracy 106
Fabian Socialism 107
Socialism on the Continent 108
American Welfare Liberals and Social Democracy 110
What Divides Welfare Liberals from Social Democrats? 111
The Problems of Contemporary Social Democracy 113
Summary 114
Critiques 115
Suggestions for Further Reading 115

Chapter 5: The Radical Left: Marx's Vision **117**
The Downfall of a Colossus 117
The Origins of Modern Socialism 118
The Utopian Socialists 120
Georg Friedrich Hegel 122

Karl Marx   125
    The Young Hegelians   125
    Marxist Materialism   127
    Bourgeois Dictatorship   128
    The Concept of Alienation   129
    Capitalism's Revolutionary Role   131
    The Contradictions of Capitalism   132
    Boom and Bust: The Intensifying Crises of Capitalism   133
    The Dialectics of Liberation   134
    The Revolutionaries in Power   136
    Future Communist Society   137
        Critiques   139
Suggestions for Further Reading   143

Chapter 6: The Radical Left: Marxist Practice   144
Pre-revolutionary Russia: Radicalism and Backwardness   144
    Revolutionary Prospects   144
    The Two Voices of Russian Marxism: Mensheviks and Bolsheviks
        145
    Bolshevik Voluntarism   147
    The Bourgeois Revolution and the Peasantry   148
    The Revolutionary Ferment Begins   151
    Ten Days That Shook the World   153
The Post-Revolutionary Years   154
    Civil War and the NEP   154
    Leninism and Marxism   155
    Stalinist Totalitarianism   156
The Chinese Revolutionary Experience   160
    The Historical Context   160
    Mao's Marxism   162
    Mao as Military Tactician   163
    Maoist Victory and the Great Cultural Revolution   164
The Non-Marxist Radical Left   167
    Anarchism: Pacific and Violent   167
    Anarcho-Syndicalism   170
    The New Left   171
        Critiques   172
Suggestions for Further Reading   173

Chapter 7: Fascism: Dead or Alive?   174
Fascism in Historical Context   174
The Rise of Fascism and Naziism: Historical Parallels   175
Fascism: A Perplexing Phenomenon   179
Fascism: The Contours of an Unprecedented Phenomenon   183

Fascism as a Reactionary Mass Mobilizing Movement   183
Fascism and the Crisis of the Middle Class   185
Fascist Ethical Idealism and the Middle Class   188
Fascist Totalitarianism: Organic Society, Nation, and State   189
Fascism and Racism   192
The Fuhrer (Leader) Principle   195
Fascist Corporatism   196
Theories of Fascism   *199*
Class-Based Theories   199
Mass-Based Theories   201
Fascism: Dead or Alive?   *203*
Suggestions for Further Reading   *205*

Chapter 8: Nationalism: Very Much Alive   206
Nationalism as an Ideology: Some Initial Considerations   *206*
Nationalism and World-View Ideologies   207
Summary   210
Modern Nationalism as a Historical Novelty   *210*
The Pre-Nationalist Era   211
The Dawning of National Consciousness   212
Summary   213
The Affinity Between Nationalism and Democracy   *213*
Nationalism and the Activation of the Masses   214
Summary   217
Nationalist Discourse: Rhetoric and Substance   *217*
The Idea of the Nation-State   217
Nations as the Building Blocks of Humanity   217
Nations as Organic Entities   219
Nationalism as Collective Egoism   219
Summary   220
What Constitutes a Nation?   *221*
Objective or Subjective Criteria?   221
Are Nations the Source of Nationalism?   222
Summary   225
Pluralism Undermines the Classical Nation-State Idea   226
The Melting Pot vs. Multi-Culturalism   228
Challenges to the Denationalized State   229
Summary   229
Nationalism: For and Against—A Historical Balance Sheet   *230*
The Case for the Prosecution   230
The Case for the Defense   232
Summary   233
When Nationalism Becomes Pathological   233
Suggestions for Further Reading   *235*

Chapter 9: Contemporary Ideological Currents: Feminism, Environmentalism, and the Storm over the University **237**

The Legacy of the Sixties   237
Feminism   239
    The History of Feminism   239
    Feminism's Unique Revolutionary Challenge   242
The Varieties of Feminist Thought   244
    Moderate/Liberal Feminism   244
      Critiques   246
    Socialist Feminism   247
      Critiques   249
    Radical Feminism   249
      Critiques   252
Environmentalism, Ecology, and Green Politics   253
    Environmentalism as an Ideology   253
Planetary Crisis   254
    The Rise of an Ecological Consciousness   255
    The Challenge to Anthropocentric Humanism   257
    Light Green, Middle Green, Dark Green   258
      Critiques   262
The Storm Over the University   263
    The Challenge to Academia   263
      Critiques   267
Suggestions for Further Reading   269

Chapter 10: Epilogue: Toward the Third Millennium   **270**

Civil Society v. Grand Mobilizing Ideologies   270
    A Contemporary Ideological Balance Sheet   271
The Right-Left Continuum: How Relevant Is It?   273
Ideology in the Global Village   274
Ideology in a Relativist Age   275

Glossary   **277**

Index   **285**

Preface

It was above all dissatisfaction with the existing ideology texts that prompted me to undertake this project. The available texts seem to divide into two broad categories. There are, first of all, those that present modern ideologies as cut-and-dried doctrines ready for ingestion. They deal in what used to be called "cepts," concepts truncated to bite-size portions that can easily be memorized. Why these ideas are important, or why "the best and the brightest" so often become passionate about them, a reader may well fail to grasp. Frequently these texts display a palpable impatience with abstract political thinking—perhaps because it resists easy summaries—and a tendency to escape into the world of practice where ideology is transformed into manageable political programs.

The other textbook variant deals with modern ideology as if it were roughly identical with modern political theory. Despite a welcome respect for ideas, these texts display a certain inert academic quality remote from the ardor and commitment that attends authentic ideological debate. The genealogy of ideas traced back to Plato and Aristotle often takes precedence over conveying the intensity and vitality of these ideas for our age. What can be easily overlooked is that these modern ideologies are in active competition for the reader's loyalty.

My objective has been to write a text that is idea centered but at the same time faithful to the real dynamism of contemporary ideological debate. Beyond attempting to engage readers at the level of the ideological arguments themselves, I have tried to draw them into the spirited give and take that ideological controversy ignites.

To accomplish this, I have presented most ideological positions as if they were being argued by a convinced advocate (although I could not bring myself to do this when it came to the chapters on totalitarian ideologies). The absence of any obvious authorial point of view is intended to heighten the sense of personal challenge with which the reader is confronted.

More importantly, I have attempted to capture the atmosphere of ideological debate by closing the presentation of each ideological position with a series of critiques and counter-arguments such as those that might be levelled by a sophisticated antagonist. Although these critiques are quite earnest in the points they raise, at times they are deliberately provocative. They raise arguments designed to catalyze thought and prompt a response. Occasionally a certain stridency of tone, so familiar to ideological debate, is introduced in order to incite animated rejoinders. The questions and criticisms raised in these sections may serve as the basis for classroom discussions or written assignments.

Totalitarian communism and fascism are excepted from this practice—for obvious reasons—although Marxism itself is not. Nationalism, with its essentially primordial quality of identification, is difficult to deal with at the level of reasoned critique. Instead, I have confronted the arguments of defenders and detractors of nationalism in the context of a grand historical balance sheet.

One impediment to holding a reader's attention that is prevalent in contemporary textbooks is the practice of dividing the text into fragments—normally not more than a few paragraphs each—in the hope that they will be more easily digestible by restless students. A boldface heading begins each fragment, as if a new subject is being broached. This practice, I believe, is counter-productive. It chops integral arguments into unnatural pieces and makes it difficult to develop sufficient intellectual momentum with which to carry the reader along.

Although the chapters below are broken into broad constituent sections, I have preferred to keep arguments intact insofar as I could. To ease the reader's way, I have chosen to place summaries of a few words each in the margins of the text. In this way, the reader can quickly scan the text via these helpful markers while preserving the natural flow of ideas and arguments.

A word about the opening theoretical chapter. It may be daunting for some students. Abstract thinking is required to grasp the different theories of ideology and the cognitive uniqueness of modern ideological discourse. I am convinced that without such an analysis the discussion of ideology would be irreparably flawed. Passing over the essential theoretical issues, as is so often done, leaves a gaping hole right at the center of comprehension. Moreover, the opening chapter can have substantial pedagogical utility: the various theories can be profitably tested against the ideological positions as they are presented in the subsequent chapters.

I have departed from the standard practice of placing social democracy in the chapter on left-wing ideologies. Instead, it is juxtaposed to welfare liberalism in the context of two chapters (Chapters 3 and 4) that cover the ground from liberalism to social democracy. Contemporary social democracy clearly has far more in common with the liberal democratic tradition than it does with Stalinist or Maoist communism. Placing it alongside the totalitarian left is didactically misleading and, moreover, would not provide the opportunity to compare it with those welfare-liberal positions that are among its main ideological sparring partners. Whatever its historical genealogy, social democracy is today a mainstream ideology in West European politics and should be dealt with as such.

The signs of the times are very evident in all that follows. The collapse of communism, for example, looms large throughout the entire discussion. On the other hand, some ideological phenomena no longer merit attention. Titoism, for example, has been dealt a double coup de grace: communism has disintegrated, and Tito's own brand of this discredited position has been violently overrun by tragic events.

One further sign of the times is a full chapter devoted to nationalism as an ideology. (To the best of my knowledge, this has no parallel in other comparable texts.) With the alarming resurgence of ethnic nationalism in the countries of the former communist world, an extended discussion seems mandatory. Nationalism, however, is not an orderly set of beliefs that can be logically pursued from premise to conclusion. Hence, the chapter is more in the nature of a description and analysis of nationalism as a phenomenon than an exposition of nationalism as a systematic doctrine.

There is poetic justice in closing with a section on the current struggle over the canon that rages across American university campuses. With the ideological struggle brought right to our academic doorsteps, it becomes difficult to relate to ideology either as a lifeless adjunct to the real world of politics or as an academic exercise in political theory. This, as I have said, is the book's underlying message.

I would like to thank my colleagues, who read all or part of the manuscript, for their helpful criticism: Gordon P. Henderson, Widener University; George Klosko, University of Virginia; Michael E. Kraft, University of Wisconsin; and John Stanley, University of California.

Chapter *1*

The Nature of Ideological Discourse

What Is Modern in Modern Ideology?

Comparing the modern and medieval

Consider the life-prospects of two children: one born into our modern Western environment as it approaches the year 2000, the other coming into the world one thousand years ago at the height of the European Middle Ages. What kinds of choices would these two children be likely to face in the course of their respective lives? How do they compare in regard to the variety of options available to them? Finally, how many of their decisions would be so overwhelmingly dictated by traditions, authorities, and orthodoxies that to speak of "decisions" at all would be to stretch the meaning of the word? Beginning with the most practical choices such as those relating to work, marriage, and place of residence, and ending with the more subtle and intangible preferences about life-style and world view, how do our two youngsters match up?

Already at birth the medieval child is a known and predictable quantity; the course of her life will hold few surprises. Her options for work, marriage, economic and social status, religious belief, place of residence, educational attainments, travel, personal joys, world view, etc., are strictly controlled by a cultural code that leaves little room for exceptions. If she is born a serf, she will marry a serf, work as a serf, live and be treated as a serf; she will be baptized and given last rites by the church; she will be illiterate. It is unlikely that she will travel more than a few score miles from the place of her birth. Her daily routine, the stages of her life, indeed the range of her thoughts are virtually given at birth. To have a birth date in the year 1000 is to have few significant options in the fashioning of one's life. By contrast, the contemporary child of Western culture travels light. No one, of course, is free from historical constraints, from socio-economic conditions, from racial, ethnic and sexual givens; no one begins life with an empty slate. But even the most timid contemporary conformist is confronted with a gallery of choices so vast that it would cause acute vertigo in his medieval counterpart. Careers are, for the very most part, chosen. Only rarely does one inherit a life-pursuit—and even then it is an inheritance one chooses to accept. Whom one chooses to marry, how many times one will marry, what the respective roles of the marriage partners will be, whether they will choose to have children and so on, all these can hardly be anticipated at birth. Even sexual preference has become a legitimate area for choice.

The economic fortunes of a contemporary youth, although significantly related to initial social circumstances, are nowhere near as predetermined as those of our medieval precursors. Nor are religious beliefs, or the lack of them. Geographic mobility and the portability of life open up choices for contemporary youth not even dreamed of in earlier ages. The style of life one elects, the world-view one espouses, the human relations one chooses to forge are all part of a modern kaleidoscope of choice that has no parallel in the lives led a millennium ago. This contrast between medieval and modern individuals carries through, of course, to their respective societies. Parallel to the restricted and predictable quality of private life, medieval social organization exhibited a static quality that stands in stark contrast to the tumultuous character of modern public life. Medieval and modern social thought also provide a study in contrasts. If medieval ideas on politics and society reflected an authoritative and encompassing orthodoxy, modern political thought has a dynamic, inventive, and unfinished quality. To better appreciate these unprecedented qualities of modernity, we would do well to take a brief detour into the mental world of medieval society. By understanding what preceded the modern style of political debate, we will become more sensitive to the unique qualities that mark contemporary ideological discourse.

Medieval political discourse   Above all, medieval thought conceived of social organization—the ways in which ranks, offices, resources, power, privileges, duties, and rights were to be distributed—as rooted in an eternal and immutable order of things. What justified the privileges of the lord, the subordination of the serf, and the authority of the priest was no mere historical accident. Authority and privilege were not the consequence of fleeting struggles for power or for economic dominance. Least of all were they the result of deliberate human choice and design. Human social order mirrored the absolute, God-willed, universal nature of things. Like the celestial hosts and the laws of nature, social order inhered in the very order of Creation.

It was an order against which there was no appeal. A **great chain of being** linked the most high to the lowliest in a God-sanctioned and God-mandated hierarchy. The form of medieval public life was not, therefore, one among many ways in which power and privilege could be distributed; it represented the single legitimate form of human association. Metaphorically speaking, the social order was chiseled out of cosmic stone. Beyond it there was only barbarism, blasphemy, usurpation, and chaos. When a serf mutinied against his lord, he not merely violated the lord's legal and traditional authority; he violated, in a fundamental sense, the essential order of things. Political revolt, understandably, was often next of kin to charges of religious heresy. Might did not make right as some cynical moderns have been known to observe; might was right.

It should come as no surprise then that anyone advocating a political viewpoint in medieval society confronted challenges quite different from those with which we are familiar today. Above all, there was no room for debate about **first principles**, the unconditionally accepted and piously affirmed assumptions of all public discourse. Hence, rival political camps did not justify their positions by arguing for incompatible world-views or opposing conceptions of public life. The premises of hierarchy and tradition, religious faith, ecclesiastical authority, royal and aristocratic privilege, etc., were the indisputable pillars upon which the entire medieval edifice stood. If you dared to challenge these ancestral truths, you as much as declared yourself a pariah—one whose views were best dealt with by excommunication or the gallows.

Traditional societies

Societies such as these are often described as **traditional** in character, that is, their members think and act within the compass of a single unchallenged way of life. At times, these prescribed forms of life are so dominant that no awareness of viable alternatives exists. For many traditional societies there is simply no other way of doing things. Indeed, in the absence of substantial challenges to their ideas and practices, some traditional societies may find it unnecessary to defend them at all.

None of this means, of course, that medieval society was a world of harmony and agreement. Traditional societies, such as those of the Middle Ages, are often no more peaceful than modern ones. What stands out, nonetheless, is the sharp contrast between the medieval and the modern style of political discourse. Medieval political opponents, as hostile as they might have been to each other, operated within a single, mandatory intellectual frame of reference. Although political enemies might make spirited arguments for different interpretations of Scripture, emphasize different precedents in the tradition, or give greater or lesser weight to different authorities, there were recognized borders of discourse outside of which only the foolhardy would dare to venture. As with our medieval child, the range of available options was strictly limited.

Pre-modern ideology

This restricted mode of socio-political discourse may be characterized as **pre-modern ideology**.[1] This is not meant to imply that the political thought of a traditional society like that of the Middle Ages was free from those values, interests, and self-justifications that ideologies typically express. In this very basic sense, all societies—traditional and modern alike—have ideologies. What traditional medieval political discourse lacked was precisely the quality that is essential to the modern ideological contest: the clash between numerous, fundamentally incompatible, often belligerent world-views.

Modern ideology

Modern ideology is a bustling, not always friendly, marketplace of ideas in which a host of political positions contend with one another in a Babel of dissonant voices and combative accents. Sharp disagreement is probably more prevalent than

---

1. The "age of ideology," we might say modern ideology, is generally thought to have commenced in the mid-eighteenth century. See for example F. Watkins, *The Age of Ideology: Political Thought 1750 to the Present* (Englewood Cliffs, N.J.: Prentice Hall, 1965).

accommodation or consensus. And these disagreements range over the most basic of questions: from incompatible assumptions about human character, to differing interpretations of human history, to conflicting blueprints for social organization, to irreconcilable visions of the human future.

Modern and medieval political debate also differ in the way in which one's competitors are to be treated. When a medieval political contender heard the opposition denying the divinity of the Scriptures, the debate ceased and the Inquisition began. There was no need, indeed it was positively demeaning, to respond to such blasphemous talk. Modern ideological advocates, by contrast, know very well that beyond presenting their own ideas attractively they must also consider, criticize, and disqualify what the competition is offering. Indeed, a great deal of modern ideology commences with a critique of adversarial positions. Contemporary ideological debate typically involves both discourse and counter-discourse; it defends and attacks simultaneously.[2]

Modern ideology's typically dynamic and conflict-ridden character is clearly related to the decline of the medieval view that our social order reflects the Divine order. Ideological discourse takes on its characteristically volatile modern qualities when this central assumption of medieval political discourse loses its hold on the Western imagination. Today, late into the twentieth century, it has become a truism that human societies are human designs, that they result from human decisions and human will. Political choices are exactly that: choices. What has been constructed so might have been constructed otherwise. Human political arrangements are conventions that have been adopted; they represent the sum of decisions, pacts, agreements, and covenants that we have made. To put it aphoristically: social arrangements are not natural "givens" at all; they are in fact "takens"—decisions taken by real people at some concrete time.

Summary   To summarize the argument to this point:

1. Modern ideology involves the (often bitter) clash of many competing world-views.
2. Modern ideology involves counter-discourse, or the disqualification of opposing views through critique and reasoned argument.
3. Modern ideology involves the recognition that social arrangements are conventional and what has been arranged in one way may be reconstructed differently.

Taken together these three elements provide the typical context of modern ideological debate, one in which many incompatible world-views compete with each other to design social conventions in accordance with their outlooks. But why has the ideological style we have just described become an irremovable fixture in the public life of all modern political communities? Why are ideology and modernity so closely related?

---

2. See Alvin Gouldner's *The Dialectic of Ideology and Technology* (New York: Seabury Press, 1976).

What is modern in
modern ideology?

Answering this question brings us close to the very center of what is modern in modern political life. With the collapse of the medieval theo-political monolith, a new and strikingly different framework of political discourse arose.[3] From this historical crucible emerged a brave new world in which political reasoning could no longer rely on transcendent, ancestral, orthodox—that is to say, non-political—arguments. To justify a political position now required arguing for it in explicitly human and political terms; it required arguments that were, to use Alvin Gouldner's term, "world referring." Political argument now needed to be justified by the nature of human character, the attributes of human social and economic life, the logic of human history, and the vision of a human future.

Justification
of ideology

This probably sounds easier than it is. Having lost the absolute anchor of medieval theo-political certainties, modern political reasoning was left stranded and disoriented. What, after all, could compare with the confidence inspired by a God-sanctioned social order resting on unconditional conceptions of right and wrong? Having eaten from the fruit of modern knowledge and having suffered expulsion from the Eden of certainty, what could legitimate the standards by which we choose to order our public life? What kind of political argument could now justify the apportionment of power, resources, and privilege when the collapse of definitive standards seemed to leave us without any standards at all? The problem is not, of course, that there are no such standards available to political actors, but that there are too many. And each of them possesses a certain plausibility. What criteria are we to use in selecting between the many different political ideals and programs that so ardently vie for our loyalty?

Let us put the problem more concretely: political communities may be organized around innumerable organizational and moral principles. Some societies allocate their resources according to the standard of military valor—the great warrior is also entrusted with political leadership. Others see religious or spiritual virtues as paramount. Still others put great stock in genealogy: those of aristocratic origins are accorded special privilege. Western democracies apportion their power and resources according to the criteria of majority rule, due process of law, and individual rights. Often the historical destiny of the nation is used to justify political action. Other standards that have been put into practice (or at least proposed for use) are racial purity, philosophical knowledge, gender, age, merit, wealth, tradition, scientific expertise, and equality—and the list could go on interminably. Just as a modern youth confronts the necessity for choice, modern citizens confront a virtually limitless supply of contending criteria for the organization of political life.

This great variety of incompatible principles, many of them competing within the same political community, makes the justification of choice mandatory. The modern mind simply cannot rest content with the argument that "It must be done this way because this is the way it has always been done" or that there is a single

---

3. One much admired attempt to describe at least a part of this transition is Quentin Skinner's *The Foundations of Modern Political Thought*, 2 vols. (Cambridge: Cambridge University Press, 1978).

divine recipe for social organization. Nor can we easily deny that there are many who are neither crazed nor obtuse nor evil who advocate political principles different from those we cherish. Justification is, therefore, of the essence. How are we to justify the apportionment of resources—almost always in short supply—when every Tom, Dick, and Sally clamor for their hefty share of the pickings and offer plausible but incompatible arguments for their entitlements?

The consequences of choice

Choosing between the many available political options and justifying one's choice is not merely an intellectual problem. These choices have very concrete consequences for real people. If a political community chooses to adopt the criterion of military valor or scientific expertise by which to organize its entitlements and policies, pacifists and poets are not likely to rejoice. They would have to live their lives in the shadow of those whom these principles favor. Even justifying "one person, one vote" requires denying the not-unfounded claims of the well-informed to a special voice in public life. Every criterion, including the most democratic and representative, necessarily entails denying another criterion, thereby disadvantaging specific groups in society.

The arguments justifying these choices, therefore, must do more than merely present a reasonable case. They must convince those who stand to lose that their sacrifices are necessary and fair; they must underwrite and legitimate a public life in which some will inevitably be unhappy with the outcomes of the political process. Ideological conviction requires the capacity to endure even in the face of loss, adversity, and crisis. The well-informed in a democracy, for example, must recognize that, however defensible their claims to a special hearing may be, the rights of the many to equal representation must come first. It is not surprising then that ideological belief tends to require considerably greater passion, depth, certainty, and commitment than most other preferences and tastes.

Ideologies pursue power

Conviction, however, is not enough. Convictions are notoriously capricious and unstable. To justify the controversial choices that modern societies must make requires something more: that ideological convictions be wedded to power. Ideologies refuse—if they can help it—to remain at the level of inspiring ideals or philosophic speculation. Ideologies are ideas in pursuit of power. They strive to transform their convictions into living practice by capturing the organs of political control. Ideology's most unique and unprecedented feature may well be its attempt to authoritatively design social systems according to its espoused ideas.

As children of the "age of ideology," for whom all of this is overwhelmingly familiar, we may be forgiven for not being startled by its uniqueness. After all, it is difficult for us to imagine a political world not constructed by the ideas we choose to put into practice. But for virtually all pre-modern societies, the notion that political communities are designed according to conventional principles that are freely chosen and then publicly enforced would have appeared odd, probably even incomprehensible.

Ideology transforms political power

Although we have contended that all modern societies strive to wed ideological justification with political power, the full import of this union is not as yet entirely apparent. It needs to be added that ideological justifications transform the nature of political power. To understand this let us try to imagine what a political community

Cheered by thousands of East and West Berliners, the infamous wall dividing the city is torn down (February 1990).

would look like if it chose not to justify its policies and preferred to rely entirely on coercion. Would such a regime be a viable political unit? It can be said very confidently that purely coercive political systems are non-starters. Rule by force and fear alone is simply too costly to be sustained over time.

If a coercive regime had to assume that each unguarded and unthreatened individual would invariably act against the regime's will, the regime would be confronted with a policing enterprise of colossal proportions. Were obedience nothing but the consequence of unmitigated force, a regime's resources would be rapidly squandered on the simple task of maintaining its existence. Even the most violent totalitarian regimes (perhaps one should say especially the most violent) seek to mobilize mass support for their programs. For a political community to be a going concern, at least some of the people, at least some of the time, must identify with the aims of the sovereign power.

Power, Karl Deutsch explains in a memorable analogy, is like money in the bank. Only the hopelessly simple-minded believe that somewhere deep in the bank's vault is a place in which my deposits sit, clearly marked with my name, awaiting my return to withdraw them. Not much less naive is the belief that banks have on hand at all times a quantity of cash equivalent to their total amount of deposits. In fact, available liquid cash represents only a small fraction of the money on deposit. If all a bank's depositors demanded to withdraw their cash, there would not be enough to go around. Are we then to conclude that banks are fraudulent institutions?

The question, of course, is meant to be rhetorical. Banks would indeed fail if their depositors demanded their cash simultaneously, as in fact happened during the Great Depression of the 1930s. Banking is not based on the dollar for dollar availability of cash for deposits, but on the trust felt by the vast majority of depositors that when they appear at the teller's window, their withdrawal slips will be honored. Were it not for this trust, we would all be breaking down the bank's doors; because of it, we feel no anxiety when our cash disappears into the teller's drawer in return for a stamped receipt.

Political power, like cash, will never be available in sufficient quantities if all citizens challenge a regime simultaneously. Like banks, states require a large measure of trust—**legitimacy**, in the terminology of political science—if they are to survive. What they lack in legitimacy, they need to make up for in the costly, ultimately bankrupting currency of coercion. A regime perceived as legitimate by its citizens will enjoy a considerable measure of obedience and cooperation without the need to employ force or even the threat of force. When legitimacy is prolonged and profound, obedience will go beyond simple compliance with government directives; it will become an internalized and habitual form of civic life. In such cases, we are justified in saying that power—the simple capacity to demand and enforce compliance—has been transformed into authority—the rightful and accepted exercise of control over others.

Ideology transforms power into authority

Ideology is instrumental in effecting this crucial transformation of power into authority. By providing justifications for rights and duties, it helps to render the actions of government legitimate and acceptable. Governments perceived as legitimate are able to focus more on coordination and direction and less on policing and repression. Politics becomes more a consensus-seeking activity and less an exercise in compulsion and submission. In other words, the road from brute power to rightful authority invariably passes through the justifications of ideology.

Power transforms ideology

Although ideology transforms power, it must be added that power transforms ideology as well. First of all, ideologies usually undergo processes of adaptation and reformulation when confronted by the realities of power. Rarely if ever does the purity of an ideological system survive its successful rise to power. Implementing ideological programs in the real world of practice tends to be a sobering experience. (Mirabeau, one of the key actors in the French Revolution, noted that when the radical Jacobin revolutionaries became ministers, they rarely acted as "Jacobin ministers.")

Power effects ideology in profounder ways still. As idea systems, ideologies are more or less plausible, more or less attractive political hypotheses contending in the marketplace of ideas. The accession to power transforms an ideology into a commanding and dominant public agenda in control of social resources and political choices. It becomes (to the degree it succeeds) a familiar, tangible, densely real fact of social life. An ideology in power is no longer supported simply by the persuasiveness of its arguments; it is confirmed and reinforced by our daily round of sights and sounds, by the educational institutions that shape the minds of the young, by the subtle and ever-present socialization process we all undergo, by the inducements of peer-group pressures, by the desire for personal, social, and professional advancement, and much, much more.

Empowered ideologies are no longer merely plausible intellectual alternatives. Because they are integrated into a pervasive social reality, the intellectual dilemma of choosing among the many contending ideologies is, very significantly, put to rest. Dominant ideologies cease being contenders in a free-for-all intellectual debate. When an ideology is securely wedded to power, its theoretical contestability tends to be overshadowed by the uncontestable nature of its political control. Dominant ideologies are usually absorbed unconsciously rather than selected deliberately. They become established and authoritative political axioms that we do not so much freely choose as routinely accept.

Summary   Let us recap the argument as it has developed up to this point.

1. The context of modern ideology is one in which many incompatible, often hostile political world-views contest each other for the control of political power.
2. Because a great many competing political principles seek to organize human life—principles that necessarily favor some and prejudice others— the justifying mission of ideology in political life is indispensable.
3. Without the justifications of ideology, political power would be indistinguishable from brute coercion—and coercion is far too costly and inefficient a means of social control.
4. Supported by the justifications that ideology provides, power undergoes a critical transformation and emerges as legitimate authority.
5. When ideology is securely wedded to power, it undergoes a critical transformation from a speculative political world-view competing in the marketplace of ideas to an authorized force that firmly directs the choices we make.

Ideology: Definitions in Pursuit of an Elusive Concept

Few writers on ideology have not been heard muttering about the frustrating elusiveness of the term. Although periodic efforts are made to close the definitional debate with a definition to end all definitions, spoilsports always surface to express this or that critical reservation. Why should dozens of definitions exist, but no Definition? After all, our opening discussion appears to have made a promising start towards pinning down what is involved in the ideological phenomenon. Besides, the reader is surely entitled to ask, why should the definitional wrangles of the professionals be of any interest? Why don't we simply patch together a serviceable definition and set off on more interesting and productive explorations?

Defining ideology   The answer is that the definition of ideology is not a technical issue that can be casually sidestepped. Understanding why ideology poses such insuperable definitional problems is a critical part of understanding the nature of ideology itself. We take up the obstacles to definition therefore, not out of any particular concern with narrow technicalities, but rather because there is probably no finer introduction to the ins and outs of a complex and dynamic subject.

Definitions do not come easily, first of all, because the term ideology often serves as a political insult. In one conventional usage, to be called ideological is to be accused of rigidity, fanaticism, shallowness, and conformity. In other contexts, it is to be dismissed as impractical and starry eyed. In still other usages it denotes the cynical manipulation of ideas for the sake of selfish interests. No wonder we tend to define ideology as that which our opponents have. For our own favored political ideas more honorable terms like political philosophy are preferred. Notably, almost every major political world-view, at some point in its self-portrait, will protest that it is not an ideology like the others.

Even a brief analysis of the alleged defects of ideology—as enumerated in the previous paragraph—will make it clear that they are not always compatible with one another. Ideology is said to be a cynical manipulation of ideas, yet prone to high-flying, impractical theories. But how can a system of ideas be shrewdly cynical and naively romantic at the same time? Furthermore, if ideological belief entails shallow conformism, if it is the conceptual equivalent of a uniform, how can it also be excessively theoretical or the shrewd and selfish exploitation of ideas? The received popular understanding of the term seems to include fundamental inconsistencies. What accounts for this curious muddle in our thinking?

The conservative understanding of ideology

In fact, these three alleged defects—ideology as (1) irresponsible theorizing, (2) dogmatic rigidity, and (3) ideas masking ulterior motives—correspond to the different understandings of ideology prevalent among **conservatives**, **liberals** and **radicals** respectively. For conservatives, ideology is that form of thought which conceives of political development as a rational, systematic, and deliberate process shaped by the application of human intelligence. Such hyper-rationalism falls into the category of ideology rather than genuine social understanding because it is excessively theoretical and ahistorical. In the conservative lexicon, ideologies are hasty speculative blueprints designed by pompous theoreticians who like to show off their philosophical sophistication, but have little relevance to the complex texture of real political life. For a conservative, liberal notions of enlightenment and progress—to say nothing of the radical's vision of revolution and equality—are archetypically ideological. By contrast, conservative prudence and caution are not.

The liberal understanding of ideology

For liberals, ideology smacks of fanatical conformism. Ideology is the intellectual bulldozer that crushes individual responsibility and in its place creates the faceless mass public. By replacing the pragmatic lessons of common sense available to every enlightened, self-interested individual with the quasi-religious orthodoxies of some allegedly infallible thinker or leader, ideology cultivates intolerance. A liberal would characterize ideology as that form of political thought so convinced of its own truth that it is unwilling to tolerate dissent. Moreover, by being fanatical and intolerant, ideology raises the political temperature dangerously. Ideological politics loses its character as a civil and dignified meeting of responsible individuals who accommodate each other in order to sustain a common life. For liberals, ideology destroys public life; it converts politics into a messianic pursuit, and because one does not compromise about messianic deliverance, ideology means hatred and violence. By contrast, liberalism is the soul of pragmatic intelligence. It is open-minded and open-ended, that is, non-ideological.

The radical understanding of ideology

For radicals, especially Marxists, ideology is a form of mental pathology that especially afflicts the **bourgeoisie**, i.e., the ruling class, who are systematically blind to the distorting interests that underlie their thinking. Typically, bourgeois conservatives and liberals speak as if their political programs were the incarnation of some universal logic. What they conveniently ignore, and what Marxists love to remind them of, is how perfectly their allegedly wise and humane ideas accord with their own material interests. For radicals, therefore, ideology involves an inevitable element of duplicity because it presents selfish and partisan ideas as if they were altruistic and universal. To be sure, not all such distorted ideological formulations represent deliberate trickery or outright deception. Usually, in fact, liberals and conservatives appear to sincerely believe what they say. But material interests have a way of dominating their thoughts and controlling their programs. For Marxists, the pathology of ideology is especially deadly because its distortions are so imperceptible and devious.

Definitions are ideological

Would-be definers of ideology are caught in a particularly vicious form of the Catch-22 paradox. Definitions of ideology appear to rely on prior ideological commitments. Indeed, arguing for a specific ideological position often begins with defining ideology in a specific way. Definitions are therefore not a prelude to the study of ideology, a mere preliminary formality; they are already ideological weapons in the thick of the ideological battle.[4]

Of course, not all definitions of ideology have been avowedly ideological in character. Numerous attempts at value-free, neutral descriptions have been proposed as well. But the term ideology appears to have a charged and inherently controversial character. It is sometimes spoken of as an essentially contestable term. Hence, non-committal, dictionary-like definitions are often forgotten as soon as they are offered. Avoiding the controversy seems to render these definitions hopelessly lifeless and trite—not so much false as uninteresting. Ideology may be one case in which neutrality does not add to understanding.

Even if we could adequately define ideology without entering the ideological struggle, other serious difficulties lie in wait. Definitions of ideology frequently fail for a simple reason: they attempt to reduce a great variety of phenomena into a single undiscriminating category. An analogy will clarify the point. Imagine what would happen if human language had only a single word to describe all forms of mental activity. Whether it was the abstract speculations of philosophy, the process of composing music, the cognitive capacities used in reading the funnies, or the

---

4. See William E. Connolly, *The Terms of Political Discourse* (Lexington, Mass.: Heath, 1974) especially Chapters 1 and 2.

kind of mechanical reflexes involved in tying one's shoes—they could only be referred to with a single word. The ensuing confusion would be enormous. Imagine trying to define such a term and the problems facing a definition of ideology become somewhat clearer.

The many levels of ideological discourse

Ideology is an umbrella term that simultaneously refers to numerous levels of political discourse. It includes everything from the highly self-conscious and quasi-philosophical thought systems proposed by great thinkers to the fragmentary and inconsistent belief systems of the masses. It reaches great heights of theoretical sophistication just as it descends into mindless sloganeering. At one level it serves to direct political leaders in their choice of concrete policies and practices—what are often spoken of as **operational codes**. At another it forms the basis for the way we socialize children. At times it is appealed to in order to mobilize a populace to action or sacrifice, while at others it serves the more mundane need of transforming coercion into legitimate authority. Clearly, each of these levels of ideological discourse involves us in a very different kind of venture.

For starters, each level has its own unique intellectual substance and style. Arguments formulated in the philosophical mode will be profoundly different from calls to action made at a political rally, or from the presentation of civic ideas to school children. Each domain of ideological discourse has its unique objectives—persuading the intellectual, arousing the crowd, socializing the child—and hence its own standards of success and failure. What succeeds in speaking to the social theorist will not be effective for mass audiences, and vice versa. Ideas that work in a theoretical treatise may be of little use to politicians who need to resolve a pressing political crisis. The kind of ideological formulation that effectively bestows legitimacy on a political system may be totally inadequate when the objective is to inflame political passions.

Each form of ideological discourse makes a different appeal: to critical reason, to practical wisdom, to the need to conform, to the sense of justice, to the desire for emotional catharsis, to fears and hatreds, etc. Each level of ideological discourse has its characteristic kind of proponent: the philosopher, the political leader, the publicist, the propagandist, the teacher, or the electrifying public speaker. One kind of discourse is more likely to be spoken, another will almost always be found in written form. And so on.

It should not be surprising then that attempts to forge a single definition out of these many forms of discourse face great difficulties. Because what applies to one level will often be thoroughly inappropriate to the others, it becomes a formidable task to compose a single definition that will be both comprehensive and meaningful. If the definition is narrowly focused in order to increase clarity, it will miss ideology's multitude of different levels. If on the other hand it attempts to flatten out the multi-tiered complexity of the ideological phenomenon into a blandly general summary—like a doctor who asks for the average temperature of the patients on his ward—nothing much will have been gained.

Distinguishing between ideology and political theory

And yet, despite all that has been said and difficult though it may be, some tentative form of identification is nevertheless necessary. Rather than attempt a full-scale definition of ideology, however, and be threatened with all the pitfalls we enumerated above, it would be wiser to set ourselves a lesser (although by no means little) task: to distinguish between ideology and political theory. (For our present purposes, political theory and political philosophy are understood to be identical.)

Political theories are idea systems whose core concern is persuasion and understanding. They are not distinguished by an overt drive to power. They are not judged by their practical success in translating ideas into reality. It cannot be said, for example, that the failure of Hobbes to create a great Hobbesian community of political activists dedicated to his authoritarian ideas diminishes the *Leviathan*'s importance. Hence, political theories do not normally come with a complex infrastructure of levels dedicated to doing, changing, operationalizing, or mobilizing.

Even when they originate in the heat of sectarian battles, political theories have a tendency to rise above the fray, to take the long view of things. Rather than present us with urgent concerns expressed in insistent language, political theory tends to speak with a more tranquil voice. Rather than addressing us in a variety of different voices, each directed to different practical objectives, political theory tends to be heard in a single thoughtful register.

Ideology, by contrast, operates at many different levels simultaneously, from the speculative to the most concrete and mundane. Ideologies are inevitably more than pure intellectual systems. They are ideas in pursuit of self-realization in the real world of practice. If they are not operationalized, ideologies fail to fulfil their declared purpose. Plato's admission in the *Republic* that the political ideas he presents may be unrealizable is foreign to the world of ideology.

Ideology is philosophy in overalls, ideas with a job to do. Like all theoretical ideas that must stand the test of application, ideology is concerned with what works. Imagine a theoretical mathematician, for example, who must certify the sturdiness of a bridge. Ideology tends to be more concerned with immediate consequences and with concrete dilemmas than with pure issues of principle. It aims at directing action at least as much as it is dedicated to directing thought. Ideologies present their ideas not only to convince, but also to energize the converted to go beyond reflective conviction.

Distinguishing between theory and ideology

This is clearly true of those levels of ideological discourse concerned with mobilization, socialization, and operationalizing policy. But is it true of ideology at its most speculative level as well? Disregard for a moment the infrastructure of practice underlying ideological discourse and focus exclusively on its most theoretical expression. Can we easily distinguish between political theory and ideology?

If the key word in this question is "easily," perhaps the only fair answer is a non-committal statement about its being a controversial matter. To be sure, there are those who would insist that, isolated at this level, little difference exists between ideology and political theory. Ideology, they might say, is only political theory in a dynamic mood.

Ideology requires certainty

Nonetheless, a convincing argument can be made for the existence of a significant distinguishing mark between ideology and political theory, even at this speculative level. Political theory tends to have a tentative, unfinished character. The debate is never closed. It is an expected part of philosophical discourse that the contentions in a compelling philosophical work defending a particular world-view will be met with objections and counter-contentions. Ideology, by contrast, tends to be presented with a certainty and finality that attempts to close debate. Otherwise the ensuing call to action would be difficult to justify. If ideology must justify a social order—including the apportionment of scarce resources, the distribution of power, and the meting out of punishment—it is imperative that its principles be more than debating points of uncertain standing.

Politics, in the end, is killing—a life and death enterprise. Traitors, terrorists, and revolutionaries who would overthrow our established form of life face a violent death. We consider it legitimate to use lethal force against them because of our conviction that the principles embodied in our institutions and laws are basically as they should be. Hence, giving the signal for the gallows trap door to be dropped is a solemn moment of commitment to a certain way of doing things and of thinking about things. Indecisiveness and doubt have no place in this grim ceremony.

Ideology's vital role in a functioning society is to provide the certainty necessary for resolute action. Ideology will therefore contain a degree of decisiveness and closure, even in its most theoretical formulations, that is usually lacking in other forms of social thought. If a criterion does exist by which ideology can be distinguished, it is most likely that ideology provides the certainty required to authorize public action.

Summary   To summarize the argument in this section:

1. The definition of ideology is complicated by the term's use as a political swear word. Because of the term's negative implications, no one wants his or her own cherished political values characterized as ideology.
2. Ideology is said to involve (a) irresponsible theorizing, (b) dogmatic rigidity, and (c) the exploitation of ideas for ulterior motives. Clearly these alleged defects are not always compatible with each other.
3. The sources of these three distinct characterizations of ideology are conservatism, liberalism, and Marxism respectively. For conservatives ideology represents theorizing divorced from the real historical process; for liberals it involves shallow conformist orthodoxies; for Marxists it entails the exploitation of ideas to rationalize selfish material interests.
4. The definition of ideology is part of the ideological struggle itself.
5. Attempts at definition founder because ideology is not a single homogeneous phenomenon but includes multiple levels of discourse ranging from the philosophical, to the operational, to the propagandistic, to the mobilizing. Each level of discourse has its own unique characteristics.
6. Political theory is distinguished from ideology by its lack of a drive to power and self-realization. Theory is contemplative and concerned with long-range issues of principle. Ideology, by contrast, comes with a machinery of practice and with various levels of discourse.
7. Even at its most theoretical, ideology differs from political theory in its need for the kind of certainty that can authorize real political decisions.

Ideology's location on the map of human experience can be specified; it lies on the border between the domains of philosophy and politics. Its ideas derive from the one; its practice pertains to the other. And yet, neither philosophy nor politics are particularly proud of their bastard offspring. Viewed from the heights of philosophy, ideology appears to be a noisy step-child that violates the serene open-endedness of philosophic debate. With its insistent declarations and unjustified certainties, it fails to respect philosophy's reflective and theoretical character.

When seen from the perspective of politics, by contrast, ideology appears either as ivory-tower thinking that suffers from excessive rationality (conservatives), or as closed-minded and intolerant dogma (liberals), or as material interests masquerading in the cloak of reason (radicals). Despite its indispensability and pervasiveness, ideology tends to be an orphan—disowned by its philosophical and political parents.

Beyond its lack of popularity, ideology, as we have seen, suffers from a basic ambiguity in regard to its defining characteristics. But a way of progressing a bit further toward clarification is to trace the history of the concept. In what ensues, we shall follow the dramatic transformations that have overtaken the meaning of the term ideology from its strange origins to the present day.

Ideology: The History of a Concept

The French Revolution

The concept
of ideology

Ideology is a modern concept. When the American colonists rebelled against the British Crown, for example, the term did not yet exist. Until the events associated with the French Revolution, there was no specific word in the European languages to describe the public advocacy of political ideas. Of course political ideas and their advocates have always existed, with or without a specific term to describe them. What came to maturity toward the end of the eighteenth century was both a new understanding of the nature of political ideas and a new terminology to characterize them. As the opening section of this chapter was at pains to show, modern ideological discourse differs significantly from the way in which political ideas were debated in traditional society. If there is a date that can be placed on the advent of political modernity, it is surely those momentous events surrounding the revolutionary turmoil in France.

Left and right

Not only the term ideology has its origin here. Many of the familiar categories by which we classify the ideological world arose in the context of the French Revolution as well. For example, our habit of referring to political ideologies as **left-wing**, **right-wing**, and **centrist** derives from the seating of the delegates in the revolutionary National Convention. Those occupying the left wing of the hall were the radical Jacobins. Facing them on the right were the conservative Girondists. Between them—and since the seats were graduated, below them as well—sat the centrists, who were regularly derided by both sides as comprising the wishy-washy middle ground of French politics.

Despite vast political changes across the past two centuries, this left-right classification is far from being obsolete. To be sure, political scientists regularly complain that it is insufficiently precise and that it is often misleading. And undoubtedly, they are right. But whatever its failings, the left-right continuum of political positions continues to be our single most useful and prevalent form of ideological classification.

The coherence of ideological positions

Consider for a moment how certain political positions have tended to cohere with each other, to cluster into idea-families. To be a left-winger, for example, is to support egalitarian policies, both politically and economically. But it is also, normally, to oppose religious intervention in politics, if not to support a thoroughgoing secularism. Together with these ideas we usually find a tendency to cosmopolitan internationalism, or at least a rejection of nationalism in its more strident forms. A certain progressive ardor, sometimes mixed with messianic overtones, rounds out the picture. What accounts for the affinity that these ideas have had for each other? Why has the left-wing position persisted as a totality for so long?

One obvious response would be that a strictly logical bond exists between the various elements of leftist thinking. But even a hasty mental experiment should make it clear that there is nothing essentially egalitarian about secularism (or secular about egalitarianism) or cosmopolitan about messianism (or messianic about cosmopolitanism.) And surely the same could be said about the elements that constitute the centrist and right-wing positions.

These ideas cohere not for deductive rational reasons, but because in the context of the debate set into motion by the rise of modern politics they have a certain social, economic, and psychological attraction for each other. The various elements tend to go together because they represent reasonably coherent and integrated responses to the controversial issues thrown up by the context of modern politics. They offer a satisfying and coordinated outlook that promises to orient the believer through the often confusing maze of concerns initiated by the revolutionary events in France. In other contexts of political debate, the pre-modern for example, we would find the battle lines drawn according to a very different kind of logic.

Given the centrality of the French Revolution to the formation of modern politics, it is no surprise that ideologies of the left, right, and center received some of their most powerful expressions within its setting. Modern conservative ideologies arose in reaction to the reckless dogmas and murderous consequences of the revolution. The germ of radical ideas makes its appearance here as well, although a number of decades passed before political radicalism matured into a systematic creed. And if there is an axis for liberal thought, it is the revolutionary era as well, despite the many illiberal acts committed in the name of revolutionary justice.

De Tracy and the Origins of the Term Ideology

In 1795, after the first flush of French revolutionary activity had subsided, an Institut de France was established to give the official version of the ideas that had directed the revolution. Its head, Antoine Destutt de Tracy, proposed undertaking a "science of ideas" that he dubbed "ideology." In the optimistic and progressive spirit of the Enlightenment, de Tracy believed that ideology would be able to explore human thinking in the same way that zoologists examine physical specimens. Indeed, ideology was to be a branch of zoology; it would eventually be possible to describe and understand the formation of ideas much as we are able to understand the anatomy and physiology of biological species.

Ideology as true knowledge

Ideology in de Tracy's mind was not mere description, but the definitive exposition of what was true and what was false. Its aim was twofold: first, to present systematically what could be counted as authentic knowledge, and second, to trash all the vague metaphysics, theology, and sentimental morality that had warped European thinking prior to the Enlightenment and the Revolution. Knowledge would finally be placed on a secure and incontrovertible footing. The study of ideology would distinguish genuine human needs from their false impersonators. De Tracy and his followers promised that reason triumphant would mean an end to social strife and suffering—ills rooted in inadequate understanding and false opinions. When authentic knowledge of real human needs emerged, the definitive blueprint for an ideal human society would be within reach.

The term ideology was launched, but de Tracy's program did not get very far, despite being initially welcomed. The tide began to turn when Napoleon, aspiring to dictatorial powers, fell out of sympathy with the revolution and its aims. De Tracy and his followers, as supporters of liberal revolutionary ideas, became a thorn in the emperor's side, their influential identification of "true ideas" with such revolutionary staples as freedom of speech and freedom of the press provoking him into action. Napoleon sarcastically dismissed de Tracy and his disciples as "ideologues" and effectively dismantled the Institut de France.

The derisive name stuck; what had originally signified an enlightened project to distinguish true from false political ideas became a term with an unsavory ring to it. Ideology came to denote pompousness and unwarranted self-confidence, a theoretical arrogance that was linked to practical irrelevance. This shade of meaning has accompanied the term ever since. The attempt to lend philosophical authority to partisan political ideas would henceforth carry disturbing undertones. Already at its inception, then, the term ideology carried within it the sense of tainted goods, ideas whose claim to truth was somehow problematic.

Marxism and the Concept of Ideology

What Marx meant by ideology

Enter Marx. No one has done more to give ideology a bad name than the great revolutionary social thinker and activist. Oddly perhaps from our perspective, the person whose thought created the most intense and sustained ideological efforts of modern times found the ideological enterprise fundamentally flawed. What did Marx understand by ideology and why has it become, in Marxist discourse, a term of rebuke? In sharp contrast to de Tracy, who saw in the study of ideology a search for truth, Marx labels as ideological ideas that are basically false, or at very best, self-serving, partial, and misleading. To study ideology, in Marx's view, is to explore distorted forms of human thinking. Essentially, ideology is political thinking dominated and directed by partisan interests.

This distortion of political thinking is particularly noxious because it is usually not deliberate or even conscious. Our world-views, Marx explains, take shape in the context of our lives, and our lives are part of the universal struggle for power, wealth, and position. We do not as a rule choose our broad ideological attitudes any more than we choose the lives we are born into. For most of us most of the time, our ideological perspectives are given with the particular forms of life we lead. We are either financially comfortable or struggling, manager or laborer, urban or rural, white or black, natives or immigrants, male or female, old or young—not to speak of the innumerable foci of identification related to nationality, religion, and language. There are no generic human beings. We are inevitably particular creatures with specific characteristics. Each of these characteristics lends a typical color to our outlook. The concerns of someone whose stomach growls from hunger will be different from those of an individual who worries about the effects of an over-rich diet. We would be surprised if it were not so.

Ideology reflects interests

Political perspectives are, therefore, not immaculately conceived. Not being disembodied spirits, our political ideas are unlikely to possess Olympian detachment. Inevitably, our views take form within the real interests we pursue, the particular social group that is our frame of reference, and the socio-economic position we occupy within the community. Our competing interests tend to be reflected in the kinds of ideas we accept and advocate. Ideological struggles are material struggles carried on by intellectual means. The notion that ideological positions reflect some ultimate cosmic truth rather than being a particular historical creation representing real interests is, for Marx, an infantile thought worthy of being taught in the kindergarten of social analysis.

If the impetus behind our political ideas derives from the interests we seek to defend and advance, ideologies are best understood as cognitive weapons in the struggle between real people. As a cognitive expression of our different life-situations, ideological competition is really a struggle between the interests of different groups. When ideologies clash over questions of principle, Marx recommends that we uncover the deeper needs, the more basic material concerns that underlie the seemingly theoretical principle. Studying ideology is, therefore, an exercise in unmasking. The astute critic looks beyond the fog of sentimental pronouncements to the soft underbelly of ideas: the critic wants to know—or rather to unmask—the lurking interests, the real social groups, the practical consequences that an idea involves.

Ideology as false consciousness

But ideology's distortions are not limited to the intrusion of partisan interests into what pretends to be objective thinking. There are cases—and critically important ones for Marx—in which ideology is, in a sense, a double distortion. When ideological thinking accurately reflects the life-situation out of which it derives, at least it can be said that there is a reasonable harmony between interests and thought, between a group's practical needs and its political outlook. Despite the distorting influence of interests on ideas, at least *my* ideas are being distorted by *my* own interests. But more serious pathologies arise when a group's ideas are overpowered by alien interests, when they serve causes that are in fact hostile to their own welfare. In other words, there are cases when ideology, beyond being a form of rationalization for interests, becomes a means of domination. This Marx refers to as **false consciousness**.

Ideas, when effectively planted in the minds of people, can be vehicles of repression no less than truncheons or tear gas. In fact, they are more effective than physical force because the people coerce themselves into obedience. Marx contends forcefully that one of the most potent weapons of control wielded by the dominating groups within liberal capitalist society is the control of ideas. These ruling groups control the production and consumption of ideas no less than they control a society's wealth and power. In innumerable subtle and not-so-subtle ways, the ruling group's ideology (which not surprisingly justifies the system that gives them dominance) is incorporated into the minds of those who serve them. The authentic interests of the subordinated classes are dismissed as mutinous talk, rabble-rousing, and treason. Like the butler who becomes an ardent defender of aristocratic privilege, the subordinated underclass is taught to praise the very forces holding them in thrall. This is a form of cognitive imperialism, a penetration of foreign ideas into the very center of consciousness. When Marx proclaims that the proletariat has nothing to lose but its chains, he means among other things that most proletarians have even lost effective control over their own minds.

These are highly provocative contentions, as Marx intended them to be. They stir up a hornet's nest of questions and counter-attacks. And we will take them up systematically when we come to the chapter on Marxism as an ideology (Chapter 5). For now, all that can be added to this initial thumbnail sketch is Marx's visionary belief that, come the revolution, ideology (in the sense of political ideas subordinated to partisan interests) will become obsolete. Together with exploitation, coercion, repression, violence, and conflict, it will become a museum piece belonging to the happily overcome pre-history of the human species. Liberated from the ballast of distorting interests, human thought will be free to dedicate itself to authentic human needs, to creation, and to self-realization.

From Ideology to the Sociology of Knowledge

Marx's impact on the political thought of the past century and a half is arguably greater than that of any other thinker. And yet, perhaps the greater part of those who found Marx's ideas worthy of serious consideration were far from being Marxists in any orthodox sense of the term. They appropriated an insight here, a method there, without adopting the world-view in toto. One such thinker is Karl Mannheim, a gifted sociologist of Hungarian-German stock who was witness to the disintegration of the German Weimar Republic in the 1920s. In this period of fierce ideological struggle, Mannheim, particularly in his major work *Ideology and Utopia* (1929), was moved to confront and explore the nature of ideological discourse.

Mannheim and Marx

Mannheim's basic premise derives from Marx: ideas do not generate spontaneously; they are invariably born out of the push and pull of real human needs. Our social thought arises in the context of our social existence; our political outlooks are conditioned by the concrete settings in which they arise. To fully understand a specific social conception, therefore, it is incumbent upon us to pass beyond the abstract, reasoned arguments in which an idea presents itself. Whatever its formal status as a logical construct, an idea will not tell us—indeed often it will attempt to hide—its real social purpose. Only by assessing an idea against the background in which it originated can we appreciate its full significance. The analysis of political ideas must go beyond what was actually said and consider the no less important issue: why it was said. To this point, Mannheim and Marx would concur.

But whatever his debt to Marx, Mannheim opposes the Marxist tendency to debunk ideological positions by unmasking the selfish motives and hidden interests that underlie them. Marxists, he believes, tend to trivialize ideology into a sinister social conspiracy. They disqualify ideas rather than try to understand them. Nor is it surprising, Mannheim complains, that once Marxists define ideology as the expression of dubious partisan interests, it is found exclusively in their opponent's thought. As long as the study of ideology is taken up with unmasking the distortions in an adversary's position, Mannheim warns, it will fail to provide a general understanding of the ideological phenomenon.

Mannheim's
argument In point of fact, *all* ideas, my own included, are accountable for in terms of their social context—not only those ideas I happen to find disagreeable. When we unmask the interests lurking in our opponent's position, we are only doing to others what honesty behooves we do to ourselves as well. Indeed, we should entirely depoliticize the study of ideology. Ideas, Mannheim argues, are not so much distorted by social interests as they are routinely and universally shaped by them. Although selfish needs are clearly involved in the formation of political outlooks, ascribing great social world-views to the intrusion of egoistic motives misses the point. It is not the subjective inclinations of individuals and groups that are primary in the creation of ideology, but rather the objective logic of the total social setting. Only when it becomes clear to us that our political ideas are an inherent and unavoidable part of the global social process will the concept of ideology be rescued from its debasing political use.

Ideology: total
and particular In this spirit Mannheim distinguishes between two different approaches to ideology: the "particular" and the "total." The **particular conception of ideology** relates to political ideas as the expression of partisan interests. It fastens onto the self-centered elements in a thought system in order to discredit a specific enemy. When ideological analysis is no longer used as an intellectual battering ram but transforms itself into a general method of social and historical research, then we have risen to the **total conception of ideology**. If the "particular" conception involves us in mistrust, cynical unmasking, and the imputation of sordid motives, the "total" conception, Mannheim insists, has no ax to grind. Its concern is fundamentally theoretical: to clarify the historical regularities and sociological laws that bind specific social ideas to certain social realities—what Mannheim calls a **sociology of knowledge.**

Mannheim's
struggle with
relativism If all ideas are equally conditioned by social context, however, can any perspectives be spoken of as superior to others? If ideas are essentially social reflexes, should we not banish terms like good and bad, or right and wrong, from our moral and political vocabulary? Would it then be fair to say that Mannheim's sociology of knowledge leads us to the relativistic conclusion that there are no general standards by which to judge ideas? Mannheim expended the greater part of his considerable talents agonizing over this question without reaching either sharp or really satisfying answers. His troubled equivocations are highly instructive for us as we embark upon a study of modern ideologies: they teach us that once our political ideas are understood to be expressions of underlying psychological or sociological needs, the threat of relativism—with all its tortuous problems—is never very far away.

The intellectuals   If Mannheim found it impossible to offer definitive criteria for the truth or falsehood of ideologies (as de Tracy and Marx had set about to do), he nevertheless singled out a particular social group that in his view had a significant advantage over all the others in orienting themselves in the ideological labyrinth: the intellectuals. To be sure, intellectuals cannot lift themselves above the setting in which they think, for the same reason that all other mortals cannot. Like the rest of us, they are conditioned by the historical and sociological environment in which their thought takes shape. Nevertheless, because their view of the public domain is invariably broader than those of the partisans to the political struggle, their perspective offers a unique promise of detachment and comprehensiveness.

Whatever their own social status happens to be, intellectuals are not merely learned representatives of the upper, middle, or lower classes. Intellectuals have a singular need to comprehend their world that cannot be reduced to the simple pursuit of material interests. They are in a sense free-floating, not tied to any one specific partisan perspective. This unique social character, Mannheim claims, endows the intellectuals with a privileged point of view. On the one hand, they are very much part of their reality and hence able to penetrate its meaning. On the other, they are reasonably detached from any specific political camp and hence able to view the political drama from the broadest possible perspective.

As opposed to political rivals who dismiss competing positions with scorn, intellectuals are trained to penetrate the sources, character, functions, and significance of ideas, even if they find them repugnant. They are especially adept at putting themselves in the other side's shoes, at understanding a rival ideological position from within. Because of their relatively uncommitted and autonomous stance, they are also able to integrate the various ideological positions into a total picture. Putting all the ideological pieces together from a detached and general viewpoint—rather than viewing them all from one fixed partisan position as, for example, the Marxists do—is the intellectuals' main claim to social authority.

More than any other group, the intellectuals are equipped with an accurate and comprehensive map of a society's ideological terrain. Although even the most accurate map cannot tell us where we should be going, properly used it can provide an indication of potential trouble spots and prevent head-on collisions. Viewing a society's ideological strife from a detached and comprehensive standpoint holds out the hope of managing the conflict through an impartial understanding of its underlying dynamics. By comprehending the totality of the social process, the intellectuals can orchestrate a communal effort aimed at coping with the divisions that set group against group. For Weimar Germany in the throes of disintegration, this was a hope that Mannheim held onto desperately.

Whatever their differences, both Marx and Mannheim conceive of ideology as the cognitive expression of deeper social forces. Ideology, from their perspective, is both less and more than it appears to be. Less, because it is never the reasoned expression of pure principle it would like us to believe it is. And more, because it always has a hidden agenda, an unspoken program of concrete and partisan objectives.

Ideology as Fanaticism: A Restrictive Definition

The tendency to discredit ideological thinking has also found a home among many Anglo-American social scientists. Although they are uneasy with the Marx/Mannheim conception of ideology as political thought in the service of interests, they nevertheless contend that ideology is a fundamentally shady enterprise. What intrudes into ideological thinking, they believe, is not so much a concealed socio-economic agenda as fanaticism and uncontrolled passion. Ideology is what happens to ideas when they are overheated and oversimplified by political fervor. They become emotive, inflated, and jingoistic rather than detached and analytical—philosophy that has deteriorated into mass propaganda. The niceties of logic and empirical testing are trampled underfoot by one's higher duty to the cause. The civility and fair-mindedness that ought to mark dialogue between members of a political community degenerate into a shouting match between ideological advocates whose commitment is usually far more substantial than their knowledge. Ideology is, therefore, an intellectual malady: thought perverted by blind loyalty and shallow conformism.

Qualifying as ideologies from this perspective are political doctrines at the extreme poles of the ideological spectrum, such as fascism, National Socialism, Bolshevism, communism, McCarthyism, the New Left, and radical feminism. Typically, these ideological doctrines divide the world into an honorable *we* and an irremediably evil *they*. Ideologies of this kind demand total devotion and blind obedience. They claim, moreover, to be in exclusive possession of the one and only political truth. Perhaps most abhorrent of all is their unwillingness to even entertain the possibility of compromise. Their mission is nothing less than the creation of a radically new human world, and those who stand in their way cannot expect to have their rights read to them.

A non-ideological view?

What, then, would qualify as a non-ideological point of view? Clearly, one that lacked the pathologies enumerated above. It would be pragmatic, pluralist, tolerant, compromising, civil, and open-ended. In other words, it would be some form of liberalism. However powerfully liberalism may contend in the political marketplace of ideas, from this perspective it is not an ideology. These theorists make a sharp distinction between ideas that have become a fetish for their believers and those that, as a matter of principle, are open to critical examination. Ideas that serve as tentative hypotheses to be tested in practice belong, they claim, to an entirely different category than those that are unquestioned articles of faith. A pragmatic, compromising attitude in regard to political principles cannot be counted an ideology because pragmatism, by its very nature, is not wedded irrevocably to any one policy or program.

As opposed to the views of Mannheim but like those of Marx, advocates of this point of view argue for a **restrictive** understanding of ideology. They pejoratively label certain political positions ideological, while excluding others—in this case pragmatic liberalism. For these theorists, liberalism lacks the parochialism and rigidity of ideology; in its humaneness and open-mindedness, it represents everything that ideology is not.[5]

The end of ideology

Interestingly, in the mid-1950s this same camp of theorists broached a controversial (and since then largely discredited) claim that the West was entering an era marked by the **end of ideology**. They discerned a pattern of transformation in European politics marked by a sharp decline in extremist politics and radical ideologies. Repelled by the devastation wrought by National Socialism and Stalinist Communism, post-war Western democracies were repudiating ideological politics and moving toward a pragmatic bargaining style.

The left had abandoned its dream of revolution, the right its hope of crushing the labor movement. Grand ideological programs were disgraced and disowned. The prevailing order of the day was to divide the communal pie in a manner that would satisfy, at least minimally, all sides to the political debate. "Give and take" had replaced "all or nothing" as the key phrase of European politics. Political maturity had triumphed; ideology, like other unfounded prejudices, was on its way to extinction.[6] Historically, the end of ideology did not survive the 1960s. The Vietnam War, the Civil Rights Movement, student rebellions, and the "events of May 1968" in Paris constituted precisely the revival of ideology that these theorists had discounted.

Ideology's Positive Role: The Non-Restrictive Definition

Critiques of the restrictive liberal definition

Opposition to the "end of ideology" thesis was not a monopoly of political radicals. Liberals too rejected the "end of ideology" position—as well as the restrictive definition of ideology—at a basic principled level. Pragmatism and liberalism, these critics claimed, were every bit as much ideologies as all the others. Defenders of the restrictive definition were only throwing stones out of a glass house. They begged every imaginable question by defining ideology so that it excluded their preferred position—not to speak of the sins involved in describing liberalism in such beautified and self-serving terms. Besides, using "ideology" as a synonym for "depraved political thinking" is unacceptable in basic academic scientific terms. How would we react, asks one critic, to an analysis of religious ideas that was framed in terms of superstition?[7]

For these critics (for example, Apter, Geertz, and Seliger)—many of them committed liberals—the single-mindedly pejorative understanding of ideology

5. Some of the main protagonists of this viewpoint are Giovanni Sartori, Edward Shils, Lewis Feuer, and Seymour M. Lipset. For an extended discussion of the "restricted" versus "inclusive" understanding of ideology, see Martin Seliger, *Ideology and Politics* (London: Allen and Unwin, 1976) 25–169.

6. See Chaim Isaac Waxman, ed., *The End of Ideology Debate* (New York: Funk and Wagnalls, 1968).

7. See Clifford Geertz, "Ideology as a Cultural System," in *Ideology and Discontent*, ed. David Apter (New York: Free Press, 1964) 51, as well as Apter's introduction, 15–46.

must be abandoned. To define it as a shady enterprise marked by ulterior agendas or unruly passions fails on a number of grounds. First, because such definitions are overly conspiratorial and unjustifiably restrictive. They confuse the pathological with the prototype. Some ideologies may be blindly conformist, but this is not part of the definition of ideology itself. Second, and more importantly, these kinds of definitions ignore the necessary and positive role that ideology plays in the maintenance of social systems and individual mental well-being. Because they focus on ideology as a cognitive malady, they miss its more constructive, day-to-day significance. What neither the Marxist nor the restrictive liberal view sufficiently appreciates is how indispensable ideology is as the cognitive glue that binds a society together. They fail to comprehend ideology's importance as a consensus-fostering, community-creating phenomenon.

Ideology's indispensable functions

Without a common ideology, social solidarity would be quite unattainable. Lacking a collective ideological idiom, we could not communicate easily with our fellow citizens. Neither could we transmit a political culture from one generation to the next. Leaders would be unable to lead were there no accepted reservoir of political values in terms of which they could justify their actions. Without the impact of a legitimizing ideology, brute power would hardly stand a chance of being transformed into accepted authority. This is true most especially in newly emerging nations. In the absence of solid communal traditions, ideology provides the galvanizing focus around which a new national consciousness can be constructed.

While traditional societies are governed by implicit and unchallenged value systems, modern states require the self-conscious services of an ideology to foster cohesion. When the face-to-face familiarity of pre-modern communal life is replaced by the impersonal and formal ties of mass industrial society, only a common ideology can recreate the sense of unity and purpose that animate a vital society. Were it not for the services of ideology, therefore, modern political systems would be impossible to sustain.

Ideology, moreover, provides the template or road map that allows societies to respond to the vast quantity of political information they regularly absorb. Ideology orders our world for us and, in so doing, makes it meaningful and coherent. In a sense, ideological belief tames the anarchic reality we confront by transforming it into a relatively clear and intelligible picture. It creates a world of standing categories and concepts that reduce political dilemmas into previously solved problems. It resolves political questions according to an established scheme of ideas and values. This spares us the intellectual exhaustion and practical paralysis that would ensue if we had to consider every moral-political question that confronted us as if for the first time.

To these indispensable social functions there needs to be added the critical importance ideology has for the formation of individual identity. Ideological commitment is a perceptual lens that helps each of us organize our world and, hence, act as integrated individuals. It creates a convincing and manageable account of the often very complex events that surround us; it provides the navigational equipment to guide us through the political turbulence that at one time or another we all face; it imposes a reasonably satisfying fit between our ideas and the facts accosting us daily. Without a system of socio-political ideas to guide us in our daily behavior, we would be quite lost.

All this relates to the cognitive level of human perception. But ideology has important emotional functions as well. It constitutes a clearinghouse that directs and regulates the flow of our feelings. Ideology affords moments of catharsis, of inspiration and dedication, of moral indignation and hatred, of pride, of solidarity and belonging. In other words, it contributes toward a satisfying inner emotional life. Ideology furnishes a roster of heroes and martyrs with whom we can identify, and no less important, a gallery of rogues and traitors against whom we can vent our spleen. It creates a world of symbols, myths, rituals, anthems, and flags to which we respond instinctively—whatever their historical accuracy or formal rationality. By grasping complex, often contradictory phenomena in metaphoric and emotive language (e.g., "Workers of the world unite; you have nothing to lose but your chains," or "Give me liberty or give me death") ideology can communicate to its followers a living sense of social reality that is unavailable to the cold language of science. It is no wonder then that the young, whose search for identity and emotional outlet is singularly intense, should prove to be unusually vulnerable to ideological appeals.

But if the language of ideology tends to the metaphorical and emotive, if it deals in catharsis, propagates myths, and simplifies complexity into energizing slogans, would we not be justified in saying that ideology does indeed distort the cool and detached language of social analysis? So understood, how far is ideology from mass indoctrination? Have we not then returned to something very much like the restrictive liberal view of ideology as a form of irresponsible and dangerous political expression? Furthermore, don't we violate the obvious lessons of common sense if we understand ideology as the beneficent provider of social cohesion and intellectual coherence? That ideology is about conflict and partisan interests, that it misleads as much as it clarifies, is a basic lesson that every mature observer of the political world will have learned somewhere along the way. It would appear that we have not escaped the vicious cycle after all!

Summary   Let us summarize the central elements discussed in this section:

1. The modern concept of ideology originated in the French Revolution. Familiar ideological categories, such as the left-right classification of ideological positions, had their origins in the revolutionary turmoil as well. The historical context of modern ideology, ushered in by the French Revolution, remains central to our contemporary political experience.

2. The initial use of the term ideology by de Tracy entailed distinguishing between true and false political ideas. The term ideology gained negative resonance after Napoleon ridiculed de Tracy and his followers as ideologues.

3. Karl Marx's understanding of ideology reinforces this pejorative sense by claiming that ideology is really the exploitation of ideas to rationalize material interests. Ideology does not usually distort thought deliberately; it naturally takes shape within the context of our social interests.

4. Marx contends that ideology can be an instrument of repression. When ideas expressing the interests of the dominant elements of society are inculcated into the minds of the subordinate classes, their thinking becomes doubly perverted: not only is their thought in the service of interests, it is in the service of interests that oppress them.

5. Karl Mannheim rejects the Marxist tendency to disqualify ideology as a social conspiracy. The general, as opposed to particular, approach to ideology understands all social thought as routinely and universally conditioned by social forces. So understood, the study of ideology properly becomes a sociology of knowledge.

6. In Mannheim's view, the intellectuals have a privileged position in the understanding of ideology because of their relatively detached, general, and independent perspective. By viewing the many ideologies comprehensively, they may be able to aid in coping with dangerous ideological conflict.

7. A restricted view of ideology, held by some Anglo-American, liberal social scientists, associates it with fanatical social thinking of the kind prevalent among the Nazis and the Bolsheviks. Ideology is a cognitive malady involving mass conformity, blind loyalty, intolerance, and messianic political dreams. Accordingly, liberalism, with its pragmatic, compromising style, cannot be classified as an ideology.

8. Other Anglo-American social scientists—with many liberals among them—offer a **non-restrictive** and considerably more positive view of ideology. They claim that ideology has indispensable social functions to discharge—functions critical to the well-being of modern states and individuals. It is bound up with social solidarity, a common political culture, efficient decision making, personal identity, emotional health, etc.

9. But if ideology provides emotional catharsis and electrifying myths, have we not returned to a view of ideology as a dangerous form of political expression? Besides, common sense tells us that ideology does not simply provide social cohesion; it is obviously about conflict and partisan interests. We do not seem to have found our way out of the labyrinth after all!

Where does all this leave us? Confused perhaps. We may be excused for feeling impatient and frustrated. Nor can we be faulted for wishing to cut through all these complications with a simple resolution that sets all the difficulties to rest. And yet it is entirely possible that journeying this long and tortuous route will have contributed a great deal to our understanding of ideology—more perhaps than a simple definition neatly offered up at the outset. It may well make us sharper critics of the ideological systems to be presented in the coming chapters. Some may even be moved to try out the various theories of ideology we have presented on the ideological systems we shall consider. At very least, we end this journey with a greater appreciation of why the phenomenon of ideology has raised such formidable obstacles on the path of those who have attempted to master it.

Suggestions for Further Reading

Althusser, Louis. *Essays on Ideology*. London: Verso, 1984.

Apter, David, ed. *Ideology and Discontent*. New York: Free Press, 1964.

Barth, Hans. *Truth and Ideology*. Los Angeles: University of California Press, 1976.

Bell, Daniel. *The End of Ideology: On the Exhaustion of Political Ideas in the Fifties*. New York: Collier Books, 1961.

————. "The End of Ideology Revisited (Parts 1 and 2)," *Government and Opposition* 23 (Spring and Summer 1988).

Carsnaes, W. *The Concept of Ideology and Political Analysis*. London: Macmillan, 1974.

Connolly, William E. *The Terms of Political Discourse*. Lexington, Mass.: Heath, 1974.

Eagleton, Terry. *Ideology*. London: Verso, 1991.

Feuer, Lewis. *Ideology and the Ideologists*. Oxford: Blackwell, 1975.

Gouldner, Alvin. *The Dialectic of Ideology and Technology*. New York: Seabury Press, 1976.

Larrain, J. *The Concept of Ideology*. London: Hutchinson, 1979.

Lichtheim, George. *The Concept of Ideology and Other Essays*. New York: Vintage, 1967.

McLellan, David. *Ideology*. Milton Keynes, England: Open University Press, 1986.

Plamenatz, John. *Ideology*. London: Macmillan, 1971.

Seliger, Martin. *Ideology and Politics*. London: George Allen and Unwin, 1976.

————. *The Marxist Conception of Ideology*. Cambridge: Cambridge University Press, 1977.

Skinner, Quentin. *The Foundations of Modern Political Thought*. 2 vols. Cambridge: Cambridge University Press, 1978.

Susser, Bernard. *The Grammar of Modern Ideology*. London: Routledge, 1988.

Watkins, F. *The Age of Ideology: Political Thought 1750 to the Present*. Englewood Cliffs, N.J.: Prentice Hall, 1965.

Waxman, Chaim Isaac, ed. *The End of Ideology Debate*. New York: Funk and Wagnalls, 1968.

Williams, Howard. *Concepts of Ideology*. New York: St. Martin's Press, 1988.

Chapter 2

Conservatism: What Conservatives Want to Conserve and Why

From Traditionalism to Conservatism: Old Wine in New Bottles

Conservatism's meaning is contextual

Conservatism is a slippery term. Like its arch-rival radicalism, its meaning often depends entirely on context. In the context of the contemporary Western democracies, being conservative normally means sympathizing with ideologies of free enterprise, property rights, and individualism. To be a Western radical, by contrast, entails advocating economic equality, the redistribution of property, and a concern for the rights of the impoverished. Ironically, in the post-communist Soviet Union these same terms have precisely the opposite meaning. To be a conservative is to support retention of state-enforced equality, collectivist economics, and authoritarian politics. Radicals in contemporary Soviet politics—as odd as it may sound to Western ears—are those who support free enterprise, property rights, and individualism.

To confuse matters further still, Muslim radicals are generally religious fundamentalists who advocate return to a strict code of traditional morality including an emphasis on chastity, doctrinal purity, and the primacy of the clergy. In the context of Catholicism, by contrast, those who advocate such practices are likely to be called conservatives. The point is clear: in itself, the term conservative has little or no substantive meaning. The very same ideological program that is characterized as conservative in one place will be dubbed radical in another. Context is paramount.[1]

---

1. See Martin Seliger, *Ideology and Politics* (London: Allen and Unwin, 1976) 91 ff.

Our first task is therefore to specify the context in which the term conservatism is to be used below. It is the context of those religious, cultural, scientific, economic, and social transformations associated with Western development from the Middle Ages to modernity, or in other words, the context of modern Western political thought. Within this context, conservatism takes on a reasonably distinct and enduring ideological character. It comprises a rich, loosely knit family of ideas with a specifiable style, typical motifs, and predictable programs.

Conservatism and traditionalism

Many have noted that conservatism bears a certain temperamental and conceptual likeness to those ideas we spoke of (in the opening chapter) as traditional. Assuming that in fact conservatives do wish to conserve the traditions of our past, this likeness should come as no surprise. Conservatives and traditionalists share a profound concern for continuity and a keen suspicion of those short-lived cultural novelties that strut and fret today and are gone tomorrow. Both hold in highest esteem the reservoir of wisdom offered up to us by past experience. Neither is comfortable with the frantic pace of change that has overtaken the modern world.

Traditional societies and the pre-modern style

But conservatives and traditionalists are worlds apart in the kind of political discourse they conduct. Traditional societies retain the pre-modern style described in the opening pages of the first chapter. They operate within a single mandatory form of life that is sealed off, either naturally or deliberately, from others that might challenge it. Indeed, traditional societies feel no need to confront alien cultures, not even in order to present reasoned criticisms of them. For such criticism would necessarily mean becoming engaged with the challenge that these foreign ideas present—a prospect considered either dishonorable or dangerous or both. Traditional societies see no reason to provide others with accounts of their own world-view. They are especially reluctant to translate their beliefs into terms that can be understood by those outside the tradition. If modern ideology is a bustling marketplace of contending ideas, traditionalists definitely are not part of it. They seal themselves off from its challenges. They decline the invitation to compete.

Traditional cultures, of course, are not always passive and serenely self-contained in their ideological responses. When a traditional society feels itself threatened by foreign influences—Iran of the Ayatollahs is a good example—it may lash out violently at its enemies. But to lash out is not to compete. The foreign threat will be denounced, but the argument will not be joined. From behind the secure walls of tradition, the enemy will be dismissed as a satanic force that menaces all that is good and right. A few choice expletives may be thrown in as well. But the external challenge will not be confronted as an alternative way of life that merits serious consideration.

What happens, however, when the threat to the traditional order is too close at hand to be deflected or simply denounced? What if the challenging force has succeeded in breaching the walls of tradition and appears on its way to victory? Apart from simply abandoning the tradition, two very different responses are possible. In one case, traditionalists might dig in their heels, rededicate themselves all the more fervently to their beliefs, and redouble their efforts to keep the contaminating influences at bay. They might, in other words, attempt to insulate the traditional community from non-traditional ideas. The pressures on such a defensive traditional community would be far more acute than in the past, and yet many such communities continue to thrive in the modern era.

But the defenders of the old ways may also choose to fight fire with fire. They may resolve to defend their world-view by challenging the challengers, presenting an attractive, carefully reasoned account of their conceptions and practices. If this defense is to be effective in rallying sympathy among wavering traditionalists and in convincing outsiders that the tradition is worth taking seriously, it must contain some very untraditional elements. After all, traditional arguments traditionally presented are precisely what have failed to protect the tradition against its enemies.

Tradition joins the modern ideological debate

Above all, the tradition will no longer be able to act as if it is the only game in town. It will have to tailor arguments to an audience that no longer assumes the tradition to be binding or beyond criticism, compare rival points of view with the tradition and prove them inferior, and effectively answer critiques levelled at the tradition from outside its confines. Non-traditional knowledge will have to be mastered in order to successfully speak the language in which the debate is conducted. The tradition's arguments will have to go beyond the narrow traditional community and address themselves to the public at large. In other words, the traditional point of view will have to join the modern ideological debate.[2]

From traditionalism to conservatism

These are the birth throes of conservatism. As a first and very makeshift rule of thumb we may say that conservatism arises as an adaptation and defense of traditional ideas. This adaptation, nevertheless, may depart significantly from its source. Indeed, this is usually the case. Conservatives do not often defend an entire traditional system of ideas intact. Frequently the many elements that make up a traditional outlook become fragmented into separate themes that are defended by different conservative advocates. The traditional legacy with its monolithic character becomes a loosely knit collection of allied but distinct positions.

All this is admittedly rather abstract. We must, therefore, add flesh and muscle to the intellectual skeleton by placing these abstractions in the specific historical context of modern conservatism. To understand how modern conservatism emerged out of the traditional ideas that preceded it, we will make a brief historical detour and reexamine the political conceptions that reigned as Europe emerged from the Middle Ages into the modern era. By examining this traditional network of beliefs we should be able to identify the distinct themes that would later make up the different varieties of conservative thinking.

---

2. The French counter-revolutionary conservative Joseph de Maistre claimed that "formerly royalism was an instinct, now it is a science." Cited by Richard A. Lebrun in the introduction to de Maistre's *Considerations on France* (Montreal: McGill–Queens University, 1974) 6.

Let us begin by enumerating these traditional themes without comment.

Traditional themes

1. Precedent: Custom and precedent—often spoken of as **prescription**—determine the validity of claims to rights and privileges and provide the criteria by which to judge the legitimacy of social practices generally.
2. Absolute Truth: Truth is one, eternal, and universal and therefore properly governs human social and political life.
3. Human Limitations: Human beings are flawed, imperfectable creatures. Sordid desires and selfish interests regularly overcome principle and reason. Individual and communal conflicts are, therefore, inevitable. Human designs for reform (to say nothing of revolution) cannot fundamentally alter the basically defective nature of social life.
4. Hierarchy: Because human abilities are unequally distributed, some individuals are meant to lead just as others are meant to follow. Hierarchy, the subordination of some individuals and groups to others, is therefore an integral and irremediable part of the human condition.

Today many of these themes appear independent of each other; we may find ourselves sympathetic to one while remaining uncomfortable with another. For example, the belief that a single, universal truth should guide our social arrangements (theme 2) is not always compatible with the idea that age-old custom (theme 1) should be decisive in our choices. After all, customs vary from place to place while universal truth, by definition, does not. And yet, for the medieval mind they were parts of a single broadly accepted world-view.

Tradition undermined by modernity

The religious, scientific, commercial, and cultural transformations that created modern Europe profoundly undermined this traditional medieval world-view. As a consensual orthodoxy it progressively lost its hold—displaced by the network of fresh and forceful ideas usually referred to as liberalism. To be sure, some well-organized traditional groups like the Catholic Church succeeded in holding out by reaffirming their faith and adapting to the new reality, but it was clear the old ideas had suffered a great fall and would never be put back together again—certainly not in their traditional form.

Nonetheless, many of the individual elements in the traditional belief system survived the fall. Fragmented off from the system to which they had originally belonged, they evolved in different, sometimes surprising directions. For example, traditionalism's reliance on ancestral rights and privileges was converted into theories of history that praised the depth of wisdom contained in long-enduring human practices. Ideas that had derived originally from religious inspiration were often reformulated in secular and civic terms. To mention a single example, the Christian doctrine that humankind is tainted by **original sin** became secularized into the view—associated with thinkers like Thomas Hobbes—that human character is naturally selfish and pleasure-centered.

Let us now take a more detailed look at these conservative themes as they have developed in the modern world. In what follows we shall take up each of these themes in turn by focusing on the thought of a key conservative thinker.

Conservative Themes

The French Revolution and modernity

The move from traditionalism to conservatism took place in innumerable stages from the Renaissance to the Enlightenment. Traditional ideas and institutions lost ground continually on a great many different fronts—ground that the anti-traditionalists quickly occupied. The explosive culmination of these anti-traditionalist pressures took place centuries after the close of the Middle Ages when the French Revolution of 1789 violently assaulted the privileges of the monarchy, aristocracy, and church. It comprises the great historical fault line that divides the modern from the traditional.

The revolt against tradition

Drawing on ideas that the **Enlightenment** had made popular (for greater detail see Chapter 3), the revolutionaries of 1789 insisted on a radical break from the conventions of the **ancien regime**. Nothing so enraged these uncompromising visionaries as the conspiracy they perceived among the various forces of reaction: the church, the crown, the army, the landowners, and the official guardians of public morality. Taken together, the beliefs these groups fostered served to justify unthinking submission to "the way things have always been," keeping the masses blind, ignorant, passive, and in a permanent state of superstitious awe toward their "superiors." Systematically hidden from the French citizenry was that they could think for themselves and become masters of their own future. The revolutionaries charged that traditionalists preferred to envelop human life in impenetrable mystery because that justified treating the people as if they were children lost in the dark.

Voltaire as Enlightenment thinker

Voltaire, perhaps the most representative Enlightenment thinker, enjoyed employing his dagger-sharp wit to puncture traditional orthodoxies and demonstrate their self-serving character. An international grandmaster in the art of exposing the mischief and nastiness that lurked behind pious ideas, he heaped derision on religious claims to special knowledge. Arguments that humans were imperfect and hence incapable of self-improvement were only conniving justifications for maintaining injustices. Precedent and custom were more often than not synonyms for villainy and unreason. History, according to Voltaire, was not to be taught to children because it was the record of human enslavement, folly, and boorishness. Indeed, Voltaire liked to sign his letters with the belligerent declaration, "Wipe out the infamy"—presumably the combined infamy of superstition, tyrannical custom, and crippling ignorance.

Fortunately the errors of the past, Voltaire declared confidently, do not necessarily control the future. We need not remain the victims of a path we never chose. By directing the light of reason onto social life, human beings can liberate themselves from the traditional forces that control them. The dead weight of custom can give way to the vital powers of real knowledge. History can, in fact, become a truly human history, that is, one directed toward the realization of authentic human ends. Voltaire held out a vision of progress toward a community of mature and enlightened adults who designed their institutions according to the dictates of their reason. His message was constructive and destructive at once: a powerfully optimistic appeal to a future illuminated by rationality, and simultaneously, a declaration of war on the constraints of the past.

Rousseau and the social contract

Rousseau, the most influential of the Enlightenment's political thinkers, shared some of these ideas with his rival/ally Voltaire. Although Rousseau rejected parts of the rational thrust of the Enlightenment—his thought is often seen as the starting point for the **Romantic reaction** against Enlightenment rationalism—he fully agreed that autocratic political power is illegitimate. The legitimacy of authority, he contended, did not derive from ancestral traditions, from Divine ordinance, or from the genealogy of aristocratic families. Rousseau refused to accept the legitimacy of any political power not founded on the will of the people. To be genuinely legitimate, Rousseau wrote in his masterwork *The Social Contract*, political power must express the **general will** of a community. Political communities properly arise out of contracts made among free, morally united peoples. These contracts embody the essential communal will; they consolidate a common purpose. Implicit in the idea of a social contract is the understanding that political communities are human designs, agreements that embody human will—perhaps even a daily plebescite of the contracting parties. Political communities are most definitely not mysterious unions shrouded in the clouds of history.

Precedent and Prescription—Edmund Burke

Burke's conservative response

These bold claims did not go unanswered. As is so often the case, the more spirited and compelling the attack, the more sustained and forceful the defense, and from across the English Channel came a defense that has become recognized as the most influential formulation of conservative thinking in the modern era. Its author was Edmund Burke (1729–1797), a thirty-year veteran of the House of Commons, a Protestant Irishman by birth, and a defender of the old order by conviction.

Burke vs. Voltaire and Rousseau

There is something perverse in presenting Burke's ideas as a series of systematic and theoretical propositions about politics, for it was precisely the systematic and theoretical qualities of Enlightenment thinking that he found most offensive. For Burke, politics was not an arena suitable for abstractions, but an intensely practical activity requiring prudence and sobriety rather than brilliance or contrived hypotheses. Voltaire and Rousseau were never more wrong-headed than in their attempt to systematize the rational and timeless principles upon which public life should rest. Human societies, Burke declared, were far too complex, unique, and intractable to be successfully penetrated by such flimsy inventions.

Burke was not a political philosopher. Both as a matter of personal disposition and as a conscious political principle, he found the philosophic style of political analysis objectionable. He would have preferred being described as a learned but practical individual who had amassed a rich experience in public life. His knowl-

Edmund Burke (1729–1797). A conservative politician who rejected abstractions.

edge, he would have liked it said, derived from an intimate familiarity with both the limits and possibilities offered by the real world of politics. Above all, his apprenticeship in politics had taught him that the texture of lived experience was always more diverse, unruly, and subtle than mere ideas could capture.

Not surprisingly, Burke had difficulty sustaining an abstract argument for more than a few paragraphs. His thought more naturally tending toward the specific and accessible, he felt most at home responding to real events and issues as they presented themselves. Much of his writing is therefore in the form of pamphlet essays that address the pressing issues of eighteenth-century English politics. In fact, many of his most memorable arguments come in the context of speeches he gave to the House of Commons. As he once explained his rejection of abstractions: "I must see the things, I must see the men."[3]

Burke's critique of the revolutionaries

No event in Burke's lifetime had as dramatic effect on "things" and "men" as the French Revolution. The sixty-year-old Burke, at the height of his career and his powers, rose to the challenge in his most celebrated work, *Reflections on the Revolu-*

---

3. Quoted by Russell Kirk in "Burke and the Philosophy of Prescription," *Journal of the History of Ideas* 14 (1953):365–66.

tion in France. For Burke, the French Revolution was a revolution of doctrine and theory—a bloody academic exercise. The revolutionaries responsible for the upheavals in France were radicals with half-baked ideas and no political experience. Armed with these dubious virtues, Burke wrote sarcastically, they set out to tear down the social edifice painstakingly built by centuries of human effort. They were sure they knew better, this band of philosophical fanatics, merely because their heads were filled with bits and pieces of pretentious ideas. Confident of what needed to be done to satisfy the dictates of reason, and lacking the restraint that comes with real political experience, they had set France on the course of catastrophe.

The limitations of political theories

Despite Burke's defense of continuity and tradition, he was no unconditional enemy of reform; he supported the American Revolution and, more broadly, advocated government by the consent of the governed, because these causes were rooted in established historical rights that reached back to the Magna Carta — as opposed to the French Revolution that relied on mere theory. The revolutionaries in France, enamored by theory, failed to understand that society is not a simple mechanism to be taken apart and put together again at will. They were like theoretical biologists who, without ever having held a scalpel in their hands, unhesitatingly performed radical surgery based upon a pet theory they happened to hold. In Burke's view, the institutions a nation builds up over time do not derive from consciously designed theoretical principles. Hence, theory is irrelevant to their understanding.

Institutions reflect historical trial and error

Enduring social practices, Burke believed, develop out of the thousands of daily experiences undergone by countless individuals in an endless variety of circumstances. Institutions like religion, the crown, social hierarchy, the family, and private property never leap into being simply because they are convincingly demonstrated by eloquent theoreticians or because they are in accord with the abstractions of reason. Only slowly, almost glacially, as the consequence of a massive historical exercise in trial and error, do human practices strike root and endure:

> *The science of government being therefore so practical in itself and intended for such practical purposes—a matter which requires experience, and even more experience than any person can gain in his whole life, however sagacious and observing he may be—it is with infinite caution that any man ought to venture upon pulling down an edifice that has answered in any tolerable degree for ages the common purposes . . .*[4]

In each enduring social institution, Burke insisted, lie buried the cumulative results of innumerable adjustments to changing circumstances. Long-enduring institutions are therefore always more than they appear to be. What seems senseless in the impatient theoreticians' eyes may well be part of a delicate social balance finely tuned through centuries of trial and error. As with complex ecological sys-

---

4. *Reflections on the Revolution in France* (New York: Bobbs-Merrill, 1955) 69–70.

tems, even small human interventions can have devastating effects. These long-standing social institutions continually bear the pressures exerted by human needs and interests. If they fail to meet these demands, obsolescence follows. Ill-suited social conventions, Burke was convinced, are dealt with harshly by history itself; they do not require revolutions to undo them. Their very inappropriateness will, in time, send them packing. By contrast, if a social usage shows great resilience over long periods of time, it must contain elements that are indispensable for our existence. From Burke's point of view, nothing speaks so strongly in favor of an institution as its staying power.

The species is wise

Although individuals, however brilliant, often commit preposterous errors, the species taken as a whole is a true genius. The knowledge of the solitary thinker or a generation of thinkers is necessarily limited by the minimal experience on which it is based. Compared to the wisdom residing in age-old institutions, theoreticians are invariably light-weights. They have every reason to be humble. After all, Burke cautions repeatedly, "the nature of man is intricate; the objects of society are of the greatest possible complexity." There are no simple answers that "can be suitable either to man's nature or to the quality of his affairs."[5]

Theoreticians may be seduced by a little knowledge, but humankind, with its lengthy historical perspective and infinitely various experiences, has a way of separating the wheat from the chaff. Given sufficient time, Burke declares, "it almost always acts rightly." Continuous experience will not long be taken in by impostors, intellectual fashions, or failing ideas—whatever their alleged theoretical perfection. It embodies the collective verdict of humanity on the great political issues. We ignore this verdict at our peril.

Burke's critique of social metaphysics

Those like Rousseau who devise fanciful theories and then declare them to be superior to the lessons of history are the worst offenders. Concocted ideas such as the general will or the social contract are weightless and ahistorical—"social metaphysics," in Burke's mocking phrase. They lack any appreciation of how real societies arise or endure. These ideas fail, therefore, because (1) they are simple while social life is always complex; (2) they are based on hypothetical ideals while social life is always rooted in concrete experience; (3) they claim to be rational and time-less while social life is always practical and particular; (4) they claim that societies are created and sustained through the exercise of our sovereign will while, in truth, social life emerges organically in a slow and painstaking process of collective experimentation.

Rationalist politics encourages fanaticism

The most dangerous flaw in the rationalist's position is the fanaticism it encourages. In Burke's mind, rationalist politics and fanaticism are inseparable. Since reason is notoriously unsteady—what is reasonable here may be outrageous there—controversy over theoretical principles is virtually inevitable. Moreover, lacking a recognized authority before which these disputes can be resolved, theoretical conflict has a way of deteriorating regularly into violence. Burke warns that rational principles do not come equipped with mechanisms of

---

5. Burke, *Reflections on the Revolution*, 70.

compromise or resolution. They tend to be all-or-nothing affairs that incite all-out conflict. How astute Burke was in this analysis can be judged by his canny prediction—made a few months after the fall of the Bastille—that the French Revolution would deteriorate into terror and finally be taken over by an order-restoring leader.

By contrast, historical-based claims to property rights or political legitimacy can be validated by reference to the historical record. They can be arbitrated, legally adjudicated, or become the object of practical compromise. Indeed, to speak the language of historical precedent is to enter a world of practical wisdom that cultivates deference to others and the honorable resolution of conflicts.

Prescription vs. rationalism

Political claims, Burke concludes, should be submitted to the great tribunal of history. **Prescription**, not abstract principle, is the surest guide to political action. By prescription Burke means to convey a sense of the compelling weight of historical precedent. He also recommends **prejudice** to his readers, although not in its contemporary negative meaning. Prejudice, for Burke, is the well-founded judgment of those who are attached to a rich political tradition and wish to preserve it. In the following very graphic passage he portrays the difference between those who exercise "wise prejudice" and those who are in the grip of the rationalist delusion. Political actors

> *should approach to the faults of the state as to the wounds of a father, with pious awe and trembling solicitude. By this wise prejudice we are taught to look with horror on those children of their country who are prompt, rashly to hack an aged parent in pieces and put him into the kettle of the magicians, in hopes that by their poisonous weeds and wild incantations they may regenerate . . . their father's life.*[6]

In surely the most often cited passage from the *Reflections*, Burke expounds his conservative thinking with an eloquence and power that make it worth reading with great care:

> *Society is indeed a contract. Subordinate contracts for objects of mere occasional interest may be dissolved at pleasure—but the state ought not be considered as nothing better than a partnership agreement in a trade of pepper and coffee, calico, or tobacco, or some other low concern, to be taken up for a little temporary interest, and to be dissolved by the fancy of the parties. It is to be looked on with reverence because it is not a partnership in things subservient only to the gross animal existence of a temporary and perishable nature.*

If not for momentary gain, in what sense is society a contract? Burke's answer could hardly be more majestic:

---

6. Burke, *Reflections on the Revolution*, 109–10.

It is a partnership in all science; a partnership in all art; a partnership in every virtue and in all perfection. As the ends of such a partnership cannot be obtained in many generations, it becomes a partnership not only between those who are living, but between those who are living, those who are dead, and those who are to be born.

He concludes by evoking the image of a contract that transcends particular states, to become linked with eternity and universality.

Each contract of each particular state is but a clause in the great primeval contract of eternal society, linking the lower with the higher natures, connecting the visible and invisible world, according to a fixed compact sanctioned by the inviolable oath which holds all physical and all moral natures, each in their appointed place.[7]

Summary

To summarize the elements of Burke's conservatism that we have presented:

1. Politics is a practical, experience-based activity. Abstract theories are irrelevant as a guide to political action.
2. Human society is far too complex and delicate to be encompassed by rational schemes. Such schemes will inevitably be revealed as inappropriate to the real world of practice.
3. Institutions are not the creation of conscious will or rational contracts. They develop in a slow and painstaking process of historical trial and error. Hence, long-standing practices must be presumed to contain a full measure of wisdom.
4. Because the thinking of individuals is always based on limited experience, it is to be approached with suspicion. By contrast, the species as a whole is wise.
5. Because rational doctrines lack the suppleness that comes with experience, they tend toward extremism and rigidity. When they come into conflict, violence is likely to ensue.
6. The proper guides to political action are prescription and prejudice. They provide the criteria by which to judge competing claims to rights, duties, and privileges.

Burke's position has a certain undeniable plausibility. But let us take up the challenge that Burke himself lays down and refuse to accept his ideas merely because of their apparent reasonableness. In the spirit of Burke's own teachings, we need to confront his conservatism with concrete political realities and see how it fares. Are prescription and prejudice reliable guides in the real world of public life? Are they relevant to political realities very different from those of eighteenth-century England? In

---

7. Burke, *Reflections on the Revolution*, 110.

other words, how universally applicable are the insights he offers? Judge for yourselves.

Critiques

A. Consider the case of a society that has always been based on slave labor. If a group of slaves mounts a rebellion in the name of equal treatment—a concept without precedent in their society—would it, in Burkian terms, be defensible? To make the case even more flagrant, what if the traditional practice is cannibalism, which a group of sensitive souls rejects because of unprecedented notions of human dignity?

B. Consider a community that is and has always been profoundly divided in its political traditions — for example, a society composed of two ethnic or religious groups who have no choice but to live together, or alternately, two groups within a single society who have always held incompatible worldviews. What would prescription mean in these circumstances? Could it be a guide to the legitimacy of political claims?

C. What of a society that incorporates racial discrimination into its life and appeals to the historical record to justify it? Racial prejudice, this society argues, is as old as human history. Probably no people has ever been entirely free of its effects. It has thrived on all continents, in all historical periods, in virtually every conceivable cultural setting. How are we to deal with this kind of justification? Can we continue to claim that as a species we are wise? Does the age and universality of racism add anything to its acceptability? If our answer is no, is it based on no more than a flimsy rational theory?

D. Particularly challenging is the case in which a certain group within society has gained ascendancy over all the others. It controls the sources of wealth as well as the instruments of physical coercion, such as the police and army. Most critically of all, its control extends to the society's culture, to its approved ideas, even to the authoritative version of its own history. All these instruments of control are effectively exploited to legitimize the controlling elite's regime. Let us assume further that this control has existed for as long as anyone can remember. Should the compelling weight of precedent act to deter potential revolutionaries from pursuing their radical objectives?

Hypothetical cases such as these are likely to give Burke's sympathizers second thoughts. They appear to expose some fatal defects in his conservatism. But do they? Are his principles irreparably compromised by these examples? Can they be reformulated in a way that would meet these challenges? What distinctions and arguments would be necessary in order to mount an effective defense?

Whatever our final verdict on the Burkian position, actively grappling with its inner dynamics will surely convince us of its resilience and pertinence. If we enter into thought experiments of this kind, the logic and limits of the world-view are likely to become clear, present, and alive. But modern conservatism is not exhausted by Burke. Let us turn now to another of its typical contemporary forms.

Truth is Universal and Unchanging—Leo Strauss

The variety of political traditions

Political traditions are notoriously different from one another. What counts as civic virtue on one side of a border may well be considered villainy on the other. If one political tradition highlights rationality, another celebrates instinctive urges. Some traditions are pacific, others violent. Some enforce rigid hierarchies; others tend to egalitarianism. Many cultural traditions are closed and tribal in outlook. Others strive toward a broadly universal significance.

Although this profusion of traditions is all too obvious and familiar, what are we to make of the jumble of ideas and practices that confront us? Are we to understand the diversity of political traditions, like the diversity of human languages, as a fact of life beyond which there is no appeal? Is each tradition to be understood as a separate truth? Or is there a way of introducing order into what appear to be mutually exclusive viewpoints? Should we be searching for a larger, more encompassing truth, one that transcends specific political traditions in a single integrated vision?

It would not have occurred to the medieval political mind to ponder questions of this sort. For medieval thinkers, the traditional and the universal were not two separate modes of approaching political thought. What had come down through tradition was assumed to be divinely ordained. The theocratic-hierarchic-monarchic political tradition was, in their mind, sanctioned by the cosmic order itself.

When the medieval political world collapsed, these two approaches—the traditional and the universal—became unstuck. Arguments from tradition, such as the one we encountered in the thought of Burke, no longer necessarily linked up with the very different contention that what was traditional was also authorized by some ultimate natural reason. Contemporary tradition-based conservatives[8] counsel sticking close to the actual qualities that animate a particular culture of political behavior rather than indulging in vacuous philosophizing about universal principles. Only through experiencing the inner sense and natural rhythms of a specific tradition—in much the same way that native speakers experience their mother tongue—are we genuinely able to participate in a culture of political discourse. Indeed, many latter-day disciples of Burke have nothing but scorn for conservatives who seek the proper guiding principles of political life through speculative reason and soaring abstractions.

Conservatism as universal reason

In sharp contrast, there are others for whom conservatism has become identified with the existence of a transcendent universal reason. In and of itself, they contend, tradition possesses no authority. Political traditions are notorious in preserving nonsense on a vast scale. A tradition of political behavior is authoritative only to the degree that it incorporates the binding dictates of a timeless and absolute reason. To justify traditions merely because they happen to have survived is to encourage subordination to what were often historical accidents and political conspiracies.

---

8. See for example Michael Oakeshott's *Rationalism in Politics* (London: Methuen, 1962).

Besides, accepting each political tradition as a law unto itself encourages a moral and political chaos that undermines the prospects of civilized life.

The contemporary voice of conservatism is therefore heard in (at least) two different registers. Although both traditional and philosophical conservatives champion many of the same policies, they speak a fundamentally different political language. If they act as allies in their common struggle against liberals and radicals, they nevertheless tend to emphasize different elements within the conservative heritage.

Strauss

Few contemporary philosophical conservatives compare with Leo Strauss (1899–1973) in the intellectual influence they exerted or the personal loyalty they inspired. His biographical details are easily recounted. After taking a PhD in philosophy in his native Germany, he immigrated to the United States prior to World War II and took up a position teaching political philosophy at the University of Chicago. Although he wrote widely on many different aspects of political ideas, it was the classical thought of Plato and Aristotle as well as that of the medieval Arab, Jewish, and Christian thinkers with which he felt the greatest sympathy.

Strauss was anything but a conventional professorial academic. Although a profoundly learned and bookish scholar who championed the life of philosophical contemplation, he was also something of an intellectual guru. Around him developed a Straussian academic circle dedicated to preserving and disseminating his ideas. More than two decades after his death, his disciples constitute what may be the most cohesive fraternity in North-American political science. His followers have made substantial inroads into the upper echelons of government, and it is not unusual for his name and teachings to be appealed to on Capitol Hill or Pennsylvania Avenue.

Critique of tradition

Tradition held little interest for Strauss, who in a typical argument notes that tradition can justify nothing unless we make the prior decision to accept tradition as the proper source of our political judgments. Appealing to tradition requires that we first make a convincing case for tradition as authoritative. Otherwise, why should we follow it? Surely not because we are conformist sheep who lack other alternatives. If we choose to honor ancestral traditions, it must be because they have been shown to be the most reliable guide to political life. But if this is the case, is it reason or tradition that has carried the day?

Careful consideration of Burke's plea for tradition will prove the point. Burke presents a reasoned defense of tradition, one that attempts to persuade us of the superiority of prescription over Enlightenment rationalism in the resolution of political issues. But if Burke's appeal to tradition rests on a rational demonstration of its appropriateness, then the choice of tradition rests on a rational rather than on a traditional foundation. In fact, Strauss taunts, tradition-based conservatives invariably turn to reason to justify their arguments. It could hardly be otherwise since tradition does not have the power to justify itself. Tradition must be justified by nontraditional means. And if it is reasoned argument that moves Burke and his followers to accept tradition as decisive, then clearly arguments in regard to political principle must be met at the level of reason rather than be disposed of by simple appeal to the ancestral.[9]

---

9. *Natural Right and History* (Chicago: University of Chicago Press, 1953) 294–323.

Straussian reason   But Strauss would not have us employ reason in its everyday sense. For Strauss (as for conservatives of virtually all types), the idea of John and Jane Doe relying on the dictates of their own very limited reason to guide political life is the stuff of which nightmares are made. The reason of the "common man" is, predictably, all too common. In the Straussian view, leadership belongs to the wise, and the divide between the masses and the truly wise can never be bridged; it is radical and abiding.

Nor is he referring to the reasoning prevalent in the natural sciences—the kind of reasoning so often championed by Enlightenment thinkers. Modern science, with its narrowly empirical character, is capable of illuminating the trees, but not the forest. It cannot perceive the Whole, the overarching Truth, of which the many empirical scientific truths are only a small part. Moreover, scientific reasoning encourages the pernicious illusion that to reach the truth we need merely follow a certain prescribed scientific research method. In this, science promotes the most foolish of democratic beliefs: it appears to equalize unequal minds, that is, to reduce the pursuit of truth to a standardized, mechanical activity broadly available to the mediocre.

Strauss champions reason that is speculative, comprehensive, and eternal in character, and he is fully aware that it has fallen on hard times. With few exceptions, Strauss complains, contemporary public discourse disdains the pursuit of the transcendent principles that underlie authentic political wisdom. What passes for political reasoning has no interest in or capacity for this noble enterprise. Instead, fashionable intellectuals like nothing better than to deride the very possibility of such knowledge. Like other medieval superstitions, they assure us, it has been overcome.

The culprit in all of this, Strauss believes, is a loss of faith, an erosion of the age-old belief that wise human beings can know what is good and bad, right and wrong. Not what is "good for me" or "right for my lifestyle," but rather the good and the right in themselves. Strauss insists that without the belief in eternal truths that are beyond our power to affect, we stand at the brink of **nihilism**.

Relativism   This loss of faith can be condensed into a single highly charged word: **relativism**. According to this very popular modern notion, our ideas are always part of a concrete context; they express changing historical needs and are born in the dynamic of real events. Ideas are the instruments by which we orient ourselves in the real world. Relativists deny that social ideas can possess a timeless validity or that they can be immaculately conceived. They are always human devices that originate in the framework of specific human needs. Hence, there is little point in evaluating them as if they were candidates for some transcendent truth.

Gaining genuine political knowledge, Strauss contends, is fatally compromised by this repugnant modern fashion. By assuming that all our thinking reflects socio-economic interests, psychological drives, or historical peculiarities, the relativist discredits the possibility of distinguishing the true from the false. Political ideas, like tastes in food or clothing, are ultimately personal commitments dressed up in impressive-sounding language. At the end of the day, there is no real difference between ideological sloganeering and sophisticated political philosophy: both express the changing needs of real people confronting concrete situations. Ideas are only functional, appropriate, or serviceable. Nothing more can be said about them.

Relativism leads to nihilism

But if there are no independent criteria by which to adjudicate between rival arguments, if all one can say about an idea or practice is that it is appropriate to its historical setting, if political philosophy turns out to be little more than an intellectualized justification for underlying interests, why bother? Why bother embarking on the laborious process of study and disciplined thought? Why pursue "truth" at all, Strauss protests, if the entire project has become so questionable that the very term needs to be enclosed in a pair of mocking quotation marks?

Strauss identifies the "crisis of modernity" with the abandonment of this belief in an ultimate truth. "Until a few generations ago," he observes nostalgically, "it was generally taken for granted that man can know what is right and wrong, what is the just or the good or the best order of society."[10] This is no longer the case. At the end of the twentieth century, an era in which doing your own thing has become almost a sacred duty, terms like eternal verities and transcendent truths seem quaint echoes from a past age.

Relativism suits modern mass society

But why has the relativist pathology spread so rapidly, and why has it found so large and receptive an audience? Relativism has become prevalent, Strauss replies, because it is perfectly appropriate to the sensibilities of modern mass society. Relativism is just the kind of self-serving position that would attract the small-minded, the conformist, and the mediocre, i.e., the qualities dominant in contemporary mass society. Relativism flatters their half-baked ideas by assuring them that they are no worse or better than those of the learned and the wise. They are only different.

The effects of modern relativism

By abolishing the standards that convicted them of their own inadequacy, relativism relieves the mediocre of the sense of inferiority that they should, by right, feel. In fact, it entirely wipes out the distinction between the vulgar and the sublime and places the lowliest and the highest on equal footing. It places mindless consumerism and television comas on a par with inspired literature and profound ideas. Grand Old Opry becomes every bit as good as grand opera, and the creations of Walt Disney stand alongside those of Milton and Spinoza.

This infinite tolerance does not arise out of deep respect for the intelligence and sincerity of an adversary. Relativist tolerance is the direct consequence of reducing all beliefs to the same sorry state. If one belief is no better than another, what is there to be intolerant of? Relativist tolerance is not a high-minded principle; it is the lack of any principles at all—a mark of intellectual and moral bankruptcy.

---

10. "The Three Waves of Modernity," *Political Philosophy, Six Essays of Leo Strauss*, ed. Hilail Goldin (Indianapolis: Pegasus, 1975) 81–82.

The self-contradic-
tion of tolerance

Beyond condemning this kind of permissive tolerance on ethical grounds, Strauss believes it is impossible to defend intellectually. In a strikingly acrobatic argument (that brings us back full circle to the one we heard in regard to tradition at the opening of this section) Strauss asks whether the tolerant ought to be tolerant of the intolerant. If toleration "is in accord with reason" and based on the assumption that we "can know the good," we should be intolerant of the bad or, in other words, reject the premises of relativist tolerance. If, on the other hand, we ought to be tolerant of the intolerant, we have violated our own rule and shown that tolerance is baseless and no better than intolerance.[11]

This argument does more than refute the relativist position. Through it Strauss emphasizes his most fundamental thesis: without an appeal to a binding and definitive reasoned standard, our beliefs founder. Even when we wish to defend tolerance of highly divergent points of view, we can only do so by committing ourselves to a single unambiguous point of view—that tolerance is right. Indeed, even the belief in relativism itself is either true or it is worthless. Strauss would have us understand that without accepting the existence of discoverable ultimate standards of judgment, and without recognizing that the pursuit of such standards is the primary objective of political thinking, our intellectual life is shallow and fraudulent.

Apart from the obviously conservative and elitist qualities that mark these arguments, it must be noted that Strauss and his disciples are convinced that the transcendent reason to which they appeal supports the main outlines of the conservative position. In practical terms, in fact, Strauss's operative political platform is not very different from that of other contemporary conservatives. Revolution and political adventurism are unacceptable, law and order are essential, egalitarianism is a dangerous delusion, intervention into private concerns is corrupting, social hierarchy is unavoidable, mass democracy is far from ideal, institutions and practices like the family and chastity are desirable.

Burke vs. Strauss

What separates Burkians from Straussians is the manner in which these beliefs are derived. For Straussians, the confidence that Burke and his followers place in the good sense of the many over time is unwarranted. By adding up the ignorance of the many over the centuries, they contend, all we are left with is compounded ignorance. Only by appealing to those standards that defy time and place do we rest our position on unshakable foundations.

Summary

To summarize the elements of Strauss's conservatism:

1. Political traditions cannot be the basis of our political judgement because they are widely discrepant in their characters. Moreover, much of what is traditional has been preserved because of accident or conspiracy.
2. Political traditions as well as our other political beliefs require justification in the light of reasoned principles. Such principles derive from universal

---

11. Strauss, *Natural Right and History*, 5–6.

and absolute standards accessible to philosophical understanding.

3. Philosophical reason is radically different from common sense or scientific reason. It is comprehensive and eternal in character and is only available to the truly wise. The pursuit of unconditional truths is the object of genuine political thinking.

4. Relativism—the belief that ideas can have no truth independent of the context in which they function—is the great enemy of genuine political thought and the most prevalent pathology of the modern mind.

5. Relativism is entirely appropriate to modern mass civilization because it flatters the philistines and the vulgar. Because it disqualifies standards, relativism denies that the common are inferior to the noble and virtuous.

6. Relativist tolerance derives not from respect for rival ideas but from the absence of any standard by which to judge them. In the end, if a reasoned case cannot be made for tolerance (or relativism or tradition) it must collapse in self-contradiction.

Critiques   A number of concluding questions (like those searching dilemmas we directed at Burke) are necessary if we are to grapple with the character and consequences of Strauss's ideas.

A. Most basically, how convincing is the claim that there exists a single, eternal, and unconditional truth that we can discover? Surely the virtually infinite variety of human cultures speaks eloquently against it. More than a little ethno-centrism and patronizing naivety are displayed in the view that the truth has been discovered by a handful of people and in only some cultures but is sadly lacking in all of the others.

B. Can it be purely coincidental that the universal dictates of reason seem to accord with the political platform of modern, Western conservatism? Why should we be convinced by Strauss's version of these ultimate standards when he has so many competitors who are equally certain that the truth is in their possession? Is it not just as credible, for example, that the truth lies on the side of equality and a politics of liberation (as Jefferson and many other worthy thinkers were convinced)?

C. How can we speak of accessible ultimates when even the greatest of philosophers—ostensibly the custodians of reason—are so often divided among themselves on the most basic issues? Shouldn't all of this teach us a little intellectual humility? At very least, shouldn't it make us feel a bit queasy with bombastic talk about final and absolute truths?

D. In the end, how far is Strauss's doctrine from a non-demonstrable declaration of faith? Oddly enough, for all his talk of reasoned standards, little in his argument appeals to what we familiarly call reason. Strauss tends to rest his case on the esoteric qualities of the philosophic experience itself rather than on any demonstration available to the non-initiated. Strauss's conservatism does not even have the virtue of Burke's in that at least Burke rested his claims on a broad historical thesis that is open to reasoned investigation. Strauss offers only a maddeningly elusive position that claims to reflect a truth systematically denied to almost everyone else.

E. How compatible is Strauss's world-view with the democratic faith? This is an important question not because demonstrating its incompatibility with democracy would necessarily disqualify it, but rather because it is important to follow ideas to their practical consequences. On its face at least, Strauss's credo gives every sign of being inimical to democratic values. What else is one to make of a doctrine that is based on an esoteric truth available to the few, a doctrine that is deeply disdainful of the wisdom of the average citizen? Why indulge in the entire undignified political hullabaloo of interest groups, electoral competition, and political bargaining if there is a single truth and it is binding and knowable?

These queries and critiques are not necessarily fatal to Strauss's position. Indeed, some of them are deliberately overstated. Nevertheless, they are likely to compel those who found his ideas attractive to reconsider, or at least to struggle a bit harder. Even Strauss himself would applaud such an effort. Burke and Strauss based their conservative views on an understanding of history and philosophy respectively. But many highly influential political analysts argue for a conservatism that rests on the flawed nature of human character. To these thinkers we now turn.

Human Imperfectability: Saint Augustine, Thomas Hobbes, and Sigmund Freud

Enlightenment optimism

Whatever their other differences, conservatives are unanimously uneasy with the liberal vision of humanity progressing toward enlightenment and liberation. At the heart of this typically modern outlook lies a critical assumption that conservatives emphatically do not share. Most simply, the liberal proposition can be stated as follows: the source of human adversity and suffering derives from the faulty character of our social institutions rather that from the nature of humanity itself. Flawed societies produce flawed individuals—not the other way round.

Progressives believe that human character is a *tabula rasa*, an empty slate; it is all potential and can become whatever is made of it. Its specific content and attributes are determined by whatever our personal and social experiences happen to be. We are socialized to become what we are; our personalities and perspectives reflect the historical, racial, cultural, sexual, class, ethnic, familial, and political settings in which we live. It follows clearly that the source of social evils and human tragedy lies in society itself. Whether we search for the roots of war or poverty, repression or ignorance, the culprit is to be found in the social circumstances in which these failings arise.

The optimistic conclusions to be drawn from this line of reasoning should be clear. Insofar as human problems derive from social problems, and social problems are subject to our reforming efforts, the future seems to be rosy indeed. As we progressively apply the tools of enlightened analysis to failing public arrangements, the symptomatic human pathologies arising out of them will gradually fade away. If we can relieve social ills, we have come a long way toward relieving human ills.

Conservative pessimism

Conservatives are more than a little skeptical. Besides rejecting pie-in-the-sky predictions about future bliss as immature wishful thinking, conservatives insist that the liberal/progressive outlook is flawed at a far more basic level. Progressive thinkers fail to recognize how deeply human character itself is implicated in the shortcomings of social life. Progressives obscure the immediate link between our ingrained human perversity and the often failing quality of our lives as social beings. They do not understand that aggression and greed are prevalent in society not for accidental and hence correctable reasons; they are prevalent because they are inextricable from the very constitution of the human psyche.

Augustinian conservatism

This is perhaps the oldest and most durable of conservative themes. Some sixteen-hundred years ago the great theologian Saint Augustine (354–430) gave it a profoundly somber Christian reading. He proclaimed that human character was so fundamentally contaminated by original sin that social justice was forever beyond our reach. Lust, venality, and irrational urges were incomparably stronger than rational or virtuous motives. Politics and the state are, at best, remedial institutions. Like police officers or jails, political institutions are designed to keep our belligerent and selfish character under control. Human history could not progress toward any lofty goal for the eminently simple reason that human beings could not progress beyond their own corruption and weakness. After all, they could reproduce only themselves. The very belief in progress, Augustine tells us, the self-flattering idea that human beings could overcome their creaturely limits through purely human efforts, was the essence of the mortal sin of pride.

Hobbesian conservatism

This same pessimistic picture reemerges more than a millennium later in the thought of the eminent English political thinker Thomas Hobbes (1588–1679). Hobbes's presentation is secularized and full of scientific trappings, but it is no less gloomy or forbidding. Here too the insatiable and violent character of human behavior is the central fact of social life. Uncontrolled humans would be little better than beasts. In fact, they would be worse than the dumb creatures of the fields and forests because human reason adds cunning and calculation to natural selfishness. Only the threatening presence of a powerful state ready to punish infractions can prevent the bloody anarchy that is humanity's natural state. Political institutions are therefore the determined enemy of and the deliberate counterweight to human nature, not the vehicles through which some higher form of human life can be progressively realized.

Freudian conservatism

Transposed into the language of contemporary Freudian psychoanalysis, the enduring Augustinian/Hobbesian world-view goes through yet another transformation—without altering its essential message. If anything, the portrait of human character that emerges from the writing of Sigmund Freud (1856–1939) is even more somber. Our deepest and most savage tendencies are, in Freud's view, outside our control, even outside our conscious knowledge. Reason is equipped to penetrate only the relatively shallow and accessible levels of our human existence. Only where reason ends do our authentic motives begin. In fact, what we cannot know about our motives is likely to have far greater effect on our actions and feelings than the rational accounts we are able to give of them. If we can deliberate about our intentions dispassionately, Freud would warn, there is every reason to believe that we are far from their vital source.

In the Freudian image, civilization is a frail bridge over the swamp of our murderous and incestuous desires. Civilization is in fact an unnatural state. By systematically frustrating our elemental impulses and forcing us into the role of buttoned-down, law-abiding individuals, civilization itself becomes the source of deep human discontent. We pay an especially high price for civilization's success in creating restrained and ethically disciplined individuals: we suffer from restless desire and vague desperation. We are caged and tamed, but not happy.

To believe, in the manner of the progressives, that the solution to the regular outbursts of human savagery is increased education, greater refinement, and more effective control over anti-social desires involves a tragic misunderstanding. For it is precisely the repression of our savage needs that is the real source of our desolation. More refinement means more, not less, discontent. Intensifying the restraint and good taste in our lives will only make the explosive frustrations that underlie civilization all the more uncontrollable and the return to our basic predatory state all the more likely. Paradoxically, the repressed desire to throw off the bonds of civilization and revert to passions of the most barbaric kind may be greatest in those who are, to all appearances, the most genteel and cultured. Freudians note how close the abominations of the Nazis were to the flowering of high German culture.

In this light, the progressive's fixation on issues such as social conditions, political rights, national self-determination, the distribution of property, etc., appears to be hopelessly irrelevant. Reform these all you want, Freudians declare; they are not the real source of human woes. Political revolutions are powerless to transform the human material out of which social life is constructed. (As in the old Soviet joke: all a revolution can do is transform a czar into a commissar.) Property can be equalized, social conditions substantially altered, political rights ensured; all this will not touch the deeper springs of human hostility and discontent. In fact, institutions like private property only express more fundamental ego needs for control and dominance. By abolishing property, we only displace these basic drives to other areas. Henceforth, cutthroat competition for dominance will simply take on different forms: who will have the more powerful position in the party hierarchy, who will be the fiercer warrior or even the more ingenious philosopher.

At best, civilization is a delicate balancing act between the need to restrain our primordial urges and the equal necessity to nevertheless allow for their expression. The notion that we are on a journey of self-perfection, that through the progressive rationalization of our social institutions we will be able to liberate ourselves from war, want, and injustice, cannot, in Freud's view, be taken seriously. Indeed, these baseless hopes, by encouraging infantile fantasies, only endanger the fragile equilibrium we have so precariously achieved.[12]

---

12. Freud's political ideas are found primarily in *Civilization and Its Discontents* (New York: Norton, 1961).

Summary   To summarize the central elements of that form of conservatism which bases itself on human frailty and imperfection:

1. Human beings are fundamentally flawed and limited.
2. The source of social imperfection lies in human imperfection.
3. Political life is powerless to perfect these flaws because they inhere in human nature.
4. Political life can do no more than prevent human beings from acting on their naturally selfish and predatory intentions.
5. Attempts at fundamental political reform and social revolution will invariably fail because they can only deal with the symptoms rather than the sources of human problems.
6. Equalizing property or political rights does not overcome human rivalries, exploitation, or selfishness. These vices will merely resurface in new (and not necessarily more desirable) forms.
7. By encouraging baseless hopes that human existence can be fundamentally overhauled, progressives threaten the social order and are responsible for a great deal of human suffering.

Critiques   These powerful ideas have attracted powerful criticisms.

A. Consider, first of all, that these irrational and perverse creatures have done a remarkably responsible and fearless job in diagnosing their own distress. Wisdom, honesty, and perception have been employed in order to convince us of humanity's depravity and treachery. It is hardly what we would expect from irremediably flawed beings. If we grant that the conservative's analysis of human nature is on the mark, do we not also commit ourselves to a more positive role for reasoned analysis than they allow?

B. What balanced individual would care to deny that human nature has a seamy side to it? None but the most wildly quixotic of ideological partisans would care to differ. Conservatives who make much ado about human weakness appear, therefore, to be crashing through an open door. Recognizing the human potential for corruption is only a preliminary step to virtually all political analysis; it hardly commits us to conservatism.

C. When we free the argument for human imperfection from its melodramatic rhetoric, how convincing is it? When destitute slum dwellers for whom desperation and anger have become a way of life turn to violent crime, is it because of original sin or homicidal tendencies lurking in their subconscious? We would surely want to know why these supposedly fundamental human characteristics tend to pass over the prosperous suburbs. Would anyone deny that if the same individuals were brought up in more satisfying surroundings they would likely develop less anti-social behavior?

D. When ravaged and repressed people turn to terror as a last resort, do we not entirely mystify what has happened if we understand it as a question of radical human evil? Would we be closer to understanding any of the major concerns of contemporary politics (such as the rise and fall of communism, the feminist movement, political and technological modernization, the rise of religious fundamentalism) if we viewed them through the lens of human imperfectability? Human imperfectability always seems to be saying too much and to be saying it too vaguely to be of much use for political analysis.

E. How credible is the conservative tendency to debunk progress and insist that history cannot truly advance because human character is irremediably twisted and perverse? Surely the rise of modern democracy, universal franchise, the unprecedented spread of human rights, popular education and the prevalence of literacy, the growing recognition that racial, religious, and sexual prejudices are unacceptable, and the decline of corporal punishment make a very eloquent refutation of this argument. To deny that we can progress and improve our lot would mean that public beheadings, illiteracy, feudalism, slavery, debtor's prisons, autocracy, marriage at age ten, and mass superstition are every bit as good as what has developed at the end of the twentieth century. Put in this concrete way, does not the human imperfectability argument appear contrived and implausible?

The Necessity for Hierarchy: Ortega y Gasset

Mass vs. elite   All humans are imperfect, but many conservatives are convinced that some are considerably more imperfect than others. At very best, conservatives contend, the belief in human equality is a theoretical abstraction. In practice, it is overwhelmingly refuted by our simplest observations. Summarized in its starkest form this argument insists that there will always be a sharp divide between the mass of people on the one side and humanity's natural aristocracy on the other. Healthy societies respect this distinction; the masses recognize their station and its duties, deferring instinctively to the special role that elites must play.

Since Plato's scathing attack on egalitarian democracy in *The Republic*—as the revolt of the low against the high, the base against the noble, opinion against knowledge—arguments for a hierarchical organization of society have taken many forms. In our time probably no single formulation of this position has reached so wide an audience as *The Revolt of the Masses* by Ortega y Gasset (1883–1955). The book appeared in 1930, some thirteen years after the Russian Revolution, less than a decade after Mussolini's rise to power in Italy, and a short three years before the Nazi takeover in Germany. Ortega wastes no time in getting to the point; he begins with the following blunt declaration:

There is one fact which, whether for good or ill, is of utmost importance in the public life of Europe at the present moment. This fact is the accession

*of the masses to complete social power. As the masses, by definition, nei-
ther should nor can direct their own personal existence, and still less rule
society in general, this fact means that actually Europe is suffering from
the greatest crisis that can afflict peoples, nations, and civilization.*[13]

"Heap after heap," the multitudes have been "dumped on the historic scene." If
they continue to control the European future, Ortega predicts, "thirty years will suffice to send our continent back to barbarism."[14]

The character of
the masses

It is not that our century has for the first time created ordinary people. Ordinary
has always been the norm. But the run-of-the-mill individual typically has had a
clear recognition of and a healthy respect for those whose qualities were out of the
ordinary. What has changed in our era is that the masses no longer recognize the
limits imposed by their ordinariness; they now insist on unlimited political power.
No area of life is safe from their aggressive interventions. They install themselves
as the arbiters of taste when they have no taste; they wish to dictate to the world of
politics although they cannot be bothered with its responsibilities; they insist on
ruling even though they are incapable of self-discipline. Lacking all humility, incapable of self-criticism, and rejecting any standard that transcends their own,
they constitute an unprecedented historical phenomenon: "the brutal empire of the
masses."[15]

Mass man

For Ortega, "mass man" is not identical with the great unwashed or an impoverished underclass. The concept has as little to do with economic status as it has to
do with the savoir faire involved in ordering wine at an elegant restaurant. "Mass
man" can be rich or poor, professional or laborer. The label involves a state of
mind, or to be more precise, a weakness of mind. To be part of the mass is to feel
just like everybody and not be concerned about it. It is to demand nothing of oneself, to be exactly what one happens to be: "mere buoys that float on the waves."
Alarmingly, Ortega warns, conformity has become more than a commonplace trait;
it now insists upon imposing itself universally. The mass wishes to crush "beneath
it everything that is different, everything that is excellent, individual, qualified and
select."[16]

Like heirs who have come into a lavish inheritance they did not work to create,
the masses have come to control the heritage of Western civilization. They have little
sense of the human genius and the prodigious efforts that went into creating the rich
legacy they now claim as their own. Still less are they willing to admit that its preservation is a demanding responsibility. Not recognizing what went into its construction,
they have no appreciation of what is necessary for its perpetuation. They want to
enjoy civilization while remaining unencumbered by its burden. These spoiled masses are unintelligent enough to believe that it is simply there for the taking. Civiliza-

13. *The Revolt of the Masses* (New York: Norton, 1960) 11.
14. Ortega y Gasset, *Revolt of the Masses*, 51–52.
15. Ortega y Gasset, *Revolt of the Masses*, 19.
16. Ortega y Gasset, *Revolt of the Masses*, 18.

tion for them is a great windfall and, Ortega believes, they have set about squandering the accumulated capital of the centuries with "radical ingratitude."

For the masses who rule **mass society**, rights are simply birthrights—they have no sense of human achievements attained with difficulty and sustained with effort. Born into the relative ease and abundance that modern civilization provides, they never learn the elementary lesson—known to all other ages—that there are profound limits to our human designs. The very idea that there are authorities higher than themselves is greeted with jeering disbelief. Deference and restraint are, of course, foreign to them. They know only how to demand their rights and expect them to be fulfilled without delay. Not surprisingly, caprice and permissiveness are their second nature. Ortega does not mince words about this repellent "mass man":

> *He is satisfied with himself exactly as he is. Ingeniously, without any need of being vain, as the most natural thing in the world, he will tend to consider and affirm as good everything he finds within himself: opinions, appetites, preferences, tastes. Why not, if nothing and nobody force him to realize that he is a second-class man, subject to many limitations, incapable of creating or conserving the very organization which gives his life the fullness and contentedness upon which he bases this assertion of his personality?*[17]

Can it surprise us that this "mass man" typically creates a cult of youth? Like the young, "mass men" are free of the burden of the past. They enjoy rights more than they assume obligations. They are only very partially responsible for the things they do. They live on the allowances provided by others. Revolting against the authority of the accomplished and the venerable is presumed to be part of their natural process of development. They live for the moment only. And they feel themselves invincible.

These "mass men" hanker after equality—but not because they perceive human worth in other individuals. For them equality is the ability to throw off the uncomfortable truth that others are more deserving than themselves. As opposed to the noble idea of equality that elevates all humanity to dignity and worth, the vulgar equality of "mass men" is merely a levelling device to bring all others down to their pitiful state. Similarly, liberal democracy for these "mass men" is not a higher form of social organization dedicated to human rights and mutual tolerance; it too is merely an instrument by which the masses can pursue their pleasures without being haunted by the sense of inferiority.

A learned ignoramus

Oddly enough, those for whom Ortega reserves his sharpest arrows are not the semi-literate working class. Rather, he sees in the "doctors, engineers, technicians, financiers and teachers," the "prototype of the mass man." These techno-barbarians are specialized until they know everything about nothing. They are modern savages

---

17. Ortega y Gasset, *Revolt of the Masses*, 62.

who reject broad cultivation and general learning as unacceptable dilettantism. Ortega describes them as "extraordinarily strange," neither learned nor ignorant. They are not learned because outside their specialty they are boors. But they are not ignorant either because they are amply trained (as opposed to genuinely cultivated). They are "learned ignoramuses," and they are dangerous. The confidence that comes with expertise drives them to insist on *all* their opinions—ignorant and primitive though these may be—with dogmatic certainty. Accustomed to the authority and deference that come with social and professional position, these "partially qualified men" are constitutionally unable to face the fact of their own ignorance. In Ortega's mind they represent the cutting edge of the revolt of the masses.[18]

Bolsheviks and fascists as mass men

For Ortega, nothing better exemplified the collective character of "mass man" in revolt than the political movements that had just triumphed in Russia and Italy and were soon to rise to power in Germany. Whatever their differences, both Bolshevism and Fascism are mass movements that accurately reflect the character of "mass man." They fully embody what can be expected from the triumphant revolt of the mediocre. They tear down the culture of centuries in order to enthrone their own childish notions of what art, music, and literature ought to be—whether in the form of socialist realism or aryan art. They are not only addicted to tasteless kitsch, they insist on its being universal. They harbor the greatest hostility for the non-conformist and the truly original. The rote repetition of shallow ideological formulae is their typical form of political expression. At times they simply refuse to give reasons for what they do—"Let us be done with discussions," they cry—and consider this a moment of greatness. Their ideas, Ortega declares, are nothing more than instruments in the service of crude desires—"appetites in words."

The threat of mass man

The unconditional submission demanded by "mass man" accurately reflects his basic character: he is a "primitive" with a smattering of technical skills. If **direct action** has taken the place of measured action, and groupthink has come to replace individual responsibility, it is only because the "mass man" has no patience with complexity, responsibility, or challenging ideas. Mass movements declare the right of vulgarity and ignorance to be dominant. In the light of all this, it will surprise no one to hear that, for Ortega, resisting the triumph of "mass man" is nothing less than "keeping back the invading jungle."[19]

Only if humanity's natural hierarchy can somehow reassert itself will tragedy be averted. Only if the culture-bearing elite is permitted to lead and the masses are content to follow can Western civilization set itself aright once again. And Ortega is not particularly hopeful.

Summary

Summarizing the main elements of Ortega's conservatism:

1. "Mass man" has displaced the natural cultural elites in the West. "Mass man" is defined by a specific psychopathology: he demands nothing of himself, he is content to be exactly what he is—just like everybody.

---

18. Ortega y Gasset, *Revolt of the Masses*, 109–14.
19. Ortega y Gasset, *Revolt of the Masses*, 89.

2. Masses have always existed; what is different at present is their demand for political power. They insist that their shoddy tastes, values and standards be imposed universally.

3. The masses do not understand that a culture, to be preserved, requires care and cultivation. They are interested only in their rights; they lack appreciation of duties and responsibilities. The masses have no respect for any authority above them or for any limits upon their will. Like the young, they live for the moment and feel themselves invincible.

4. Equality for the masses is a levelling device by which to pull everyone down to their pathetic level. Similarly, liberal democracy is a means to pursue their pleasures without being haunted by the sense of inferiority.

5. The technocrats—those who are trained in some narrow specialization rather than broadly cultured—represent the "mass man" in his most dangerous form. Accustomed to authority and deference, these "learned ignoramuses" are unable to perceive their own lack of understanding. They insist on their opinions with dogmatic certainty.

6. Modern mass movements like Fascism and Bolshevism represent the mentality of the "mass man" exactly. They lack a sense of history, believe there are no limits to what they can do, impose their crude cultural tastes on all, and speak a political language that is shallow sloganeering.

7. Only by allowing the natural hierarchy of human social organization to reassert itself can catastrophe be averted. Deference to the cultural elite on the part of the masses is the only way civilization can be preserved.

Critiques   Many of the objections directed to the previous conservative thinkers are clearly relevant to the case of Ortega, and it would be well for the reader to reconsider them at this point. But Ortega has come in for some critiques that are unique to him.

A. Ortega's prediction that only thirty years separated us from barbarism is badly mistaken. Thirty years have twice passed, and we do not seem in any imminent danger of being overtaken by the "invading jungle."

B. Ortega's contention that relying on the mass of common people in public life would bring catastrophe seems to be decisively refuted by the evidence of the last two centuries. If anything, the wisdom of the common people has proved itself generally reliable over time, while the alleged superior knowledge of the elites, vanguards, and intelligentsia constitutes quite a sorry record.

C. Neither does Ortega's account of Bolshevism and Fascism appear to square with the factual record. These movements derived from very specific complexes of historical forces that owed far more to economic crisis and political instability than to the soul of the "mass man." Ortega's tendency to reduce them to some elusive psychopathology of mass society is, at best, fanciful speculation—more esthetics than history.

D. Isn't Ortega's revulsion with the rise of the specialist precisely what we would expect from the typical patrician "man of letters" who can afford to be vaguely cultivated but is useless for any practical task? (More cynically stated: patrician intellectuals seem to put forward their claim to leadership on the grounds that they are incapable of doing anything else.) Isn't Ortega's defense of the cultural patriciate a transparent rear-guard action on the part of a class that is rapidly becoming historically extinct?

E. Wouldn't a late medieval theologian witnessing the rise of a secular intelligentsia (of the kind that Ortega currently represents) have reacted with doomsday predictions every bit as menacing as those we have just heard? Prophesies of doom, like prophesies of liberation, will be with us for a very long time to come.

F. Finally, doesn't Ortega have it all wrong? It seems perverse to bemoan the unprecedented education of the masses, to understand it as a retrograde step. (Only those who regret the loss of their monopoly over education are likely to be unhappy with its universalization.) No less perverse is the argument that Western culture is on the verge of collapse. Never before have so many universities flourished, never before have so many scholarly publications been available, never before has high culture been so widely accessible, and never before would a book like *The Revolt of the Masses* have become a major best-seller. Why does Ortega insist on seeing "barbarians" where solid common sense would lead us to appreciate the indispensable services of doctors and engineers without whose skills our lives would be that much poorer? If there is someone who lives off the fruits of civilization and is guilty of "radical ingratitude," perhaps it is Ortega himself!

Some readers may be puzzled by the absence of one very familiar ideological position that is often placed in the conservative category. This form of conservatism normally includes a vigorous defense of free enterprise and property rights, opposition to big government, rejection of the welfare state, etc. It has been excluded here because, formally speaking, it is really a pure, classical version of the liberal point of view. To more fully understand it, we need to leave the conservatives behind and go on to explore the significantly different logic of modern liberalism. It is to this task that we now turn.

Suggestions for Further Reading

Eliot, T. S. *Notes towards the Definition of Culture*. London: Faber and Faber, 1972.

Freud, Sigmund. *Civilization and Its Discontents*. New York: Norton, 1961.

Germino, Dante. *The Revival of Political Theory*. New York: Harper and Row, 1967.

Huntington, Samuel. "Conservatism as an Ideology," *The American Political Science Review* 51, no. 2 (1957).

Kirk, Russell. *The Conservative Mind*. Chicago: Henry Regnery Co., 1953.

Lippmann, Walter. *The Essential Lippmann*. Ed. Clinton Rossiter and James Lare. New York: Random House, 1963.

Lorenz, Konrad. *On Aggression*. London: Methuen, 1963.

Morganthau, Hans. *Politics Among Nations*. 2nd rev. ed. New York: Alfred A. Knopf, 1959.

Niebuhr, Reinhold. *The Children of Light and the Children of Darkness*. New York: Scribner, 1960.

———. *Moral Man, Immoral Society*. New York: Scribner, 1960.

Nietzsche, Friedrich. *The Portable Nietzsche*. Ed. Walter Kaufmann. New York: Viking, 1969.

Oakeshott, Michael. *Rationalism in Politics*. London: Methuen, 1962.

Scruton, Roger. *The Meaning of Conservatism*. Totowa, N.J.: Macmillan, 1980.

Viereck, Peter. *Conservatism Revisited*. New York: Scribner, 1949.

Voegelin, Eric. *The New Science of Politics*. Chicago: University of Chicago Press, 1952.

Will, George. *Statecraft as Soulcraft*. New York: Simon and Schuster, 1983.

From Liberalism to Social Democracy (1)

(Chapters 3 and 4 comprise a single extended essay that covers the ground from classical liberalism to social democracy.)

Modern Liberalism: Dominant and Ambiguous

If ideological success is measured by the sheer prevalence of a political world-view, then liberalism must be counted the most successful modern ideology. For the past three centuries, liberal thought has been the defining quality and the most fundamental experience of Western political civilization. It has become the normal condition of the industrial Western democracies. Liberalism's basic credo—comprised of such familiar items as **individualism**, civil rights, private ownership, and **pluralism**—is inseparable from the modern Western political outlook. With the collapse of communism in the late 1980s, this dominance became all the more thoroughgoing. So much so, in fact, that one contemporary analyst could make the bold and controversial claim that ideological struggles, as we knew them in the past, have come to an end. Liberalism, he proclaimed, has triumphed.[1]

American liberalism includes conservatives
In the United States, liberalism has had a near ideological monopoly. Throughout the greater part of American history, there have been few serious challenges to its primacy.[2] To be sure, some American political activists prefer to be described as conservatives. It is also true that the term liberal has come to be identified with the left branch of the liberal family tree. Nevertheless, for the sake of

---

1. Francis Fukiyama, "The End of History?" *The Public Interest*, Summer 1989 and responses in Winter 1989 issue. Also see his *The End of History and the Last Man* (New York: Free Press, 1992).
2. See Louis Hartz's classic study, *The Liberal Tradition in America* (New York: Harcourt, 1955).

historical and terminological accuracy it is important to understand that political debate in the United States takes place within a single tradition of ideological discourse: liberalism. Strictly speaking, American conservatives and liberals are both liberals—estranged members of a single ideological family. Conservatives champion a position known as **classical liberalism** while liberals support a more recent variant often described as **welfare liberalism**. For all of their substantial differences, they remain bound to a set of commonly accepted moral and political axioms.

The ambiguity of "liberal"

Liberalism is flexible and inclusive in its meanings, more an evolving tradition of ideological discourse than a single sharply defined political credo. The wide variety of uses to which the term liberal can be put becomes strikingly evident when we compare phrases such as liberal arts, a liberal education, a liberal attitude toward sexuality, a liberal contribution to charity, a liberal spender, and a liberal-minded view of world affairs. In some instances the term connotes broad cultivation and a generosity of the spirit, in others it entails permissiveness and tolerance. But it can also mean material generosity, even a tendency toward wastefulness. It may at times refer to a form of open-mindedness that takes an active interest in the diversity of human life and seeks to appreciate the points of view held by others.

Two senses of liberty

The term *libertas*, from which liberalism derives, has also had a long history that goes back to classical civilization. In its older classical significance *libertas* meant something quite different from its modern equivalent. In the ancient world, liberty was understood as a positive entitlement; it related to an individual's right and civic duty to share in public deliberations and decisions. A free person was one who was able to participate in public life. The modern meaning, by contrast, carries a fundamentally negative sense. It connotes an individual's immunity from communitarian intervention, a guaranteed sphere of privacy and independence. As opposed to classical liberty that drew an individual into public life, modern liberty offers protection from it. To possess liberty in the modern sense means, therefore, to be free of interference in the pursuit of one's own personal objectives.

American vs. European liberalism

When we consider the more specifically modern political uses of the term, its possible meanings expand further still. In the American context, those called liberals belong to the left; they advocate government intervention in favor of the weak and needy, the redistribution of wealth, and a generally reformist attitude toward the institutions of government. By contrast, liberals in continental European politics oppose these very same measures. They support free market economies and resist the attempts of left-wingers to introduce welfare legislation and expand the role of government. As odd as it may sound to American ears, European liberal parties belong to the conservative center-right of the political spectrum.

Liberalism's pervasiveness in the modern world is matched only by its unsettled, ambiguous character. It has no catechism, no orthodoxy, no authoritative texts, and no single revered thinker. Compared to communism with its canonical Marxist writings and systematic creeds, liberalism is a grab-bag of loosely related beliefs and behavior. Even the most celebrated liberal treatises, like those of John Locke and John Stuart Mill, do not command the authority or inspire the reverential textual commentary typical of the masterworks of other ideological traditions. To be sure, liberalism possesses the basic historical unities that characterize every evolving tradition of ideological discourse. Nevertheless, three centuries of evolution have created so rich a mixture of liberal species and sub-species that contemporary liberalism resists easy characterization. Indeed, modern liberalism is generally thought to include within itself a wider range of disparate views than any other ideological family.

Liberalism's Substance: The History of an Idea

Classical Liberalism

Modern liberalism emerged in the seventeenth century during the long and stormy English Civil War, especially its climactic resolution, the Glorious Revolution of 1688–1689.* It represented the revolt of a rising urban middle class of merchants and entrepreneurs against the pre-modern alliance of throne, sword, and altar—the absolute monarchy, the feudal aristocratic order, and the vast powers of the church.

Early liberalism's program

Early liberals challenged the legitimacy of the traditional medieval order and championed the right of individuals to pursue their own lives unimpeded by the heavy-handed, often arbitrary control of kings and clerics. They sought to loosen the constraints imposed on the dynamic commercial classes by a static, authoritarian regime that defended established hierarchies and orthodoxies. In place of obedient subjects, liberalism sought to create autonomous citizens. Each individual, liberals argued, possessed a sovereign and inviolable private space into which the authorities were prohibited from entering.

Negative freedom

The best form of government, they declared, was government that governed least. Such government would subject the social and economic behavior of its citizens to a bare minimum of regulation, and jealously safeguard each individual's natural rights to life, liberty, and property. Hence modern liberalism, from its origins onward, has regularly been associated with a fear of the overbearing state. It has been dedicated to carving out a domain reserved exclusively to individual choice. The commitment to what is commonly called **negative freedom**—the freedom *from* public interference in private matters—has been perhaps its most enduring characteristic.

Note: After nearly fifty years of civil war, William and Mary of Orange were invited to assume the role of king and queen of England in place of the unpopular James II. They accepted a Bill of Rights that made Parliament sovereign over English government. This has come to be known as the bloodless or Glorious Revolution.

John Locke

The state of nature

John Locke in his *Second Treatise on Civil Government* (published in 1690 but written earlier) gave these rising anti-authoritarian sentiments their most eloquent expression. In a dramatic departure from the accepted view of political power as a divine endowment, Locke asserted boldly that the powers of government derive directly from the consent of the governed. Government has no legitimacy but that which it draws from the will of those who voluntarily establish it. But if states are legitimated by popular will, Locke faces a novel dilemma—one that did not even occur to the earlier divine right theorists. Why would free and rational individuals choose to empower a state if states irresistibly mean police, executioners, conscription, and taxes? Why would a state be established if it exacts so high a price? Why not remain at the level of a non-regimented, stateless society? The answer to this cardinal question must be sought, Locke argues, in the hypothetical period that preceded the creation of public authority: the **state of nature**.

Natural right to life and liberty

By nature, Locke asserts, individuals are free, equal, and self-governing. These fundamental human qualities inhere in our very character as living and willing

beings. Most fundamentally, Locke argues, we each have a right to our bodies and our lives: they constitute the most inalienable form of property. They are ours essentially, beyond all conventions or historical accidents. Our rights to life and liberty are, therefore, absolute.

The fruits of our body's labor are ours by right as well. As Locke puts it: "Every man has a property in his own person. This nobody has any right to but himself. The labor of his body and the work of his hands, we may say, are properly his."[3] When an individual changes a natural object into a human artifact by investing labor into it— say by transforming a wooden log into a table—more has happened than an objective

John Locke (1632–1704). He asserted that individuals are free, equal, and self-governing.

---

3. Peter Laslett, ed., *Two Treatises of Government* (Cambridge: Cambridge University Press, 1960) 329.

change in the wood's form. By "mixing our labor" with the log, we make it ours. It is no longer an unappropriated part of nature's bounty. The table carries the imprint of a specific individual's labor and creativity. It has become inextricable from the self whose creative powers it now embodies. It has become property in the original sense of the word: that which (like life and liberty) inheres in the self.

Natural right to property

Others, recognizing that this object is no longer ownerless, are duty-bound to respect its new private status. Similarly, when they mix their own labor with nature's bounty, they are entitled to expect that the property so created will be broadly respected as well. Property is therefore *natural*; it precedes the formation of the state and is not dependent on any institution for its legitimacy but forms an intrinsic part of what it means to be a willing, active human being. Prior to the creation of public authority, therefore, the normal state of affairs is one in which property, created by individuals investing their labor into unowned objects, is broadly recognized as belonging to specific persons.

Broadly but not universally. There will always be those cases, Locke cautions, where the rule of reason breaks down. Whether because of genuine conflict over ownership, or as the result of willful misappropriation, or out of simple negligence, individuals will at times feel that their property has been wrongfully taken from them. Understandably, they will attempt to recover what they think is rightfully theirs and punish those who have violated their rights. But such attempts at recovery and punishment pose a serious problem: they threaten to shatter the peace and to plunge the state of nature into feuding and violence. Worse still, the cycle of revenge and retaliation threatens to spiral out of control and to engulf many otherwise uninvolved individuals. The normally peaceful state of nature is, therefore, in danger of degenerating into a frightening state of all-out war.

The role of the state

Public authority comes into being in order to deal with this latent, ever-present peril. Governments, Locke contends, are created for the specific purpose of preserving order by arbitrating between the rival claims of clashing individuals. Much like a referee at a sporting match, the state is charged with guaranteeing that the rules of the game are honored. Without actually becoming part of the contest, the state insures that fair play prevails. It may not go beyond this regulative role. Not having created individual rights, the state may do no more than arbitrate between them. On no account may public authority infringe or undermine them.

The limits of state power

When individuals enter a political community, Locke contends, they do not surrender their natural rights to life, liberty, and property. On the contrary, the entire purpose for which public authority is created is to guard against the violation of personal rights. Individuals, bearing their rights to life, liberty, and property with them, contract with a public authority to safeguard the peace so that they may each more fully enjoy their own natural entitlements. Because property rights predate the state, they are immune from state interference. Locke's conclusion is simple and dramatic: legitimate government is limited government—limited by the individual rights of those it has been created to serve.

Rights are
individual

An important corollary of this argument is that rights are always individual rights. Because rights derive from the property we each have in our own lives and bodies, they must always inhere in specific persons. The community, or society as a whole, has no rights. Indeed, the community is simply an abstracted figure of speech; apart from the real individuals that comprise it, it has no moral or political standing. There can be no general will, no single unified perspective transcending the interests of a society's individual members. Individual interests never add up to more than many individual interests; they do not become transformed into the public welfare. Hence, there can be no justification for sacrificing one individual's rights for the sake of another's—even for the sake of the so-called common good. Government oversees the interactions between autonomous self-seeking individuals; it ensures that the natural market mechanisms of buying and selling, contract and performance, injury and restitution operate with a minimum of friction. Nothing more.

Summary

Locke's liberalism, then, is based on the following ideas:

1. A view of humans as rational, self-interested creatures who naturally possess the rights to life, liberty, and property.
2. Although humans normally respect the rights of others, without an arbitrating authority clashes between individuals can endanger the peace.
3. The state is established to safeguard our natural entitlements. By arbitrating conflicts, it allows us to enjoy our rights in peace.
4. Not being the source of human rights, the state may not violate them. These rights, most notably the right to property, are absolute.
5. Rights are always individual rights. No communal rights exist. Hence, the community many not violate individual rights for the sake of some ostensible common good.

But it would seem that this kind of unmitigated individualism is a recipe for catastrophe. A society of self-seeking atoms, each pursuing different objectives, lacking any overall plan or purpose seems likely to degenerate into chaos. How could it survive without coordination? A free-for-all of unregulated individuals would also wreak havoc with the market itself. If every responsible business must plan its marketing strategies with great care, how can general prosperity be expected to issue from a random collision of interests?

Adam Smith

Private vice,
public virtue

The undesigned nature of the capitalist market, liberal theorists tell us, is the paradoxical secret of its great success. In his classic study of free enterprise economics, *Wealth of Nations* (1776), the great Scottish liberal Adam Smith argued that the spontaneous actions of innumerable separate individuals each pursuing their own personal benefit added up to a marvelously efficient, prosperous, and free form of human association. "It is not from the benevolence of the butcher, the brewer, or the baker that we expect our dinner, but from their regard to their own interests." In fact, Smith writes, "I have never known much good done by those who affected to trade for the public good." Smith continues:

> *every individual necessarily labors to render the annual revenue of the society as great as he can. He generally, indeed, neither intends to promote the public interest, nor knows how much he is promoting it . . . he intends only his own gain, and he is in this, as in many other cases, led by an invisible hand to promote an end which is no part to his intention.*[4]

Paradoxically, our private vice of selfishness becomes, in the self-regulating capitalist market, a public virtue.

Capitalism's efficiency
Driven by the dependable motor of self-interest and regulated by the sensitive mechanisms of price, supply, and demand, the liberal free-market system succeeds—far better than any deliberately designed system could—in coordinating individual actions. Prices constitute a highly efficient signaling system that synchronizes the actions of innumerable individuals who lack firsthand knowledge of each other. Seeking the best for the least, consumers keep quality up and prices down. Seeking the greatest profits, producers are beholden to do the same. **Capitalism** therefore succeeds in utilizing resources optimally, meeting the most varied demands, assuring the best service and producing at the lowest cost. An apparently random collision of interests is in reality a finely tuned network of stimuli and responses that regulates vast numbers of individual decisions in the most efficient manner possible.

Capitalism's virtues
Capitalism, for all its selfishness—indeed precisely because of the way it utilizes human selfishness—is socially benign. Most significantly, it is benign without relying on that rarest of human qualities: altruism. Without imposing unnatural sacrifices in the name of the general good, capitalism creates public wealth. It encourages human cooperation spontaneously rather than imposing it by authoritarian means. The free market fosters precisely the blend of human cooperation and competition that is appropriate to the peaceful/aggressive realities of human nature. Besides, capitalism insures that each person—whether laborer, proprietor, or consumer—possesses the greatest liberty compatible with a similar liberty for every other person. Above all, the invisible hand that coordinates the market gives the last word to the countless ordinary individual consumers freely pursuing their own lives. Capitalism's greatest virtue lies in its being a daily referendum in which final authority resides in the desires of real individuals.

---

4. *Wealth of Nations*, ed. Bruce Mazlish (New York: Bobbs-Merrill, Library of Liberal Arts, 1961) Book 4, Ch. 2, 166.

Smith's
individualism

Like many other early liberals, Smith insists that personal and economic freedom are primary—even more significant than civil and political freedoms. Liberty begins with the ability of individuals to pursue their careers, family lives, patterns of consumption, and contractual responsibilities without a busy-body government telling them what they should be doing. Smith's liberalism, like Locke's before him, is therefore radically individualist. The free, self-seeking, rational individual is the ultimate source of the wealth of nations. There is no general welfare apart from the individual pursuit of interest. Defeating the free interplay of individual interests through public interference in the market mechanism will only undermine efficiency, reduce prosperity, and diminish liberty.

Summary   Smith's contribution to the liberal idea:

1. Individuals pursuing their own interest are led, by a kind of invisible hand, to add to the public wealth.
2. The free market, relying on price, demand, and supply, coordinates the activities of countless individuals far better than any deliberately designed system could.
3. Individual self-interest is the most reliable motive toward the production of wealth for all. Hence, public interference in the workings of the free market is to be strenuously avoided.

The Revision of Classical Liberalism

Oddly enough, modern liberalism was at least a century and a half old before it received its name. When John Locke and Adam Smith defended individual rights and praised the free market, liberalism was a nameless phenomenon. Ironically, when the term liberal finally made its way into our political vocabulary (its first use was in 1810), liberalism was already departing from the heritage of Locke and Smith to assume a new and substantially different character.

Capitalism's problematic consequences

The classical liberal belief that uncoordinated, spontaneous market mechanisms were best left undisturbed was beginning to be challenged by a powerful new liberal conception of social needs. This newer form of liberalism was not always happy with the results of unrestrained capitalist competition. It recoiled at the festering slums of underfed and overworked laborers who toiled at their rote jobs for 14 to 16 hours a day. Widespread prostitution, illiteracy, homelessness, recurrent epidemics, violent crime, and child labor deeply disturbed many a sensitive conscience. In addition, capitalism did not seem to be encouraging the beneficial form of individualist competition it promised. Market mechanisms had given rise to all-powerful monopolies that made a mockery of competition: they controlled entire industries, set prices arbitrarily, produced shoddy goods to which there were no alternatives, and exploited their work force with brutal indifference.

This new conception also challenged the classical liberals' identification of freedom with economic freedom. The new theorists were unhappy with classical liberalism's only lukewarm commitment to popular democratic government.[5] They were particularly disturbed by its prevalent tendency to link civil and political rights to the size of an individual's economic holdings. To vote, for example, one needed to be the owner of a substantial amount of property. In England at the beginning of the nineteenth century property qualifications limited the vote to the upper middle class and above. In the United States, property qualifications, although more lenient, were also quite common.

But these new liberals challenged more than property qualifications for voting. They called into question classical liberalism's most inviolate rules: (1) that popular will was powerless before each individual's property rights; (2) that government's sole function was to protect property and arbitrate between individuals when they came into conflict with each other. Classical liberals insisted that whatever the pressing social needs governments wished to pursue and however great the majority that supported these measures, there could be no justification for abridging the rights of individuals to their property. Being the inalienable and absolute possession of individuals, property rights formed a natural barrier beyond which others, especially the organized community, were prohibited to venture. States that trespassed onto property rights, classical liberals had warned, violated the covenant upon which their existence rested and, in so doing, called their legitimacy into question.

The welfare
liberal's
alternative

If classical liberals tended to value property rights over citizens' rights, the new brand of liberalism that emerged during the nineteenth century felt that these respective claims needed to be reassessed. These new liberals—revisionist or welfare liberals—did not, of course, seek to discredit property rights or renounce individualism. Individualism and property rights are principles that unify liberals of all varieties. Yet the revisionists departed from the classical understanding of liberalism in two major ways: first, in wishing to modify the stark doctrine of absolute property rights that was leading to acute social ills and crippling the market mechanism itself, and second, in tending to perceive of liberalism and of popular democratic rule as indissociable from one another.

These new liberals argued that the classical doctrine was failing on its own terms because it destroyed in practice what it professed in principle. Individualism and personal autonomy—liberalism's deepest commitments—were being stunted by the very doctrine that championed them. As one twentieth-century liberal, John Dewey, put it:

Instead of the development of individuality which it prophetically set forth,

---

5. See Giovanni Sartori, "The Relevance of Liberalism in Retrospect," in *The Relevance of Liberalism*, ed. the Research Institute on International Change, Columbia University (Boulder, Colo.: Westview Press, 1978) 1–31.

there is a perversion of the whole ideal of individualism to conform to the practices of a pecuniary [money-centered] culture. It has become the source and justification of inequalities and oppression.[6]

Revising classical liberalism

Rather than sticking to obsolete dogmas that were miscarrying in practice, the revisionists called for a reconstruction of liberalism to make it more suitable to the new world it had helped create. To preserve its original intent, liberalism would have to revise its earlier commitment to the untrammeled free market and to the inviolability of private property.

A new role for government

The role of government also required rethinking. Instead of acting as an impartial referee in the free competition between autonomous individuals, governments were, in reality, enforcing rules that consistently favored some and prejudiced others.

To uphold the sanctity of contracts is doubtless a prime business of government, but it is no less its business to provide against those contracts being made, which, from the helplessness of one of the parties to them, instead of being a security for freedom becomes an instrument of disguised oppression.[7]

Revisionist liberals insisted that beyond the indubitable right to contract freely and to own property securely, the actual realities of public power had to be considered; otherwise individualism and liberty were in danger of becoming worthless slogans.

Property rights favor the propertied

Protecting property rights indiscriminately, the revisionists argued, in effect meant safeguarding the rights of those who were already in possession of vast amounts of property. If government existed to protect property, was it any surprise that the propertyless fared so badly both legally and politically? If the purpose of government was to enforce contracts between individuals whatever their content, can we wonder that the weaker partners to the contract—say starving laborers who have no choice but to accept unjust work agreements—regularly find themselves lawfully exploited?

States, revisionist liberals declared, were different from joint stock companies in which one's standing in the community of investors was determined by the amount of property one held. There was no escaping the sense that human society was more than an aggregation of independent investors each possessing separate interests. To be sure, liberalism's dedication to safeguarding the rights of self-interested individuals could not be questioned. But important as these rights were, they were insufficient to adequately comprehend the nature of social life. Social interdependence went beyond contracts, commodity trading, and formal employer-employee relationships. It involved more essential human bonds. One might even

---

6. Cited by D. J. Manning in *Liberalism* (New York: St. Martin's Press, 1976) 104.

7. Dewey cited by Manning, *Liberalism*, 20.

speak of a common good or a public welfare without violating the commitment to individuality and property rights. Rights were held not by individual Robinson Crusoes seeking their separate fortunes; individual rights were held by persons sustained by a rich social life and by traditions of communality. If the rights of some had to be modified in order to protect the individuality and rights of many others, the trade-off was both necessary and legitimate.

Perhaps, the revisionists added, classical liberal conceptions such as absolute property rights and minimal government regulation had been appropriate in an era of staunchly independent proprietors, isolated homesteaders, and rural landowners. But a century and half of massive socio-economic transformations had made these early capitalist ideas woefully anachronistic. The complex patterns of social interdependence, economic concentration, and large-scale industry that marked modern urban society meant that the proper role of government as well as the place of property rights required a new kind of ideological dispensation.

Utilitarianism

One very influential version of these new liberal ideas was incorporated into the philosophical movement known as **Utilitarianism**. Beginning with Jeremy Bentham in the late eighteenth and early nineteenth centuries, carried on by his disciple James Mill and finally by the latter's son John Stuart Mill, the Utilitarian idea became toward the end of the nineteenth century England's dominant socio-philosophical school. Its core idea can be simply stated. The proper criterion for a morally legitimate social policy is whether it serves to advance "the greatest good of the greatest number." Bentham had conceived of a "calculus of pains and pleasures" that ought to direct our actions. We must carefully consider the effect of a proposed policy on society as a whole. If the overall benefit for the greatest number outweighs the displeasure it causes for the rest, the policy is morally desirable.

Utilitarians vs. classical liberals
This sounds deceptively simple and obvious. Consider, however, what classical liberals might say in response. The paramount good of even an overwhelming majority does not grant the right to violate the natural entitlements of individuals. Rights are not public property to be allocated according to an alleged common good. Rights may not be bartered or redistributed. Policies that deprive me of my rightful property—for example, to shelter the homeless—are nothing but theft and no less objectionable than being coerced into contributing to charity. By strict utilitarian logic, classical liberals would charge, individuals could be stripped of all they have in order to serve social purposes for which they have no sympathy.

Utilitarians would dismiss this charge as a wild exaggeration. Because private property and individual rights are among the most beneficial of all social institutions, it is inconceivable that these would be capriciously set aside for some dubious policy objective. Nonetheless, if it should happen that an individual's property rights stood in the way of a critical social objective, the pressing needs of the many might well take precedence over the property rights of the few. Revisionist liberals of all kinds, Utilitarians among them, would therefore accept the following principle: individual property rights, although possessing presumptive validity, must be assessed in terms of their effect on the broader social context.

A number of dramatic examples will illustrate the point. If—to begin with a very extreme instance—an individual's legitimately acquired land had the only water source in an arid region and he subjugated the local populace by charging exorbitant prices for water, it would be entirely legitimate for the public authorities to abridge his property rights by regulating the distribution of water and setting maximal prices for its purchase.

Or, consider a corporation that buys up a town—its land, factories, homes, stores, utilities. It then contracts with workers who, needing jobs badly, agree to live and work within this company town. But as a provision to the contract, the corporation stipulates that the town will not be run as a democracy. Strikes are forbidden, civil rights will not be honored, and elections will not be held. Since the town is now entirely private property, the owners argue, it is outside the limits of public control. To make the case even more severe, what if the contract provides that the town's children must forgo their education and begin working in the company factories at age five? In such cases, overriding social concerns should clearly have priority over property rights. Government would be authorized to step in and annul the offending provisions of the contract. Although both sides had entered into the agreement in a state of formal freedom, the clearly desperate conditions that coerced the workers into accepting so dehumanizing a contract would provide adequate justification for government to disqualify it.

Implicit in this last case are a number of important principles. First, the protection of property rights is not the sole function of government. For revisionist liberals, government serves equally as a guardian of the public welfare. The attempt to use property rights as a legitimation for suspending popular self-determination is, therefore, unacceptable. Second, the necessity for education appears to be so critical that governments are duty-bound to override contractual rights in order to protect it. Because education is a primary means to personal self-realization, the safeguarding of individuality requires that it be mandatory. Individuals can be required to receive an education—even if this limits their natural liberty and their contractual rights—because without education their personal autonomy would be permanently stunted.

Positive
government

Liberalism in its revisionist-welfare form is, therefore, partial to a more positive understanding of what governments ought to be doing. Revisionism rejects the classical liberal's negative conception of both personal freedom—as the freedom from interference—as well as the negative conception of the state's role—states have only the minimal role of protecting property and contracts. Welfare liberals interpret their commitment to individualism, liberty, and property rights in a broader, more activist way. Paradoxically, the only way to protect individual rights is for government to prevent some individuals from exploiting their entitlements in a way that undermines the ability of others to exercise theirs.

Individualism
redefined

Individual rights, they insist, go beyond those related to property and to non-interference. Individuality can only be developed under certain favorable social conditions. Destitution, for example, is as great an enemy of individual liberty as is autocracy. Freedom from external interference, therefore, although important, is not the single defining quality of personal autonomy. Individual rights, if they are to be meaningfully exercised, must be the possession of those who are in a position to utilize them. Otherwise they are mere legal fictions. The genuinely free person is the self-possessed one: an individual who is able to act according the dictates of a mature and informed conscience. To speak to a homeless person about individualism, non-interference, and property rights is to indulge in a particularly heartless joke.

John Stuart Mill

This tendency to perceive of liberty in its broader social context characterizes the work of perhaps the greatest liberal thinker of the nineteenth century: John Stuart Mill. In his essay *On Liberty* (1859), Mill goes well beyond the property-based liberty as simple non-interference doctrines that had characterized classical liberal thinkers. What, he asks, is the justification for the freedom of ideas and opinions? What is liberty for? Why is it important?

Liberty is
utilitarian

Liberty is important, Mill believes, for a number of complementary reasons. As a Utilitarian, he justifies liberty because of its beneficial effects on society. When the free flow of ideas is present, "wrong opinions and practices, gradually yield to fact and argument."[8] Allowing the unimpeded competition between rival ideas, even marginal and unpopular ideas, sharpens our thinking and weeds out arguments that cannot withstand careful scrutiny. A plurality of contending positions is the best guarantee

John Stuart Mill (1806–1873). He believed in the free flow of ideas.

---

8. *On Liberty*, Everyman Edition (London: Dent, 1972) 82

that truth will emerge triumphant. Liberty serves society by fostering the cause of knowledge.

Liberty ennobles   But beyond such explicitly utilitarian justifications, Mill also appeals to the essential human worth of liberty, to the caliber of person it fosters. Of what value are ideas, even true ideas, Mill asks, if the believer does not understand the reason for their truth? Ideas held as "dead dogma" rather than "living truth" are "but one superstition the more."[9] Conformity of any kind, even to a broadly accepted opinion, diminishes our human potential for intellectual creativity and for moral self-mastery. When, however, truth is sought among many differing points of view, when each rival perspective needs to be critically evaluated, it is we as sovereign moral agents who gain. Beyond its practical dividends for society, therefore, liberty is humanly ennobling.

The new liberal ideal   A society of rational, informed, morally engaged, and autonomous persons is among the highest of liberal ideals. "The worth of a state," as Mill puts it, "is the worth of the individuals composing it . . . With small men no great thing can really be accomplished."[10] To enhance the worth of a state's individuals, the protection of personal property, is indeed of great importance. Property entitlements provide the inviolable personal space critical for autonomous human development. But if they are critical, they are nevertheless often insufficient. Individuals who are prevented by illiteracy, grinding poverty, or an overbearing state from being autonomous cannot form the basis of a healthy political community. Authentically liberal government will, therefore, set its full authority against threats to individual self-development, whatever their source. It will seek to create a free, intelligent, and participating citizenry by advancing the conditions that encourage basic human autonomy.

Summary   To summarize the central tenets of revisionist liberalism:

1. Absolute property rights and minimal government often do not advance the cause of liberty. An unrestrained free market creates poverty and monopolies, both of which are enemies of personal autonomy.
2. By understanding liberty in terms of property rights, classical liberals had unjustifiably made one's public standing conditional on one's economic holdings. No less than property rights, the civil and political rights of participatory democracy are critical for the development of free individuals.
3. Hence, the liberal ideal must be expanded to include creating the material and spiritual conditions for the development of informed, intelligent, and morally responsible individuals.
4. The radical individualism of classical liberalism should be moderated to allow for considerations of the common good and the public welfare, i.e., to accommodate the potentially positive role that government can play in safeguarding liberty.

---

9. Mill, *On Liberty*, 96.
10. Mill, *On Liberty*, 170.

Welfare Liberalism's Practical Program

Safety nets   When translated from the abstractions of social theory into concrete historical practice, these revisionist liberal ideas gave rise to many social programs aimed at remedying severe cases of poverty, exploitation, and degradation. A series of safety nets were erected to catch those who faltered in capitalism's relentless competition, to prevent individuals who could not sustain themselves by their own efforts from falling into the depths of helplessness and desperation. Unemployment insurance provided a soft landing for those who had lost their source of income. For those unable to support themselves for longer periods of time, welfare programs were established. Social Security payments assured older people of a minimal income in their declining years. Health care for the indigent and the aged made certain that the most important human resource of all, health, would not be the privilege of the young and the well off.

A progressive income tax provided that a disproportionate part of public expenses would be shouldered by those who could afford it most. Industry and trade were regulated to prevent significant injury to the public welfare. The purveyors of dangerous or deceptively marketed products became liable to prosecution. Health standards were instituted in many industries, especially those dealing with food preparation. Monopolies were broken up to encourage trade. Uniform safety and quality standards went into effect for a wide variety of businesses. Working conditions and hours were regulated by government. Child labor and the labor of pregnant women were severely limited and strictly supervised. Minimum wages were imposed. Mandatory education was legislated. Needless to say, all of these involve a substantial departure from liberalism in its classic form.

In the twentieth century these measures expanded to include the rights of trade unions to organize and represent the interests of workers. Many measures assuring job security, pensions, days off, benefits, severance pay, etc., became commonplace. The Great Depression of 1929 ushered in an era of even deeper government penetration into business and trade. As President Franklin Delano Roosevelt put it: "The age of enlightened administration has come."[11] During the **New Deal** of the 1930s Roosevelt initiated public works projects to put many of the unemployed back to work. Public assistance programs expanded, banking and stock market practices were carefully regulated, public utilities came under government supervision, and huge government conservation projects like the Tennessee Valley Authority (TVA) were embarked upon.

Keynesian   Influenced by the liberal British economist John Maynard Keynes, the idea that
economics   governments should borrow money against the future to stimulate a weak economy—more commonly known as **deficit spending**—became increasingly prevalent. Governments primed the pump, administered a jump start for economic growth.

---

11. From *Addresses on American Democracy*, Classics of Western Thought: The Modern World (New York: Harcourt, Brace and World, 1968) 519.

Money was pumped into the economy in the anticipation of sustained economic growth after the initial burst of activity had passed. Understandably, government's role expanded further still when it marshalled and coordinated the massive national effort involved in fighting World War II.

Following World War II, public regulation turned to less overtly property-related issues. Governments began to intervene in unprecedented areas such as the civil rights of racial and ethnic minorities, women, criminals, etc. School desegregation and affirmative action policies meant the imposition of federal standards on regions and institutions that were often unhappy with them. Government became embroiled in the explosive controversies related to birth control, abortion, and pornography. Toward the end of the century regulation spread to a number of novel and highly charged issues such as environmentalism, multi-cultural education, and gay rights.

The failures of big government

The agenda of welfare liberalism had, in the early post–World War II years, become the public agenda. Classical liberalism, although it retained a small ardent following, was clearly in retreat. But a number of serious cracks in the dominant liberal edifice began to show. Deficit spending had created a national debt of monstrous proportions that raised serious obstacles to further economic growth. Moreover, the old policy of government spending no longer seemed to be stimulating the economy; it was now creating an ornery problem of it own: stagflation—inflation without economic growth. Staggering health costs, in which government was deeply involved, were making the American economy uncompetitive in the world market. Widespread reports of welfare fraud, of welfare families on the dole for three or four generations, of welfare recipients involved in violent crime, created the public perception of something gone very wrong with a humanitarian effort. Perhaps most basically of all, the common feeling that individual autonomy was being suffocated rather than enhanced by public intrusion into private affairs raised serious questions about the direction that liberalism was taking.

The revival of classical liberalism

If welfare liberalism held the historical stage for much of the century, since World War II, and particularly in the last three decades, there has been a significant revival of the classical liberal position. Reacting against the failures of big government and the limits of deliberate social engineering, the idea that "a free market is the finest guarantor of individual freedom" gained both new converts and a fresh theoretical sophistication. The collapse of the Soviet planned economy made free enterprise capitalism seem all the more attractive to many, especially those in East Europe who were emerging from the painful inadequacies of collectivism. At present both the classical and the welfare versions of liberalism coexist in the marketplace of ideas. Because each has developed many variants and offshoots of its own, modern liberalism has become a busy hive of intellectual activity in which many of those who use the title liberal feel quite uncomfortable with others who do the same.

The varieties of liberalism

For one school of American liberals—the conservatives—the economic market should not be regulated but public morals should. For their adversaries—who usually answer to the name liberal—moral issues should be left to private choice while economic concerns should be carefully scrutinized by government. Some liberals preserve the optimistic belief that reason can effectively control and direct human affairs, while others are deeply suspicious of any rationally conceived and deliberately designed public order. Some associate liberalism with the spirit of scientific experiment. Others—often referred to as **Social Darwinists**—believe that capitalism is the preferred economic system because, by creating stiff competition between producers, it fosters excellence and progress as well as ensuring the survival of the fittest. Some are partial to **natural rights** theorizing, which for others is (in Bentham's old phrase) "nonsense on stilts." For some, liberalism is based on the notion of a social contract; others remain committed to the utilitarian principle of the greatest good of the greatest number; others still relate liberalism to the live-and-let-live tolerance required in an era of relativist skepticism. The one benefit to liberalism from all this disunity is that it is probably too various and multifaceted to be easily done in by any single enemy.

Liberalism: The Enduring Themes

However multifaced liberal discourse may be, a number of themes have endured throughout its historical evolutions. To be sure, even these enduring themes are differently interpreted by the various schools of liberal thought. Some will be central to one version of liberalism while being only secondary to another. With these reservations kept in mind, what would a generic liberalism look like? Which ingredients persist in all or nearly all of its many versions?

Rational, self-directed individuals

1. Liberals understand human beings as enlightened, rational, active, sovereign, self-interested creatures. Hence, the final authority in human affairs ought to be the conscience of the private individual. All mature persons ought to be responsible for their own conduct, for choosing their own life-plans, for determining their own ethical and intellectual credos. Although liberals recognize that social interaction is imperative for the realization of these individual life plans, they insist that the social collective must not be endowed with privileged moral standing. A human community represents a network of private interests interacting with each other, not a self-standing organic unit possessing a will and objectives of its own.

   This image of the self-directed, autonomous individual lies at the heart of liberal beliefs. It underpins the liberal's highly positive attitude towards competitive, free-market economics. The sanctity of private property is grounded in each person's ability to transform the natural world through the use of will, creativity, and labor. Understanding the self as an inner-directed, inviolable private space entails that certain human and civil rights must not be infringed. Deriving from this same basic image is the liberal tendency to favor tolerant, live-and-let-live social policies.

Liberal egalitarianism

2. Liberals are egalitarians insofar as they view each individual as endowed with the same moral status as all others. Hence, equality before the law and equality of basic human entitlements are mandatory. This equality extends to the identical ability of all to freely contract with each other, to transfer property, and to sell labor. Liberals also support the principle of

equality of opportunity—if it is defined as the equal opportunity of each individual to compete in the free market. If, however, equal opportunity is expanded to entail government's actively equalizing opportunity by assisting the disadvantaged to compete more effectively, the liberal camp would find itself deeply divided. Liberals of all shades strenuously reject egalitarian ideas if they lead to a policy of levelling unequal human talents.

Reason as universal

3. The view of individuals as rational and enlightened implies a certain universality to human character. Notably, it was Jeremy Bentham who coined the term "international." Liberalism is not a parochial creed with local objectives; it understands its commitment to both human rights and to the international capitalist market as a reflection of the most essential and abiding qualities of the human character. Of course, violent passions may temporarily distort reason, and duress can undermine informed self-direction; unimpeded however, the essential human qualities of discernment and autonomy will reassert themselves. This view often leads to an optimistic appraisal of the human future.

The right and the good

4. Liberals distinguish rather sharply between the "good" and the "right." These two terms, so often used interchangeably in everyday speech, have very different meanings in modern ideological discourse. The "good" involves specific, substantive objectives that individuals, as moral agents, set for themselves. It denotes the life plans or broad human goals towards which people strive. Very obviously, different individuals are committed to incompatible conceptions of the good: for some it is wisdom, for others hedonism; many pursue riches while others are dedicated to body building. "Right," on the other hand, has to do with means, not ends. It deals with the proper procedures to be followed in the pursuit of the good. Right relates to the rules of the game that must be adhered to whatever one's particular conception of the good may be.

Liberals insist that states must remain neutral and passive in the matter of the good, but take an active role in the matter of the right. In other words, states ought to be agnostic about the proper aims of human life. They should not set ethical goals for society as a whole. (As we noted above, society is not an organic unit and hence can have no substantive goals of its own.) Ethical choices, in the liberal view, are properly the province of the private individual's conscience.

What public authority must do is ensure that individuals are free to pursue their own version of the good as long as this does not infringe upon the rights of others to do so as well. Government does far better in restraining ignoble human impulses than in realizing noble ones.

For liberals, therefore, government is **instrumental**: it safeguards the conditions necessary for each of us to engage in our different human pursuits. All government regulation, arbitration, and administration properly serve to guarantee a more basic goal: the preservation of our individual human autonomy to chose and to act upon our conception of the good.

Skepticism and pluralism

5. Liberals tend toward skepticism in regard to moral absolutes. Human conceptions of the good, after all, will always be variable and plural. Besides, even those many moral ends we espouse as individuals may not be compatible with each other—we may, for example, feel that individual entitlements are inviolate while simultaneously (and without contradiction) we are drawn instinctively to a noble vision of human equality.[12] Liberals tend to be uncomfortable with official versions of the virtuous life or the true human vocation. Especially distasteful are those single-minded doctrines that tell us what our conception of the good would be were we only authentically rational and liberated individuals.

The moral ends of even reasonable and decent individuals, liberals insist, are irreducibly complex and various. No moral benefit will be gained, but much injury will be suffered, if we force our different moral commitments into a single streamlined ideal. Hence, moral pluralism has been a crucial component of the liberal credo.

Negative vs. positive freedom

6. Liberals are wary of conceptions of "positive freedom," which hold that, to be truly free, individuals must follow the dictates of their higher selves. Individuals are not free if merely unhindered by obstacles in the pursuit of their goals. Drunkards, for example, may voluntarily drink themselves into a daily stupor even though it would be difficult to speak of them as free. Advocates of "positive freedom" conclude that true freedom is the pursuit of genuinely rational ends, or in other words, acting so as to realize our true human potential. It is "freedom to," not simply "freedom from."

Liberal suspicion is aroused by such doctrines because they have so often led to rationally constructed, monolithic, and coercive political systems. Once freedom is identified with accepting certain ideas or practices, how far are we—in Rousseau's notorious words—from being "forced to be free"? How far are we from the total loss of individual autonomy that is part of totalitarian thought control? Whatever the theoretical attractiveness of freedom as a lofty, positive quality, it is in practical terms a very high-risk strategy.

Negative freedom, by contrast, understands free persons as those whose actions are free from external restraints—so long as these actions are not injurious to others. This negative view may lack some of the moral boldness and clarity of positive freedom, but it is more secure, cautious, and humane.[13] It also takes very seriously the significance of individual moral autonomy. Better that we should struggle with our own weaknesses and act

---

12. The most eloquent contemporary liberal theorist defending the plurality and incompatibility of moral goods is Sir Isaiah Berlin. See for example his "Two Concepts of Liberty" in *Four Essays on Liberty* (Oxford: Oxford University Press, 1969).

13. See Berlin's "Positive and Negative Freedom" in *Four Essays on Liberty*.

Pragmatism and
piecemeal reform

according to our own lights than be forced, in the name of freedom, into some dubious notion of the good.

7. Liberals like to think of themselves as pragmatic, moderate, and accommodationist. They prefer piecemeal reform to the massive overhauling of governmental institutions. Radical restructuring, they argue, fails for a number of reasons. First of all, when transformations are wholesale, they unavoidably violate the natural rights of some individuals. Second, when changes are too sweeping, social experiments lose all accountability. It is impossible to determine which results derive from which causes. So many factors have been set into motion that isolating the reasons for success or failure becomes a hopeless task. Third, because liberals reject the political imposition of values and recognize that many different moral ends must necessarily coexist, they fear large-scale reforms that follow a rigid blueprint. Change, if it is cautious and gradual, if it derives from the spontaneous interaction of many free and non-directed individuals, is beneficial and necessary. By contrast, change inspired by ideological master plans is a menace to liberty, to efficiency, and to social stability.

Ordinary vs. epic

8. Liberalism lacks the moral drama and the epic qualities of many other ideologies. It normally fails to generate emotional heat or **utopian** dreams. Interestingly however, liberals are genuinely contented with this ordinary "politics as usual" character. It is difficult to lose one's head, they might say proudly, about a doctrine set on healing, compromise, and fair play. By contrast, it is far easier to delude oneself into condoning all manner of historical mischief if radical solutions are involved.

On the other hand, liberalism's detractors see these same qualities in a negative light. Liberalism is for middling people who are incapable of great things. Its advocates do not hold to deep or firm beliefs; they are, critics continue, small-minded bargainers, pragmatic problem-solvers—an uninspired lot. One contemporary liberal spoke for a broad constituency when he responded:

> *If one seriously believes that the purpose of history is to provide a stage for heroes, then the detractors are right. Liberalism recognizes that heroes there will be . . . but it believes that politics has failed when heroism has become necessary.*[14]

Contemporary Liberalism: A House Divided

The enduring liberal themes we have just enumerated should not encourage the impression that classical and welfare liberalism are separated by issues of only marginal importance. They are two very different positions divided by a common idea.

---

14. Charles Frankel, "Does Liberalism Have a Future?" in *The Relevance of Liberalism*, 112–13.

In fact, the ideological distance between welfare liberals and social democrats may at times be less than that which separates welfare liberals from their classical liberal namesakes.

The twentieth century's closing decades witnessed an unusually vigorous and high-level debate between classical and welfare liberals. Both positions underwent profound intellectual revivals, with major restatements of each appearing in quick succession. After a lengthy period of the intellectual doldrums, liberalism was treated to an embarrassment of riches. The enduring themes were reformulated in contemporary terms. The old critiques, sharpened by newly accumulated historical evidence, were presented with brashness and originality. One day we may find the contemporary debate between welfare and classical liberals as indispensable to our intellectual heritage as we today consider the debate between Hobbes and Locke.

Contemporary Classical Liberalism

Friedrich A. Hayek

Hayek's warnings

Socialists and welfare liberals found a formidable adversary in the Noble Prize–winning economist Friedrich A. Hayek. In dozens of books and articles, written in his native Austria and later in his adopted countries England and the United States, Hayek warned that collectivist economic planning posed a profound threat to liberty.[15] At first he had few allies. When *The Road to Serfdom*[16] appeared in war-torn Britain, government intervention was at its height and social democracy commanded the loyalty of much of the intelligentsia. Not many gave credence to his doomsday prophesies. Fifty years later, however, Hayek's writings and the classical liberal position they defend command a wide and enthusiastic audience.

Hayek's most persistent argument is that modern societies cannot be deliberately designed and directed without risking the direst of consequences. Our tendency to believe otherwise rests on an understandable error: since it seems obvious that we have created the institutions of our social life, it would seem equally plausible that we should be able to recreate them as we see fit. Imperfections in the functioning of our social machinery, we imagine, should be analyzed and repaired much as we would a leaky faucet or a flat tire. This analogy, Hayek insists, is dangerously mistaken. It assumes that since order exists in society, it must have been consciously designed. It fails to appreciate that the great organizing networks of human life arise out of the unplanned interaction of human interests.

Unplanned order vs. design

Consider the growth of human language. No central academy master-minded its pronunciation, grammar, and vocabulary. It is a living code created by the inter-

---

15. While at the University of Chicago, one of Hayek's colleagues was Milton Friedman, whose free-market conceptions overlap and reinforce Hayek's own. See Friedman's *Capitalism and Freedom* (Chicago: University of Chicago Press, 1962).

16. London: Routledge, 1944.

action of countless speakers pursuing their own objectives. Language presents a strikingly complex case of unplanned order. Consider further the short-cuts across the grass—they exist on every campus—that over the years have become beaten tracks. No coordination between the scores of daily short-cut takers was necessary to create it. Some began to cut the corner to get to the library more quickly, others to avoid the crowds on the pavement, others still because they didn't want to meet someone. The number of individual reasons is probably incalculably large. But the convergence of different objectives gave rise to a cooperative, although unplanned, creation.

Social institutions, Hayek claims, are fundamentally of this kind. They are not created in order to pursue society's common goals; they represent the selfish/cooperative interactions of innumerable individuals attending to their own affairs. Although no single purpose binds us all, the overall result is ordered and regular. Enduring human institutions are built out of reciprocity, overlapping interests, and the need to divide labor and share services. Patterns of social life emerge out of the spontaneous and uncoordinated actions of many persons who usually have no knowledge of each other. Neither do these different individuals necessarily agree about which human purposes ought to be valued. What should be clear, Hayek emphasizes, is that with so many different, indeed incompatible, individual interests being pursued, the social equation can never be reduced to a single common denominator.

This is precisely what the planners believe they can do. Typically, they contemplate a social problem as if it were a logical conundrum with a single neat solution. Political principles are derived from philosophical theorems, and the untidy jumble of unique individuals is set aside in favor of intellectual rigor and economy. These would-be political engineers fail to understand that if there is no single social objective, reconstructing society according to a master plan must end in tragedy. Because social blueprints are invariably less complex than the reality they seek to design, they always abridge and distort the irreducible interests of the many into a streamlined rational construction. In their rush to create an enlightened administrative state, Hayek warns, they will disrupt the finely tuned, spontaneous interactions of individual interests and invite either totalitarianism or chaos.

Individuals vs. bureaucrats
Compare the knowledge at the disposal of a central planner with the sum total of knowledge possessed by the innumerable individuals who make up a complex society. Even the most gifted administrator aided by the largest databanks of information does not begin to compare with the firsthand, on-the-ground, exhaustive knowledge possessed by all those who are daily involved in millions of different human pursuits. All the more so when it comes to individuals determining what their own interests are. The knowledge utilized by individuals freely seeking their own fortunes cannot be surpassed, certainly not by an artificially constructed, centrally run board of bureaucrats. Compared to the host of individual experts on their own lives, the administrator is a patent ignoramus.

The planner's response
Although they might grudgingly grant the point, the administrator and his welfare liberal supporters would respond that this kind of argument unwittingly serves

their purposes. True, they would concede, policies conceived and administered centrally cannot match the diversified, minute, and individualized knowledge available to an entire population. But the problem with all this knowledge is precisely that it is individual; it doesn't "cumulate." The total cumulated knowledge of the many individuals that we compared to the administrator's is, in fact, a theoretical abstraction. Nowhere does it transcend the selfish and unruly desires of separate individuals. It is the administrator's job to make sure that out of this babel of interests a consistent and unified policy emerges.

Beyond their tendency to create disorder, unplanned societies, in which individual interests are pursued without restraint, lead to a number of wasteful consequences. They create unnecessary duplication: a single public utility, for example, saves the cost of a dozen competing bureaucracies each repeating the same tasks. It avoids squandering vast sums on unproductive advertisements. Simple economies of scale—the greater the scale of production the lower the per unit cost—will reward us handsomely. Perhaps most critically, pressing social concerns are not likely to be addressed by the pursuit of individual interests. Individuals invariably direct their energies toward personal gain. Many selfish interests, even cumulated, do not add up to one public interest.

Hayek's counter-attack

These kinds of arguments will occupy us for the remainder of this chapter and for most of the following one. What concerns us immediately is Hayek's spirited rejoinder. All of these criticisms revolve around a single dubious contention: individual interests do not coordinate naturally; hence, order must be consciously imposed. For Hayek this view is egregiously mistaken. On the contrary, the capacity of individual interests to coordinate naturally is the genius of the free-enterprise system. Market economies are superior to all others because, without any conscious design, a wonderfully self-balancing order is achieved. The unimpeded flow of information between free persons acting on their own interests creates an efficient self-regulating communications network that synchronizes countless individual actors without resorting to authority.

Prices and unplanned order

How is this remarkable feat of satisfying countless diverse interests accomplished without any deliberate plan? How can an aggregation of individuals lacking a single goal or firsthand knowledge of each other be made to operate as a harmonious whole? The answer, Hayek contends, is that all of them respond to a single set of signals called prices. Prices tell us when and what we should sell, buy, produce, and consume. If the price is right, we will buy a laptop computer or take a trip to the Caribbean. Similarly, if there are good profits to be made, laptops will be produced and airlines will add flights. Without knowing who the laptop buyer is or if the Caribbean is being visited to escape the winter cold or pursuit by the police, buyer and seller have been brought together in a mutually beneficial way.

Prices, in short, match up the diverse interests of different individuals. They coordinate our activities and choices naturally. Businesses may have no high-minded desire to feed the hungry or clothe the naked, but they end up doing just that. Individual consumers may have no desire to enrich an enterprising producer, but end up doing just that. The price mechanism may be blind, but it miraculously synchronizes the choices of innumerable individuals without the need for any further supervision.

What is most remarkable about this unplanned process of coordination is how it encourages peaceful coexistence between otherwise deeply inimical human ends. Without making incompatible value systems any more friendly to each other, the price mechanism reconciles these cross-purposes by having them all benefit from the arrangement. It binds individuals not by the ends they seek (which is impossible) but by the means—the market system—they employ to achieve these ends. The price mechanism therefore pacifies what might otherwise be an irresolvable clash of human interests.

Planning means coercion and conflict

By contrast, all centrally administered economies must choose one human value over another. Because they suppress the price mechanism that naturally registers the diversity of human needs and interests, designed economic systems are necessarily blunt and coercive instruments. They can only pursue selected, simplified, and partisan interests. Despite the humanitarian impulses that sometimes underlie them, collective goals are nothing but the politically sanctioned goals of a dominant social group. Irresistibly, they disadvantage individuals whose interests are not publicly favored. Moreover, they encourage conflict and coercion because they attempt to bind people by ends rather than means.

The free market and planned economies might be compared to two different types of electoral arrangements: the plurality system and the system of proportional representation. Planning, like the winner-take-all plurality system, can only register a single victor. It is unable to represent the wills of the many (sometimes even the majority) who did not prefer the candidate with the largest number of votes. A candidate or socio-economic objective supported by only five percent of the population is destined to be permanently unrepresented. By contrast, proportional representation systems, which apportion representation according to the percent of the vote each party received, are highly sensitive to even small variations in the vote. Our five-percent party, for example, would be entitled to a full five percent of the representation. Free enterprise economies, like proportional representation systems, express the actual diversity and irreducibility of human interests. Minority consumers are not outvoted; the needs of even the smallest and most eccentric market will be accommodated.

The virtues of free competition

The pricing mechanism not only fosters a minutely adjusted communications network between producers and consumers, but tends to ensure lower prices and better service as well. Hoping to undersell competitors, manufacturers seek the cheapest way to produce a commodity. This encourages vigorous research and development programs as well as the quest for alternate sources of scarce materials. The suppliers of raw materials must also keep their prices competitive or they will lose orders to other suppliers who do. Consumers add their input into the communications network by favoring those sellers whose products and service are consistently of high quality and low cost. In a word: prices and competition direct human creativity and natural resources into channels that maximize the benefits of all. (Quite obviously, Hayek notes, no similar pressures exist in planned economies.) In the end, the rewards the market confers on particular individuals are a good indication of the real benefits they have conferred on others.

Liberty underlies the free market

The key to the system's remarkable success, Hayek believes, is the liberty of individuals to pursue goals of their own choosing without artificially imposed constraints. Because only free individuals are in a position to register their genuine interests, only a free market has available to it all the relevant and necessary economic information. Beyond its indubitable moral and human value, therefore, individual liberty underpins the entire market system. In a sense, the market is a perpetual referendum that depends for its operational success on free and universal suffrage. By side-stepping the market's information grid, we lose something irreplaceable. Curtailed liberty translates directly into curtailed system success.

Why socialism fails

Socialism fails, therefore, not merely because it violates personal liberty or because it goes against the grain of an individualistic human nature; it fails because it is, strictly speaking, impossible. The colossal quantity of economically significant information that would be needed to regulate a vast and complex modern economy is beyond anything that can be absorbed, analyzed, and acted upon by mere mortals. Planned economies, when they are not emitting disastrously misleading signals, are suffocating from the lack of vital information. Long before the collapse of the Soviet Union—when so many discovered they had known all along that planned economies don't work—Hayek had predicted its inevitable failure.[17] Learning subsequently in hair-raising detail of the giant snafus that tangled the Soviet economy, the harvested crops that rotted in the fields, the production of goods for which there were no consumers, the omnipresent corruption and institutionalized payoffs that seem to have lubricated an otherwise immobilized system, leaves Hayekians with a triumphant sensation of "I told you so."

The proper function of government

Government, Hayek concludes, has no business directing economic activity or coordinating human ends. Progressive income tax, rent and price controls, social services, minimum wages, etc., are all illegitimate intrusions.[18] What then is government's proper function? For Hayek, public authority's legitimate objective is to provide the framework in which the market can operate undisturbed. The object of political power is to guarantee economic freedom; it has no goal of its own. For classical liberals like Hayek, economic freedom is the core freedom from which all the others derive. Unless the freedom to buy and sell, to negotiate

17. See Hayek, *The Road to Serfdom.*

18. See Hayek's *The Constitution of Liberty* (Chicago: University of Chicago Press, 1960) for his thoughts on what the institutions of a free society should look like. Chapters 17–24 deal with issues such as taxation, labor unions, town planning, government support of research, minimum wages, etc.

and contract, is preserved, the others will slowly disintegrate. Hayek dismisses the stock charge that this economic conception of liberty is only a mean-spirited trader's ethic lacking vision or inspiration. He argues, on the contrary, that to be able to chose one's goals, to calculate the best means by which to achieve them, to use one's energies and talents to actually realize them, this is the very definition of a free person.

Summary

Summarizing Hayek's main arguments:

1. Human institutions arise out of the unplanned interaction of individual human interests. Without firsthand knowledge of each other and without any necessary agreement about values, the spontaneous, self-seeking activities of separate individuals create order and cooperative enterprises.
2. Without imposed authority or deliberate design, the free market efficiently disperses economic information about individual preferences and interests. Through the signalling mechanism of prices, the diverse interests of various individuals are finely coordinated. Competition drives prices down just as it drives quality and service up.
3. Planned economies fail because they are unable to artificially duplicate the communication network that is natural to the free market. Moreover they are necessarily coercive because they authoritatively impose certain human ends rather than allowing different ends to be reconciled through the medium of an open market that serves the general welfare.
4. Liberty is crucial to the operation of the market because it facilitates the full and accurate expression of differing human needs and interests. Economic freedom—the freedom to conceive, calculate, and carry out one's individual interests—is the condition for all other kinds of freedom.
5. The object of government is to guarantee the unhindered functioning of the market. Politics is a means to economic freedom, not an end itself. Hence, government's role should be minimal. It must not interfere with normal market activity—neither by correcting the outcome of market competition through redistributing income, nor by pursuing the allegedly collective ends of society.

Robert Nozick

At times, Hayek's ideas bring to mind Edmund Burke's disdain for rationally designed social schemes. At others, they are reminiscent of Adam Smith's invisible hand that naturally coordinates individual interests. The venerable liberal idea of inalienable property rights, however, is largely absent from Hayek's teachings. As an economist, Hayek is principally concerned with the actual mechanisms of the free market rather than with the essential entitlements of individuals. It is the utility of private property and free enterprise, not their ethical character, that is the master thread of Hayek's thought.

A rights-based
defense of liberty

We need to turn to another contemporary theorist, Robert Nozick, for a restatement of the older Lockean idea that our natural property rights act as an ethical barrier against governmental activity. Nozick, a Harvard philosopher whose book *Anarchy, State and Utopia*[19] presents a boldly unconventional rights-based defense of the free market, is probably the most discussed figure in the current revival of the liberal right. In Nozick, the **libertarians** (as supporters of the liberal right are often called) have found their philosophical champion.

Nozick's arguments are of an ethical rather than an economic nature. He explicitly rejects justifications of state authority that rest on its allegedly beneficial consequences for the public welfare. This kind of utilitarian argument, as was noted above, can justify all kinds of highly problematic policies, including unconscionable assaults on individual rights. Nozick seeks to draw the line between permissible and forbidden government activities, not by appealing to their effects but rather by assessing their compatibility with individual human rights. Given that individuals have certain rights inherent in their very character as rational beings, which intrusions into their private space can be justified without doing violence to their natural liberty? How far may the state go in coercing individuals—for that is what states, in fact, do—while respecting the entitlements that are naturally theirs?

The minimal state

Nozick's controversial answer is: not very far at all. Beyond a **minimal state** that provides basic protection and indispensable administrative coordination, public authority is an illegitimate usurpation. Governments should provide public safety—and little else. Hence, many of the governmental activities that we have come to take for granted, Nozick claims, are indefensible. These include social services for the needy, redistributing wealth, and most forms of economic regulation. These measures are rejected not because they necessarily fail to achieve their ends; they are illegitimate because they rest upon the violation of individual rights. Even the imposition of taxes is illegitimate. In Nozick's stark phrase, it is the equivalent of "forced labor."

The separateness of
individuals

Human beings, Nozick insists, are rights-bearing creatures. By virtue of our reason and free will—i.e., our ability to shape our lives in accordance with some chosen conception of the good—we are all entitled to be treated as ends, not means. Treating people as a means to an end that is not of their own choosing constitutes an infringement of human individuality. For Nozick, therefore, no person's liberty or welfare may be legitimately sacrificed in order to enhance those of another. The separateness of persons is basic and inviolable; it may not be compromised by aggregating individuals, amalgamating different human objectives, or subsuming individual interests under categories like the public good. Nozick says it flatly: "There are only individual people, with their own individual lives."[20]

---

19. New York: Basic Books, 1974.

20. See Nozick, *Anarchy, State and Utopia*, 32–33.

There is no social pie to be cut up and distributed. Imagining that we all have a common claim on the total property existing in a political community overlooks the elementary fact that property invariably comes with its natural owners; it is not "manna from heaven." Distributive criteria for apportioning wealth, such as equality or neediness or merit, are based on the indefensible assumption that property is a social resource or a collective asset. In fact, the theoretical hocus pocus involved in socializing private property accomplishes little more than providing a flimsy excuse for taking what is rightfully mine and transferring it to another. Nozick concludes that property, if it is rightfully acquired through labor, exchange, or inheritance, is an entitlement against which organized society has no claims.

This includes claims based on the alleged moral unworthiness of the owner. Even if we were to agree that the stupendous wealth accruing to Madonna or Michael Jackson is undeserved, it is still theirs. The roulette-wheel millionaire, the gigolo heir to a fortune, the porno king, although we may well disapprove of their actions, are nonetheless the proprietors of their holdings. Ownership is not a spiritual endowment that is based upon the moral worthiness of the recipient; it derives from the right of the pop-music audience, the casino, the millionaire parent, the consumer of pornography to part with their money as they see fit.

Altruism, not coercion

Nozick would dismiss the charge that he is defending a heartless, dog-eat-dog world. On the contrary: acts of voluntary altruism are deserving of the highest praise. He advocates not amoral selfishness, but a world in which moral decisions are the free decisions of moral agents using their entitlements according to their own lights. What he objects to is not benevolence, but the coercive imposition of alien moral objectives onto individuals. Pursuing these objectives by depriving individuals of their property rights only adds economic injury to moral insult.

Benevolence, not rights

Welfare liberals and social democrats fail to understand that humanitarian impulses cannot be realized through coercive measures that reduce some individuals to the means that advance the welfare of others. Furthermore, they err dramatically in claiming that disadvantaged groups have a right to demand their share of the social pie. Typically, they confuse benevolence with rights, voluntary moral acts with proprietary entitlements. Although a moral principle may enjoin me to help the needy, this is very different from the claim that the needy have a right to my possessions. The source of this confusion is, once again, the fallacious notion that wealth is a collectively held asset.

Redistribution's problems

To puncture this myth of a reservoir of common wealth, Nozick offers a number of raucously unconventional counter-examples. He asks his readers to imagine the claim of a disgruntled married individual. My spouse, this person contends, is far less desirable than those of others. Society therefore should redistribute spouses to insure that we each have our fair share of the social pie. Or consider the case of an exam in which one student argues that, to be fair, we really ought to redistribute our grades so that all of us receive a mediocre but passing grade. Does the student with the grade of 40 have the right to demand of student who received a 90 that they divide the 50 points between them so that they both pass with a 65? Our moral intuitions revolt at the notion! Clearly, my grade is mine because it reflects my effort, my talents, and my performance. Similarly, my spouse is mine because he or she has chosen me rather than someone else. Redistribution makes no sense because the present apportionment, if it has come about freely and legitimately (i.e., no cheating, no forced marriages, no extortion, etc.), is inextricably related to my choices, my abilities, my luck, my self. And Nozick queries: Doesn't property fall into exactly the same category?

Nozick asks us to consider the case of ten sailors who, surviving a shipwreck, find themselves marooned on ten different islands. Each of them, according to temperament and talent, utilizes the time differently. Some build and plant industriously, others loll in the sun and subsist on berries. Imagine now that after years they discover each other's presence and meet to talk over their situation. What would we make of a claim, advanced by one of the lolling berry-pickers, that they really ought to redistribute their wealth because it is unjust that some should have so much while others have so little? I do not ask this, our loller insists, as a matter of charity but as a matter of right. Again our moral instincts revolt. After all, the current distribution reflects just what each of them has done with their time. Isn't it perfectly obvious that the rights they have in their own accomplishments are independent of the needs that others may have? And again Nozick presses the point: Doesn't property accumulated in less exotic circumstances fall into precisely the same category? Why should one individual have any rights to a neighbor's accomplishments and possessions?

Collectivism's flaws
:   The collectivist impulse is, therefore, misguided in (1) its confusion of benevolence with rights, (2) its cavalier disregard for property entitlements, and (3) its stubborn tendency to view wealth as a common social resource. But there is more to the collectivist's wrong-headedness, and it goes deeper still.

End-state theories of justice
:   Their conception of justice, Nozick declares, is badly skewed. Rather than accept as just whatever economic reality is created when sovereign individuals freely pursue their own goals, the collectivists insist on deciding, right from the start, what a satisfactory outcome will look like. Certain voluntarily arrived at **end states** are deemed unworthy. Although individual rights have been scrupulously respected and property has been accumulated in an unobjectionable manner, collectivists feel compelled to rectify the outcome through economic regulation and income redistribution.

End-state theories of justice predetermine that a certain pattern of ownership must prevail. They reject the proposition that the chips should be allowed to fall where they may—even if all the players have played by all the rules all of the time. Defenders of end-state theories have a clear agenda: the preferred end state, reflecting a certain desired value pattern such as egalitarianism, takes precedence over the free choices of autonomously interacting individuals.

Rejecting end-state theories
:   In opposition to end-state theories of justice are those approaches that focus on the procedure rather than on the outcome. No end state is privileged, just as no freely arrived at outcome is disqualified; restrictions apply only to the manner in which these outcomes are to be pursued. If all the steps leading up to an outcome are unobjectionable, there can be no grounds for meddling with it.

The problem with end-state theories, Nozick complains, is that they are always rectifying what free and autonomous people decide. They regularly deflect the invisible hand's movements, replacing the natural order with an artificially imposed one. But artificial order requires constant surveillance and regular intervention. Free, uncoordinated actions will tend to upset the desired end state. To survive, it must aggressively resist these counter-tendencies and perpetually reassert itself. Hence, political systems wedded to end-state preferences are necessarily unstable and coercive. Unstable, because they must constantly readjust natural tendencies in the direction of the desired end state. Coercive, because in so doing they unavoidably disqualify voluntary acts between free people.

Rejecting end-state theories

Consider a political community in which end-state theorists have had their way. After much effort, they perfect the distribution of social resources in a way that is entirely to their liking, that is, precisely in accordance with their view of the just society. If this society is to be maintained over time in its just state, it must police virtually all free exchanges between individuals. After all, if Jane wishes to part with some of her justly distributed resources in return for a service that Mary performs, it will upset the definitive end state. Mary will have more and Jane less than the end state mandates. Either the authorities, jealous to preserve the just society, must prohibit such acts outright, or they will be forced periodically to return to Jane what she willingly has transferred to Mary. Either they must be coercive and vigilante-like, or create turmoil through constant redistributions—Nozick suspects they will have to be both simultaneously. End-state theories thus thwart the normal interaction of free individuals. As Nozick bitingly puts it, they prohibit "capitalist acts between consenting adults."

Summary

Summarizing the central points of Nozick's argument:

1. By virtue of our ability to create a life in accordance with our individual conception of the good, each human being is entitled to be treated as an end rather than as a means. Human separateness may not be diminished by levelling, averaging, or amalgamating different human ends into a composite public welfare.

2. Government may not infringe our basic human entitlements without our consent. For example, the right we each have to our own property, so long as it has been legitimately acquired through labor, exchange, or inheritance, is not subject to public regulation or redistribution. While individual benevolence is praiseworthy, property rights may not be compromised in order to further collective social ends such as aiding the poor or providing health care or fostering education.

3. There is no social pie to distribute. Property comes with owners; it is not a collective asset. Property rights are not to be assessed in terms of their social utility or by what others may think of the moral qualities of the owner. They are entitlements that do not require social justification because they precede and are independent of organized society.

4. The only legitimate function of the state is to provide protection and make sure that the rules of the game are being honored. This minimal state has no autonomous objectives of its own.

5. End-state theories of justice thwart the voluntary interactions of autonomous individuals by determining in advance what their outcome must be. Rather than allow free individuals to pursue their own objectives and accept any outcome that is arrived at without violating personal entitlements, end-state theorists regularly reject and rectify what free individuals have achieved. End-state theories are, therefore, inexorably destabilizing and coercive.

Suggestions for Further Reading

Barry, Norman. *On Classical Liberalism and Libertarianism*. New York: St. Martin's Press, 1987.

Berlin, Isaiah. *Four Essays on Liberty*. Oxford: Oxford University Press, 1969.

Dahl, Robert. *A Preface to Democratic Theory*. Chicago: University of Chicago Press, 1956.

Friedman, Milton. *Capitalism and Freedom*. Chicago: University of Chicago Press, 1963.

Gould, Carol. *Rethinking Democracy*. Cambridge: Cambridge University Press, 1988.

Gray, John. *Hayek on Liberty*. Oxford: Basil Blackwell, 1984.

———. *Liberalism*. Minneapolis: University of Minnesota Press, 1986.

Hall, John. *Liberalism: Politics, Ideology and the Market*. London: Paladin, 1987.

Hartz, Lewis. *The Liberal Tradition in America*. New York: Harcourt, 1955.

Hayek, Friedrich. *The Road to Serfdom*. London: Routledge, 1944.

———. *The Constitution of Liberty*. Chicago: University of Chicago Press, 1960.

MacPherson, C. B. *The Real World of Democracy*. Oxford: Clarendon Press, 1966.

———. *Democratic Theory: Essays in Retrieval*. Oxford: Clarendon Press, 1973.

———. *The Life and Times of Liberal Democracy*. New York: Oxford University Press, 1977.

Manning, D. J. *Liberalism*. New York: St. Martin's Press, 1976.

Nozick, Robert. *Anarchy, State and Utopia*. New York, Basic Books, 1973.

Pateman, Carole. *Participation and Democratic Theory*. Cambridge: Cambridge University Press, 1970.

Paul, Jeffrey, ed. *Reading Nozick: Essays on Anarchy, State and Utopia*. Oxford: Blackwell, 1978.

Research Institute on International Change, Columbia University, ed. *The Relevance of Liberalism*. Boulder, Colo.: Westview Press, 1976.

Rothbard, Murray. *For a New Liberty: The Libertarian Manifesto*. New York: Macmillan, 1973.

Ruggiero, E. *The History of European Liberalism*. Boston: Beacon Press, 1959.

Sartori, Giovanni. *Democratic Theory*. New York: Praeger, 1965.

Chapter *4*

From Liberalism to Social Democracy (2)

Critiques of Classical Liberalism

Classical
liberalism's
comeback

Classical liberalism has made a remarkable comeback. Thinkers such as Hayek and Nozick succeeded in restoring the lustre to an idea that, by all indications, had been mortally wounded by the Great Depression, Keynesian economics, and the New Deal. The collapse of communism only made their arguments appear that much more convincing. Predictably however, classical liberalism's return from ideological limbo has not been greeted with universal acclaim. Many of the same criticisms that were levelled at its defenders during its mid-nineteenth-century heyday are once again being levelled at its more recent proponents. For many of its enemies, classical liberalism has, if anything, become even less tenable at the end of the twentieth century. What is certain is that the heated debate between contemporary classical liberals and their critics has produced some of the most acute ideological polemics in recent historical memory.

Critiques

Before turning to welfare liberalism, we therefore should take stock of the arguments directed against the classical liberals. If classical liberalism is to be a viable ideological alternative, it must respond convincingly to the following critiques.

Radical
individualism's
flaws

A. The radical individualism that stands at the heart of classical liberalism is a wildly improbable, visibly false doctrine. It violates the most familiar and common of all our perceptions: human beings are social animals—not merely in the obvious sense of living together and dividing labor with each other, but in the far more essential sense of being human by virtue of our common lives. Aristotle said it definitively some twenty-three centuries ago: outside organized society only beasts or gods can dwell. We are not isolated island dwellers any more than we are unconnected atoms each calculating personal gain. This kind of Robinson Crusoe individualism and the backwoods capitalism it underlies represent a laughable caricature of the densely social reality with which we are all familiar.

Exaggerated individualism leads to inevitable errors. Typically, it views ownership as unrelated to social life: property is acquired in some fictional private space, as it were, behind society's back. But leaving aside the contrived cases of shipwrecked sailors and state-of-nature dwellers, wealth is, very obviously, always produced through human cooperation. Every commodity or service or technological achievement is shot through with social interdependence and common efforts. The way we farm, manufacture, buy and sell, consume, even the ways in which we love each other and fight with each other are parts of our social existence. Our very cultural and moral selves, indeed our specific form of consciousness, are social constructions.

Consider even the most authentically individual of human enterprises: the hermit researcher, working alone without any assistance, associates, or public support. This researcher too is the repository of an enormous quantity of social knowledge and historical experience. Indeed, there would be no problems to research and no method by which to research them were they not provided by a tradition of social discourse and inquiry. Even what this lone researcher discovers is, therefore, not a private creation. It is, in a fundamental sense, a social product.

Property as social product

Clearly, property is also a social product. Ownership entails cooperative activity. For the modern institution of property to flourish we require social rules that govern acquisition and trade, market conventions, a common currency, a judicial system to arbitrate claims, and a public authority to impose judicial decisions. Property reflects human interconnectedness at least as much as it mirrors our separate existences. To speak of property, therefore, is to acknowledge that claims to ownership are necessarily mediated through social institutions and conventions. At the end of the twentieth century, in an intricately interdependent global village, claiming that private property lies outside social jurisdiction is to indulge in a particularly bizarre form of fantasy. The idea of self-contained individuals, creating property out of themselves, unconnected and unindebted, is quite absurd. Their demanding absolute rights to this property is simple affrontry.

But wealth and property are cooperative in yet a deeper sense. Cooperative activity is not merely the activity of many separate individuals added up together. Were it so, the social product could, at least in principle, be decomposed into its constituent parts, with all individuals receiving their separate due. But this is just what cannot be done to a truly social product. The sum is more that the collection of its parts. The French nineteenth-century radical thinker Pierre-Joseph Proudhon put it in the following way: If it took a hundred workers an hour to set on its pedestal a great stone obelisk (which sits to this day at the center of the Place de la Concorde in Paris), would it take a single worker a hundred hours to do the same job? Isn't it perfectly obvious that a single worker would be unable to do the work however long he labored? Most significant social products are cooperative in this sense; only the concerted effort of many makes the achievement possible at all.

All this leads to a single conclusion. Beginning one's social analysis with the image of radically separate persons pursuing individual ends is so fundamental a distortion of the human condition that it leads irresistibly to a dangerously skewed ideological program.

Radical individualism is morally repugnant

B. The classical liberal image of radically separate individuals each moved by selfish concerns is morally repugnant. It runs against the grain of everything that Judeo-Christian ethics has taught us. It celebrates egoism, applauds fierce competition, reduces worth to cash value, and denies any social responsibility to care for the infirm and unfortunate. Seen from the perspective of the thundering orations on justice of the Hebrew prophets and the Christian message of compassion and love, the classical liberal ethic represents the morality of Sodom and Gomorrah. The suggestion that the needy ought to be cared for through private charity only adds insult to injury.

Charity is inappropriate

C. Private charity, however laudable, is not an effective instrument to deal with complex and pervasive social ills. More importantly, it is an entirely inappropriate response to such problems. If slums, poverty, and illiteracy affected only a random sampling of individuals who were down on their luck, perhaps private charity would be the appropriate response. But it should be obvious to any fair-minded observer that poverty is not random; it persistently afflicts some social groups more than others.

Poverty embedded in social structure

Patterns of poverty, in other words, are deeply structured into our social and economic lives. Blacks, Hispanics, women, residents of Appalachia, etc., are considerably more likely to be afflicted than others. And it would be laughable to make the claim that these groups are where they are only because of the random individual qualities of their members. Their standing within the socio-economic system—no less than the standing of those are who well-heeled and privileged—is at least in part a social rather than an individual phenomenon. Hence, discussing property rights as if they were acquired by ahistorical and asocial individuals makes no sense at all. For example, is it possible to evaluate the problems that African-Americans currently confront without considering the heritage of slavery? Can the prevalent practice of unequal pay for women be disentangled from the inferior place that women have historically occupied in society?

As soon as the disadvantaged position of certain groups is understood to be deeply embedded in a social context rather than the private difficulties of many separate individuals, it becomes apparent that advocating individual charity as the solution to the problem represents a confusion of categories. Socially created problems are the responsibility of society.

A loser for every winner

D. Capitalism, whatever its virtues, necessarily makes for both winners and losers. In the sweepstakes of market competition, we cannot all come out on top. In fact, the success of some is inevitably at the expense of others. Buying a Toyota weakens General Motors. If you get the job, someone else doesn't. Like victory and defeat in battle, wealth and poverty go hand in hand. Power and privilege are, therefore, never self-standing facts. They always entail casualties. There is an underside to every success, pain for every gain, a debtor for every creditor, a factory worker for every CEO, a housekeeper for every successful professional.

The propertied are therefore bound to the propertyless more closely than they would prefer to imagine. Dissociating their wealth from the destitution of others represents both willful blindness and callous arrogance. To enjoy the perquisites of wealth requires creating a service class whose unenviable position is the direct outcome of this very wealth. Hence, claims made by the affluent that they bear no social responsibility for the disadvantaged ring hollow.

Let us state this argument at the level of principle. Property does not, as the classical liberals claim, endow its owners with rights against society. Neither is ownership a warrant for claims of immunity from the needs of one's associates and co-citizens. On the contrary, ownership is the very source of such responsibility.

E. Classical liberals claim that laissez-faire economics supports both freedom and democracy. This claim must be rejected for a number of related reasons.

Freedom from want

1. Unrestrained capitalist competition always creates great disparities of wealth and poverty. Alongside the wealthy and powerful we find a large underclass of destitute, helpless, demoralized, sometimes homeless individuals. These pauperized individuals are not members of the body politic in any meaningful sense. The formal status of this underclass as "citizens equal to all others" is a cruel mockery that only the most legalistic and insensitive can take seriously. (The French writer Anatole France once quipped: "The law in its majestic equality forbids the rich as well as the poor to sleep under bridges, to beg in the streets, and to steal bread.") The idea of government of, by, and for the people has no real significance if it does not include the right of all to minimal human dignity. For those who live in want and squalor, lacking the ability to fashion their lives or lead independent existences, all the beautiful words pledging "liberty and justice for all" are so much claptrap. Without elemental human dignity, freedom and democracy are empty words.

Economic inequality creates political inequality

2. One need not be a left-wing radical to concede that economic power begets political power. A great concentration of economic power in the hands of a few—which unrestrained capitalism tends to create—is therefore not compatible with truly popular government. Societies divided along sharply drawn economic lines, with a typically small owning class controlling a vastly disproportionate share of the wealth, will necessarily reflect this economic imbalance in other spheres of public life as well. Economic dominance has a way of becoming political dominance. In fact, nineteenth-century capitalism, which classical liberals wish to revive, was just such a case: the rule of a patriciate only mildly moderat-

ed by the trappings of democratic government. It was just for the sake of meaningful democracy and individual liberty that these practices were abandoned. Their return would only mean a regression to "democracy" and "liberty" in name only.

Democracy and social solidarity

3. Genuine democracy involves the presence of a communal ethos, a sense of solidarity and kinship. As much as it requires certain legal-constitutional features, democracy is dependent upon an inner psycho-social reality that binds citizens together into a unit. Understood merely as adherence to formal rules of the game, to the principle of "honor my rights and I'll honor yours," democracy is a thin, unsatisfying, and ultimately non-sustainable political arrangement. Flourishing democracies are first of all cohesive, morally bonded societies with a distinct ethical character and a shared sense of purpose. It is precisely this moral unity that fosters honoring the rules of the game and respecting the rights of other individuals.

Classical liberalism dissolves the glue that binds a democratic people together by disintegrating society into radically separate and atomized individuals. As imagined by a classical liberal, society can have no more cohesiveness than potatoes in a sack. By conceiving of rights as barriers erected by individuals against the intrusion of others rather than as part of a human condition that draws us together in our common humanity, the classical liberals allow no significant room for moral community. And without moral community, the long-range prospects for authentically democratic community life are quite dim.

Economic inequality causes social strife

4. Stable democracies are those that avoid the extremes of wealth and poverty. When the divide between haves and have-nots is too great, anger, resentment, and envy tear at the social fabric. After all, the dispossessed have little to lose. Neither do those who wish to maintain order have much choice but to resort to repression and violence. This kind of revolutionary situation is the typical product of a political system in which property rights are unrestrained by any conception of an overriding common good.

Only when the far greater part of the citizenry has a stake in society does democracy avoid the ravages of civil strife. (It is no accident that all the stable contemporary democracies have large middle classes and substantial social programs to help the needy.) Classical liberals, with their belief in free market competition unmoderated by any social responsibility for the casualties of such competition, seem bent on creating the kind of revolutionary situations in which freedom and democracy have little chance of surviving.

Democratic publics reject classical liberalism

5. The incompatibility of democracy and classical liberalism is most ironically evident in its consistent rejection by democratic publics. Democratic publics are composed of large groups for whom the dismantling of social security or the scrapping of progressive income tax would spell catastrophe. Wherever universal suffrage is a reality, true laissez-faire

economics do not stand a chance. (Even the most classically liberal of recent regimes—Reaganism and Thatcherism—kept the lion's share of social service programs intact.) The full expression of a sovereign popular will is not compatible with the untrammeled freedom of each individual to own and do as she or he pleases.

Failures of the profit motive

F. One article of faith common to all classical liberals is that the general welfare is best served by the free exercise of the profit motive. Government intervention must be rejected because it undermines the benefits accruing from the unplanned coordination of many private desires.

No one would care to dispute the power of the profit motive or deny that trading between individuals will often work to the advantage of both. But to believe that the selfish interests of many different individuals always add up to the good of the whole involves a breathtaking leap of faith that is as perverse as it is naive. To start with, what would be the response of the great mass of poor, propertyless laborers—the typical product of an unregulated market—to the idea of the good of the whole? A bitter laugh, perhaps. Free trade may indeed create wealth, but its concentration in a few hands subverts rather than promotes the good of the whole.

Moreover, the individual profit motive is incapable of dealing with many critical public issues that, by their very nature, require a single community-wide perspective. Can we imagine a military defense establishment that was anything but government run? Even with intensive government monitoring, the desire for a handsome profit has often enticed defense contractors to produce goods that were overpriced and/or shoddy. If our highway systems were planned and constructed by many different firms each according to their own bottom-line economics, probably they would be as redundant and incompatible as computer programs. Would auto safety and emissions standards be what they are had government not imposed its will on an unenthusiastic industry? Corporate profit and loss concerns are surely not the same as the national interest.

Can we take seriously the idea of drug companies regulating themselves, subject only to the considerations of "will the public buy it"? How many tragedies would it take until the public stopped purchasing an injurious medicine? Can a national education system be run from anything but a national perspective? Can consumer demand be the deciding factor in what children will or will not study in schools? Can the ability to pay be a relevant consideration in whether children receive an education?

Health care, the one American social service that was run on a largely private basis for years, only demonstrates how incompatible are the profit motive and the good of the whole. Drug companies, doctors, hospitals, and medical supply manufacturers, exploiting the special urgency and sensitivity of the market for health care, raised prices until they became an intolerable drag on American economic competitiveness. Vast numbers of Americans were left uninsured and under-insured. (The lure of receiving enormous monetary gain—a sure spin-off of the profit-centered mentality—prompted many individuals to initiate unnecessary malpractice suits against doctors and medical establishments, further jacking up health costs.) It became patently obvious that a health care system directed by the profit motive cannot work. Only a health program conceived as a totality—a national health plan—could both lower costs and overcome the injustices created by unregulated market forces.

One final concrete example. Inner city slums rarely have supermarkets. Small grocery shops charging very high prices are the rule. Because of alarming crime rates, insurance companies—moved by profit/loss considerations—demand exorbitant insurance premiums. Supermarkets usually respond by taking their business elsewhere. The result: although considerably less well off than suburbanites, slum dwellers pay more for life's necessities than those living in wealthier areas. Uninsured, high-priced small groceries are all that is available to them. Which only reinforces the vicious cycle of poverty and dependence on public support.

Neither the insurance companies nor the supermarkets can be faulted for their behavior. After all, they operate to make a profit and cannot be expected to sacrifice their investors' money in order to do good deeds. Precisely what they cannot do is act for the good of the whole. Only a government-sponsored insurance initiative that transcends considerations of profit and loss can support the kind of program that would foster the general good of society.

What classical liberalism clearly lacks in this case, as in all the previous cases, is a conception of society as more than a collection of private interests. It is unable to conceive of individuals as tied to their peers by anything more than a "scratch my back and I'll scratch yours" mentality. And without a meaningful conception of the "social," classical liberals are trapped into a lopsided, one-dimensional individualism that does not begin to be adequate to humanity's communal and moral character.

Which economies do best?

G. Finally, the classical liberal's view of unregulated capitalism as the goose that lays golden eggs simply is not borne out by the facts. Those economies that have done best over the past three or four decades are not those that have clung to the principles of laissez-faire. States like Japan, Taiwan, South Korea, Hong Kong, Singapore (and other emerging Pacific rim economies) have set the world standard for production, efficiency, and profitability. Yet there is no mistaking the substantial public control over trade that they practice. These states are marked by government coordination of many economic activities, by significant public efforts to encourage savings, by keeping labor costs down, and much more. There is, in short, no demonstrable correlation that would bear out the classical liberal's thesis that the freer the economy from public intervention, the more it flourishes.

Moved by criticisms such as these, many otherwise unrepentant liberals set out to reconstruct the core liberal doctrine on a new basis. Discarding early liberalism's radical property-based individualism, they reformulated the liberal credo in what they understood to be a gentler, more humane form. It is to a recent, particularly influential version of this kind of revisionist or welfare liberalism that we now turn.

The Liberalism of John Rawls

Pre-Rawlsian Liberalism

Although it gradually became quite dominant in the twentieth century, the new welfare liberalism lacked sophisticated intellectual foundations. Its economic sources in Keynesian theory had no real parallel in a systematic liberal political theory. Supporters tended to justify it on ad hoc, pragmatic grounds and with vague references to its commendable morality. Usually its defence consisted more in a rejection of the alternatives than in a reasoned presentation of its own principles. Welfare liberalism was that reasonable, tried-and-true ideological position that lay roughly mid-point between classical liberalism and democratic socialism. More a practice than an ideological system, it nevertheless seemed to muddle through successfully enough, and that was usually deemed sufficient by its advocates.

A theoretical basis for liberalism   Part of the unprecedented stir occasioned by the appearance of John Rawls's *A Theory of Justice*[1] derived from its ambitious attempt to provide just such a theoretical basis for contemporary welfare liberalism. In 600 densely reasoned pages, Rawls presents an exhaustive argument that attempts to uncover the ethical core around which liberal practice had been organized. The unspoken moral intuitions that had inspired welfare liberals to reject both laissez-faire economics and socialist egalitarianism are revealed to have clear and sophisticated theoretical underpinnings. No wonder then that in the past two and half decades Rawls's thought has become the focus of a major academic industry.

Rawls' Argument

Although Rawls' argument is often forbiddingly complex, its essential moral insight can be expressed quite simply. Imagine two children with a piece of chocolate cake in front of them. They wish to divide it fairly. Neither of them is to have any more than the other. What procedure should they use to insure a fair division? The solution to this old riddle is fairly obvious: the one who cuts the cake will not be the first one to choose a piece. Fairness is guaranteed because the one who cuts the cake has every reason to be scrupulously careful in dividing it equally. An unfair division would only mean getting a smaller piece.

---

1. Cambridge, Mass.: Harvard University Press, 1971.

Assuring just
decisions

Is there any way, analogous to the solution to our riddle, of fairly apportioning social resources (such as wages, wealth, entitlements) among members of society? Is there a method of distribution whose fairness is so transparently obvious that, like the cake-cutting procedure, it would be accepted by any reasonable individual? Assuming that a group of individuals are setting out to form a new society, can we devise a perfectly just method, hypothetical though it may turn out to be, that would provide guidelines for the distribution of their wealth, the drafting of their laws, and the organization of their institutions? If we can, we will have gone a long way toward solving one of the thorniest of all human socio-political dilemmas.

Rawls believes there is such a method. As in the cake-cutting procedure, it guarantees fairness by precluding the possibility that individuals will take unfair advantage of each other. Because what is at stake is infinitely more complex than hungry children and a piece of cake, the ground rules controlling their deliberations must be far more detailed and restrictive.

Rawls's thought
experiment

Creating such a transparently fair context for negotiations is the heart of Rawls's project. To ensure unquestioned fairness, he proposes the following thought experiment. Let us assume that the individuals who gather to authorize a charter for the new society are like individuals with whom we are all familiar: they are not especially altruistic folk who might be moved to sacrifice their own interests for those of others. These are average, pleasure- and interest-seeking individuals who will carefully weigh each proposal with an eye focused on "what's in it for me?"

Negotiations will not be easy; in fact, they will threaten to break down right at the outset. Each individual will naturally try to have her or his own needs and attributes given special regard. The highly intelligent will push for a society in which leadership, status, and wealth go to the intelligent. Poetic souls, business entrepreneurs, and military types will each have very different agendas. If men advocated a society in which men were dominant, women would hardly cheer the prospect. The poor will naturally seek to redress their poverty just as the wealthy will attempt to preserve the division of wealth as it is. In other words, divergent human interests will stymie the procedure. With each individual pursuing only personal gain, the deliberations will produce ragged compromises and convoluted deals in which fairness plays little or no part.

The Original Position

The veil of
ignorance

To avoid these pitfalls, Rawls proposes an intriguing twist. Let us, he says, hypothetically imagine that the deliberating individuals in this **original position** are surrounded by a **veil of ignorance**. That is, they are ignorant of any specific traits they may have as individuals. (Needless to say, no one can, in practice, efface the knowledge of who she or he is. Rawls is proposing an entirely speculative thought experiment.) They would not know if they are smart or stupid, energetic or lethargic, wealthy or poor, healthy or infirm, good-looking or ugly, woman or man, educated or ignorant. Neither would they know the geographic area of their residence, the religion they followed, or even the human generation they belonged to. They would, further, be unaware of their general philosophy of life and of the peculiarities of their personal temperament (risk taking or timid, optimist or pessimist).

Nevertheless, Rawls cautions, they would not be like the proverbial creature from Mars: they would be fully familiar with the general psychological, sociological, and historical background knowledge that every mature and sane human being possesses. (They would know, for example, that a twenty dollar bill dropped on a crowded sidewalk would not be there an hour later.)

Stripped of any interest-creating attributes, what criteria for the distribution of resources would be adopted? Clearly, there would be no point in forming alliances or in cutting deals—not knowing what my (or others') interests are precludes such a strategy. Each individual is in the same situation as every other; to know what one would decide under these conditions is to know what each would decide. To be sure, the negotiators are still evaluating the rival criteria for apportioning wealth by what the effect on themselves is likely to be—recall that these are not do-gooders. But because the interest of one now coincides with the interest of all, these calculations will take on a novel character.

A generic human perspective

Without assuming noble or self-sacrificing motives, each individual has, nevertheless, become a microcosm of the whole. Although there are no collective interests or general will, we can still say that each person possesses a generic or universal human perspective. Each participant looks out onto the society that is being formed with concerns and objectives that would be accepted by every other observer.

For Rawls, this unanimity is critical. Because the decision-making context is free of all distorting interests, it represents that transparently fair, universally acceptable perspective that recalls the solution to the cake-cutting problem. Hence, what those in the initial bargaining situation decide and the logic they use to arrive at their decision does not merely obligate them as specific individuals; it constitutes an essential human decision that binds us all. Had we been part of this perfectly fair bargaining context, we too would have arrived at the same conclusions.

Rawls insists that our personal presence at the negotiating table is, in the end, immaterial. Because the "original position" recreates in pristine form the context in which moral decisions are fairly deliberated, we are all bound by its logic whether or not we actually affix our signature to its conclusions. Although this negotiating context is entirely hypothetical, Rawls believes that it captures the heart of our moral reasoning and embodies the core of those intuitions that direct our ethical sensibilities. Indeed, if we, today, wish to evaluate a set of rival moral claims, we can do no better than to imagine how we would respond to them were we to find ourselves in the "original position" behind a "veil of ignorance."

What System Would Be Chosen?

Capitalism rejected

What would individuals freed from distorting selfish interests decide in regard to the distribution of wealth? One alternative confronting them would surely be pure capitalist competition. Would individuals who were ignorant of their place in society be likely to accept it? Would it be deemed desirable from the generic human perspective? Rawls thinks not. Because unrestrained capitalist competition causes a sharply unequal distribution of wealth, each of us, having no clue as to our natural abilities or place in society, would fear ending up at the bottom of the heap. We would be unwilling to risk finding ourselves destitute and occupied in life-long drudgery for the sake of the slim chance that we might turn out to be wealthy and well-connected. Seeking to minimize the possibility of maximal injury, we would reject the claims of pure capitalism outright.

Fair competition rejected

What about that form of modified capitalist competition in which the weaker competitors are given advantages to compensate for their initial disabilities? Would we accept the results of capitalist competition if it were mitigated by policies like progressive income tax, head start, and **affirmative action**? Although rejection would not be as unambiguous as with the previous suggestion, we would, Rawls believes, balk at this proposal as well. First of all, our background knowledge would alert us to the familiar fact that all the compensatory programs in the world will not equalize the chances of, on the one hand, an inner-city child of a broken family growing up amid poverty and violence, and, on the other, a child raised in a loving, education-fostering, financially well-off family.

Second, even if compensatory programs could bring us all to the same starting line for the capitalist race, the results of the race would still remain unacceptable. There would still be winners and losers, some whose interests would be sacrificed to the interests of others. Capitalist competition always creates a service class whose life is spent in the shadow of those who have made it. Contemplating my prospects for a meaningful life from the original position, I would be unwilling to agree to an arrangement in which I might well turn out to be a disadvantaged underling, a means to the ends of others.

Strict equality rejected

At first glance at least, strict equality seems to be the answer. Not knowing where we will all end up, why not equalize our fortunes? It would certainly do away with the risk of being unhappily subject to the wealth of others. But strict equality, Rawls declares, exacts a heavy price of its own. So heavy indeed that even our fear of ending up at the bottom of the capitalist heap will be set aside in order to avoid it.

Incentives for excellence

Consider this concrete example. Each of us, whether rich or poor, will at times need the services of a doctor. Hence, we all have an overwhelming interest in having the best trained, most expert doctors available to us. Often, our very lives depend on it. What is it, however, that fosters high-quality medical care? Foremost perhaps is attracting very talented people into the medical profession. But few would undertake the long and arduous program of medical training were they not promised substantial rewards at its end. Hence, incentives, such as an unusually good income, are probably indispensable for truly high-quality medical care.

From behind the veil of ignorance, we are always driven back to consider how we would react to a particular economic arrangement were we among the disadvantaged of society. How would we, as the least favored, react to an arrangement that permitted doctors to receive a larger chunk of communal wealth than we did? Rawls believes we would happily accept the arrangement because it would be in our interest. The idea of mediocre physicians receiving strictly equal rewards for their services would be unattractive even to society's weakest citizens. Higher quality medical care would be worth higher salaries for its providers.

Equality is in no one's interest

Much the same would be true for other professions that are especially vital to our well being. Talented scientists, mathematicians, engineers, administrators, entrepreneurs, political leaders would have to be differentially rewarded because their work leads to richer and more convenient lives for each of us. We each are paid back many times over for their extra wealth. Viewed from the "original position," we would opt for accepting those kinds of inequalities that all members of a society—including the weakest—would find congenial to their interests. It may seem odd, but as a strict principle, equality is in no one's real interests.

The perspective of the least favored

But even if equality were not our aim, expending considerable resources on the well-being of the most disadvantaged would be uppermost in our minds. Fearing that we would find ourselves in that unenviable group, every effort would be made to alleviate its discomforts. Proposals for the apportionment of resources would have to be scrutinized from the perspective of all members of society, including its least favored. If this last group would not accept a particular allocation, we, from behind the veil of ignorance, would be fearful of adopting it. For example, we would never accept a social reality in which some individuals possessed vast riches while others were forced to scrounge for scraps amid the refuse. We would reject an arrangement that allowed some to enjoy financial good fortune if that good fortune did not serve the benefit of us all.

Determining a Just Distribution of Resources

Take the case of medical care mentioned above. We concluded that high-quality medical care would be unlikely without substantial rewards. But is there a reasonable ceiling to the difference in income necessary to encourage the practice of quality medicine? From the perspective afforded by the "original position," when is a reward substantial enough? Rawls's answer: When the reward would be accepted by the least favored members of society.

Justifiable inequalities

Let us say, for argument's sake, that the average income in a given society is $35,000 a year. It should be possible, at least at the level of principle, to determine what reward would be sufficient to attract bright and ambitious people into the medical profession. In other words, it would be theoretically feasible to calculate beyond what point raising the level of reward would no longer be beneficial to society as a whole. A higher income might, it is true, attract a few more talented individuals; still, from the perspective of society's weakest members, this extra benefit would be marginal compared to the outlay it would require.

Unjustifiable inequalities

Arguably, doubling the average would do the trick. A yearly income of $70,000 would reward doctors for the training and responsibility that go with their job just as it would create the necessary conditions for the practice of high-quality medicine. This then would represent the optimal point that social policy ought to strive for: creating the level of reward for individuals who contribute to the general welfare so that (1) the contributions could be expected to continue and (2) the rewards would be accepted as justified and worthwhile by society's weakest members. Beyond that point—doctors in contemporary America often earn five, even ten times that figure—only the personal interests of the physician are served. There is no comparable gain for society at large. From the perspective of the "original position"—which is to say from the perspective of justice—such practices cannot be defended.

Viewed from a Rawlsian perspective, the salary ladder that pegs different professions at different income levels would have to be substantially rethought. The morally random way in which the market determines income levels could not be the final word. Some professions with relatively modest incomes—teaching and nursing come to mind—would look far more critical and deserving to deliberators in the "original position." On the other hand, the prodigious incomes of some CEOs, professional athletes, and rock stars would seem grotesquely inappropriate. Menial workers would have to be well compensated for their drudgery because of the real possibility that we would end up in their ranks. In general, it appears certain that the divide between the highest and lowest incomes would shrink considerably. Although Rawls is no advocate of strict equality, he does believe that departures from similar treatment and equal rewards would have to be justified in terms of their beneficial impact on society as a whole.

Justifying the free market

Considering its proven capacity to create wealth for all, our Rawlsian deliberators would surely not want to discard the market mechanism. Even for those who will turn out to be society's weaker members, free enterprise offers far more attractive prospects for independence, higher living standards, and advancement than any other available system. Moreover, the absence of private property has a chilling tendency to go hand in hand with repression and autocracy.

The free market is morally blind

Still, as we claimed above, our negotiators would reject the idea that market mechanisms ought to be the alpha and omega of the distribution process. They would conclude that the market's allocation of resources and rewards only partially overlaps with the social arrangements mandated by the "original position." Whatever free enterprise's undeniable advantages may be, its distribution of wealth is not identical to the dictates of justice. Allowing the vagaries of the market to determine social rewards means shirking one of our most critical moral responsibilities; it entails allowing the workings of a blind mechanism to take the place of a deliberate ethical point of view. Judged by the standards of an entirely fair distribution of goods, unregulated capitalism often appears to achieve its apportionment of wealth by a toss of the dice.

Talents should not determine rewards

Rawls pursues this line of argument to some very disquieting conclusions. He insists that, viewed from behind the veil of ignorance, individual talents have no self-standing moral claim to rewards. That is, we have no business allowing talents themselves to determine reward. If we reward talents, it is because of their beneficial effect on the general welfare, not because their possessors can parlay these talents into a profit on the open market. That one has a talent—whether it is exceptional mental endowments or the ability to dunk a basketball—is in itself no more worthy of reward than red hair or a size 15 shoe.

Indeed, receiving special deserts because of a high IQ or unusual physical prowess is, in a sense, doubly unfair to others not so endowed. The fortunate, having been randomly selected by nature to receive uncommon abilities, are not only granted opportunities that make their lives richer and more rewarding, the arbitrariness is aggravated by rewarding them yet a second time—i.e., financially—for their luck. (The mediocre are doubly injured: they both lack talent and are made to live lesser lives financially because of it.) Individual talents are, Rawls concludes, morally irrelevant. Seen from the "original position," our respective talents do not entitle us to individual benefits; they comprise a pool or a social reservoir to be organized and rewarded in a way to which all deliberators would assent. Our sights, he emphasizes, must not wander from the very real possibility that we will not be among nature's chosen.

Social solidarity without altruism

Ironically, although each negotiator in the "original position" has been no more altruistic than the typical trader in the marketplace, what emerges from the deliberations is something quite different: a marked tendency to perceive of social issues in terms that transcend individual interest. The musketeer's call of "all for one and one for all" would seem to be quite appropriate. Paradoxically, an exercise that began with self-interested individuals ends with our speaking earnestly of the public good and of social welfare.

Although these arguments are abstractly philosophical in character, they are brimming over with implications for social practice. A full-blown ideological system lurks in these speculative exercises. Even those welfare liberals who have difficulty accepting Rawls's philosophic system will usually have little trouble subscribing to its concrete programmatic consequences. Indeed, Rawls's writings incorporate so many of the "I believes" characteristic of contemporary liberalism that a summary of the practical conclusions deriving from his ideas reads like a checklist of current welfare liberal ideology.

Summary

1. Human beings are rational, enlightened, self-interested individuals. Their rights and welfare ought to be the central focus of social policy. Although they are bound to each other in commerce, community, and moral life, the interests of one individual should not be sacrificed for the interests of another.

2. Private enterprise and private property are basic and necessary. Not only do they hold out the promise of considerable social wealth, they are also indispensable for individual freedom and self-determination.

3. Nevertheless, the market mechanism, whatever its palpable advantages, is in itself an insufficient guide to the distribution of social resources. It often fails to take fairness, moral desert, and human dignity into account. It apportions wealth in a morally arbitrary way—frequently with obnoxious results. At times, it allows the unconscionable subjection of some to the interests of others. Hence, the mechanisms of the market need to be moderated by deliberately adopted social policies that smooth the jagged edges endemic to capitalism.

4. Private property, for all its importance, is not an absolute entitlement. It is held in the context of a common social life and, hence, may be adjusted and limited to foster important social objectives. Although never to be undertaken frivolously, appropriating private property for pressing public need is a legitimate prerogative of the duly constituted authorities representing the popular will.

5. Our responsibility for society's weaker members is basic and unshirkable. Beyond the shrewd counsel contained in the adage "united we stand, divid-

ed we fall," society as a whole is morally bound to its less fortunate fellows—and not only as a matter of personal charity. The democratic vision is not exhausted by formal practices such as periodic elections or the due process of law. No less, it involves a commitment to human dignity and self-mastery. When members of the body politic are unable to exercise their roles as active citizens because of destitution, illiteracy, or brutal exploitation, it is a social rather than merely a private concern.

6. Private businesses are profit-making organizations; they do not necessarily seek the general good. The claim that a million different businesses each pursuing its own profit invariably harmonize with each other to serve the public welfare is both false and irresponsible. The truth is often quite different. Private businesses must be monitored and, if need be, restrained so as to protect the public from their potential rapaciousness and greed.

7. The only institution that transcends sectarian interests and possesses a total social perspective is government. As the authorized representative of popular will, government uniquely embodies the common aspirations of the whole political community. Government is not the enemy! Although sluggish, top-heavy bureaucracies are a danger to be avoided, government's proper role does involve regulating, monitoring, and administrating those aspects of business and public life that require a society-wide perspective. It also entails operating the complex of social welfare programs that care for those groups disadvantaged by deep-rooted social and historical discrimination—those that the market mechanism cannot avail.

8. In more concrete terms, welfare liberals like Rawls support a series of large-scale social programs designed to mitigate the less attractive consequences of capitalist competition. The best known among these programs:

Welfare liberalism in practice

   a. Unemployment insurance that cushions the blow of losing a job by providing temporary income until new work can be found.
   b. Social security programs that guarantee workers a dignified and comfortable old age.
   c. Medical programs for the indigent and aged.
   d. Welfare assistance for those who are chronically unable to care for themselves.
   e. Educational support and other opportunity-equalizing measures for those whose circumstances place them at a disadvantage in market competition.
   f. Fair-hiring laws, including affirmative action programs, assuring those who have suffered a long history of discrimination that their needs will receive special attention in the marketplace.
   g. Low-cost housing for low-income individuals.
   h. Health, safety, and quality standards for trade, especially in potentially dangerous industries such as drugs, aviation, arms, pesticides.
   i. Standards for working hours, conditions, labor disputes, minimum wages.

j. Environmental protection laws.

k. A system of progressive taxation underlying this network of policies and programs to assure that their costs fall most heavily on those who can best afford to pay for them.

The overwhelming familiarity of these policies and programs attests to the continued dominance of welfare liberalism in contemporary political life. Although classical liberals have mounted a spirited challenge, the dominance of their welfarist rivals remains solid and secure. Dominance, however, begets critique, and a wide variety of opponents and would-be successors have set their sights on exposing what they consider welfare liberalism's feet of clay. From all sides of the political spectrum come a host of penetrating attacks directed both at Rawls and at the type of liberalism he champions. Often there is little these critiques share apart from a common distaste for welfare liberalism as a philosophy and as a political practice. Let us turn to a brief sampling of these critiques.

Critiques

A. Although superficially Rawls seems to distance himself from the far-fetched, Robinson Crusoe individualism of the classical liberals, the distance is more apparent than real. In fact, the same exaggerated image of radically separate individuals each pursuing personal interests lies at the heart of his social vision. And with a distorted basic image of human life comes a distorted image of the human political community.

Rawls's exaggerated individualism

Rawls's negotiators in the "original position" lack any common context. They are pre-social atoms thrown together by the practical necessity of establishing a society. (Even the need to establish a society is not really a common one; it derives from the benefits that social life endows on each individual.) Only the contrived device of a veil of ignorance can neutralize the stark incompatibility of their interests. After being artificially maneuvered into a single perspective, they still lack any essential bonds or human community. They have no more in common than two investors in the same joint stock company.

What Rawls, like the classical liberals, fails to appreciate is that human society is a bond that transcends interest and gain. Human beings are essentially communal in character. Society is not merely a contract (note the unabashed terminology of the marketplace) entered into by calculating negotiators. Hence, the image of pre-social, non-associated, identityless individuals bargaining with each other in a speculative void is terribly misleading. To derive the moral obligations, institutions, rights, and duties of organized human society from these distorted origins is to poison the well at its source. Insofar as welfare liberals hold to this core individualistic image, their views will remain fundamentally wrong-headed.

Equally flawed is the notion that our moral obligations derive from abstract reasoning or from contractual obligations. Contracts do not create either societies or moralities or identities. People come with their social identities. These are not afterthoughts. Indeed, our moral obligations are inextricable from the very identities that link us to other individuals in specific communal settings. Far from being radical individuals as the liberals imagine, human beings are radically situated in particular communal contexts. We are each who we are due to the specific social world in which we live. Conceiving of individuals as pure, self-enclosed bargaining units who only later fill in their characters and moral sensibilities involves a fatal misunderstanding of human ethical behavior. In order to rest on realistic foundations, therefore, political and moral reasoning must commence with the human social bond as primary and fundamental.[2]

Classical liberals' critique

B. Classical liberals find Rawls's blurring of the lines between individuals an affront to both logic and to private property. Rawls's entire speculative exercise is illegitimate because collectivist conclusions are already present in the very nature of the thought experiment he asks us to make. Although he presents the negotiators as separate individuals pursuing their own interests, this is in fact a transparent fiction. They are flattened-out, generic creatures—maneuvered into a single identical point of view. Whatever is unique and different about each of them is artificially set aside. With their individuality veiled in ignorance, what other perspective is there but that of the nondescript everyman? If only a single perspective is permitted, is it surprising that collectivist conclusions ensue? Perceiving of justice as that which faceless individuals in a condition of ignorance would accept already prejudges the argument in the collectivist's favor.

Claiming that individual talents and properties are part of a common social pool to be dealt with according to social need is the deepest kind of affront to human individuality. If my own talents are not mine, what is? If what I can make of myself is subject to a collective determination, what sense does the idea of the autonomous individual possess? Similarly, if property is viewed as a sort of public trust, is it any wonder that it ends up being distributed according to the standards of the entire collective?

Rawls's most fundamental error lies in failing to appreciate that what is mine depends on what I do, not on what others decide. Because they belong inherently to my person, my efforts and my property are outside the reach of collective determinations. They are natural entitlements that antedate political life, not moral rewards granted by the public will.

Setbacks for welfare liberalism

C. In its broader and less philosophical form, welfare liberalism has suffered some severe setbacks in recent years, and its critics have wasted no time in using these obvious shortcomings in attempts to discredit the doctrine as a whole.

---

2. See Michael Sandel, *Liberalism and the Limits of Justice* (Cambridge: Cambridge University Press, 1982) and Alasdair MacIntyre *After Virtue* (Notre Dame, Ind.: University of Notre Dame Press, 1981).

1. Keynesian economics with its reliance on deficit spending, i.e., government's borrowing money for public expenditure in order to stimulate a sluggish economy, has proved to be less than a blessing. In recent years it has created a painful mixture of inflation and economic stagnation, or stagflation.

2. The vast amount of funds required to cover the expenses of the social security system, medicare, unemployment insurance, welfare, etc., are quite literally bankrupting the country.

3. Apart from the massive financial outlays involved, these programs have spawned some of the most byzantine bureaucratic structures ever created. Not only are they notoriously redundant, inefficient, and mired in red tape, they only prove the old adage that the larger the bureaucracy the greater the opportunities for corruption. Lacking the pressures exerted by profit and loss, government expenditures always seem to balloon out of control. It has become a truism for us that work done under the pressure of bottom line economics regularly turns out to be cheaper, quicker, and of higher quality than similar work done by public agencies. The humiliating collapse of the communist economies renders this truth incontrovertible.

4. The expenses involved in running a vast governmental bureaucracy have increased the tax load on the average hard-working family in an alarming way. This insatiable governmental colossus seems to do nothing so well as eat up personal income and bury fresh initiatives under suffocating regulations. Taxing and spending, welfare liberals have lost sight of their original purpose: a commitment to individual freedom and personal autonomy.

5. Programs designed to help those in need have too often turned into sources of easy money that discourage incentive and foster dependence. They create a population of professional takers who are as adept at playing the system as they are in avoiding real productive work. Rather than provide help in times of need, these programs seem to perpetuate the conditions that make them necessary in the first place. Welfare payments, for example, are too generous and too simply available; they generate a self-reinforcing cycle of dependence and despair. Too often they serve to perpetuate socially destructive behavior, ranging from rampant promiscuity, to drug use, to violent crime. When third and fourth generations continue to live on welfare handouts, must not the fair-minded individual conclude that there is something seriously wrong with the system?

6. There is a well-known corollary to the righteous illusion that providing for the needy out of public funds is the answer to their ills. Destitution and anti-social behavior, we are told, derive from unfortunate social environments. Change the environment—so goes the familiar liberal tale—and the problem will dissolve on its own. More and more this

seems a questionable hypothesis. Blaming the environment for one's failings is a sure way of perpetuating them. By shifting the burden of responsibility from the individual person, where responsibility belongs, to all-excusing conditions, the opportunity for true improvement is lost. All it does is breed a culture of complaint in which everyone is a helpless victim of some condition or other. And make no mistake: complaining and self-victimization have no constructive consequences.

In hard-nosed practical terms as well, tinkering with the social environment often proves quite futile. (Certainly the most radical attempt to change conditions and thereby to change human behavior—the communist experiment—failed dismally.) More often than not, changed conditions only change the external shape of the problem. What gets pushed out the door comes back in through the window. When one set of symptoms is erased, another set—no less problematic—takes their place. For example, attractive public housing projects built in order to remove the indigent from festering slums quickly disintegrate into squalid, crime-ridden super-slums. As one impatient opponent of welfare liberalism put it with cruel starkness: there are no slums, only slum dwellers.

To give the poor a genuine chance at improving their lot involves rewarding their initiatives, not padding their welfare checks. Pride comes from accomplishments, not from handouts. Encouraging free enterprise with its mechanism of reward for socially useful effort is, therefore, the effective treatment for the ills of society.

From Welfare Liberalism to Social Democracy

Up to the beginning of the twentieth century, **socialism** was, for the very most part, associated with revolutionary political action. The term could be counted on to cause a tremor of panic in middle-class hearts. In fact, socialism and **communism** were essentially synonyms—our current distinctions between the two were yet to be made. Only slowly and falteringly did dissidents establish an alternative socialist agenda that rejected revolution and authoritarianism and instead committed itself to parliamentary democracy and individual rights.

Socialists vs. communists

Breaking away from Marxist orthodoxies was a traumatic affair. Hostility between democratic socialists and radical communist revolutionaries—each claiming to be the true standard bearer of the socialist cause—flared at the very outset and did not subside until the communist movement collapsed nearly a century later. At times this hostility was irrational and obsessive; at one point it even undermined their ability to create a united front against the Nazi threat. For social democrats, Bolshevik communism had besmirched a noble cause with ruthlessness and autocracy; for communists, the **social democrats** were back-stabbing traitors who, while using the language of Marx, were in practice doing the work of his enemies.

The fusion of socialism and democracy

We will follow the course of radical socialist thought from its origins onward in the next two chapters. Here our concern is with the fusion of democratic and socialist ideologies that became a major force in European politics roughly a hundred years ago. The heart of the social democratic argument can be simply stated: political democracy is incomplete so long as profound economic inequalities persist. If political democracy is to be more than a fig leaf masking the real control of the haves over the have-nots, political equality will have to be matched by an economic bill of rights. The right to basic material well-being is no less fundamental than the right to vote. This, social democrats insist, is not merely a matter of elementary justice; it is an essential implication of democracy itself.

John Stuart Mill, who toward the end of his life flirted with mildly socialist ideas, described the grotesqueness of nineteenth-century laissez-faire capitalism with indignant irony. Capitalism, he writes, apportions wealth in inverse proportion to labor.

The largest portion to those who have never worked at all, the next largest to those whose work is almost nominal, and so in descending scale, the remuneration dwindling as the work grows harder and more disagreeable until the most fatiguing and exhausting bodily labor cannot count with certainty on being able to earn even the necessities of life.[3]

Fabian Socialism

Prompted by much of the same moral indignation that moved J. S. Mill, a group of outstanding English intellectuals founded the Fabian Society in 1884. (George Bernard Shaw, H. G. Wells, Beatrice Webb, Sidney Webb, and Graham Wallas are only the best known among the **Fabian socialists**.) Adopting an explicitly anti-dogmatic, practice-centered socialism, they turned their backs on the grand historical theories and the romantic utopian yearnings that were so typical of French and German socialists. Socialist democracy, they believed, would triumph because political freedom and economic egalitarianism were natural allies. Indeed, each was the necessary condition for the genuine realization of the other. Socialism was the economic aspect of democracy, just as democracy was the political aspect of socialism.

As intellectuals, the Fabians believed in the power of reason. Their strategy was encapsulated in a single word: permeation. Straight thinking had to permeate society. If only the practical advantages of socialism could be convincingly argued—again not as theory but as facts on the ground—it could count on victory. Hence, they avoided high-flying abstractions and concentrated their efforts on specific and systematic analyses of particular institutions and policies. They proposed creative reforms in city planning, in the tax structure, and in social welfare programs. They offered concrete scenarios for the transfer of extravagant private wealth—which undermined social cohesion and public welfare—to communal control. Rejecting a violent takeover by a vanguard of ideologically enlightened

---

3. *Political Economy*, Book 2, Ch. 1, Sec. 3.

revolutionaries, the Fabians championed a program of gradual reform rooted in popular will expressed within constitutional government. They even proposed reimbursing wealthy capitalists for some of their holdings that would become communal property.

Although not a few Fabians soon became disillusioned with the ability of John and Jane Doe to reason politically—they were appalled by the irrationality and intellectual sloppiness they found in popular opinion[4]—their influence on British politics was out of all proportion to their small numbers. The British Labor Party, one of the most venerable of social democratic parties in Europe, owes much of its ideological inspiration to them. Again and again, when the Laborites came to power in the twentieth century, the Fabian heritage of moderation, pragmatism, and reasoned argument provided them with their political ideals.

Socialism on the Continent

Continental European socialists were cut from different cloth. Deeply indebted to Marxist thinking, continental socialists at the end of the nineteenth century were more ideologically systematic and theory-centered than their British counterparts. They were prone to confrontational politics, to heroic stands of principle, and to utopian visions of a radically altered human reality. What is more, their power was clearly on the rise. As opposed to the small band of Fabians, continental socialist parties enjoyed vast voting constituencies. Their human and material resources grew continually.

The erosion of ideology

Paradoxically, their very successes ate away at their ideological commitments. Position and power created interests they wished to preserve. After all, they now controlled established organizations that wielded substantial political influence. Inevitably, their unconditional revolutionary fervor began to wane. Yet social democratic leaders continued to speak as if they were still mounting the barricades. Old revolutionary slogans, it appears, die hard. Even though most European socialists by the turn of the century had, in practice, ceased being revolutionary firebrands, the old rhetoric of class struggle and violent insurrection persisted.

Bernstein vs. Marx

Eduard Bernstein, a prominent German Socialist, shook the socialist establishment by challenging its outmoded revolutionary rhetoric as well as the Marxist theories upon which it rested. In his influential book *Evolutionary Socialism*[5] Bernstein called upon socialists to acknowledge that economic and political realities had changed since the days when Marx and Engels had authored the *Communist Manifesto*. What had changed, Bernstein argued, was that the poor were not growing poorer as Marx had predicted. The lot of the working class was, on the contrary,

---

4. See for example Graham Wallas, *Human Nature in Politics* (Boston: Houghton Mifflin, 1916).
5. (New York: Scribner, 1961). A more recent edition of this work is *The Preconditions of Socialism* (Cambridge: Cambridge University Press, 1993).

generally improving. Careful scrutiny of the relevant data made it clear that workers were making some real gains. Income was growing and social benefits were covering more individuals. What is more, the power of the social democratic parties was growing. And the prospect for these trends continuing was good. Revolutionary posturing was, therefore, a dishonest, self-defeating charade. Socialists of integrity needed to abandon their anachronistic formulas and adjust to the new world of political opportunities. Many of these opportunities, Bernstein believed, lay in the world of parliamentary democracy.

Implicit in these arguments was a fundamental challenge to Marxist dogma. Revolutionary Marxists had rejected parliamentary politics because it was, in their view, only a facade for ruthless class rule, distracting working class attention from the uncompromising class struggle at the heart of capitalism. Parliamentary coalitions and political deals that served to blur class lines were to be strenuously avoided. Workers could never share power with their oppressors. Revolution was the only appropriate response to the dictatorship of the wealthy.

Evolutionary socialism

Bernstein's findings cast serious doubt on this doctrinaire position. The interests of the poor, he was convinced, did not lie in boycotting the political process. Even limited participation had already caused significant improvements in their social and economic position. And there was no reason why working-class parliamentarianism could not extend and deepen these accomplishments. Workers would be better served if they used their voting power and parliamentary clout to reform what could be reformed now rather than awaiting a revolutionary big bang that would miraculously catapult us all into an age of freedom. Parliamentary democracy was an ally of the working class. It could translate the great voting potential of the working class into genuine economic and political attainments. Fought for in parliaments rather than on the streets, socialism would come to be in an evolutionary rather than a revolutionary manner. Ideas such as these laid the foundation for modern European social democratic parties.

Few are the European or Anglo-American countries that have not had a labor or social democratic government (or at least a coalition that included social democrats) during the twentieth century. Like liberalism, however, social democracy comes in many varieties. Each social democratic party, apart from being a member of a broad ideological family, is also rooted in a unique national political reality that determines its character and idiosyncracies.

The varieties of social democracy

French, German, and Italian social democracy have, for example, preserved a certain affinity for their Marxist ideological origins that tends to be absent in the more pragmatic, evolution-centered British Labor Party. Some social democratic parties have substantial anti-clerical components (generally in countries where there has been a strong religious right), whereas in others this element is relatively marginal. Challenged recently by the **Greens**—a brash, young environmentalist party—the German Social Democrats have attempted to steal their opponents' thunder by incorporating environmental issues into their own platform. Social democrats in the poorer European democracies such as Ireland and

Greece tend to be more favorable toward policies like nationalization, economic planning, and the redistribution of property than in wealthy states such as Germany. (In the latter, talk of large-scale nationalization is avoided like the plague.) The Israeli socialist tradition, because of its pioneering origins, has emphasized cooperative and communal ventures such as the **kibbutz**. Swedish social democracy, by contrast, has not made public or cooperative ownership central to its program. Rather, it has adopted a system of cradle-to-grave social services, a **welfare state** system that claimed to be the third way between capitalism and communism.

The character of social democratic parties has changed fundamentally since the days when they were adjuncts to crusading labor movements. No longer are their parliamentary representatives rough workers who leave the lathe or forge in order to speak out for their comrades' needs. The vast majority are presently university-educated professionals. Their tone tends to be business-like rather than declamatory. They often feel themselves as at home in the corporate board room as they do in the labor union hall. Similarly, the electoral constituency of social democratic parties, particularly in wealthier democracies, has ceased to be predominantly working class in character. In some cases, working-class support for social democratic parties accounts for only a third to a half of their total votes; notably, most of it comes from the middle classes and the intellectuals.

American Welfare Liberals and Social Democracy

Social democracy[6] has made little ideological headway in American public life. It has always had an alien, European odor about it. Apart from some sporadic flirtations with socialist thinking during the Great Depression of the 1930s and a strange kind of Woodstock socialism during the 1960s, socialism has usually served as a term of abuse in the American political vocabulary. Nevertheless, moderate social democrats and the more ardent American welfare liberals share significant areas of ideological overlap. Comparing the policies of social democratic regimes in Western Europe with those of unreserved American welfare liberals reveals some striking parallels.

Welfare liberalism:
U.S. vs. Europe

It is often observed that American welfare liberals have a greater potential to move leftward than welfare liberals in the European context. They tend to display more sympathy towards socialism than the European liberals. American welfare liberalism has in fact been viewed as a bootleg social democracy. In the absence of a significant social democratic tradition, American welfare liberalism has been prone to expand and fill the social democratic vacuum. Welfare liberalism in Europe, by contrast, because it has always had an established social democratic movement on its left flank, has not shown a similar elasticity.

The substantial similarities between social democracy and welfare liberalism

---

6. Democratic socialism is generally understood to be somewhat more radical than social democracy, but for this discussion the differences between them have been disregarded.

prompted one distinguished American social democrat to speculate that welfare liberalism and social democracy are on the path of convergence:

> *The difference between social [i.e., welfare] liberalism and democratic socialism keeps growing smaller, so that at some point it may become no more than incremental. Both traditional liberal thinkers and Marxist theoreticians would deny this; a good many social democrats, in effect, believe it.*[7]

Although many of welfare liberalism's beliefs would serve social democrats fairly well, we must remember that even if the two are converging, it is from very different starting points. Welfare liberalism developed out of the individualistic, free-enterprise tradition of classical laissez-faire economics, while social democracy evolved out of the radical left with its very different political agenda. No wonder then that their respective political styles, the kinds of issues to which they show particular sensitivity, even their roster of historical heroes and villains have remained unmistakably different. (Karl Marx, for example, is more a hero than a villain for social democrats, and more a villain than a hero for welfare liberals).

What Divides Welfare Liberals from Social Democrats?

Welfare liberals are individualists

Probably the deepest fault line dividing the adjoining terrains of welfare liberalism and social democracy relates to their assumptions about human nature. Welfare liberals, whatever their critiques of classical liberalism, are liberals nonetheless; their fundamental social image is that of the autonomous, rational, self-interested individual. Society is an aggregation of such individuals seeking to realize their own life plans. One hears relatively little talk in the welfare liberal camp about the moral qualities of the community itself or about the essentially social character of human life. If welfare liberals believe that the infirm and the poor need assistance, it is so that they too may pursue their individual lives in dignity and autonomy.

Rawls's conception of justice illustrates the point nicely. Despite his distaste for the unregulated market, Rawls begins his exploration of justice with an unmistakably liberal image: separate individuals calculating their individual interests. It is true that he goes as far as a liberal can go in mitigating classical liberalism's uncompromising individualism. He insists, as we have seen, on the social responsibility of each for all. But we must not forget that this responsibility derives from our calculation of our own self-interest and not from a deep sense of mutuality or communality. Rawls rejects outright the suggestion that social solidarity can be assumed at the outset of the bargaining process. If society does nevertheless become a moral unit—and Rawls sees this as one of the most attractive elements in his conception of social justice—it is an unintended consequence of the private interests pursued by separate individuals.

---

7. Irving Howe in *The Relevance of Liberalism*, ed. Research Institute on International Change (Boulder, Colo.: Westview Press, 1978) 39.

Constrained by the conditions of ignorance prevailing in the "original position," they will end up with an "all for one, one for all" mentality without having abandoned their essentially individualistic perspectives.

Social democrats arrive at their typical policy preferences from the opposite direction. Their credo begins with precisely the assumption that Rawls avoids: the fundamentally social character of human life. Human beings are not, in the social democratic view, discrete atoms linked to each other by their need to exchange goods and services. Our social needs and social nature transcend the world of instrumentality and enter into the very heart of what it is to be human. Autonomy is, therefore, not a characteristic belonging to separate individuals; it must always be autonomy within the communal setting. Social democrats will resist speaking of individuals as if they were self-enclosed centers of behavior. Individuals may bargain and calculate, but these activities take place against a prior and more basic social bond.

Social democrats often prefer a distinctly **organic** image to describe society. The social union must be understood, they might say, as a living organism that is more than an aggregation of its constituent individuals. It has a life and a moral standing of its own. Indeed, society precedes the individual in much the same way as the whole precedes the part.

Doctrines of this kind have often issued in suffocating collectivism and authoritarianism. If the individual is a limb contributing to the life of the social organism, the road to repression is, potentially, very short. Social democrats are highly sensitive to this danger. Having seen some of their own ideological kith and kin embark on seemingly noble quests for social justice only to be destroyed by collectivist authoritarianism, they are permanently on their guard. The desire for a just and egalitarian society, they warn, must not be allowed to swallow up the no less critical need for democratic freedoms. Any doctrine that fails to accommodate both these needs is too narrow to fit a fully human political agenda.

When society is sharply divided into haves and have nots, not only justice is violated. For social democrats, individualism and autonomy are in danger as well. Extremes of wealth and poverty so empower the wealthy and so devastate the poor that talk of individualism and political liberty ring hollow. Freedom of the press, for example, is a distinctly secondary concern for the illiterate subsistence farmer. Chronic hunger makes the right to vote seem a paltry privilege. Nor are the homeless likely to place political activity high on their list of priorities. To be equal politically, therefore, requires at least a minimal degree of equality in the citizenry's social and economic position. The marketplace needs to be suffused with some of the same communal, egalitarian, and democratic spirit that prevails in the political arena.

Social democrats recognize that differences in income, standing, and power will always be with us; these seem an eradicable part of our human condition. And they have no trouble acknowledging the positive contribution that competition makes in the marketplace. But, they insist, economic differences and competition must be kept within limits that preserve society as a moral union of equal persons. When socio-economic differences create a dehumanized underclass, or when individuals and classes are so fundamentally set against each other that it becomes difficult to speak of social solidarity, political pathology has set in. The parts have

Social democrats are community centered

The dangers of collectivism

Poverty undermines democracy

A moral union of equal persons

substituted themselves for the whole. The moral cohesion of the political community has become unstuck.

Ideological
mirror images

Both welfare liberalism and social democracy may be spoken of as compound ideologies: both begin with a core doctrine—in the one case liberalism, in the other socialism—whose excesses they deplore. Welfare liberals seek to mitigate the starkness of liberal individualism with a substantial dose of social responsibility that often approaches a mildly socialist position. Social democrats, on the other hand, in a kind of ideological mirror imaging, insist on preserving liberal staples such as individual rights and political freedoms. If liberals seek to protect society's weaker members against the destructive consequences of unbridled competition, social democrats are dedicated to avoiding the conformism and authoritarianism that have so often accompanied simple collectivist ideas. The basic elements of both are, therefore, roughly parallel; they each balance a commitment to a rights-based democracy and private property with a concern for social justice. Nevertheless, as liberals and socialists respectively, they will often differ energetically in regard to the spot on the equality-individualism continuum that best satisfies both demands.

Admittedly, the lines between the two at times blur and their rhetoric becomes difficult to disentangle. One illustration will have to suffice. Ramsay MacDonald, the influential British socialist who twice served as Prime Minister (1924, 1929–1935), energetically denied that social democrats were against private property. On the contrary, private property is a critical human need. For each of us to express what is unique in our personality we must own our share of property. What social democrats reject, he continues, is the concentration of private property in a few hands. When the wealth of some is the cause of the propertylessness of the many, it is the right to property that suffers. This is not property in its healthy sense—as an instrument of self-development—but rather its abuse and negation. Precisely because property is so fundamental to human self-development, it must be made widely available. The social democratic objective, he concludes, is the realization of private property's optimal potentialities. To this end, socialist measures become necessary. Even a sharp scalpel will not neatly divide liberal from socialist arguments in this case. Liberal axioms and socialist conclusions so thoroughly dissolve into each other that the search for pure categories becomes hopeless.

The Problems of Contemporary Social Democracy

Whatever its power as a moral and ideological vision, all is not well with contemporary social democracy. There are signs that it has lost its way. From the 1920s until well after World War II, social democratic ideas were linked to a reasonably clear political program. Nationalization (i.e., government ownership and control) of key industries as well as central economic planning were their favored policy choices. These practices reflected antagonism toward the injustices caused by free-market economics, as well as the belief that central economic planning was superior to the hit and miss anarchy of an unregulated market. Planning, they predicted, would rationalize production by eliminating wasteful competition. It would be directed toward the general welfare and not merely by the hunger for immediate profits. Finally, it would utilize natural and human resources more efficiently.

In recent decades, the shortcomings of nationalization and centralization have become a familiar cliche. Inevitably, this has caused a vacuum in social democratic politics. Social democrats have been forced to recognize private enterprise as the irreplaceable center of any modern economy. This creates a dilemma to which there is no easy answer: How do we translate social democracy's distinctive moral sensibilities and its vision of social responsibility into an effective political program? If capitalist competition is accepted as indispensable, what credible program can social democrats offer that is both morally distinctive and practically workable?

Moreover, the growing affluence of the Western democracies has made the egalitarian socialist message—so appropriate to periods of want and crisis—somewhat out of date. Clearly, social democracy is no longer the crusading presence it once was. Its moral urgency is blunted when simple working people can afford a comfortable home, two cars, and a substantial degree of leisure. Oddly enough, social democracy has ceased being a fighting force because much of its fight has been won. It is in ideological limbo precisely because it has succeeded in establishing the legitimacy of its moral concerns. Many of the issues it fought for in the past (such as minimum wage, labor unions, progressive income tax, free education) have become the commonplaces of today. They have also been taken up by many other ideological groups making social democracy seem redundant and without a distinctive voice of its own. Does social democracy stand for anything beyond a somewhat vague commitment to democracy, pragmatic policies, and a developed social conscience?

Summary
Let us recap briefly the fundamental elements that go into the contemporary social democrats world-view:

1. Social democrats are unconditionally committed to democracy, individual rights, and the due process of law. They reject violence and revolution.
2. Society as a whole has a basic responsibility for all its citizens, their dignity, welfare, education, health, and physical subsistence. Hence, government must act to encourage full employment, social security, health care, educational opportunity, old age pensions, and a wide variety of social services.
3. Nevertheless, private property and market competition ought to be preserved. Only when they significantly undermine communal solidarity or create unacceptable disparities of wealth and poverty are they to be limited by government regulation.
4. In the past, social democrats tended to believe that central planning and the nationalization of critical industries (utilities, railroads, mining, steel, health care) was the answer to society's ills. This has become less and less the case in recent decades. The current social democratic slogan is "as much competition as possible, as much planning as necessary." This can be expanded to read: private enterprise wherever possible; government control only when it is not.
5. Ideologically, social democrats have a pragmatic, ad hoc quality to their thinking. Sharply defined, systematic doctrines are foreign to them. They

lack the certainties of the radical left. Nor do Marxist ideas such as dialectical materialism, economic determinism, or the withering away of the state (all to be discussed in the next chapter) have much appeal for them.

Critiques   Although we will put off to the next chapter the main critical questioning of socialist principles, two brief but very pressing difficulties should already be obvious.

> **A.** Having conceded that capitalist competition must form the center of any successful modern economy, what is left for contemporary social democrats to offer? Recognizing further that nationalization of major industries is no panacea for social ills—indeed that it creates insuperable problems of its own—only compounds the social democrat's troubles. Neither has planning fulfilled socialist expectations. It has proven to be wasteful, insensitive to consumer needs, and a drag on economic growth. Social democrats do not seem to have a single leg left to stand on.
>
> **B.** Although they are often ideologically nondescript, social democrats can rely upon a coalition of beneficiaries who are tied to the party by their pocket books. In reality, social democracy is less an ideology with a vision and more a partnership of interests. It succeeds above all as the advocate of special needs. To this one they promise free college education, to that one free rides on public transportation, to yet another tax breaks and salary supplements. Social democracy has ceased to be a clearly definable ideological position. It has taken on the character of a super interest group.

Beginning with conservatism, traversing classical and welfare liberalism, we have followed the ideological spectrum to social democracy. This portion of the spectrum—from conservatism to social democracy—forms the heartland of modern western ideological thinking. It contains those positions most prevalent in Western democracies, those that give the tone to contemporary Western political discourse. In different degrees, they all share a respect for law and democracy, for individual rights, and for private property. Beyond the borders of this ideological heartland lie the radical ideological poles: communism and fascism. It is to them that we now turn.

Suggestions for Further Reading

Bernstein, Eduard. *Evolutionary Socialism*. New York: Scribner, 1961.

————. *The Preconditions of Socialism*. Cambridge: Cambridge University Press, 1993.

Blocker, H. G. et al., eds. *John Rawls' Theory of Social Justice: An Introduction*. Athens, Ohio: Ohio University Press, 1980.

Bottomore, Tom, ed. *Socialism of the Future: A Journal of Political Debate*. London: Pluto Press, 1992.

Crick, Bernard. *Socialism*. Minneapolis: University of Minnesota Press, 1987.

Crosland, C. A. R. *The Future of Socialism*. New York: Schocken, 1963.

Daniels, Norman, ed. *Reading Rawls*. Stanford: Stanford University Press, 1989.

Durkheim, Emile. *Socialism*. Ed. Alvin Gouldner. New York: Collier, 1962.

Fried, Albert, and Ronald Sanders, eds. *Socialist Thought: A Documentary History*. New York: Anchor, 1964.

Fromm, Erich, ed. *Socialist Humanism: An International Symposium*. New York: Anchor, 1966.

Galbraith, Kenneth. *The New Industrial State*. Boston: Houghton Mifflin, 1967.

Gay, Peter. *The Dilemma of Democratic Socialism: Eduard Bernstein's Challenge to Marx*. New York: Collier, 1962.

Harrington, Michael. *Socialism*. New York: Bantam, 1973.

Lichtheim, George. *A Short History of Socialism*. London: Weidenfeld and Nicholson, 1970.

MacIntyre, Alasdair. *After Virtue*. Notre Dame, Ind.: University of Notre Dame Press, 1981.

Myrdal, Gunnar. *Beyond the Welfare State: Economic Planning and Its International Implications*. New Haven: Yale University Press, 1960.

Nove, Alec. *The Economics of Feasible Socialism*. London: Allen and Unwin, 1983.

Rawls, John. *A Theory of Justice*. Cambridge, Mass.: Harvard University Press, 1971.

Sandel, Michael. *Liberalism and the Limits of Justice*. Cambridge: Cambridge University Press, 1982.

Shaw, G. B., and others. *Fabian Essays*. 1889. Reprint, London: Allen and Unwin, 1958.

Waltzer, Michael. *Radical Principles: Reflections of an Unreconstructed Democrat*. New York: Basic Books, 1980.

————. *Spheres of Justice: A Defense of Pluralism and Equality*. New York: Basic Books, 1983.

Chapter *5*

The Radical Left: Marx's Vision

The Downfall of a Colossus

Communist ideology discredited

"And so, in a single lifetime, the whole misconceived enterprise has had its day, and collapsed amid almost universal execration."[1] So wrote the Sovietologist Robert Conquest shortly after the disintegration of the Soviet empire. Not only had the Soviet political system collapsed in disgrace, but its communist ideology was thoroughly discredited as well. In a matter of months, political ideas that had claimed the allegiance of a third of the world's population and been the nightmare of liberal Western regimes faded into oblivion. The depth of popular resentment toward the communist system and the rapidity with which its ideological principles were repudiated astounded even veteran observers of communist affairs.

Left-wing reactions

Western leftists had long been dissociating themselves from Soviet ideology and practice. Nevertheless, the extraordinary speed and thoroughness with which communism was abandoned in the homeland of the revolution made for some painful soul-searching. Reactions varied. A number of isolated islands of orthodoxy, such as China, North Korea, and Cuba, held tightly to their communist creeds—even though their long-term life expectancies appeared doubtful. Most European communist parties changed their names and did all they could to distance themselves from old-style Soviet Communism. Some underwent a profound process of organizational and intellectual renewal, emerging as authentic democratic socialist parties. Interestingly, many Western leftists greeted the Soviet collapse as good news. Finally, they declared, Marxism could free itself from its heavy

---

1. Robert Conquest in the *Times Literary Supplement*, 20 September 1991, 3.

Soviet burden and return to its true roots. Others turned to what is sometimes called the cultural left and led the university-based struggle against racism, sexism, and the old canon (see "The Storm Over the University," Chapter 9). Finally there were the hopelessly disillusioned, those who simply conceded that their god had failed.

Is Marxism discredited?

After the Soviet downfall, we are tempted to dismiss the entire Marxist tradition as an unfortunate episode best consigned to the trash bin of history. This would be a serious mistake. Although it provides no consolation for the millions who perished in the **Gulag**, we should remember that communism grew out of some of the deepest roots in our Western moral and philosophical tradition. Marxist theory has engaged some of the finest minds of our time. Nor can it be denied, even by its enemies, that Marxism provides tools for political/historical analysis that, in terms of sheer intellectual ambition and complexity, have few parallels in other ideological systems. Indeed, a great deal of contemporary liberal democratic thought is inconceivable without the catalyst provided by the Marxist challenge. Moreover, many of Marxism's basic ideas and intellectual methods have migrated well beyond their radical left-wing origins. We find them today in the best of ideological homes. Lastly, Marxism is not a single phenomenon. It has always been made up of rival factions with competing ideas. Hence, we must ask: (a) How true to Marxist conceptions were Soviet ideology and practice? (b) Is the collapse of Soviet Communism identical with the discrediting of Marxism? (c) To what extent are Marxist doctrines responsible for Soviet crimes?

Communism and fascism

Horror at the outrages of communism inevitably brings fascist parallels to mind. The **totalitarian** repression and the surreal camps of death seem to bond these two ostensible rivals into a single political category—as if the left and right extremes of the ideological spectrum had bent over and touched each other. Such parallels, understandable though they may be, strike some thinkers as egregiously wrong-headed. They fail to distinguish between a noble idea gone sour and an evil idea that remained evil in practice. Marxism, they point out, was born out of the most humane aspirations. It was a philosophy of liberation that, tragically, turned into its opposite. Fascism, by contrast, was poison from the start. It became in practice just what it had predicted in theory. As one observer, Shlomo Avineri, puts it: If fascism is the devil, then communism is best described as a fallen angel.

The Origins of Modern Socialism

Nineteenth-century capitalism

A time-machine visit to one of Europe's capitals in the mid-nineteenth century would be a harrowing experience for most moderns, bringing us face to face with a very large class of impoverished laborers who owned nothing but the sweat of their brows—which they sold, when they could, to whoever would pay them a bare subsistence wage. We could not miss the festering slums in which they lived, the crime, prostitution, and sickness that surrounded them. Their work, which often lasted for 12 to 16 hours a day in dank, suffocating surroundings, was mind numbing and body destroying. They had no rights against their employers, who could fire them at will, no social security benefits to fall back on, and their political rights, when they had any, consisted in voting periodically for this or that patrician statesman. Their children, we would learn, were sent to work at an early age—schooling was often an unaffordable luxury. We would be impressed that the phenomenon of illiterate children working 10 hours a day was quite an ordinary one.

All this would seem doubly distressing in light of the immense powers of production and wealth unleashed by the Industrial Revolution. Production more than quadrupled in a matter of decades, yet the workers received none of its benefits—if anything, their situation became even more desperate. Moreover, the widespread squalor, suffering, and dehumanization would seem to us utterly unconscionable in light of the obscene wealth and luxury enjoyed by the few. Our rising sense of indignation about these injustices would put us in touch with the moral urges that

Karl Marx (1828–1883). The major theorist of modern socialism.

lie at the heart of modern radical left-wing thought. Whatever other currents fed into left radical ideology, moral outrage was at its center.

Radical conceptions of a reordered society did not begin with the Industrial Revolution; they had been broached long before Karl Marx gave them definitive formulation. The dream of an egalitarian, propertyless society in which rationality and tolerance prevailed had inspired Thomas More in his *Utopia* (1516). At the radical fringes of the English Civil War in the seventeenth century, and once again at the left-wing periphery of the French Revolution in the eighteenth, radically egalitarian ideas had flourished. But it was only in the nineteenth century that these ideas came into their own. Prompted by the painful reality created by industrial capitalism, visions of a different and better world began to proliferate. And these ideas were no longer speculative romances like More's work, but earnest political programs with names like socialism and communism.

The Utopian Socialists

Marx derided many of these early thinkers as utopians—dreamers out of touch with the real forces shaping the world. But Charles Fourier, Robert Owen, and Claude Henri de Saint Simon captured a certain simple enthusiasm that would later be lost when socialism became an established ideology. Unencumbered with the realities of power, they seemed to spin their ideas innocently and effortlessly. Nevertheless, later reformers and revolutionaries, especially Marx, derived important insights from these **utopian socialists**, and their message has often come down to us via the treatises of more influential radicals.

Fourier   Fourier (1772–1837), a strange bird if ever there was one, spent much of his time sitting in a Parisian cafe awaiting the benefactor who would fund the implementation of his schemes—and all the while he scribbled endlessly of the harmonious society that would be both completely free and yet wonderfully ordered. Blending mysticism, sexual permissiveness, human engineering, and a little lunacy, he sketched the profile of the self-sufficient commune he called the phalanstery.

His central insight was that work, in itself, is not distasteful. By nature we wish to create and to be actively involved in demanding projects. Work only becomes unpleasant when it is forced upon us, when it is repetitive and boring, when it goes against the grain of our natural impulses. To create an ideal society, therefore, we would have to discover the key to synchronizing our natural desires with those of others and of society. To this end, Fourier catalogues human needs, desires, and capacities (passions, as he calls them) and builds his commune on the deliberate coordination between them. The natural variety of human inclinations, when properly ordered in harmonized voluntary association, will issue in a society where all work diligently and yet all are free. Those who love the outdoors will not find the duties of a forest ranger drudgery any more than those with a taste for the culinary art will find preparing wondrous meals a chore. Even garbage collection can be matched to a group that positively enjoys dirt: children. By varying activities, schedules, partners, and locales, we would be simultaneously doing just what we wanted and serving others as well.

Owen   Robert Owen (1771–1858) did more than dream of social harmony; he turned his ideas into a functioning community. Nor did he have to await a benefactor. A wealthy industrialist, he used his own wealth to pursue his socialist/philanthropic objectives. Owen's central contention was that human beings are the product of the conditions in which they live. Perverse social systems create deformed human beings. Greed, unscrupulousness, and anti-social characteristics prevail because the world of the factories and the capitalist market sets a premium on just these traits. An enlightened reality is the best antidote to everything from drunkenness to shoddy production.

Seeking to demonstrate his contention that human nature is pliable and capable of vast improvements, Owen set up a model village and factory in New Lanark, Scotland. Here, in the best tradition of paternalism, he played the role of benevolent law-giver. Shorter working hours, limitations on child labor, and improved working conditions were to foster the emergence of a new kind of person. Rules related to cleanliness, sobriety, and leisure pursuits would encourage workers to take pride in their homes and communities. Children were educated at Owen's expense in the belief that education, in the broadest sense, was the key to the formation of character.[2] Hoping to create an international network of such enlightened communities, Owen exported his ideas to the new world. On a large plot in Indiana, he set up the socialist community New Harmony. Although it failed soon afterwards, the idea that human character can be altered by transforming the social realities that underlie it remains an integral part of the optimistic world-view of socialism.

Saint Simon   Saint Simon (1760–1825), an aristocratic cavalier, adventurer, and eccentric, believed that human history progressed in predictable stages. Each stage, he argues, carries with it a system of ideas and a corresponding social structure. Medieval Europe, for example, matched a static theological world-view with a fixed feudal social structure that gave special eminence to the clergy. Our present, post-Enlightenment era has dispensed with such theological notions. In their place, the truths of science have become preeminent. The social structure corresponding to the scientific world-view is based on industry and technology. Hence, the task facing our new world is to eliminate the anachronistic remnants of the past and to adjust our thinking and practice to a science-based world.

Two conclusions follow from Saint Simon's premise:

(1) the leaders suited to our new world are scientists and industrialists, and (2) the intricate, highly interdependent nature of industrial society requires expert planning and centralized coordination. Ignorant, old-style politicians interested in power for its own sake, and the hit-or-miss chaos of laissez-faire capitalism are as obsolete as the parasitic idlers of the feudal aristocracy. Saint Simon announces that through enlightened, professional planning, poverty can be eliminated, efficiency

---

2. The subtitle of his most famous book, *New View of Society*, was *Essays on the Principle of the Formation of Human Character*.

improved, and social needs met. Socialism is then the rational control of social affairs through the rule of experts.

The utopian legacy   The legacy of the utopian socialists constituted a network of related ideas:

1. Work can be the vehicle for human self-realization rather than mindless toil.
2. Human nature, since it reflects the social realities in which it develops, can be radically transformed.
3. The world of ideas and the concrete social world are inseparable from one another.
4. Conscious rational control of social affairs is preferable to random, individual decisions.
5. Social organization and political practice can become scientific, that is, based on reliable methods and secure knowledge.

For the young Karl Marx, these ideas were electrifying. Although he found their schemes hairbrained and their doctrines hopelessly out of touch with the real socio-economic world, he sensed that the utopians caught sight of real things to come.

Georg Friedrich Hegel

Hegel's philosophy of history   Not so in regard to the great German philosopher Georg Friedrich Hegel (1770–1831). Marx was convinced that Hegel's views were backward looking. Although his thought represented an intellectual breakthrough of enormous promise, Hegel consistently refused to embrace the progressive potential implicit in his ideas, preferring to justify the past and present rather than advance the cause of the future. Nevertheless, for Marx, as for all of his contemporaries during the first half of the nineteenth century, Hegel was the undisputed high priest of German philosophy. His philosophical perspective, most especially his view of history, was the framework within which all aspiring philosophers had to formulate their ideas. Because the road to Marxist socialism runs through Hegel's philosophical-historical conceptions, we will have to make a Hegelian detour before we proceed to Marx.

The progressive unfolding of spirit   Hegel's philosophy of history is on a truly grand scale—perhaps the boldest, most ambitious attempt ever undertaken to comprehend the human past. Its great difficulty and forbidding complexity resist easy summary. Even in highly simplified form, it remains very challenging for the novice reader. (Fortunately, only a general sense of Hegel's thought is necessary in order to proceed to Marx's. It is Hegel's vocabulary and basic method that are most important.) Hegel contends that history records the unfolding of an inner human spirit that undergoes recurrent, progressive transformations as it seeks to comprehend the world as well as itself. This spirit (*Geist* in German) has two aspects: on the one hand, this spirit is incarnated in the human drive to venture ever forward in understanding, self-mastery, and self-realization; on the other hand, however, this spirit is none other than the essential logic of the divine itself. In venturing forward, humankind progressively reveals the divine presence immanent in the world.

Human
understanding is
historical

Human understanding, Hegel believes, is inevitably historical. Each era can see only the intellectual horizon appropriate to its own stage of development. Hence, at every station along the path of human growth, only certain partial and imperfect elements in the divine logic become visible. Although our human spirit strains against these limits, it is confined to the particular point it has reached on its historical journey. In other words, the world-view of a particular era is the embodiment of spirit at an unfinished point of its historical unfolding. It follows, therefore, that later eras are further advanced in their understanding than earlier ones.

Human progress
and divine design

Hegel concludes dramatically that humanity is God's partner in creation. Through our thought and action we drive the divine plowshare through the hard sod of reality. The stages of our human historical development record the phased revelation of the divine idea. Our historical world incorporates progressively more of the divine spirit as we proceed on our human odyssey. Yet, even though human progress is the vehicle through which the divine design is realized, human beings do not usually sense the part they play in this great "world-historical" drama. Innovating philosophers, political leaders, and scientists believe that they have revealed only what became apparent to them as they struggled with a specific problem. They do not appreciate that in their natural process of discovery they have come upon and exposed the divine idea. They do not sense that human progress proceeds along a pre-ordained divine track.

The Hegelian
dialectic

But what pushes this human/divine progression forward? Hegel answers that the engine of change and progress is the **dialectic** (the term derives from the Greek word for talking or discussing, as does our term dialogue). Dialectic describes the inner logic through which ideas move forward from stage to stage in their development. We noted above that at any particular phase in the unfolding of spirit, what is believed represents only an incomplete and imperfect grasp of the divine idea. It is precisely this unfinished quality that does not permit ideas to remain static. Perceiving the weakness in a certain prevailing way of thinking (the thesis, as it is often referred to), opponents arise who criticize its shortcomings and propose an alternative (the antithesis) to remedy its failings. But the initial way of thinking does not remain passive in the face of criticism. It too mounts a defense and a counterattack. The two positions, locked in intellectual battle, expose each others' weaknesses. By the same token, the enduring strengths of each position become clear. When the point-counterpoint of this disputation exhausts all its intellectual possibilities, a third and more complete position (the synthesis) built on the strengths of each of the previous positions becomes visible on our intellectual horizon.

This third position is not merely a scissors and paste combination of the two earlier ideas. Because it preserves what was valuable and rejects what was faulty in the prior conceptions, the new idea represents a positive advance, a raising of the intellectual level to a new height of understanding and completeness. But this new synthetic position, despite its relative comprehensiveness, is merely a limited historical contention. It too suffers from partiality and imperfection. As such, it generates antagonists who point out its deficiencies and propose remedies. Which leads on to new synthetic positions. And so on, ceaselessly. In this way, spirit strains toward completeness, carried forward by human agency progressing in dialectical steps. History, in the Hegelian view, is then a vast working out of the immanent reason of the divine through the mechanism of the dialectic.

Philosophical idealism

Hegel realizes, however, that ideas never remain simply ideas. They inevitably make their way into the world. Once conceived, ideas create the world in their own image. The institutions, societies, laws—the civilizations—we establish are, therefore, the embodiments of our ideas at a specific point of their forward march. For example, the dawning of the modern idea of liberty receives its concrete embodiment in the French Revolution. Or the advances in our scientific knowledge turn into the Industrial Revolution. Although it is at the level of ideas that essential changes are wrought, these ideas then beget realities that are appropriate to their character. Philosophically, this idea-centered interpretation of history is known as **idealism**.

Real and rational

One implication of this conception is that history and philosophy are profoundly related to each other—two sides of the same coin. The progress of human thought and the progress of human civilization constitute a single progression. History is philosophy in its concrete form, just as philosophy is history in its intellectual form. What actually exists historically is reason in concrete embodiment. Or, in Hegel's famous phrase, "The real is rational and the rational is real." Thus history is not a random series of events, but rather a consecrated procession of necessary stages in the divine drama. It should not surprise us then that Hegel (most especially the older Hegel who became the philosophical master of Imperial Germany) used his considerable talents for conservative purposes: to justify the form of things as they were, that is, to read philosophical necessity into concrete economic and political structures as they existed in Germany at the beginning of the nineteenth century.

The state's moral status

Hegel's specific interpretations of the course of Western history are beyond our purposes here, but it should be clear from the foregoing that modern civilization, and for Hegel especially modern European civilization, constitutes the highest point in the progression of the human spirit. Hegel cites many different modern developments to justify this view, but among the most exalted is the modern state. In Hegel's view, the modern state, with its legal-constitutional equality for all citizens, represents an unprecedented moral accomplishment.

Forms of association

He justifies this contention in typically dialectical fashion. Three different forms of association are available to humankind: the family, civil society, and the state. The family is a biological unit in which altruism reigns. Parents work in order to support their children. Property is held in common and an "all for one and one for all" spirit prevails. But despite its magnanimous, loving character, Hegel reasons that the family cannot be the final stage of our human development. Familial relationships have two shortcomings that drive us dialectically beyond it. First, familial altruism derives from biological instincts rather than from voluntary moral decisions. Second, familial altruism is limited to a specific set of individuals. It is altruism, but of a very particular kind.

The final synthesis

We emerge from the altruistic family at young adulthood and enter civil society, the world of the economic marketplace. Here egoism reigns, for we each seek our own advancement. Conflict and competition between individuals is the prevailing mode of association. Clearly this cannot be our final destiny, even though as Hegel notes the prevalent egoism of civil society has one positive feature absent in the family: it is universal in scope. The dialectical progression beyond the family and civil society seems clear. The altruism of the family without its particularism needs to be fused with the universalism of civil society minus its egoism. What emerges from this progression, Hegel asserts, is universal altruism or the state.

The state's fusion of altruism and universality endows it with a privileged status. It represents an ultimate moral resolution to the problem of human association. Its altruism consists in the fact that state actions—for example, the redistribution of wealth to aid the poor—cannot be accounted for in simple egoistic terms. Nor can national pride or heroism on the battlefield be reduced to individual interests. They reflect a deep moral union in which individuals are bonded into something far more substantial than an aggregation of atoms. Moreover, the modern law-based state does not represent narrow sectorial interests. It transcends such selfish concerns in favor of a universal perspective that pursues the good of the political community as a whole. Equal treatment before the law, neutrality in the face of controversy between interests, universal standards of bureaucratic procedure are all manifestations of the state's universal and altruistic character.

One last element in Hegel's teachings requires brief mention. Hegel claims to have revealed the underlying structure and purpose of human history. In this light, he conceives of his own thought as an ultimate synthesis that resolves the dialectical restlessness which heretofore has driven history forward. Insofar as it reveals the deepest structure of human thinking and resolves the tension that has driven it forward, Hegel understands his thought to be final, that is, an end-point to conventional philosophizing. He believes that his philosophy not only grasps the particular historical point to which spirit has advanced, it maps spirit's entire trek, comprehends its total character, and most importantly, reveals its ultimate purpose.

The nature of freedom

The spirit's ultimate purpose, Hegel asserts, is freedom. As befits a thinker for whom the world of ideas is preeminent, freedom refers to the understanding that comes with identifying the logical course of spirit in the world. To be free is to acknowledge the shape that history has taken as necessary, to appreciate what is as what ought to be. In Hegel's philosophy itself, the spirit's striving for freedom finds its definitive manifestation.

The modern reader may well see these highly intellectualized speculations as a strange foundation for revolutionary Marxism. But it was above all in Marx's explosive confrontation with Hegel's ideas that his own position took shape. Indeed, Marx initially conceived of his thought as a revolutionary exercise in Hegelian logic.

Karl Marx

The Young Hegelians

Karl Marx was born in 1818 in Trier, Germany, to an assimilated Jewish family with a distinguished rabbinical past. His father, a successful lawyer, converted the family to Christianity because Jews were forbidden to practice law. He had hoped that his son would study law, but Karl preferred philosophy because, as he said, it did not deal with the fixed precedents of the past but with the demands of critical reason. It was while studying in Berlin, at the same university at which Hegel had taught a decade earlier, that the confrontation with the Hegelian philosophical system took place.

Right- and left-wing Hegelians

The philosophical legacy that Marx encountered in Berlin was that of Hegel's orthodox followers, who continued to emphasize the conservative elements in the master's thought. History, they taught, was a divine plan that had to be understood, not resisted. Unhappy with the merely justificatory role given to philosophy, a group of dissident students with more dynamic and reform-minded ideas organized for discussions and research. They challenged the Hegelian orthodoxy, most especially its conservative implications. These "young" or left-wing Hegelians,[3] including Marx, argued that Hegel's thought had a potentially radical message which, if properly decoded, could act as a guide to revolutionary change. They reminded their right-wing adversaries that alongside the contention that the real is rational, Hegel had also insisted that the rational had to be real as well. This meant that it was not enough to search for the reason allegedly hidden in history; it was the task of philosophy to sound the alarm when it was not. Philosophy needed to take up the cause of reason rather than to blindly champion the cause of the powers that be. Philosophy meant rationality, not rationalizations.

After completing a Ph.D. in philosophy, Marx considered an academic career, but his Jewish background and unconventional ideas closed the university world to him. Instead he began his career as a fighting reporter committed to parliamentary democracy. In short order, however, he became disillusioned with the supposedly universal and altruistic character that Hegel had ascribed to the state. Marx saw that the state was an outright partisan in the political struggle, consistently favoring the well-placed and affluent over the poor. In Hegelian terms, the state did not transcend civil society at all; on the contrary, it was a political instrument utilized by those who controlled civil society to consolidate their rule. Marx concluded that the political dominance of the moneyed classes was neither accidental nor easily remediable. Political democracy, for all its declared ideals, could not foster the good of all its citizens as long as some were in control of society's wealth while others were economically at their mercy.

Standing Hegel on his feet

At the age of twenty-five, seeking to order his thoughts, Marx undertook a serious rereading of Hegel, from which he emerged with two primary conclusions. On the positive side, the Hegelian dialectical framework picturing human history as a series of progressive transformations leading toward freedom was essentially correct. On the negative side, the idealist or idea-centered substance with which Hegel had filled his dialectical framework was seriously mistaken. Marx would later quip that Hegel was, "standing on his head," that is, resting his conceptions

---

3. Right-wing Hegelian thinking later found its way into National Socialist doctrines, just as left-wing Hegelianism found a home in Soviet Communism. It has been quipped that right- and left-wing Hegelianism finally met during World War II at the Battle of Stalingrad.

entirely on abstract ideas. Hegel had to be demystified, made to stand squarely on his feet. Only then would "the rational kernel within the mystical shell" become visible.[4]

What would an inverted Hegel look like? History would remain a record of our straining forward toward freedom, but the real freedom of concrete individuals would now be its subject. Rather than spiritualizing history into a march of divine reason, we would focus on its tangible material character. The engine of history would be the human desire for liberation, self-realization, and mastery over the world. Where Hegel says spirit or reason, we would read real people and their actual interests. Where he describes the dialectical clash between ideas, we would focus on the actual clash between groups struggling for dominance. Where he speaks of freedom in philosophical terms, we would read real political and economic freedom.

Marxist Materialism

A materialist view of history

At the most basic level, Marx observes, our human aim is to subsist. We organize our social lives in order to satisfy our physical needs. Whatever else we do—from creating culture, to establishing states—this elementary imperative is the foundation upon which all else rests. Because we live in a world of scarce resources, different groups with irreconcilable interests will constantly find themselves ranged against each other in the struggle for survival and satisfaction. Whatever one groups succeeds in getting, other groups will not have. This constant struggle between rival groups over the material wherewithal of existence supplies history with its dynamic qualities. It is not, as Hegel had said, ideas that evolve through history, but the material conditions of our existence. (In philosophy, this material-centered view of human history is known as **materialism**.) As material conditions change, the protagonists in the great historical drama change as well. In the classical era, slaves were pitted against their masters; during the middle ages, serfs were ranged against their lords. In our industrialized market society, economic classes—proletarians (workers) and the bourgeoisie (capitalists)—oppose each other.

Class status and world-view

Economic **classes** are defined by Marx as groups that are differently related to the **means of production** (sometimes referred to as **forces of production**) prevailing in a society. Some classes may own the means of production, others may manage them, still others may do nothing more than labor to operate them. In Marx's view, this relationship to a society's means of production is the critical factor in defining an individual's economic interests, social status, and political power. Indeed, class position is decisive in determining how we view the world. Our ideas tend to be appropriate to our class background. Thus, ideas do not embody themselves concretely in history as Hegel had taught, but concrete material conditions are manifested in our ideas. We think as we actually live. Social conditions determine consciousness, not the other way round.

4. From Marx's preface to the second edition of *Capital* (New York: The Modern Library, 1936) 25.

Infrastructure and
superstructure

There are, therefore, two distinguishable kinds of human creation: those involved with producing the material necessities of life, and those, like ideas, that derive secondarily from these more basic needs. Marx dubs these, respectively, the **infrastructure** (or base) and the **superstructure**. Belonging to the infrastructure are the prevailing patterns of ownership and production, as well as the available kinds of resources and technology that obtain in a given society. The superstructure includes all those creations that derive from and reflect the essential character of the infrastructure. In this category Marx includes a society's legal system, its patterns of political power, its reigning ideas, its culture, morality, and religion. Because the essential character of the infrastructure is projected onto a society's superstructure, the two always go hand in hand. Marx insists that there cannot be a glaring incongruity between them, certainly not for any lengthy period.

Bourgeois Dictatorship

The rule of the
dominant class

What follows directly is that those who control the material infrastructure also control the political superstructure. The ideas of those who dominate economically are also the dominant ideas of society. More specifically, the perspective and interests of the bourgeoisie are decisive in politics, culture, and morality. Even though the number of slaves, serfs, or workers is invariably greater than those of the ruling group, the interests of the latter regularly prevail. In a manner of speaking, the society belongs to them because the lives and labor of all others serve to enhance their interests and pleasures.

All states are
dictatorships

In this sense, Marx declares that all states are dictatorships. States represent the organized victory of one group over others in the struggle to control the material necessities of life. The very existence of a state—an institution with a monopoly over the use of force—indicates that there have been winners and losers in the battle for scarce resources. The winners, seeking to consolidate their victory, utilize the state's powers to shore up their position and preserve themselves against challenges by rival groups. The fact that, historically, minorities have always held majorities in thrall only makes the necessity for such dictatorships all the more pressing.

Hegelian ideas about the state being an ethically noble institution with a universal, neutral, and altruistic character have to be understood as just the kind of idea bourgeois thinkers would want to foster. What is better designed to keep the exploited classes in their place than the comforting idea that the state is above the fray, interested only in the general good? In practice, Marx writes, the state in capitalist society plays the reverse role; it is the executive committee that manages and enforces bourgeois control. The state is the public face of the dictatorship of the bourgeoisie.

Bourgeois control
of ideas

At times there is no choice but to beat back challenges to the ruling class's authority by violent means. In these cases, the police, the army, the prison system—what Marx calls the **state apparatus**—are called into play. But these are costly means of assuring dominance, and the ruling class prefers to avoid them. Domination through control of ideas is more efficient and more effective. If bourgeois ideas can be made to permeate into working-class consciousness, self-sustaining control would be implanted. If the working class can be led to believe that bourgeois dominance is in their best interests, economic and political arrangements will be legitimized without the need to rely on the troublesome apparatus of coercion.

On its face, making proletarian ideas serve bourgeois interests would seem to be a formidable task. After all, in the Marxist scheme of things, proletarian ideas should reflect the material conditions in which they live, and these are radically different from those of the wealthy bourgeoisie. Bourgeois ideology surely does not seek to advance proletarian interests. The world-view that arises out of the conditions of proletarian existence should reflect the subjugation and degradation they suffer. They should, Marx observes, but usually they do not.

Instead, the ideas of the ruling class, disseminated in countless subtle ways, insinuate their way into the proletarian consciousness. The ideological superstructure of capitalism justifies its belief systems and institutions through a variety of highly effective channels: it markets them through formal education, through moral lessons taught in the family, through religious dogmas, through nationalist indoctrination, through a wily system of rewards for conformity and punishments for dissidence. What emerges is a typically reverential attitude toward the political community, its authorities, and its laws. Deference to one's betters is inculcated to the point where it becomes instinct. The division of property—even if it is obscenely lopsided—appears sacred and inviolable. Judges, scientists, academics, experts, and clerics wear the halo of objectivity and integrity. Being honest, hard-working, and law-abiding, whatever the indignities that are suffered, appears as the highest ideal to which one can aspire. On the other hand, revolutionaries who call for liberation from these destructive illusions are denounced as depraved renegades.

False consciousness　　When ideas of this kind take up residence in the minds of the **proletariat**, bourgeois control becomes that much easier. Marx characterizes this phenomenon as **false consciousness**: ideas that dominate despite their inappropriateness to the real material interests of a group. False consciousness can be understood as a form of cognitive imperialism in which foreign ideas serving hostile interests penetrate the mind and dominate it. Proletarian thinking so distorted by the ideological superstructure that it can no longer perceive its own interests but instead champions the ideas of its oppressors represents capitalist cunning at its craftiest.

The Concept of Alienation

Marx describes this loss of self as **alienation**. When one's ideas are no longer one's own, alienation, or the pathological separation from what is essentially human (from our "species essence" as Marx calls it), has taken hold. Capitalism, Marx wrote in 1844,[5] is responsible for more than the alienation of the proletariat from their ideas. It violates their essential humanity in regard to (1) work, (2) the products of their work,

---

5. Upon completing his rereading of Hegel, Marx wrote the *Economic and Philosophic Manuscripts of 1844*. Unpublished in his lifetime, this work appeared only in the late 1920s and early 1930s.

(3) their social relations, and (4) their human world. It creates a reality that, rather than expressing their human aspirations and talents, represses and cripples them.

1. **Work:** Naturally, human beings are creators—Marx uses the term *Homo faber*, "man the maker." We seek to embody in the world those visions and images that we freely conceive. We wish to objectify externally what our mind's eye perceives internally. But capitalist production thwarts this process of free creativity and turns it into its deformed opposite. Rather than enabling us to create in a way that expresses our essential human nature, capitalist production crushes our creative powers and disfigures our specifically human capacities. For the assembly-line worker or the miner, work is oppressive and deadening, the very negation of creativity and humanity.

2. **The Products of Work:** Not surprisingly, the product of such alienated labor does not seem to be our own. What we make has the quality of a foreign body with little relationship to our creative efforts. Moreover, the fragmentation of the industrial process by which the product is created—with each laborer performing only a small part of the total labor—renders the final commodity unrecognizably remote from our own efforts. Marx adds that products so created become my "enemy," they enrich the capitalist powers that subjugate me. With each turn of the lever, I empower the world that impoverishes my existence. Painfully, the products in the store windows are my handiwork, but they mock me in their inaccessibility.

3. **Social Relations:** Capitalist competition turns person against person in a no-holds-barred battle for material advantage. Our basic human need for solidarity, camaraderie, and partnership in creation have no place in such a world. Here, there are only potential rivals for jobs and profits. For each striker there is a scab, for each successful entrepreneur a competitor. Love, the prototypical human capacity to approach other human beings essentially, becomes a rare exception to the rule—limited to family and romance. Hence, the humane Judeo-Christian ideal of loving one's neighbor as oneself is entirely lost in the capitalist reality. In short, capitalism is an affront to our essentially social nature.

4. **The Human World:** The world designed by capitalism confronts us as an oppressive and inhuman creation. Not only do the soot-filled cities and the befouled countryside violate our essential conceptions of beauty and serenity, the human dimension of capitalism offends against our deepest sensibilities as well. The armies of penniless laborers, the illiterate children, the hovels, the prostitution and sickness are a standing offense against our "species essence." Moreover, although I, as laborer, have created this world and its wealth, it is beyond my reach to enjoy.

Capitalists
alienated too

Marx insists that the capitalists, although surely more comfortable than the proletariat, suffer from alienation as well. They too have sacrificed their humanity to an alien god: capital. Their capital lives in their place. Indeed, it is their bankbooks, Marx argues, that appear to be endowed with a real living soul. Their money talks, creates, produces, and builds. It even fosters culture by bankrolling artists and thinkers. In essence, their dollars are ciphers that measure the lives they have squandered. For each dollar they have amassed there is a song they have not sung and a dance they have not danced; for each property they have acquired there is music they have not been inspired by, art that has not moved them, and thoughts that have not enriched their minds; for each deal they have made there is another human being they have not loved. In capitalist society it is things that live and we, their creators, are their appendages: we are homeowners, employers, debtors, mortgagees, and stockholders. In the end, the capitalist appears to be the shadow cast by what he owns.

Capitalism's Revolutionary Role

The confrontation between the bourgeoisie and the proletariat is not just another passing struggle between rival interests. It is, Marx declares, the ultimate historical battle. The class struggle we now face, he believes, differs from all previous confrontations (such as that between serfs and lords) because the Industrial Revolution and capitalism have created material and human capacities without historical precedent. For the first time in human existence, the possibility of overcoming scarcity and triumphing in the struggle for survival has become a real prospect. Through mechanization, automation, and mass production, industrial capitalism creates an unparalleled productive capacity that can amply supply our needs. It promises to liberate humanity from the grinding poverty and resignation that were so long the fate of most individuals.

Marx can hardly praise capitalism's dynamic and progressive qualities enough. Capitalism has unleashed "more colossal productive forces than have all preceding generations together."[6] It is the greatest dynamo that history has known: it brings civilization, commerce, and progress to far-flung geographical areas, unites humanity through great networks of transportation and communication, and subjects nature's forces to human direction. Moreover, the driving energy of the bourgeoisie punctures the sentimental illusions fostered by the feudal monarchy and church, sharply exposing the real, exploitative nature of human relations.

> *The bourgeoisie, wherever it has gotten the upper hand, has put an end to all feudal, patriarchal, idyllic relations. It has pitilessly torn asunder the motley feudal ties that bound man to his "natural superiors," and has left remaining no other nexus [relationship] between man and man than naked self-interest, than callous "cash payment." It has drowned the most heavenly ecstacies of religious fervor, of chivalrous enthusiasm, of philistine sentimentalism in the icy waters of egotistical calculation. . . . In one word, for exploitation veiled by religious and political illusions, it has substituted naked, shameless, direct, brutal exploitation.[7]*

6. Karl Marx and Friedrich Engels, *The Manifesto of the Communist Party*, in *Marx and Engels: Basic Writings on Politics and Philosophy*, ed. Lewis Feuer (Garden City, N.Y.: Doubleday Anchor, 1959) 12.

7. *Manifesto*, 9–10.

Searching for profits wherever they can be made, capitalists leave no historical stone unturned. Because technological improvements promise greater income, traditional means of production are swept aside. National barriers are no obstacle in their search for markets and resources. Customary roles befitting women and men or the high and low born, do not deter them either: capitalism is a great equalizer. Capitalists do not respect even their own industrial creations; they respect only profit. If profit demands dismantling outmoded technologies of production and replacing them with bold new advances, sentimentality will not stand in their way. If it involves sweeping away old ideas, old classes, superfluous workers, even each other, they are always ready to do so.

Capitalism's fatal flaw   Capitalism contributes all of this to human civilization. Some of it is deeply unsettling, even painful, but it constitutes a necessary and progressive step toward ultimate human liberation. Still, Marx contends, capitalism's contribution is fatally flawed. It carries within itself the seeds of its own destruction. In Marx's trenchant image, capitalism creates its own grave-diggers. True to his underlying Hegelian method, Marx understands the bourgeoisie's historical role as incomplete and, in the end, nonviable. It is only a partial, historically transient role whose defects generate an antithetical position that exposes its inadequacies. Inevitably, capitalism points dialectically beyond itself to a more complete and satisfying resolution of the human condition. Recall only that the capitalists, for all their wealth, are alienated from their true human nature and the inadequacy of capitalism becomes apparent.

The Contradictions of Capitalism

Forces and relations of production   Where does capitalism go wrong? Marx claims that capitalism fails because it is unable to either control or adequately utilize the very forces it unleashes. Paradoxically, the awesome potential of these forces is held back by those that have brought them into being. In Marxist terminology, capitalism is doomed because it cannot resolve the internal contradiction between its **forces of production** and its **relations of production**. By forces of production Marx means the actual material methods of production prevailing in a given society. Some societies sustain themselves by hunting with bows and arrows, others by labor-intensive agriculture, still others by industrial manufacture. Relations of production, on the other hand, describe the human side of the production process, the ways in which people organize in order to produce. In this category Marx places a society's typical divisions of labor, systems of authority, and patterns of ownership.

Capitalism, Marx contends, is caught in a self-destroying contradiction: the vast forces it has created through technological innovation (the forces of production) cannot be fully realized so long as the unregulated market, wage labor, and private property (the relations of production) remain unchanged. The two, Marx insists, are patently incompatible. Industrial production promises social wealth such as has never before existed, but its relations of production create unspeakable poverty. The new productive forces are highly social, based on intense forms of human interdependence, yet human relations under capitalism are unprecedentedly egocentric and hostile. Mechanized, automated methods of production promise liberation from oppressive toil while, in fact, the exploitation of labor becomes ever more brutal. These newly developed technological powers are able to design a social and physical environment suited to human needs and reflecting human esthetic conceptions; instead, the world they create affronts our humanity and violates our sense of beauty. In short, capitalism produces the means of human liberation but prevents its realization. And with the prospect of liberation within reach, the struggle over the human future is sharpened as never before.

The proletariat as universal

Pitted against the bourgeoisie, the proletariat is the embodiment of everything that is wrong with capitalism. The proletariat's very being refutes the bourgeoisie's claim to have created a just and humane society. This is no abstract Hegelian antithesis; the suffering proletarian is, for Marx, the negation of capitalism in the flesh. But the suffering of the proletariat differs from what many other groups have undergone in the past. For proletarian interests are not, as has always been the case historically, only narrow group interests. They do not wish to merely alleviate their own suffering; their aim is to abolish themselves as a class—in effect, to abolish the class system from which their suffering derives. In this sense, the proletariat are a "universal class." Because their degradation is limitless and their dehumanization total, their aims are universal as well. They do not suffer in some specific way, so there can be no specific reform that is adequate to their needs. They suffer in a generic human way for which there is no remedy but essential human liberation. Hence, their revolt is the revolt of humanity itself. Just as only the very sick are acutely aware of the blessing of life and health, so those who suffer ultimate dehumanization are the authentic voices of human liberation.

Philosophy's weapon

Marx's striking conclusion is that the concrete interests of the proletariat as an economic class are identical with the essential human aspiration for liberation and freedom. Until now dreams of liberation were inevitably utopian, that is, unrealizable. They had to be confined (as with Hegel) to the abstractions of philosophy or to the exalted realms of music and art. With the advent of the proletariat, however, these dreams cease being impotent visions; they now have a real champion. The proletarians carry the message of philosophy in their very being. They are the living vehicle for the realization of the age-old desire for human emancipation. In the reality of proletarian existence, philosophy has found a material weapon. In this light, Marx's famous dictum that philosophy needs to "change the world" rather than merely "understand" it takes on special urgency.

Boom and Bust: The Intensifying Crises of Capitalism

Capitalism's economic contradictions

The monumental historical battle between the bourgeoisie and the proletariat has a parallel economic dimension as well. Let us consider the course of industrialization in early capitalist Europe. Although the initial financial outlay for mechanization is great, the return in vastly increased production makes it clearly worthwhile. The greater the volume of production, the lower the cost per unit produced. With greater volume and lower costs, entrepreneurs can sell their goods competitively in the market. Soon, however, new technological innovations make their appearance. The financial investments necessary to incorporate these new devices is once again very great.

Only now the increase in productive capacity and profits is no longer astronomical, as it was in the initial burst of mechanization. Only big businesses, with large reserves of capital, can afford these new outlays. Smaller concerns, unable to compete, regularly go out of business and the ranks of the proletariat swell with the newly impoverished.

With only the wealthiest capitalists remaining, cutthroat competition over profits turns on greater investments in productive capacity, higher volumes of production, and ever lower cost per unit. (It is said that the American railroad magnate Cornelius Vanderbilt, in the competitive struggle for markets, lowered freight costs on his railroads to far below cost and then, when his competitors were forced to follow his example, sent his own freight on their trains.) But there is one other outlay that can be cut to reduce production expenses even further: labor costs. Although workers are already paid only a subsistence wage, there is pressure to further reduce this component of production costs in order to remain competitive. Here the profound illogic of the system appears. With vast quantities of goods pouring off the assembly line and wages low and falling, the capitalists pull the rug out from under their own feet. They destroy the very market that is to consume their goods. Who will buy what capitalists produce if the vast majority of their potential market lives at or below subsistence level?

Who will buy the products?

Great periodic crises are therefore inherent in the very dynamic of capitalism. Painful contractions of the market, followed by rapid expansion once again, constitute an inevitable, vicious cycle. Moreover, each successive crisis is more destructive than previous ones because the inner contradictions of capitalism become more intense as productive capacity grows but markets do not. Only a small elite of the wealthiest is able to survive this ever-worsening cycle of boom and bust. Simultaneously, vast numbers of proletarians—many of them recently impoverished—are drawn deeper and deeper into misery. Here then, in cold economic terms, lies the self-undermining nature of capitalism: its productive capacity is stymied by its human relations. As in the story of Moses in the Bible, capitalism gives us a view the promised land but is unable to lead us into it.

Although cast as the villains of the drama, capitalists do not act out of evil motives. Like the proletariat, they are trapped by the constraints of the system. If capitalists were to pay workers what they were worth to them, they might as well close up shop. Only by taking more from the workers than is paid to them in wages ("surplus value" in Marx's terms) are profits possible. Even more impossible is capitalist benevolence. Entrepreneurs who provides health care, shorter hours, or extra vacation time for their workers will lose out to competitors who do not. For Marx, then, capitalism is not evil. It is a historical necessity that follows an iron logic of its own. Capitalism is the formidable but flawed engine that promises but cannot deliver universal plenty.

The Dialectics of Liberation

Dialectically, the bourgeoisie and proletariat represent antithetical principles. The bourgeoisie provides a limitlessly productive force. The proletariat embodies the universal human drive toward liberation. Each, by itself, is incomplete. The one owns the material powers of liberation but lacks the human capacity to realize them; the other expresses the human longings for liberation but lacks the material means to actualize them. They seem ripe for a dialectical synthesis. The universal means of production need to be taken over by the universal human force of liberation. But as opposed to Hegel, who conceived of such dialectical resolutions as essentially philosophic, Marx saw the clash between these principles as anything but abstract. The bourgeoisie and the proletariat meet each other at the barricades.

The rise of revolutionary consciousness

But we have gotten ahead of ourselves. How have the proletarians, so effectively controlled by state force and manipulated by bourgeois ideas, finally found their voice and, as a consequence, their way to the barricades? How does a revolutionary consciousness emerge? Marx contends that first, in the boom and bust cycle of capitalism, the poor become progressively poorer and their lives more and more intolerable. Economic conditions deteriorate to the point where workers "have nothing to lose but their chains."[8] Second, because proletarian ranks have been swelled by the many who are unable to survive capitalist competition, the simple numerical contrast with the bourgeoisie becomes too flagrant to be ignored. A vast army of beasts of burden faces a tiny elite who live in lavish wealth.

Proletarian victory

Although illusions die hard, the deferential, law-abiding, "it's all for the best" mentality cannot survive the compounded afflictions of unemployment, dehumanization, hunger, and despair. How long can one watch the torment of one's children without desperation boiling over into action? To experience the indignities of starvation-wages for years leads to outrage that undermines resignation and meekness. It becomes clear that capitalists are not honorable benefactors, but the enemy. In a slow but steady process that parallels the intensifying contradictions of capitalism, working-class consciousness matures and becomes more militant. The workers realize that their agonies are intrinsic to capitalist exploitation and that they will never be free unless the capitalist system is smashed. The revolutionary moment arrives when the proletariat concludes that their bourgeois masters must be overthrown. (Although Marx does entertain the theoretical possibility that in some unusual realities—he mentions Holland and the United States—the working class may come to power by peaceful electoral means, he does not regard this as a likely prospect.)

All this does not happen overnight. At first, the workers' actions will be tentative, localized, and confused. But as their political understanding and tactical skill grow, the confrontations with their capitalist opponents will become more methodical and increasingly effective. From sporadic, unsynchronized strikes, they will turn to well-orchestrated, economy-wide work stoppages and boycotts. And when the repressive powers of the state are wielded against them—as surely they will

8. *Manifesto*, 41.

be—the workers will be driven toward armed resistance. In the end, the struggle's outcome is pre-ordained; the many will prevail over the few.

Whether the struggle will be intensely violent or relatively mild depends on the extent to which the contradictions of capitalism have been allowed to unfold. If they have developed to the point where (1) the capitalist class has been winnowed down to a tiny minority opposed by a vast proletarian class, (2) the economic possibilities of capitalism have been exhausted and its crisis-ridden character recognized as blatantly irremediable, (3) the workers' class consciousness has been heightened to a revolutionary pitch and its organizations have achieved unity and ideological sophistication—then the struggle will be swift and decisive.

If, however, the revolutionary offensive begins before these developments have had a chance to ensue, the struggle may well be bloody and protracted. Hence, Marx admonishes against premature revolutions which attempt to force the pace of history. For example, the resort to political terror as a way of accelerating the revolutionary process clearly means that the conditions necessary for revolution have not yet ripened, that recklessness has triumphed over good sense. Marx warns that when the dialectical process is impatiently short-circuited, the historical consequences can be calamitous.

The Revolutionaries in Power

Dictatorship of the proletariat

The morning after the revolution, the proletariat begins the process of consolidating its power and restructuring society. But because no economic class, least of all the dynamic and well-connected bourgeoisie, will accept their defeat gracefully, the proletariat must act resolutely. To prevent rear-guard counter-revolutionary activity, they must seize the instruments of coercion that have heretofore been used against them and turn them against their bourgeois class enemies. This Marx dubs the **dictatorship of the proletariat**. Since Marx views all states as dictatorships, the dictatorship of the proletariat is nothing exceptional; it merely turns the tables on what had been, under capitalism, a dictatorship of the bourgeoisie. For Marx, the dictatorship of the proletariat is more humane and less dictatorial than its predecessor: (1) It is the rule of the great majority over a small minority; (2) it is coercive only in order to serve the broad interests of humanity—bourgeois capitalists included; (3) it is explicitly only a transitional stage.

Dismantling capitalism

As important as consolidating political control is doing away with the class system upon which capitalist oppression rested. Here too a transitional stage is required. Proletarian victory will not, in itself, bring freedom and plenty. Because the rapaciousness of the capitalist mentality will not vanish with the proletarian victory, an interim period of economic incentives and central control will be necessary. Capitalist attitudes, like capitalist productive forces, must undergo a fundamental refashioning.

The dawning of communism

Initially, a simple, across-the-board equality will be imperative. Although Marx scorns this kind of economic levelling as crude arithmetic equality—it merely levels capitalist private property into a universal principle—it is, nevertheless, necessary in order to foster the transition to communism. The dawn of communism arrives when the workers take control of the means of production, humanize the relations of production, and unleash the forces of production, allowing them to work without impediment for the general good. In Marx's vision, releasing the forces of production from the obstructions of capitalism will make for a quantum leap in human material abundance.

The withering of the state

With the advent of plenty, the necessity for coercion declines correspondingly. Since scarce resources were the underlying cause of conflict and repressive power in all previous societies, the overcoming of scarcity would mean the overcoming of politics in its conventional power-related sense. A super-abundant, classless society would be a society without dissension or coercion. This would result in the **withering of the state**. The state, which the ruling classes had employed as an instrument of control, would lose its functions and, lacking anyone to repress, would simply wither away. In place of the state that had forcibly administered people, there would be only the administration of things for the general good. The proletariat, the universal class, will have abolished itself and created a universal society.

Future Communist Society

Marx's vision

Marx is notoriously tight-lipped about what the future communist society will look like. In all of his voluminous writings, no more than a few very sketchy pages here and there take up the subject. This was, first of all, because the dialectical developments leading to communism were premised on realities that did not yet exist. How they would evolve and what specific character they would take on were, Marx insists, beyond what could be seen from the present. Marx saw himself as a social analyst who described the present, its tensions, and the likely direction of their resolution. Second, he feared that a utopian society glowingly described would become an object of adoration that would distract from the real revolutionary task at hand.

Still, the broad lines that he did sketch describe a form of human existence that is truly unprecedented. Even if Marx disdained utopian speculations and saw his own projections as grounded solidly in the dialectical dynamics of capitalism, the echoes of those whom Marx had sarcastically rejected as utopians are here clearly audible.

1. Although Marx had only disdain for the capitalist democracies of his day, his ideal communist society is democratic in a radical sense. No longer would democracy be a bogus contest in which the victory of the affluent was a foregone conclusion. Authentic communist democracy would transcend the irreconcilable interests that had hitherto rent societies apart. Lacking conflict or coercion, it would be a harmonious meeting of minds between cooperative, autonomous, and free people.

2. Work, although it would still be necessary, would no longer be drudgery. Our innate creative-esthetic powers would be the driving force behind our

work. Artistry would become the content of labor. The world we created would, therefore, objectify the human ideals of harmony and beauty.

3. Possessiveness would disappear as its cause, scarcity, was overcome. We would be no more clinging and jealous in regard to abundant material objects than we are possessive about omnipresent air, despite our critical need for it.

4. Although Marx does not recommend central planning or centralization of economic and political control—if anything, localized initiatives seem to be what he had in mind—he did conceive of cooperative public ownership as the communist alternative to private property.

5. Human relations would be placed on a novel footing. No longer would individuals be appendages to their belongings and their social statuses. Being, rather than having, would be the key term in our unalienated human vocabulary.

6. The family as a patriarchal institution based on the economic and biological divisions of labor would be replaced by new forms of human association in which equality, free choice, love, and human need are decisive. Although he rejected "free love" (it is, for him, analogous to arithmetic equality—possessiveness levelled and made universal), what would come in place of the authoritarian nuclear family would liberate love and sensuality from their present oppressive constraints.

7. Because social conditions determine consciousness, the similar conditions that capitalism fosters wherever it triumphs will create international working-class unity. Nationalism will be exposed as a deceitful means by which bourgeois ideology artificially moderates class conflict and sows the illusion of solidarity. It will give way to a borderless, stateless humanity.

Marxism at Marx's death

This blissful vision of alienation overcome inspired generations of visionaries and political activists. For those who related to it with high seriousness, it distilled the natural human truth that has been mystified and alienated in the religious visions of heaven and paradise. It was a human ideal that could be believed by nonbelievers. When Marx died in 1883, however, there were few concrete indications that the dialectic was interested in realizing his vision. The working class, although growing by leaps and bounds in Western Europe, did not seem interested in ushering in the communist leap into freedom. Even less did the Russian Empire, the backward giant to the East, appear to incarnate the forces of human emancipation.

From Marx to the Gulag

Leaping forward a century to the last years of the Soviet Union's world-power status is, therefore, a traumatic exercise. How did we get from here to there: from Marx to the Gulag, from the rhetoric of liberation to the reality of totalitarianism? How, in a word, did an almost messianic doctrine of liberation turn into a Leviathan masquerading as the Messiah? Were there special circumstances in the Russian reality that contributed to these developments? Or were the seeds of corruption latent in the Marxist message all along? These questions will take up much of our discussion in the coming chapter.

Critiques

But before turning to the fortunes of Marxism after Marx, we first need to stop and deal with Marx's ideas themselves. A number of objections and criticisms must be considered. It is, of course, far too easy to list the failings of Soviet politics and hold Marx responsible for them. (Marxist sympathizers would say this is akin to blaming Christ for Torquemada's Inquisition). Arguments of this kind beg the obvious question of the relation between Marxism and Soviet Communism. Hence, in the critiques that follow, we shall focus on Marx's ideas themselves. Nevertheless, the careful reader pondering the difficulties in Marxist theory may get a good sense of where our discussion of Soviet ideology and practice will lead us.

The historical record

A. First, there are the errors in historical fact.

1. The growing impoverishment of the working class, which was the necessary condition for proletarian revolutionary consciousness, simply did not materialize. The ability of capitalism to improve living conditions for all became apparent even to nondoctrinaire Marxists, such as Eduard Bernstein, at the beginning of the twentieth century. Without a revolutionary proletariat, the Marxist scenario is missing its lead actor.

2. Marx's contention that nationalism is a waning force which would be replaced by international working-class amity has proved to be disastrously wrong. Nationalism has been one of the most (if not the most) potent forces in twentieth-century politics. Indeed, in many parts of the world it appears dangerously on the upswing.

Marxism is dated

B. Several elements in Marxism are clearly dated.

1. It is often contended that the very success of Marxism as a doctrine created the forces that undermined its historical relevance. In a curious dialectical irony, the fear of civil strife and revolution that Marx did so much to encourage prompted capitalist regimes to introduce measures that moderated the class struggle and aided workers in distress. Hence, social-welfare legislation establishing unemployment insurance, social security, maximal working hours, and limiting child labor, were all initiated by capitalist regimes.

2. Marxist economics is as relevant to our contemporary political analysis as is nineteenth-century economics—which is to say, not relevant at all. Virtually all of Marx's concepts, ranging from his understanding of class identity to his view of the business cycle, are anachronistic. To construct a radical position relevant to politics at the end of the twentieth century would mean transforming Marxist teachings almost beyond recognition.

Marx's exaggerations

C. Marx's argument that all historical societies are locked in life-and-death conflicts over scarce resources takes a molehill of truth and constructs a mountain out of it. The parallel contention, that all states are dictatorships, also suffers from irresponsible exaggeration. It takes the undoubted existence of coercion—quite an ordinary element in all human social interactions—and demonizes it into a sinister and systematic form of oppression.

Clearly, social relations involve conflict and coercion. Yet to perceive of conflict and coercion as radical and omnipresent involves no small violence to the realities with which we are all familiar. Solidarity and consensus—even a cooperative attitude crossing class lines—are not illusions or false consciousness. Our social natures reach out to others in ways that transcend interests or social status. Political communities are founded on authentic social consensus rooted in a common culture, history, and language. Class warfare and class dictatorship are, therefore, concepts with only limited utility.

Moreover, societies—particularly complex societies such as ours—cannot do without a division of labor. The fact that some lead and others follow does not justify conspiratorial conclusions. Those who rule do not necessarily do so for their own selfish class interests. Leadership entails that power be concentrated in a few hands because we cannot all rule simultaneously. Complex decisions can only be made in small deliberative bodies. Specialization mandates a division of labor and a hierarchy of command. Organization of any kind involves the imposition of constraints. Interpreting politics as a sinister plot is, therefore, as wrong-headed as it is unnecessary.

The arrogance of false consciousness

D. The Marxist concept of false consciousness is arrogant and dangerous. Arrogant, because it presumes to know, better than we do, what our real interests are. The workers or employers who do not see the truth as the authentic revolutionaries do are told that they suffer from cognitive pathology. Dangerous, because the next step is forcing the wayward to think as they should. If there is a right way to see things and it is known only by the leadership, how far are we from official ideologies and party lines?

E. Concepts such as "false consciousness" and the "necessary stages of historical development" place the organized proletarian leadership in a privileged position — they know what is coming historically and what is ideologically proper. This superior knowledge means paternalism, even repression. Those with differing views can be dismissed as "objectively" in error; at worst, they can be declared "class enemies"—a label that carries sinister implications.

We should not forget that under the pressures of revolutionary action and state repression, the lure of authoritarianism will only become more intense. How can we ever be sure that a Napoleonic leader, driven by intense personal ambitions, will not derail the entire well-intentioned revolutionary process and establish an authoritarian one-person rule for the alleged good of all? In the end, therefore, how surprised should we be when the dictatorship of the proletariat becomes the dictatorship of the party leadership over the proletariat?

Will the proletariat self-destruct?

F. Perhaps the most naive of Marxist predictions is that the dictatorship of the proletariat will abolish itself when it accomplishes its historical task. Although Marx coldly reminds us that the bourgeoisie will not accept their defeat at the hands of the proletariat, he has no difficulty in contending that the victorious proletarian revolutionary organization will dismantle itself at the height of its success. He would have us believe that they will impose a class dictatorship, reconstruct the relations of production, redirect the forces of production, and then self-destruct. There is nothing in human history to even hint that such behavior is characteristic of human beings as we know them. To believe this, Marxist atheism notwithstanding, is to believe in miracles.

A universal class?

The source of this belief is Marx's understanding of the proletariat as a universal class that expresses the essential human aspiration for liberation. Because they are the generic image of dehumanization, they cannot liberate themselves without liberating humanity. Out of their total alienation arises the vision of a non-alienated social reality. Because their historical role is essentially emancipatory, Marx reasons, they will have no interest in power for its own sake.

This is to indulge in unmitigated fantasy. Why should we believe that this remarkable form of human alchemy—from human dross to human gold—will take place? Why not consider the opposite possibility? Is it not more reasonable to assume that a horde of persecuted, humiliated, and enraged revolutionaries will institute a politics of vengeance and tyranny? Why should they not give back just what they got? Why expect more from them than we would from any other subjugated group that has finally turned the tables on their oppressors? The biblical adage says it sharply: "When a slave ascends to the throne," the "earth trembles."[9]

Human imperfectibility

G. Marxism suffers from an uncompromising emancipatory drive that lacks restraint or a sense of limits. It fails to recognize the tragic dimension in human life. In its breathless pursuit of perfect freedom, creative and sensual bliss, unblemished social harmony, and absolute plenty, it ignores the most oft-learned lesson of all generations and cultures: Human beings are imperfect creatures and human life is subject to serious constraints. To disregard these banal lessons, or to proclaim that "we are different," is the prelude to tragedy. In Classical Greece, human arrogance of this kind was called *hubris*—the sin of overweening pride. Notably, the biblical account of the Tower of Babel, in which a tower that would reach up to the heavens was built as a revolt against human limits, also ends in tragedy. Reaching too high has the stubborn tendency of being associated with falling very low.

1. The claim that human beings are radically transformable needs to be soberly scrutinized. Although it seems to be true that more favorable

---

9. Proverbs 30:21–22.

conditions will tend to elicit more favorable human traits, will perfect conditions create saints? Can jealousy, selfishness, or laziness ever be overcome? Can we conceive of a reality in which mine and thine have become obsolete terms? Will power needs or sexual coveting or artistic jealousies fade away after the proletarian revolution? Even if the Marxist revolution goes precisely according to plan, can we believe that it will spark a comprehensive and permanent spiritual revolution in the human heart? And if the answer to all these questions is a skeptical no, what is to prevent the resurgence, indeed the dominance of human vices in the newly created revolutionary reality?

2. Marx understands scarcity as the source of human conflict. At very best, this is a partial truth. Scarcity creates conflict, but then again, sometimes affluence does so as well. Boredom can do it too. As can competing philosophical orientations or even differing interpretations of Marxism. Actually, the sources of conflict are pretty much inexhaustible.

   The prodigious rise in the level of affluence during the twentieth century has not reduced levels of conflict or violence. Neither have growing literacy or the United Nations or psychotherapy. Conflict can be triggered by scarcity, but conflict is not essentially created by rivalry over material resources. Conflict is an inherently human trait whose sources lie far deeper in our psyches than this or that external catalyst. It is, unfortunately, compatible with all known forms of human political organization.

3. Neither are competition, possessiveness, and selfishness the result of capitalism. Capitalism is only one of an endless variety of social designs in which human beings compete, possess, and pursue their selfish interests. If capitalism is dismantled, these archetypical human traits will only reassert themselves in new ways. Instead of competing for markets, people will compete for the house on the hill or the most attractive mate or the fastest car. By refusing to accept these egoistic traits as permanent or by declaring that they are henceforth banned, revolutionary forms of government only force them underground where they cannot be regulated. Indeed, capitalism has the positive quality of recognizing human character for what it is and providing it with a constructive framework in which to be expressed.

4. Marx bemoans the fact that we are alienated from our core human character. Admittedly, the miserable existence of the mid-nineteenth-century proletariat is an especially deplorable instance of human alienation. But alienation—that is, not living in a way that is consonant with our human needs and desires—in its milder and more ordinary forms is a general human malady rather than a problem related to capitalism. It is identical with what is often spoken of gravely as the human condition and the tragic dimension of life. As most adults have learned, we shall never be liberated from the basic constraints that

confine human life. Except for the exceptional moments of creativity and love, alienation is the insurmountable human fate.

5. Theory and critique, Marx taught, must leave the world of thought and enter the world of practice. Like many other impassioned intellectuals, he believed deeply in the power of ideas. Skepticism about their own thinking comes hard to many of them. It is often difficult for them to entertain the possibility that theories to which they have devoted a lifetime are wrong. Being both inexperienced in the ways of the world and highly confident of their mastery of ideas, intellectuals like Marx have regularly created chaos. Perhaps the most dangerous thing about intellectuals' dreams is the possibility they might come true.

Suggestions for Further Reading

Appelbaum, Richard. *Karl Marx*. Newbury Park, Calif.: Sage Publications, 1988.

Avineri, Shlomo. *The Social and Political Thought of Karl Marx*. Cambridge: Cambridge University Press, 1970.

————. *Hegel's Theory of the Modern State*. Cambridge: Cambridge University Press, 1972.

Berlin, Isaiah. *Karl Marx: His Life and Environment*. New York: Oxford University Press, 1963.

Cohen, G. A. *Karl Marx's Theory of History*. New York: Oxford University Press, 1978.

Kolakowski, Leszek. *Main Currents of Marxism*. Oxford: Clarendon Press, 1978.

Lichtheim, George. *Marxism: An Historical and Critical Study*. New York: Praeger, 1961.

MacIntyre, Alasdair. *Marxism and Christianity*. Harmondsworth: Pelican, 1971.

McLellan, David. *Karl Marx: His Life and Thought*. London: Macmillan, 1973.

McMurtry, John. *The Structure of Marx's World-View*. Princeton: Princeton University Press, 1978.

Miliband, Ralph. *The State in Capitalist Society*. New York: Basic Books, 1969.

————. *Marxism and Politics*. New York: Oxford University Press, 1977.

Ollman, Bertell. *Alienation: Marx's Conception of Man in Capitalist Society*. Cambridge: Cambridge University Press, 1975.

Tucker, Robert C., ed. *Philosophy and Myth in Karl Marx*. New York: Cambridge University Press, 1972.

Chapter 6

The Radical Left: Marxist Practice

Pre-Revolutionary Russia: Radicalism and Backwardness

Revolutionary Prospects

Revolution
unlikely in Russia

If at the end of the nineteenth century a historical bookmaker had taken odds on the country most likely to be the home of a Marxist-style revolution, the favorites would surely have been France and Germany. They would have been followed, at a considerable distance, by a number of other Western European states such as England and the Netherlands. Russia would have appeared at the very bottom of the list as a highly unlikely prospect. When asked by the young Russian radical Vera Zasulich about the possibility of revolution in Russia, Marx himself had answered with a lukewarm, diplomatic lack of enthusiasm. In the eyes of European radicals like Marx, Russia represented backwardness, superstition, and reaction.

Russian
backwardness

From a Marxist point of view, nothing about Russia encouraged revolutionary hopes. It was an undeveloped agrarian country in which the Industrial Revolution had made only feeble inroads. It had no proletariat to speak of. For that matter, it had almost nothing in the way of a commercial bourgeoisie either. Capitalism was only beginning to make its mark in a few urban centers. Landholding and agriculture were the dominant forms of ownership and production. Great aristocratic landowners controlled the countryside where primitive agriculture was practiced by a vast and largely illiterate peasantry. It has been said that the Russian Empire was based on three complementary elements: a paternalist imperial autocracy, an obscurantist church, and a long-suffering, passive peasantry.

Russia had experienced virtually none of the liberal ferment that had swept through Western Europe. Its Orthodox Church had not undergone a Reformation as in the West. Nor had its traditional Czarist hegemony been disturbed by the **bourgeois revolutions** that elsewhere had moved the masses and toppled rulers from their thrones. (The French Revolution of 1789 is the classic instance of the commercial middle class rising against the old regime's aristocracy, monarchy, and church. Such bourgeois revolutions normally demand civil rights, free trade, and the rule of law.) Even the Enlightenment, that indispensable ingredient in all nineteenth-century progressive politics, had inspired only a minuscule fragment of Russian society. Recall finally, that when Marx and Engels addressed the *Communist Manifesto* (1848) to the workers of the world, three-quarters of Russia's population were serfs.

Challenges to Czarist autocracy generally ended in failure. When in 1825 a group of conscience-stricken aristocratic army officers (the Decembrists) attempted to initiate western-style constitutional reforms, the result was executions and Siberian exile. A half-century later, hoping to stir the great peasant masses out of their lethargy, urban intellectuals and students preached enlightenment and progress to the people. These populists, or Narodniki, championed a form of agrarian socialism based on the traditional Russian village commune (the mir). The peasants, they proclaimed, were the soul of Russia, the source of its vitality and its hope for the future. If they could be aroused, if the slumbering beauty of Russian village life could be reconstituted in a progressive way, Russia would save itself the ugliness and suffering of industrialization and capitalism. Descending on the bewildered peasants, these populists offered their services and agitated for reform. But the peasants had little use for these highfalutin do-gooders and quickly turned them over to the police as suspicious characters who were up to no good.

The Two Voices of Russian Marxism: Mensheviks and Bolsheviks

The founding of a Russian Marxist party

The hope that a Russian revolutionary movement could rely on the peasantry seemed discredited. Although poor peasants constituted the overwhelming majority of the Russian population, they would have to be led by others with more radical tendencies. One disillusioned Narodnik, George Plekhanov, found the answer he was searching for in the writings of Karl Marx. In 1883, the year of Marx's death, Plekhanov founded a study circle dedicated to exploring the relevance of Marxist teachings to the Russian reality. Fifteen years later these theoretical pursuits became organized into a political party. In 1898, the Russian Social Democratic Party was founded. Among those present at its founding was a twenty-eight-year-old intellectual of aristocratic origins with the name Vladimir Ilyich Ulyanov. He would later be known by his revolutionary pseudonym: Lenin.

Although the followers of the new party comprised only a tiny band that stayed one step ahead of the Czarist police, they began squabbling almost immediately over questions of tactics and principle. The majority, known as the Mensheviks, wished to emulate the forms of organization practiced by the established Socialist parties in France and Germany. They supported an open democratic party with participatory decision-making and broad-based membership. This, they claimed, was the kind of party that Marx had envisioned: an open, non-elitist organization that would be a natural conduit for the interests of the masses.

Hierarchy and discipline

But a vocal minority, the Bolsheviks,* led by Lenin, argued that organizational democracy was relevant only for open Western societies. In the repressive conditions of Russia, by contrast, a party that was open and public played right into the hands of its ruthless opponents. With Czarist informants swarming among radical groups and the threat of severe punishments hanging over their heads, the strategy of struggle needed to be substantially revised. A revolutionary party that waged war against a tyrannical state, Lenin argued, could not be organized like a debating society. They had to form a revolutionary army that was (1) highly disciplined, (2) hierarchical in its command structure, (3) secret in its deliberations, and (4) centralized in its organization.

Democratic centralism

Fearing factionalism and cracks in the chain of command, Lenin enunciated a doctrine of inner party democracy that was quite different from what prevailed among West European Marxist organizations. He asserted that differing views could be legitimately held and argued for by individual party members—with two critical limitations. First, there were to be no factional organizations within the party. One could speak out in favor of policies one supported. But one could not advance one's own views by coordinating positions with others prior to the decisive vote. One came to the vote as an individual, not as an organized group. Second, once the arguments were heard and the vote taken, the decision could not be appealed against. Opposition to a decision, especially organized opposition, was strictly forbidden. Lenin dubbed this doctrine **democratic centralism**.

Apart from preserving discipline and keeping the Czarist police at bay, the practical effect of this organizational principle was to immeasurably strengthen the party organization against its potential opponents. With partisan organizations prohibited, the only remaining organization was that of the party itself. If opposition to the party line could only be on an individual basis, there was little chance it would prevail against the organized party apparatus. Lenin well understood the power of a coherent, organized group, even a minority, when it faced an assembly of isolated and uncoordinated individuals.

Perhaps the most critical difference between the Mensheviks and Bolsheviks related to their fundamental conceptions of party membership. What did being a member of the party entail? Did membership involve broad sympathy for the party's program, the periodic payment of dues, and the occasional activity on its behalf? Or was membership a full-time vocation, a stern calling that took precedence over all other commitments? The Mensheviks contended that party membership entailed basic ideological and financial support; it was not necessarily an all-

---

*Note: The Bolsheviks received their name during the Party Congress of 1903. Lenin's minority faction won a chance victory in a critical vote. They took the title Bolsheviks (majority) and branded their opponents Mensheviks (minority). Although they did not again win an important vote, the title Bolshevik was jealously preserved by Lenin, and its propagandistic advantages were exploited to the full.

embracing career. Here again, they took their cues from the European radical parties. Lenin, for his part, was convinced that only professional revolutionaries could succeed in dislodging the autocratic Czarist regime. He was convinced that in the Russian reality being a revolutionary could not be a pastime for weekends and evenings.

Bolshevik Voluntarism

These tactical and organizational differences reflect an even more essential divergence at the level of principle. In Lenin's view, the party was not a conduit that channeled the interests of the masses rising from below. In the backward conditions of the Russian Empire, communist leaders could not act as the exponents of whatever position the populace happened to hold. The masses, Lenin declared, could not be trusted to grasp their true revolutionary interests. The full import of their historical struggle was beyond their capacity to understand. Left to their own devices, they would do no more than make demands for immediate improvements in their living and working conditions. They would fail to realize that capitalism itself was their enemy. In Lenin's terms, they could reach **trade-union consciousness** but not real revolutionary consciousness.[1]

Guiding the masses

Lenin insisted that the Communist Party did not represent mass interests as much as it expressed the more advanced views of the "revolutionary socialist intelligentsia." Hence, the communist leadership had to actively set the revolutionary agenda. The masses required firm guidance. Propaganda, geared to their limited sophistication, was necessary to convince them that bread and butter issues were only a small part of their historical mission. The party was the institutional home of those far-sighted individuals who had accurately understood the nature of the revolutionary process. Ideological qualifications rather than simple class standing were, therefore, critical. (Citing the example of Marx and Engels, Lenin notes that it would be quite normal for the revolutionary leaders to be intellectuals rather than workers.) In this sense, Lenin spoke of the party as the **vanguard** of society's progressive forces.[2]

But if the party's views were not a reflection of working-class conditions, Lenin's contention amounts to a significant departure from Marxist materialism. The revolutionary elite, wielding its privileged intellectual insight, could outstrip history and set the revolutionary agenda in advance of material conditions. The party was not only ahead of the masses, it was ahead of the material stage that history had reached. Indeed, the party's advanced ideological understanding could be directed toward changing material conditions when these stood in the way of revolutionary progress. Communist ideology could shape the form that history would take.

---

1. See V. I. Lenin, *What Is to Be Done?* in *Selected Works*, vol. 2 (New York: International Publishers, 1945) 53.

2. Lenin, *What Is to Be Done?*

Lenin vs. Marx

How does this square with Marx's view that material conditions are the basis for consciousness and that ideological maturity goes hand in hand with the unfolding of material conditions? It doesn't. Lenin has reversed Marx's order. He attributes to pure ideological dynamism what Marx had attributed to the dynamics of capitalist economics. If for Marx ideological consciousness depends on material conditions, for Lenin ideological consciousness acts as an autonomous force. So autonomous, in fact, that it can voluntarily initiate revolutionary activity and dominate the tempo of revolutionary change.[3] Lenin's view that the revolutionary leadership can autonomously dictate the pace of change is often described as **voluntarism**. Only recall Marx's warnings against embarking upon revolutionary adventures prior to the ripening of material conditions and the boldness of Lenin's ideas becomes apparent.

Lenin's voluntarism and his paternalistic view of the working class take Marxist theorizing in a substantially new direction. According to Marx, the proletariat embodied history's drive toward human liberation. *Their* ideas and *their* political decisions represented the cutting edge of dialectical advance. In their very historical existence, the proletariat united revolutionary theory and revolutionary practice. Theorists of revolution, like Marx himself, might aid the proletarians in understanding their situation more accurately, but they could never replace the working class as the engine of the revolution.

Lenin's view of revolution strikingly transposes these elements. The working class is the instrument with which revolutions are made by an ideologically advanced party leadership. Working class ideas and decisions are raw materials to be refined and refashioned by the revolutionary elite. In no event are the masses to act spontaneously. Lenin feared that spontaneous working-class actions would divert the movement away from its essential ideological goals and squander revolutionary energies on short-sighted escapades. The masses had to accept the discipline of the party's hierarchal chain of command and defer to its cadre of professional revolutionaries.

The Bourgeois Revolution and the Peasantry

Proletarian revolution in non-industrialized society

Bolshevik voluntarism led to a number of other unconventional conclusions. Although we have been using the terms working class and proletariat quite freely in the foregoing pages, they comprised only a tiny fragment of the largely peasant population. This raised a series of perplexing dilemmas for the Russian Marxists. How was a proletarian revolution going to succeed with an only microscopic revolutionary class? Could a proletarian revolution even be considered when capital-

---

3. Although Marx recognized that ideology, when it "seizes the masses," can itself become a "material force," he denies that it can seize the masses without material conditions being ripe. He would not accept the Leninist thesis that ideology can or should be imposed upon the masses by a revolutionary intelligentsia.

Vladimir I. Lenin in 1919. He viewed the working class as raw material to be shaped by revolutionary theorists.

ism and a mercantile bourgeoisie were still only embryonic presences? Could the peasantry be counted upon as an ally in the revolutionary struggle? There was also the problem of "necessary historical stages" that was so central to Marxist teachings. Russia was a largely medieval country that had never experienced a bourgeois revolution. What chance did a proletarian revolution have when the bourgeois revolution that was to precede it had not taken place? Before the proletariat could usher in the "leap into freedom," the bourgeoisie had to sweep away the debris of medievalism—and this seemed, at the turn of the century, a very distant prospect.

As with the issue of party organization, the Mensheviks remained close to the spirit of West European Marxism. The proletariat could not jump the revolutionary gun or skip historical stages; they had to await the inevitable expansion of capitalism, the growth of a bourgeoisie, the coming of a bourgeois revolution, the boom and bust cycle of capitalism, and so on. Neither did the Mensheviks accept the idea of an alliance with the peasantry. Although it would create a hypothetical revolutionary majority, a proletarian/peasant coalition was out of the question because peasant politics were profoundly conservative politics. Besides, even if such an alliance could confer certain tactical benefits, history would still have to pass through the straight and narrow path of capitalist development. History, the Mensheviks maintained, could not be short-circuited.

The Bolsheviks took a typically more impatient and voluntarist position. Although it was true that the bourgeoisie was not yet in a position to mount its own revolutionary offensive, the proletariat could help them along nevertheless. They could prod the bourgeoisie into action and direct the course of revolutionary transformation. Lenin theorized that the bourgeois revolution, masterminded and orchestrated by the proletarian leadership, might then spill over directly into a socialist revolution.* As to the peasantry, Lenin believed they should be enlisted in the service of revolution. Although he understood that proletarian and peasant politics were basically incompatible, the need to attain broad popular support for the revolution was the overriding consideration. Proletarians and peasants would part company soon enough, Lenin realized, but he typically preferred gains that were concretely available—even if they involved strange political bedfellows—to scrupulous stands of principle.

Marxism was a Western European ideological creation. Its migration to Imperial Russia brought with it important alterations in the doctrine's character and emphases. Let us take stock of the unique qualities of the Russian reality and of the doctrinal changes they produced.

Summary

1. The Russian reality differed from the Western European in having experienced only the early stages of capitalist development. It lacked a dynamic bourgeoisie or a substantial proletariat. Its Orthodox Church was singularly powerful and largely untouched by the currents of liberal European thought. Its Imperial monarchy was highly autocratic, reactionary, and repressive. Russia had not undergone a liberal, bourgeois revolution as had so many European states. Neither had Enlightenment thought made deep inroads into the Russian heartland.

---

*Note: This idea of an uninterrupted revolution, or the telescoping of revolutions, that would end in a classless society was formulated by Lev Trotsky, Lenin's sometime revolutionary comrade. It has become known as the doctrine of permanent revolution.

2. Marxism, in its classic Western European form, was basically inapplicable to the Russian reality. Lenin's revisions in Marxist doctrine are the result.

a. Tactically, in order to defend itself against an implacably hostile reality, the party must organize along quasi-military lines—with the emphasis on discipline, hierarchy, secrecy, and centralization. Full-time professional party members organized according to the democratic centralist principle would be the vanguard of the revolution.

b. The party, rather than the proletariat, becomes the central agency of revolution. Working-class spontaneity is dangerous; relying on its own ideological resources, the proletariat will fail to understand its revolutionary interests. The revolutionary elite is responsible for the proletariat's revolutionary activity.

c. It is not necessary to await the dialectical unfolding of history's stages. Revolutionaries armed with the proper ideological weapons can shorten the process. Stages of history can be collapsed, just as revolutions can be catalyzed and telescoped.

d. Russia's largely peasant character meant that this vast human resource had to be mobilized, if only tactically and temporarily, in the revolutionary cause. Incorporating the peasantry into the proletarian struggle introduces a novel factor that necessarily alters the dynamic and tactics of the revolutionary process.

The Revolutionary Ferment Begins

Having considered these tactical and principled revisions in Marxist doctrine, we are now in a better position to understand the character of the Bolshevik revolution and of the Bolshevik state that ensued. Let us return to the dramatic events that led up to November 1917—to what one reporter who witnessed the revolution described as "the ten days that shook the world."

The revolution of 1905

The revolutionary tide rose with the growing ineptitude of the Czarist regime. In 1904–5, Russia suffered a stinging defeat at the hands of Japan, a novice military power on the world scene. Fearing popular discontent, the regime made promises about granting civil liberties that it had few intentions of keeping. When the police fired on a peaceful crowd of demonstrators that had gathered in front of the Winter Palace, the gears of revolution were engaged. A general strike in October 1905 succeeded in paralyzing the country's economy. Workers councils (soviets) were set up in many different cities and towns to administer the revolution and, because of the breakdown of public order, to rule the country. As the leader of the preeminent soviet in St. Petersburg, Trotsky achieved national stature.

Attempting to cool the rising revolutionary ardor, the Czarist government announced that elections for a parliament (Duma) would soon take place. But together with the carrot went the stick. The St. Petersburg Soviet, after some fifty days of functioning, was forcibly dismantled. Trotsky was sentenced to life-long Siberian exile.

Manipulating
the Duma

When elections for the Duma approached, it became clear that the Czarist regime was hoping to create a sympathetic parliamentary majority by manipulating the electoral system in favor of conservative interests. But these manipulatory tactics were insufficient. Even though the more radical parties—the Social Democrats and the Social Revolutionaries (populist agrarian socialists, successors to the Narodniki)—boycotted the election, the results showed a majority favoring substantial political and economic changes. The largest delegation to the Duma, the Kadet party, were liberal constitutionalists of a rather cautious character. But even their moderate proposals for breaking up the largest landholdings were considered outrageous by the Czar. After a short session, he dissolved the Duma and called for elections once again. The new Duma proved no more amenable to Czarist will and he dissolved it once again. Rigging the electoral system more blatantly still resulted in a third Duma that finally returned the conservative majority the Czar desired.

World War I

The years between 1907 and 1914 proved to be frustratingly uneventful for the eager and restless revolutionaries. But these doldrums were quickly dispelled by the advent of World War I in 1914. Marxist theory had long been proclaiming that the approaching war would be a battle between capitalists over markets and imperialist domination. On no account were the workers to be taken in by the patriotic frenzy that the bourgeoisie would seek to promote. It was designed to blur working-class vision, to induce them to sacrifice themselves as cannon fodder for the imperialist war. Marxists emphasized that the war would provide a singular opportunity for the international working class to join ranks and rebel against international capital.

Social Democrats'
betrayal

Imagine Lenin's consternation when, living in Swiss exile, he heard that the oldest and most powerful of European Marxist parties, the German Social Democrats, had voted to extend war credits to the German government, that is, to support the war. (His disappointment was only heightened when, somewhat later, tens of thousands of workers in all the warring states volunteered to fight in their national armies.) At first he believed it was all a bourgeois hoax. But when the news was verified, he could not contain his rage. Apart from vitriolic denunciations of the German socialist leaders as renegades, he pondered the theoretical significance of this flagrant betrayal. Beyond reenforcing his already deep distrust of working-class spontaneity, Lenin began to reevaluate the respective revolutionary prospects of Europe and Russia.

The conventional view had always been that revolution would first break out in the advanced capitalist countries of Europe, those in which the dialectic of capitalism had intensified the class struggle to the breaking point. This had indeed been Marx's belief. Since Marx's death some thirty years earlier, however, dramatic changes had transformed the realities of capitalism. It was no longer the case that a national bourgeoisie faced a national proletariat in a self-enclosed class struggle. The international thrust of capitalism had rendered the concept of a closed national economy largely obsolete.

Capitalist imperialism

Feeling the intensifying pressures of an overripe capitalism at home, capitalists reached outward in order to find outlets in which to invest their excess capital. They sought to loosen the economic vise that closed about them as the fatal disparity between expanding production and contracting markets became more and more apparent. The result is known as **imperialism**: the struggle between national bourgeoisies for control over international markets and resources. World War I was its most serious consequence. Imperialism, Lenin concluded, was "the highest [and we might add, the final] stage of capitalism."[4]

Capitalism's weakest link

As the national bourgeoisies expanded their economic markets abroad and exploited the cheaper natural resources available in less developed countries, they could afford to improve their own proletariat's wages and working conditions. Oddly, imperialism mitigated some of capitalism's most intolerable offenses by exporting them elsewhere. Capitalism was kept alive by imperialist infusions. The war, however, would put great pressure on the international capitalist system. The wealthy states, relying on their large capital reserves and their imperial holdings, would be in a better position to survive these pressures than those states in which capitalism was relatively young and weak. The capitalist chain, as Stalin later put it, would snap at its weakest link. And this was Russia.

The betrayal of the European Marxists together with the weakest-link theory of capitalist collapse rid Lenin once and for all of his sense of being a junior partner in the revolutionary struggle. He was convinced that Russia was ripe for revolution. The advent of the war only fortified his resolve.

Ten Days That Shook the World

Abdication of the Czar

For Russia, the war was a catastrophe. Both on the battlefront where defeats and heavy casualties decimated the Russian army, and on the home front where inflation, famine, and corruption caused deep popular demoralization, the war seemed an inexcusable waste of life and resources. Russian army discipline broke down entirely; soldiers deserted their units by the droves, voting against the war with their feet. Many simply walked back home across the continent. Internally, Czarist control of public life came apart as well. The sense of government impotence and incompetence led the Duma to intervene in February 1917 and establish a ruling provisional committee. At the same time, however, the radical workers and soldiers of St. Petersburg, repeating the experience of 1905, set up a

---

4. In the pamphlet *Imperialism: The Highest Stage of Capitalism*, published in 1916.

soviet that competed with the Duma's provisional authorities. In short order, the Czar abdicated his throne and the provisional committee became a provisional government.

The October Revolution   At its head stood Alexander Kerensky, a moderate socialist, who felt that Russia should honor its international commitments and remain in the war. Attacked from both the right and the left, and lacking popular support because of his position on the war, Kerensky had only a tenuous hold on the reins of power. Sensing that the provisional government could not maintain its grip, Lenin returned from exile in a special sealed train, arriving at St. Petersburg's Finland Station. A few months later, in November 1917, the soviets of St. Petersburg were taken over by the Bolsheviks. (The Revolution is spoken of as the October Revolution because prior to 1918 Russia used the Julian calendar rather than the Western Gregorian calendar. Between them, there is a difference of thirteen days. Hence, Revolution occurred in October of the Julian Calendar, November of the Gregorian Calendar.)

The need to export the revolution   Campaigning under the popular banners of (a) an immediate withdrawal from the war, (b) the transfer of all land to the peasants, and (c) the concentration of all power in the soviets, the tiny Bolshevik minority became increasingly popular and powerful. Aided by the disunity among their opponents and by Lenin's canny sense of revolutionary timing, a resolute minority, fired by clear goals, seized state power. The Winter Palace, now seat of Kerensky's government, was stormed and overrun. Still it must be kept in mind that Lenin's boldness in calling for a minority working-class revolution in a vast unindustrialized country was tempered by his assumption that the Russian Revolution would be only the initial shot in a larger revolutionary barrage. The success of the revolution depended upon its triggering a series of revolutions in Europe as well. Lenin, like all his comrades, had few illusions about the new revolutionary regime's ability to survive as an island of communism in a hostile capitalist sea.

The Post-Revolutionary Years

Civil War and the NEP

The Civil War   As resolute as they were in seizing power, so were the Communists* resolute in implementing their program of nationalization of industry, redistribution of land, and the destruction of the bourgeois state apparatus. But as Marx had predicted, the bourgeoisie did not accept their defeat gracefully. Not only did they mount a spirited counter-attack, they called upon Western capitalist powers to come to their aid through military intervention. An interventionary army dispatched by the United

---

*Note: Roughly a half year after the revolution, the Russian Social Democratic Party officially changed its name to the Communist Party.

States, England, and other Western states joined the Russian Civil War in support of the Whites, or the anti-revolutionary cause. They were confronted in a series of fierce battles by the Red Army under Trotsky's command.

NEP   When in 1920 the Civil War ended in Communist victory, the Soviet economy was utterly prostrate. Industrial and agricultural production had plummeted far below the pre-revolutionary levels. Famine was rife. Mutinies by soldiers and sailors had to be put down violently. Lenin, a consummate revolutionary tactician, realized that continuing with an aggressive socialist policy of nationalization and redistribution of wealth would alienate support for the revolution. What was necessary was a hiatus in which the shattered economy could be rebuilt. In the typically Leninist spirit of taking one step backward in order to take two steps forward, the New Economic Policy (NEP) was instituted in 1921. Capitalism, monitored and regulated, would be allowed to make a partial return. Although the ultimate controls rested with the government, a great deal of latitude for private ownership and local initiative was permitted. Under the steadying hand of Lenin, the revolutionary turmoil was allowed to subside. By 1928, when the NEP was officially terminated, the Soviet Union's economy had made a substantial recovery.

Leninism and Marxism

Lenin did not live to see the end of the NEP. Although he recovered from an assassin's bullet that struck him in 1918, he finally succumbed to a stroke and died in January 1924. Lenin lived only some six years beyond the revolution for which he was the primary architect and preeminent theorist. It was in fact more a Leninist than a Marxist revolution. Even though he justified virtually all he did by citing chapter and verse in Marx, it was a highly creative and idiosyncratic interpretation that he put into practice. Lenin's relationship to Marx brings to mind the relationship between a wayward child and its parent. Without its Marxist parentage, the revolution would not have taken the turn that it did. And yet, in Lenin's formulations, Marx's ideas were wrenched so far beyond their original intent, it is doubtful that the parent can be held responsible for the sins of the child.

The dictatorship of the proletariat   **Leninism** departs most glaringly from the letter and spirit of Marxism in regard to the dictatorship of the proletariat. For Marx, proletarian dictatorship was only a logical turning of the tables on the bourgeois dictatorship that preceded it. The term "dictatorship" in the phrase did not entail a new and unprecedented form of repressive control. Its being a majority dictatorship rendered it milder, briefer, and more benign than its bourgeois predecessor. The victorious proletariat would have to resist counter-revolutionary activities and restructure the productive system, but it would not have to hold down a hostile population by coercion and violence. It would be called upon to redirect existing productive forces, but would not have to coerce the historical process into creating these forces in the first place. No wonder then that the dictatorship of the proletariat is mentioned only a few times by Marx and usually in passing.

In sharp contrast, Lenin places the dictatorship of the proletariat at the very heart of his teaching.[5] Standing at the head of a tiny minority determined to remake their country from the ground up, Lenin and his followers insisted upon iron discipline in party organization and doctrinal orthodoxy. Without relentless, uncompromising leadership the Communists would be overwhelmed by the medieval realities that prevailed all around them. They had to create out of nothing, and against intense and almost universal resistance, what historical development had handed European revolutionaries on a silver platter.

Adapting Marxism to Russian conditions
Virtually all Leninist doctrine is an attempt to adapt Marxist revolutionary tactics and principles to conditions they were not intended to serve. Lenin's suspicion of working-class spontaneity, his voluntarist understanding of revolutionary activity, his conspiratorial view of party organization, and his conception of revolution as a process energized and driven from above are all reflections of Soviet political and economic backwardness. Despite his overwhelming emphasis on the dictatorship *of* the proletariat, Lenin's deeper view might be more accurately characterized as a party dictatorship *over* the proletariat. Trotsky had in fact said as much long before the revolution. Reacting to Lenin's authoritarian and centralized view of party structure, Trotsky warned what this would mean:

> the organization of the party takes the place of the party itself; the central committee takes the place of the organization; and finally, the dictator take the place of the central committee.[6]

Leninism vs. Stalinism
If these warnings are apt to Leninism, they are a strikingly prophetic description of **Stalinism**. With all that can be said about Lenin's authoritarian streak, he still usually led by the force of personal example and by the power of his convictions. Stalin, by contrast, was an out and out despot. Although Stalinism would not have been possible without the doctrinal foundations of Leninism, the responsibility for Stalinist brutality and capricious autocracy cannot be ascribed to Lenin. Stalin departed from Leninism at least as much as Lenin had departed from Marxism. The resulting distance between Stalinism and Marxism is so great that there is legitimate doubt about even distant family resemblances. Indeed, it has often been quipped that the relationship between Marxism and what took place in the Soviet Union during the 1930s and 1940s is purely coincidental.

Stalinist Totalitarianism

Shortly before his death, Lenin warned the Bolsheviks about Stalin's uncouth

---

5. Lenin analyzes the dictatorship of the proletariat in his book *State and Revolution* (New York: International Publishers, 1943).

6. Cited by Bertram D. Wolfe, *Three Who Made a Revolution*, 2nd ed. (New York: Dell, 1964) 253.

and spiteful character. Trotsky and not Stalin was his choice as successor. But Trotsky's brilliant rhetorical and intellectual gifts were no match for Stalin's plodding but systematic takeover of the real power bases in the party organization. In a series of deft strokes, Stalin turned his opponents against each other, isolating and destroying his competitors one by one. By 1928 Stalin had effectively eliminated most of his opposition. For the next quarter century (until his death in 1953) Stalin ruled the Soviet Union with a degree of absoluteness and brutality that have rarely, if ever, been equalled in human history.

Born (1879) Iosif Djugashvili in Georgia (a part of the Russian Empire), Stalin was Lenin's opposite in temperament, background, and personal style. Lenin was an aristocratic intellectual with a cosmopolitan outlook—he was, for example, at home in many European languages and cultures. Stalin by contrast was of common origins, quite limited intellectually, and of provincial outlook—he spoke no languages but Georgian and Russian. His early experience was in a Georgian religious seminary, training for the Russian Orthodox priesthood. From this experience he brought to politics a heavy liturgical writing style (churning, highly repetitive, and formula based), a tendency toward tangled logic that masqueraded as profound dialectical thinking, and a preacher's capacity to simplify ideas so that even the commonest of folk would understand them. Although he was no match for Lenin or Trotsky as an orator or thinker, he understood the power of endless repetition of uncomplicated slogans and the great advantages of simple, unquestioning belief.

Stalin joins the Bolsheviks

Stalin's religious career ended abruptly when he was expelled from the seminary after a long series of infractions, most especially the reading of seditious materials. He found his way into radical politics, joining the Bolsheviks and supporting Lenin against the Mensheviks in the struggle for party hierarchy and authority. Notably, Stalin made his mark in the party not as an ideologue or bureaucrat, but as a daring bank robber who brought considerable sums into the party coffers. His strategy of placing those personally loyal to him in key positions in the party apparatus paid off handsomely in the succession struggle that followed Lenin's death.

Collectivization of the peasantry

Stalin's relentless ferocity did not take long to be manifested. In 1929 he began a campaign to collectivize Soviet agriculture. Brooking no resistance, Stalin ordered the decimation of a whole class of large and small landowners (the Kulaks), the collective transfer of vast peasant populations over great distances, the appropriation of all farms with their livestock, buildings, and tools, and the organization of the peasantry in cooperative and state farms (Kolkhozy and Sovkhozy). Thousands of peasants resisted by slaughtering their livestock and burning their fields. It is often said that Soviet agriculture, always the weak link in the Soviet economy, never recovered from this trauma.

The purges of 1934–38

But this was a mild exercise by comparison to what was soon to come. In December of 1934, Kirov, head of the Leningrad party organization, was murdered. We now know that Stalin was behind the assassination, but he accused virtually everyone in public life of treason and began a systematic liquidation of the entire party leadership. Trotsky had already been exiled (and would later be assassinated in Mexico by one of Stalin's henchmen), but those of the old revolutionary guard that remained were, one by one, paraded through show trials and sent to their deaths in the Gulag.[7] Each successive wave of arrests and show trails was more inclusive and more deadly than those that preceded it. The prosecutors in earlier waves became the defendants in later ones. In 1938, much like a conflagration that has exhausted itself, the Great Purges slowed, leaving a party without leadership, an army without officers, and an economy without managers. Witnesses to the era tell of rampant and morbid fears of the knock at the door in the middle of the night. It has never been definitively determined how many were killed in the Great Purges of the mid-1930s. Estimates run from the millions to the tens of millions.[8]

Stalin's cult of personality

All the while, a **cult of the personality**, actively directed by Stalin himself, was gaining momentum. His leadership, his thought, and his personal qualities were idealized and worshiped with quasi-religious fervor. Few religious redeemers have been attributed with more god-like qualities. Alexander Solzhenitsyn recalls the simple ubiquity of Stalin's face. His

> *likeness had been sculpted in stone, painted in oil, water colors, gouache, sepia; drawn in charcoal and chalk; formed out of wayside pebbles, sea shells, glazed tiles, grains of wheat, and soy beans; carved from ivory, grown in grass, woven in rugs, pictured in the sky by squadrons of planes in formation, and photographed on motion picture film . . . like no other likeness during the three billion years of the earth's crust.*[9]

Rewriting history

Stalin even waged ideological battles against Marx and Lenin, fearing that their versions of communism would overshadow his own. The *Marx-Engels Collected Works* as well as Lenin's *Collected Works* were suppressed or censored, their editors purged. The history of the revolution itself did not please Stalin's insatiable ego because his place in it was uncomfortably minor, so he set about rewriting history, erasing his opponents from the events they had dominated—Trotsky, for example, disappeared from history without a trace—and placing himself at Lenin's

---

7. The period has been brilliantly fictionalized by Arthur Koestler in *Darkness at Noon* (New York: Random House, 1941).

8. See Robert Conquest's *The Great Terror: Stalin's Purge of the Thirties*, rev. ed. (New York: Macmillan, 1973) and Alexander Solzhenitsyn's *The Gulag Archipelago*, vols. 1–3 (New York: Harper and Row, 1974–79).

9. *The First Circle* (New York: Harper and Row, 1969).

side as the co-equal revolutionary leader. What had been Marxism-Leninism now became Marxism-Leninism-Stalinism.

Stalin as ideologue

Apart from the introduction of unprecedented brutality, does Stalinist thought contribute anything new that would justify this triple-barreled ideological mouthful? Only one ideological development of note can be truly ascribed to Stalin: the doctrine of "socialism in one country." Mensheviks and Bolsheviks alike had believed that the revolution's success depended on its ability to spread beyond Russia to Europe. In this way, Russian backwardness would be offset by advanced Western technology and the Bolshevik revolutionary minority would be reenforced by the large European working class. As a communist fortress in a hostile world, they all initially conceded, the Soviet Union did not have much of a chance. A decade after the revolution, it was quite apparent that Europe was not about to follow the Russian example. Stalin, recognizing this fact, made a virtue of necessity and definitively undermined the internationalist character of Russian Marxism. He declared that "socialism in one country" was not only possible, it was imperative: socialism had to be fully built in one country before it could be exported elsewhere.

Stalin's ideological writings are otherwise mostly quite pathetic. In his hands, dialectics, with its play of opposites, becomes the science of proving that repression is really liberation and that totalitarianism is really the withering away of the state. When Stalin took principled ideological stands, the results were often calamitous. For example, he rejected the universally accepted scientific principle that biological changes can be brought about only by the sexual transfer of genetic material from parents to children. Hoping to buoy communist hopes that a "new Soviet man" could be created, he supported the view (championed by a quack biologist named Lysenko) that environmentally effected changes could be passed on as well. (That is, parents who sat in the sun, worked out with weights, and lived non-possessive lives were likely to have darker, more muscular, less possessive children.) Stalin's stubbornness in this regard set Soviet biology back decades.

Communism's decline and fall

In the thirty-six years from the death of Stalin (1953) to the collapse of the Soviet Union (1989), ideological innovations were very few. Russian Marxism had become a hidebound orthodoxy which invited repetition (louder and more insistent as the heart of belief eroded) rather than intellectual creativity. Marxism in the Soviet Union became a scholastic tradition of discourse about which one could write catechisms and commentaries but to which one could not substantially add. Ironically, the real home of Marxist creativity was in the bourgeois liberal Western states. Nothing better reflects the abject condition of communist thinking than the scorn that Western Marxists felt for the ideological writings of their ostensible Soviet allies. Or perhaps there is something that, nevertheless, reflects it better: its instantaneous and total rejection by the Soviet people when the threat of official retribution was removed.

The Chinese Revolutionary Experience

The Historical Context

Judged by the standards of modernization and industrialization, China trailed behind Russia by about as much as Russia trailed behind Western Europe. In 1917 China was a feudal country, controlled by local warlords and subject to Western colonial powers—not even remotely approaching the conditions that Marx deemed necessary for a successful proletarian revolution. Its dominant mode of thinking was Confucianism, an ancient religious tradition with a deeply conservative bent. Confucius (551–479 BCE) stressed the importance of deference to traditional authorities like parents, teachers, priests, kings, and Mandarins (a scholarly elite of bureaucratic functionaries).

The rise of Chinese nationalism

The dominance of Confucianism was challenged in the mid-nineteenth century by a rising nationalist movement that reacted with wounded pride to the humiliations inflicted by foreign occupation. Chinese civilization, which had achieved maturity and sophistication millennia before the West even began to crawl culturally, was now being overrun by rapacious barbarians who wanted only to exploit its resources and flood its markets with their goods. Because of their superior firepower, the Americans, British, and others were able to divide China, like a prostrate giant, into spheres of influence. The impotence of the Manchu rulers in resisting these foreign inroads lead to the anti-colonialist Boxer Rebellion of 1900 that required thousands of Western troops to put down. Many nationalists became convinced that only if China were thoroughly overhauled culturally, institutionally, militarily, and economically could it take its rightful place among the nations of the modern world.

Sun Yat-sen's liberal nationalism

Sun Yat-sen, the preeminent liberal nationalist leader, sought to create an autonomous China, free of foreign control, militarily modernized, economically advanced, and politically centralized. Imperialism, feudalism, warlordism, and rigid traditionalism were to be replaced by the Three People's Principles: nationalism, constitutional democracy, and popular welfare. A broad-based uprising in 1911 led to the overthrow of the Manchu Dynasty, and a few months later (January 1, 1912) Sun Yat-sen, as head of the Kuomintang (National People's Party), was installed as the provisional president of China.

The rise of Chiang Kai-shek

Despite these dramatic events, little changed for the mass of peasants and tenant farmers who continued to eke a bare living out of the soil. Neither were the battling warlords particularly impressed by the inauguration of the new president. When Sun Yat-sen died in 1925, China was still quite distant from his dream of political unity and economic prosperity. His son-in-law Chiang Kai-shek (a military man belonging to the authoritarian right-wing of the Kuomintang) finally succeeded in subduing the warlords and achieving formal unity in 1928.

Mao and the
Chinese
Communist Party

Although radical ideas had long had an audience among the Chinese intelligentsia, the Chinese Communist Party was founded only in 1921, some four years after the Russian Revolution. Mao Zedong (1893–1976), a young representative for the province of Hunan, was among its founding members. Working as an assistant librarian at Beijing University (1918–1919), the young Mao had read widely in Western literature and radical politics. Although he read only Chinese and had little access to most of the as yet untranslated Marxist classics, Mao educated himself by conversing intently with other radicals and through a careful study of what was available in Chinese. He was most especially impressed by Lenin's writings on imperialism because of the insights they provided into poor, colonized, third-world countries (as we would call them today) and their struggle for liberation. He early recognized that the unique conditions prevailing in China would require revolutionary strategies not anticipated in Marxist theory.

The united front

The fledgling Chinese Communist Party was at this early stage under the paternal influence of China's revolutionary neighbor to the north. The Soviet leadership watched the changes that were transforming China with deep interest. What, they speculated, was China's revolutionary potential? In the absence of a proletariat or any kind of modern industrial infrastructure, Stalin reasoned that Chinese Communists would have to create a **united front** with the liberal bourgeoisie and the peasantry. Together they could effectively struggle against feudalism and imperialism. Sun Yat-sen, because he represented progressive bourgeois forces, was commended by the Communists. Indeed, as part of the united front strategy, the Chinese Communists were instructed by Stalin to join the Kuomintang and to agitate from within for radical political and economic policies.

A new strategy

The Communist/Kuomintang coalition did not survive Chiang's accession to the presidency. In 1927 he turned viciously on his Communist allies and in a number of bloody raids decimated the ranks of the party.[10] A new kind of communist policy was now clearly imperative, one in which the Chinese Communists, independently of their Soviet mentors, would decide revolutionary strategy. A few critical principles were proposed. First, the communists would no longer accept junior partnership in a united front with the forces of bourgeois capitalism. Second, independent military strength and mass support would, henceforth, clearly be a primary objective of communist strategy. Third and above all, they would break from the Moscow-directed strategy of a proletariat-based revolution that relied on only tactical alliances with the peasantry. The party would base its strategy on the popular support it had among the poor peasants of the countryside. This wretched, exploited majority harbored explosive resentments that could be capitalized upon by the communists. The peasantry, not the proletariat, was China's revolutionary class.

---

10. The event has been powerfully fictionalized by an eyewitness; see Andre Malraux's *Man's Fate* (New York: The Modern Library, 1934).

Mao's Marxism

The peasant vanguard

Mao defended these unorthodox ideas in a series of reports and pamphlets written from 1926 onward. The Chinese peasantry, he declared, was not the conservative force that Soviet ideologues (based on their own history) imagined. In their hunger for land and liberation, the peasants had the force of a mighty storm that was set to sweep away the debris of feudalism, imperialism, and autocracy. They represented close to 80% of the population. If they were properly mobilized, no power could resist their advance. With virtually nothing to lose, their struggle would be fierce and uncompromising. Completing the peasant/proletariat reversal, Mao appropriated Lenin's term, declaring the peasants to be the "vanguard" of revolution.[11]

Encircling the cities

Beyond marginalizing the proletariat as a revolutionary force, Mao introduced the audacious idea that the revolutionary peasantry, beginning their drive in the countryside, would encircle resisting urban centers and compel them to surrender. Rather than spreading revolution from the urban nucleus to the rural hinterland as both Lenin and Marx had envisioned, Mao would steer revolutionary traffic in the opposite direction. It would be a "green" revolution in which the proletariat had only a subsidiary role. From a Marxist point of view, the thought of the revolutionary peasantry overwhelming the urban proletariat is a stunning novelty.

Class and nation

Maoism further revises Marxist theory by introducing nationalist elements into the class struggle. Mao understood the Chinese revolutionary process as a compounded one: first, as a battle of the peasant class against the wealthy bourgeoisie, and second, as a national effort of the Chinese to rid their country of imperialist domination. Hence, class and nation—antithetical principles in Marxist doctrine—become overlapping concepts in Maoist thought. The Chinese war of national liberation and the class revolution against capitalism become complementary aspects of the same struggle. Setting an ideological style that has become virtually mandatory for third-world Marxists, Mao conceived of China as an exploited and repressed country set upon by the wealthy nations of the world. Hence, China and the proletariat often appear as interchangeable terms in Mao's writings, just as the wealthy capitalist states and the bourgeoisie tend to merge into one another.

The struggle against Chiang Kai-shek and the Kuomintang had international significance; it was a campaign against the envoys of international capitalism and imperialism. Fighting Chiang was an integral part of fighting American and European capitalism. And stretching the parallel further still, Mao conceives of the third-world nations emulating Chinese revolutionary practice: they are destined to mount a concerted campaign against the rich capitalist countries, encircle them, besiege them, and finally starve them into surrendering. In Mao's version of Marxism, therefore, the class struggle, the national struggle, and the international struggle cannot be precisely distinguished from each other.

---

11. "Report on an Investigation of the Peasant Movement in Hunan," (March, 1927) in *Selected Works*, vol. 1 (Peking: Foreign Languages Press, 1961–65) 32.

Mao as a Military Tactician

It is as a military tactician that Mao made his most telling contribution to third-world revolutionary practice. His highly influential conception of **guerrilla warfare** has been adopted by revolutionary groups as far afield as Latin America, Vietnam, Africa, and the Middle East. How did Mao come upon this unconventional conception of armed struggle? To understand the sources of this idea we must return to the historical narrative and follow the course of Chinese Communism's struggle against the Kuomintang.

Cultivating peasant support

Soon after Chiang's murderous raid on Communist Party activists in 1927, Mao led a contingent of armed peasants into a remote and rugged mountainous area in Southern China. There he set up a revolutionary base, created a peasant government, and began to parcel out the local gentry's large landholdings to the poor peasantry. Sheltered from Chiang's troops by distance and by the forbidding terrain, Mao proceeded to consolidate his military power and expand his base by liberating neighboring areas from Kuomintang control. Cultivating the support of the peasantry and maintaining close ties with them, Mao ensured that the revolutionary enclave would be provided with shelter when attacked, as well as with ample resources in the way of food and clothing. (Among the guidelines for relating to the peasantry Mao includes the following: speak politely, pay for what you use, return what you borrow, pay for what you damage, don't swear or take liberties with women.)

The long march

Chiang was not about to allow the communists to create a state within a state. In a series of raids employing massive military power, Chiang's forces succeeded in leaving the revolutionaries with no choice but to escape or die. In October 1934 the surrounded communist forces broke through the Kuomintang lines and began an amazing trek of some 6,000 miles across deserts, mountain ranges, and rivers from the southeast of China to its northwest. Harassed by Chiang's troops and near exhaustion, they finally reached their destination near the Mongolian border a year later. Of the 150,000 fighters who began the trek, only 30,000 reached the new communist camp in the north. The Long March came to symbolize in Chinese Communist lore the limitless powers of sacrifice and devotion that the revolutionary struggle could inspire.

Already Chinese Communism's undisputed leader, Mao set up a second liberated camp and repeated his revolutionary strategy of expanding and consolidating his territorial base. By driving out the landlords and distributing their holdings among the poor farmers, Mao won the sympathy of the local peasantry. Realizing that the communist struggle against the Kuomintang's superior military force could neither be won quickly nor by conventional methods of warfare, Mao developed a body of strategic doctrines specifying the ways in which guerrilla wars are to be fought. For Mao, these doctrines are not merely technical lessons in military strategy; they are integral ideological elements of a peasant-based revolutionary movement.

Elements of guerrilla warfare

When bands of poorly armed insurrectionists face organized regular armies, the principles are these:

1. They must operate out of the remote countryside, live off the land, and win peasant support. The revolutionary army and the people among whom they are camped must be totally united in purpose. Peasant backing provides a reliable support system of fighters and resources, effective communication networks, military intelligence, and hiding places should these become necessary. The revolutionary peasant army could, if need be, melt into the countryside and disappear.

2. Because the war will necessarily be a protracted conflict, the aim is to gradually wear away the enemy, not attempt a decisive victory.

3. Guerrilla war is based on alertness, mobility, flexibility, and lightning attacks. Guerrillas do not fight fixed, stationary battles. They exploit their close knowledge of the terrain, their support among the people, and their ease of movement to outmaneuver the clumsier and more vulnerable regular armies.

In battle, guerrillas do the unexpected; they rely on the element of surprise. They neutralize the regular army's superior power by never engaging it directly. In Mao's own words:

In guerrilla warfare select the tactic of seeming to come from the east and attacking from the west; avoid the solid, attack the hollow; attack; withdraw; deliver a lightning blow, seek a lightning decision. When guerrillas engage a stronger enemy they withdraw when he advances; harass him when he stops; strike him when he is weary; pursue him when he withdraws. In guerrilla strategy the enemy's rear, flanks and other vulnerable spots are his vital points, and there he must be harassed, attacked, dispersed, exhausted and annihilated.[12]

Maoist Victory and the Great Cultural Revolution

The victory of Chinese Communism

From the mid 1930s to the late 1940s, Mao pursued these strategies with growing success. The invasion of China by the Japanese during World War II also provided Mao with an opportunity to link the communist cause with a highly popular patriotic struggle. His forces engaged both the Japanese and the Kuomintang. Expanding out of the initial northern camp, the communist-controlled areas grew rapidly. Presenting themselves as the champions of land reform and of the patriotic struggle against the Japanese, Mao's forces closed in on the slowly disintegrating Kuomintang army. When the Japanese surrendered in 1945, the war between the Kuomintang and the communists resumed in all its intensity. Gradually the military balance shifted in the communist direction, and from 1947 to 1949 the Kuomintang retreat turned into a rout. By 1949 Chiang's forces had been pushed off the Chinese mainland; all that remained to them was

---

12. Cited in *China: The Emerging Red Giant*, ed. DeVere E. Pentony (San Francisco: Chandler, 1964) 168.

the island of Taiwan. On October 1, 1949, Mao proclaimed the People's Republic of China.

Red vs. expert

Mao's character and temperament had been decisively molded by his decades as a guerrilla fighter. He took away from these turbulent years the sense that human will, when directed unreservedly toward a noble cause, can conquer all obstacles. How much more was this true, he reasoned, in regard to the hundreds of millions of Chinese people; if they acted with sacrifice and devotion, they could accomplish virtually any task they set their collective mind to. For Mao, therefore, being "red," that is, ideologically pure and deeply inspired, was far more critical than being "expert," that is, well trained or professionally qualified.

A Great Cultural Revolution

After the founding of the Chinese People's Republic, Mao's revolutionary dynamism became harnessed to the task of building a socialist society. But at some point in the early 1960s he began to complain that revolutionary idealism and self-sacrifice were flagging. The Communist Party apparatus, instead of keeping alive the white-hot fire of revolution, was becoming too much like that of the Soviet Union: bureaucratic, expert, and timidly sensible. Chaffing at the normalization that was setting in and fearful that an organized, rationally administered party would be less subject to his control, Mao called for a **Great Cultural Revolution** that would restore redness and drive out the weak-willed experts.

Mao Zedong (1893–1976). A theorist of revolution and guerrilla warfare, and leader of the People's Republic of China.

In the following years (1966–1969) China was shaken by an unparalleled kind of social and economic turmoil. Mao incited peasants, workers, and students to defy the authority of party functionaries, managers, and teachers. Parades of humiliation in which experts were marched through the streets draped in slogan-bearing dunce caps and capes that denounced the offenders' lack of redness became a common sight. Professors (imagine it!) were forced by their students to clean the public latrines. Party officials were brought by the droves to the countryside and made to work in the fields. In many cases these were far from merely symbolic humiliations: great numbers (estimates range from the thousands to the millions) were killed by roving bands of violent red guards whose motivations were not always ideological in character.

The return of the experts

Industrial and agricultural production were extremely hard hit. Mao's personal stature was also significantly tarnished. The great helmsman, about whom a Stalin-like cult of the personality had developed, seemed far less god-like with China in the throes of bedlam and its economy in disarray. When Mao died in 1976, China seemed ready for a period of ideological cooling down, for a respite from disorder and tumult. The pragmatic voices of the once humiliated experts were heard again. Foremost among them was Deng Xiaping (b. 1904) who attempted to steer China away from reckless adventurism and toward realistic projects aimed at modernization and raising standards of living. Tourism was encouraged, and to a degree China even became open to world communication networks. Although the primacy of the party remained unquestioned, on-again, off-again experiments in free trade and free speech made some progress.

Tienanmen Square

The fragmentation and final collapse of the Soviet Empire created serious new dilemmas for the Chinese leadership. The fall of communism left China almost alone in the communist camp. Not only was communism's ideological attraction visibly weakening within China, it now had to fend for itself in a world without substantial ideological allies. Moreover, the Soviet collapse awakened the hope, especially among students and intellectuals, that China too would rid itself of repressive communism. In June 1989, thousands of students demonstrated peacefully in Beijing's Tienanmen Square, calling for greater personal and public freedoms. The leadership reacted with a brutal tank assault that (under the eyes of international television) crushed the protest.

The future of Chinese Communism

Even though the Tienanmen challenge to its authority was decisively smashed, many veteran China watchers became convinced that the days of strict communist control in China were numbered. Communism had been discredited as an unpopular and repressive regime, and in time this would be its undoing. Others argued that the sorry fates of the Soviet Union and Yugoslavia after the fall of communism provided an object lesson for those who might be tempted to change China too drastically and too fast. Potential reformers could not help but conclude that it would be better to retain order and centralized control under the communists—moving all the while toward greater freedom and openness—than to violently open Pandora's box and brave the unpredictable consequences. With its huge population (larger than the United States, Europe, and the former Soviet Union combined) and its awesome economic and military potential, one thing is clear: no one can afford to remain apathetic to ideological developments in China.

The Non-Marxist Radical Left

Anarchism: Pacific and Violent

Anarchism's image   Not so very long ago the fearsome image of the anarchist was used regularly by parents to frighten their disobedient children. The anarchist was an alien figure who lurked in the shadows. He wore dark glasses, a wide-brimmed hat that shaded his cunning face and heavy black beard, and a nondescript flowing coat that probably hid a bomb or two in its bulging pockets. He spoke with an indeterminate Central European accent and was likely to be overheard muttering that the world had to be mercilessly destroyed before it could be properly rebuilt. His head was full of mad theories and dense ideological double-talk.

Caricatures die hard and anarchism's bad press will not easily go away. The malevolent image of the anarchist that has dominated the public mind is the handi-work of the doctrine's most violent representatives: terrorists, assassins, and violent irrationalists. To be sure, there have been significant numbers of bomb-throwing, darkly conspiratorial anarchists in the past century and a half. And "propaganda of the deed," as terrorist anarchists described their bloody work, has claimed its share of innocent lives. But, in truth, these violent rebels occupy only a relatively small niche in the anarchist universe. Anarchists are just as likely to be pacifists and pro-foundly anti-authoritarian. They oppose Marxism (and anarchism has dogged Marxism's steps from the very beginning) because of its tendency to authoritarian-ism and its emphasis on dictatorship as a necessary phase in communism's evolu-tion. For the great Russian novelist Leo Tolstoy, or his compatriot Prince Peter Kropotkin, anarchism was above all a moral doctrine that preached love, non-vio-lence, and voluntary cooperation.

Anarchism's critique of regimentation   The coercive state, anarchists claim, is the primary source of human ills. Regi-menting humanity in authoritatively maintained relationships leads to the loss of its most vital and creative powers. Anarchists observe that nothing so effectively destroys a child's natural curiosity and desire to learn as formal education. (Thank-fully, they add, our children learn their native tongue by themselves rather than through formal instruction—otherwise we would all be mute.) The institutionaliza-tion of love in the bond of marriage is another favorite example: it so often suffo-cates romance and eros. Similarly, they argue, coercive, state-monitored human relations take the heart out of personal authenticity and instinctive social solidarity. The state, they declare, is both the cause and the most glaring symptom of decay and artificiality in human associations; it fills the vacuum created by the impover-ishment of authentic human community. When we lack the capacity for voluntary association and self-created order, the state's heavy hand regulates relationships and legislates conformity. Where spontaneous human relations have withered, the state creates a uniform and docile public; where the art of social dialogue has been lost, binding legal conventions take its place. The state is in fact a pathological state, a deplorable condition of humanity.[13]

The greater part of what is now done through imposition and discipline, anarchists argue, can be done through voluntary human agreement. Order does not have to be the result of coercion—indeed coerced order gives every sign of being fragile and humanly unsatisfying. A true human order would result from the spontaneous associations between free moral agents. It would issue in a community of individuals who, without either having become saints or being intimidated by the gallows, can accept and respect the rights of their comrades.

Voluntary
non-competitive
association

Anarchists therefore focus their moral attention on the associational possibilities of voluntary local groups and leagues. Like the Marxists, they rely on the dynamism of the exploited working class to do the actual work of revolution. But in contrast to the Marxists, many anarchists contend that the process of creating voluntary liberated socialism must begin in the here and now, even before the actual revolution takes place. New kinds of social relations based on cooperatives and communes need not await proletarian victory. In the aftermath of revolution, the workers would consolidate these freely established, non-competitive associations, extending their range and scope to include all of society. Coordinated or federated with each other, these spontaneously organized workers cooperatives and communes would take the place of the overbearing state.

Kropotkin on
natural cooperation

Kropotkin argued forcefully that our conventional view of the coercive state as indispensable derives from a mistaken image of nature. We have been led to believe that nature is "red in tooth and claw," a merciless and bloody struggle for survival. According to this understanding of biological evolution, competition, not cooperation, is nature's overriding imperative. If nature is a "war of all against all," then it stands to reason that we must have a powerful state in order to prevent unbridled chaos. Kropotkin disagrees. He presents a provocative counter-argument that details the many cooperative and altruistic elements in nature that more than offset its violence. Nature displays a wonderful harmony between the different species, a harmony in which the division of labor and mutual aid are of paramount importance. Most critically, this harmony is achieved without any external authority imposing its will. As human evolution unfolds, he anticipates the growing dominance of peaceful, voluntary cooperation.[14]

Tolstoyan spiritual
anarchism

While anarchists agree fundamentally on the ideal of a stateless society, they are deeply divided over strategy. Some, like Tolstoy, believe that if the anarchist aim is a non-authoritarian, non-violent world, then authority and violence must be repudiated now. Means must be congruent with the aims they seek to foster. Violent means will lead to violent ends. Hence, only persuasion and the setting of personal examples can create a world in which reason and morality triumph. It may be slow and difficult work, but any political change brought about by force will necessarily create a force-dominated world.[15]

---

13. See Martin Buber, *Paths in Utopia* (Boston: Beacon Press, 1966) 46–57.
14. See Peter Kropotkin, *Mutual Aid: A Factor in Evolution* (Boston: Extending Horizon Books, 1955).

Bakunin's violent anarchism

Others, like the Russian Mikhail Bakunin, found this kind of spiritualized anarchism preachy and unrealistic. To clear the way for a new world necessarily meant radical destruction, complete annihilation of the old. "All that is false must be destroyed, without exception and without pity, so that the truth may triumph—and it will triumph."[16] What most especially needs to be destroyed is political power, the seed of all evil. Although Bakunin accepts Marxism's ultimate aim—a stateless society—he denounces Marxist ideology because, in his view, it perpetuates political power and thus only encourages the reemergence of oppression in a new guise. Despite his doctrine of the withering away of the state, Marx had taught that the revolution must capture and redirect the power of the state, not eliminate it. Bakunin insists that the revolutionary forces need to dismantle political power and, by means of the "spontaneous and incessant actions of the popular masses,"[17] create a non-coercive social community of free individuals.

Bakunin vs. Marx

If Marx understood political power as a symptom of the class struggle that would wither away when its cause disappeared, Bakunin was prone to denounce the state as the source of evil. If Marxists insisted that without leadership and organization the worker's movement had no chance of succeeding, Bakunin warned that with top-heavy leadership and the retention of coercive institutions, the revolutionary future might prove worse than the repressive past. Let us give Bakunin the last word. "What intellects are powerful enough," he rhetorically asks of the Marxists and their idea of a revolutionary dictatorship,

> to embrace the infinite multiplicity and diversity of interests, aspirations, wills, needs whose sum constitutes the collective will of a people? What intellects are powerful and broad enough to invent a social organization capable of satisfying everyone?[18]

Clearly, not the intellects of the Marxist dictators! Only the anarchic, that is, the spontaneous organization of society from below according to the promptings of its own freely acting membership can promise a future that will be both socially cooperative and individually free.

Anarcho-Syndicalism

Phrases like the "spontaneous organization of society from below" beg a whole slew of problems, not least of which is that the terms "spontaneous" and "organization" are patent opposites. How, in concrete terms, can anarchist society be at one and the same time both socially cooperative and individually free? Anarcho-syndicalism attempts to provide an answer to these questions by adding organizational

---

15. Leo Tolstoy, *The Law of Love and the Law of Violence* (London: Anthony Blond, 1970).

16. Cited in George Lichtheim, *A Short History of Socialism* (London: Weidenfeld and Nicholson, 1970) 123.

17. Lichtheim, *A Short History of Socialism*, 129.

18. Lichtheim, *A Short History of Socialism,* 129.

specificity to the rather abstract anarchist principles we have thus far heard from Tolstoy, Kropotkin, and Bakunin.

Worker control of industry

The term "syndicalism" derives from the French word "syndicat" or labor union, and syndicalism did in fact originate in the French trade union movement. The combination of anarchism and syndicalism points to the central content of the doctrine: a spontaneous organization of society based on worker control of industry. The workers, those who are themselves involved in production, are to supervise the standards, working conditions, resource allocations, and quotas of each industry. Industry-wide worker organization, anarcho-syndicalists claim, is the natural form of non-coercive order because it follows the actual contours of human activity. Each self-administered industry will send representatives to a coordinating council whose purpose is to effectively synchronize the activities of the various economic sectors. In the end, all the means of production and distribution will be coordinated by a federation of labor unions.

Coordination vs. political control

Anarcho-syndicalists stress that coordination differs essentially from political control. The latter is coercive in character, while the former does no more than align the activities of free people. In the anarcho-syndicalist scheme, social order derives naturally from the synchronization of freely interacting individuals. Anarcho-syndicalists vehemently deny that incompatible interests or scarce resources will lead to conflict and, inescapably, to politically coercive decisions. This kind of thinking, they charge, belongs to the typical pathology of state-dominated individuals who are so accustomed to regimentation that they are unable to even conceive of human dealings based on voluntary cooperation and mutual respect.

The general strike

Anarcho-syndicalism also has a distinctive approach to the strategy of revolution. Being a labor-centered movement, its natural tendency has been to identify revolution with labor's most potent weapon: the strike. They reason that if local strikes against specific employers can have devastating effects, how much more irresistible would their combined effect be if they were general and caused a total shutdown of the entire economy? The **general strike** would make clear that ultimate power rested in the hands of the workers because they, and they alone, were the creators of all social wealth. If they stopped working, everything would grind to a halt. The ruling class would be brought to its knees. And that would be a perfect prelude to the anarcho-syndicalist vision of a worker-controlled economy. In the hands of its most radical advocates—the French syndicalist George Sorel is the outstanding example—the general strike takes on the quality of a charmed, virtually apocalyptic myth of proletarian deliverance.[19]

Anarchism's erratic career

Anarchism and anarcho-syndicalism have had erratic careers. At times they frightened polite society witless, at others—the present especially—they sound strangely irrelevant if not a bit unhinged. For the first few decades of the century, anarchism was a powerful presence in France, Italy, and Spain. After World War II, its influence weakened considerably.

The New Left

Anarchism and the New Left

It has often been observed that the New Left of the 1960s owed at least as much to the spirit of anarchism as it did to the more orthodox strains of Marxism. Like the anarchists, the emphasis of these young would-be revolutionaries was anti-authoritarian and anti-conventional. They praised spontaneity and felt most comfortable with theatrical actions and unrestrained self-assertion. Freedom from regimented rationality was a central element in their revolt. Theirs was less an ideologically inspired class rebellion than an insurrection against establishment values. Not surprisingly the traditional Marxist parties, with their more analytic and organizationally structured character, displayed little enthusiasm for what they saw as immature revolutionary antics. Since the decline of 1960s radicalism, expressly anarchist ideas have fallen on hard times. (This is not true of right-wing libertarian anarchism, which has flourished. See Chapter 3.)

Although the student revolution of the 1960s failed to achieve its declared objectives, it shaped the agenda of the left for the decades to come. Proletariat-based radical movements had, after all, lost much of their credibility. Although the working class had carried the banner of revolution for over a century, it was perfectly clear at the end of the twentieth century that the contemporary industrial proletariat had a lot more to lose than its chains. And with the collapse of the Soviet Union and the difficulties in which mainstream Marxism finds itself, novel avenues for left-wing politics have become dominant in Western radical thought. These have included (1) liberationist movements based on race and gender, (2) green politics based on the pressing ecological crises facing the planet, and (3) the university-centered struggles over the appropriate academic syllabus in a world that is no longer dominantly white, male, and Western. These very fresh developments in contemporary ideology will be taken up in Chapter 9.

The present agenda of the left

Presenting pointed critiques of Soviet Communism is like beating someone when they are down and out. No more devastating critique can be imagined than the overnight disintegration of the system and the total disgrace of its ideological pretensions. Even Chinese Communism has recoiled from its doctrinaire communist past. Its present seems more dictated by pragmatic considerations of stability and survival than by communist principles. Approaching the year 2000, conventional communist ideology has more relevance to us as history than it does as an active protagonist in the contemporary ideological struggle. In this light, anarchism may well be fortunate in having failed to ever put its ideas into practice. At very least, they are less sullied than those of communism. A few concluding questions in regard to anarchist ideology are therefore in order.

Critiques of anarchism

A. The Marxists, and especially the Leninists, seem historically vindicated at least in one regard: revolutions will not take place without organization and leadership. Anarchist history is the clearest manifestation of this basic truth. Either the anarchists organized in order to direct the revolutionary struggle—in which case they violated their anti-authoritarian principles—or they remained true to their anarchist principles and were outflanked by their organized opponents, usually the communists. Paradoxically, anarchism cannot remain true to itself without condemning its efforts to failure.

B. Much the same can be said about the Tolstoy/Bakunin split. Tolstoy's form of spiritual anarchism is noble but practically impotent. Bakunin's violent

---

19. See his *Reflections on Violence* (New York: Collier, 1974).

anarchism may conceivably succeed in destroying the state, but its consequences are unlikely to be serenity and harmony. It seems a macabre form of mysticism to believe that, out of conflagration and violence, a gentle peace will emerge.

C. Anarchist ideology is dangerous because the vacuum in authority that it sees as a noble ideal is, in fact, a standing invitation to the unscrupulous and the authoritarian. Anarchist victories will always be short-lived because they leave themselves utterly exposed to political predators. After all, the only way that anarchism triumphant can protect itself against its enemies is to announce clear prohibitions and to set intimidating punishments, that is, to reintroduce political coercion. No doctrine so quickly turns into its opposite as anarchism.

D. Anarchism's wholesale rejection of authority misses the potentially ethical character of organized public life. Institutions have it in their power to express our unique communal character; they do not necessarily inhibit or violate our wills. In fact, a state that represents our collective wills more fully than any other institution could be the vehicle *par excellence* for expressing our ethical solidarity. The simple identification of freedom with the absence of authority is, therefore, a serious error. By destroying authority, anarchism does not create real freedom as much it creates an impoverished ethical vacuum.

E. Were anarchism's case to rest solely on humanity's instinctive social nature, it would be fairly easy, at least at the level of premises, to grant its assumptions and to give its arguments a serious hearing. But there is an additional axiom to anarchist thought that requires no little gullibility to swallow—to wit, that humanity is good by nature, and were it not for the distortions and corruptions fostered by the state, this natural virtue would shine through. In the closing years of our bloody century, can anyone make such an argument without flinching?

Suggestions for Further Reading

Chen, Jack. *Inside the Cultural Revolution.* New York: Macmillan, 1975.

Conquest, Robert. *The Great Terror: Stalin's Purge of the Thirties.* Rev. ed. New York: Macmillan, 1973.

Koestler, Arthur. *Darkness At Noon.* New York: Random House, 1941.

Malraux, Andre. *Man's Fate.* New York: The Modern Library, 1934.

Mao Tse-tung. *Selected Works of Mao Tse-tung.* 4 vols. Peking: Foreign Languages Press, 1961–65.

Miller, David. *Anarchism.* London: Dent, 1984.

Schram, Stuart, ed. *The Political Thought of Mao Tse-tung.* New York: Praeger, 1963.

Shapiro, Leonard. *The Communist Party of the Soviet Union.* New York: Vintage, 1964.

Shub, David. *Lenin: A Biography.* New York: Penguin, 1976.

Solzhenitsyn, Aleksander. *The Gulag Archipelago.* 3 vols. New York: Harper and Row, 1974–79.

Starr, John B. *Continuing the Revolution: The Political Thought of Mao.* Princeton: Princeton University Press, 1979.

Tucker, Robert C., ed. *Stalinism: Essays in Historical Interpretation.* New York: Norton, 1977.

Wilson, Edmund. *To the Finland Station.* Garden City, N.Y.: Doubleday, 1955.

Wolfe, Bertram D. *Three Who Made a Revolution.* New York: Dell, 1964.

Woodcock, George. *Anarchism.* New York: Penguin, 1962.

Chapter 7

Fascism: Dead or Alive?

Fascism in Historical Context

An elastic term Banishing the term "fascism" from polite academic conversation might not be a bad idea. A hundred different meanings crowd into this remarkably elastic word. Worse still, it has become an all-purpose term of political abuse rather than a clear ideological category. Overzealous police actions are fascist, male repression of women's rights is phallic fascism, psychiatric hospitals practice institutional fascism, even hateful parental regulations earn the fascist label.

Its more specifically political usage is no clearer. For years, the communists called the social democrats social fascists. Right-wingers like to vent their spleen at communists by dismissing them as red fascists. Indeed, not so very long ago new-left critics branded Western democratic regimes as proto-fascist. As it emerges from these assorted usages, fascism is little more than a highly charged term of disdain for brutality and repression. Such indiscriminate usage does not make the study of fascist ideology any easier.

Perhaps the greatest practical obstacle to the understanding of fascism is, ironically, its evil character. Our moral senses are so outraged by its crimes that critical analysis is somehow paralyzed. Faced with the enormity of its misdeeds, all we can do is shudder. The highly complex historical phenomenon of fascism typically becomes reduced to it worst case: Germany. And the German case becomes reduced to its most dreadful atrocities. In the end, fascism becomes equated with death camps and assembly-line genocide. Related to in this way, the study of fascism becomes an exercise in ethical sensitization, a moral nightmare that we must live through again and again to learn the great cautionary lesson of our time: if it happened once, then we must reassess our ideas about the human capacity for evil. As a historical warning, the focus on fascism's satanic character is legitimate, even mandatory. As a substitute for understanding, however, it contributes little.

The historical context
To understand fascism we must first of all place it in historical context. As a conscious and developed political phenomenon, fascism belongs to the inter-war period. It made its historical entrance during the waning years of World War I, rose to its greatest influence and power in the mid 1930s, and crashed to defeat in 1945 at the end of World War II. In Italy, the fascists came to power in the so-called **march on Rome** (see below) organized by Mussolini in October 1922. It took nearly eleven years for a second fascist leader to make his way to the top. Then, at the end of January 1933, Adolf Hitler was appointed Chancellor of Germany. By 1936 the possibility that fascism was the wave of the future could not be dismissed easily. Fascist movements were organizing with alarming success all over Europe and beyond. Moreover, a civil war between a fascist-supported right and a communist-supported left was raging in Spain. This struggle—from which, some three years later, the right under General Franco emerged victorious—was commonly seen as a dress rehearsal for the fate of Europe.

With the defeat of the Axis forces in 1945, fascism as a pervasive and threatening world presence faded into history. Mussolini and Hitler died abject deaths, and by all accounts their movements succumbed with them. Persecuted and outlawed, the fascist parties that had dotted Europe a decade earlier were disbanded and discredited. In the end, the Italian fascists had held power for twenty-odd years; the National Socialists had ruled Germany for all of twelve. Fascism rose meteorically and fell just as precipitously.

And yet, it is critically important to recognize that fascism was no historical accident, no mere freakish parenthesis in European history. As a political and as a human phenomenon, it was far more significant than what might be surmised from its short tenure in power. Fascism's roots, both intellectually and politically, lie deeply embedded in Western culture and public life. Nor can its mass psychological allure be ascribed to mere chance. Whether we pronounce fascism dead or conclude that it is merely hibernating depends on how we understand the political and spiritual sources of its vitality in the inter-war years.

Our preliminary task, therefore, will be to consider the historical background to the rise of fascism. We shall proceed by studying the intriguing similarities that mark the Italian and German cases.

The Rise of Fascism and Naziism: Historical Parallels

German-Italian parallels
A series of striking parallels between the events surrounding the fascist rise to power in Italy and Germany has long fascinated historians and political analysts. Despite the undoubted uniqueness and irreducibility of each case, it is impossible not to be struck by certain significant analogies between them. Historical parallels do not, of course, lead automatically to clear interpretive conclusions. Facts never speak for themselves; they are always spoken for. Nevertheless, even a simple and schematic recounting of these similarities should whet our intellectual curiosity.

Late
unification

1. Italy and Germany were the last major European states to achieve political unification. Whereas most European nation states became clearly defined geopolitical entities in the seventeenth and eighteenth centuries, Italy and Germany in the mid-nineteenth century were still patch-quilts of local authorities. Bitter internal conflicts as well as the machinations of rival states prevented these small units from consolidating into a single sovereign political community. Understandably, Italian and German national sensitivities were especially acute.

Unification
from above

2. When unification came—and it was complete in both cases at much the same time, about 1870—it came from above. It was achieved through diplomatic and military strategies orchestrated by political leaders rather than by movements whose dynamism derived from the people. Although the Italian Risorgimento (the movement to national unification) had substantial popular elements, unification and independence were more the result of diplomatic maneuvering than mass political activity. The shrewdness and political dexterity of Count Cavour was more critical than the popular-based movements of Garibaldi and Mazzini.

In the German case, unification was the brilliant handiwork of a single man: Otto von Bismarck. There was no popular movement to speak of. The Iron Chancellor, as he was called, conducted a virtuoso diplomatic and military campaign that succeeded both in overcoming internal resistance and in militarily overpowering rival states. In a series of ingenious diplomatic moves and triumphant military operations against Denmark, Austria, and France, Bismarck, the conservative Prussian monarchist, brought his policy of "blood and iron" to a successful conclusion.

Leadership not
representative

3. In both cases the drive to unification was spearheaded by a specific part of the national community: in Italy it was the more industrialized, wealthy north, in Germany the Prussian aristocratic landowning class—the Junkers. The very form of the unified state was, therefore, a cause for tension and recriminations.

Unresolved
tensions

4. Unification did not resolve deeper underlying difficulties. In fact, some of these problems were intensified by being brought into a single unified structure. In Italy, the great divide between the industrial north and the rural south was aggravated by the north-inspired political union. Similarly, unification prompted a virtual rupture between the newly established liberal secular state and the Vatican, with its deeply conservative teachings and policies.

In Germany, unification left the existing distribution of political power virtually intact. It remained centered in the anti-modern, rural Prussian aristocracy. Despite Germany's rapid industrialization and modernization, the structures of authority and legitimacy remained fundamentally land-based and pre-modern. The rising industrial and financial elites did not attempt to replace the older reactionary patriciate with a more liberally oriented one. On the contrary, they sought to endow their newly acquired position and wealth with legitimacy by buying their way into the traditional ruling circles.

No democratic
traditions

5. Neither Italy nor Germany possessed a solid tradition of democratic thought and government. Germany was authoritarian, conservative, and lacking in a participatory political ethos. Its intellectual tradition tended to distinguish sharply between pure inner freedom on the one hand, and the real world of domination and force on the other. From this perspective, spirit and power were constituted out of radically different materials. Pragmatic bargaining politics, which sought to realize the possible even if it departed from the ideal, was disdained as small-minded, even dishonorable. Typically, the one opportunity that Germany had to liberate itself from authoritarianism—during the revolutionary European Spring of 1848—turned into a windy theoretical debate and ended in disgrace.

The fledgling Italian parliamentary tradition was severely compromised almost from the start by the tendency to subvert the legitimacy of the political opposition. In a practice known derisively as Trasformiso (transformation), the ruling party appealed to the opposition to abandon its principles and join them for the sake of national unity and welfare—not to mention the fat political payoffs that were offered. Consequently, Italian politics became based on shifting and cynical coalitions that did nothing to inspire confidence in the democratic process.

Unification without
the unifiers

6. Count Cavour died shortly after unification while Bismarck remained in office for some twenty years thereafter. Both of them erected a delicate structure of alliances, coalitions, and power balances that controlled the underlying sources of dissension. These structures of control did not survive the departure of the architects of unification. In less practiced hands, many of the latent conflicts reasserted themselves with alarming severity.

The red scare

7. From the 1890s onward, the left-wing revolutionary parties in Italy and Germany received a substantial portion of the votes cast. Not surprisingly, the establishment perceived these radicals as a formidable threat to their interests. The red scare was incalculably intensified by the success of the Russian Revolution in 1917. Exploiting the specter of an imminent Bolshevik coup, the anti-democratic right made serious inroads into the normally liberal and centrist middle classes. Fed by the fear of left-wing subversion, reactionary themes that seemed to have been overcome by Enlightenment and universal education surfaced once again.

War frenzy

8. The outbreak of World War I prompted an unprecedented surge of hyper-nationalist identification in Germany and Italy. This war frenzy had a profound effect, particularly on the young who would reach maturity in the 1920s and 1930s. The war's unprecedented scale of violence made mass destruction a familiar phenomenon and deadened sensitivities to what previously would have been considered unthinkable.

Ex-combatants

9. The dislocations caused by the war were particularly painful and widespread in Germany and Italy. Many simply could not find their way back to pedestrian civilian life after the epic experience of war and heroism. Notably, the core of both the Fascist and Nazi "shock troops" (the Blackshirts and the Brown-

shirts) came from these ex-combatants. Germany's stinging defeat and the demeaning conditions imposed by the Versailles treaty were further grievances that the extreme right would effectively exploit.

On a lesser scale, the Italians, who had fought on the winning side, were incensed at having been cheated out of the territorial prizes of victory they had been promised early in the war. Right-wing adventurers (like d'Annunzio), whom the fascists would later emulate, dramatized this loss of honor and territory to great effect.

Economic crisis

10. Economic crisis was central to both cases as well—although, once again, the plight of Germany was far more disastrous than that of Italy. In Italy, the fascist takeover in 1922 was indissociable from the recurrent waves of strikes that Mussolini applauded when they served his purposes, and denounced when they did not. He claimed to be the true voice of the suffering Italian underclass—rather than the Bolsheviks who betrayed the workers in the name of high-sounding theories. By caring for the weak and the poor, he insisted, the fatherland would heal the class wounds that the left had opened. Without fascist exploitation of economic distress, the march on Rome might never have taken place.

The Weimar Republic established in Germany after the defeat in World War I and the abdication of King Wilhelm suffered from grievous economic difficulties. In 1923 Germany was hit by a calamitous runaway inflation that quickly wiped out the life savings of many citizens, reduced pensions to a pittance, and wrought havoc with those who lived on a fixed income. A short six years later, the Great Depression of 1929 struck with devastating intensity. Of all the major European countries, Germany was hardest hit. Unemployment skyrocketed, foreign credits dried up, and the economy ground to a halt. Three and a half years later when Hitler was appointed Chancellor, these economic woes were still acute and the Nazis were still exploiting them to the hilt. With all the necessary caution that historical what-if hypotheses require, it is still a safe bet that without the severe economic crisis, Hitler would have remained part of the eccentric side-show of Weimar politics.

Power assumed legally

11. Although both movements spurned conventional democratic politics, the fascists and the Nazis came to power legally. Neither party ever received a bona fide majority in a free election, but Mussolini and Hitler were appointed heads of state in the authorized fashion. To be sure, the fascist march on Rome threatened to resort to violence if their demands were not met. But in the end, Mussolini (who had been in Milan during the march, at a safe distance from the excitement and with a reassuring train ticket to Switzerland in his pocket) was properly called upon by King Victor Emmanuel to assume the post of Prime Minister. He took office without a shot having been fired.

The legality of Hitler's rise to power cannot be doubted. From the onset of the Depression, Weimar politics had taken a sharp turn toward instability, violence, and extremism. Hitler's parliamentary delegation, which had been a mere twelve in 1928, grew to 107 in 1930, and 230 in 1932. Although they fell somewhat (to 197) in late 1932, they were still the largest party delegation in the Reichstag, even if they fell short of a majority. After a series of parliamentary crises at the end of 1932 and the beginning of 1933, the aging and probably senile President Hindenburg faced a fateful decision. Should he appoint another weak interim Chancellor, or should he take a chance on the macabre Austrian corporal who aggressively promised to restore law and order? Prevailed upon by right-wing, anti-republican nationalists who argued that Hitler would destroy the communists but would be putty in their hands, Hindenburg appointed Hitler Chancellor on January 30, 1933. The most ruthless tyrant of the century had come to power lawfully.

This odd presence of legality continued even after the ascent to power. Neither Mussolini nor Hitler implemented their totalitarian programs at once. Both preserved, at least for a while and when it suited their purposes, the veneer of constitutionalism. They assumed their dictatorial powers by what were, at least formally speaking, legal means. Only in stages did their tyrannical objectives become obvious: they gradually abolished civil rights, closed independent newspapers, disallowed opposition parties, and set up a secret police. Above all, they began a systematic campaign to create a fully mobilized political community unanimously dedicated to the will of the Leader.

Having made our way, very selectively, through the events leading to the consolidation of power in Italy and Germany, it should be obvious that we have taken only a small first step in the direction of understanding fascism. We have, it is true, narrowed the historical and political coordinates. The striking parallels between the Italian and the German cases offer much food for the political imagination. But it is only a bit of historical scaffolding that has been set into place. We now face the more formidable task of penetrating into the interior structure and design of fascism both as an idea and as a practice. That this is no easy task will become apparent in the following section.

Fascism: A Perplexing Phenomenon

Liberalism, Social Democracy, and Marxism, despite some very critical differences between them, are part of the same extended idea family. They are all children of the Enlightenment. Each of them, in its own way, cherishes rationality and human progress. Human beings, they would all agree, through the use of their reason are able to continually improve the world in which they live, making it more and more satisfying for human life. At least in theory, each of them accepts the sanctity and dignity of human life. All of them believe in a universal human community. They all praise peace and recoil from war and violence. Education and learning are among their highest values. In the end, there would be only moderate differences of outlook were liberals, social democrats, and Marxists asked to distinguish between decent and wicked individuals.

The shock of fascism

No wonder then that when fascism appeared on the historical scene it caused such consternation in so many different circles. It was the greatest surprise of twentieth-century politics. Fascism appeared to break the ideological mold in which Western social thought had been accustomed to operate. Here was a movement that, two centuries after the Enlightenment, praised the irrational instincts, celebrated brutality, denigrated reason, exalted the cult of war, and advocated racial tribalism. It appeared to have sprung into being out of nowhere. Fascism seemed to be a throwback to a long-past age, although, confusingly for an archaic phenomenon, it utilized all that was modern in media technology to get its message across.

Initial reactions

Observing these bizarre ideological mutations, some frustrated analysts concluded that fascism was simply a fluke. Fascist leaders, they suggested, like latter-day Pied Pipers, had bewitched entire populations into following them blindly. Others attributed the puzzling phenomenon to a takeover by a political mafia, an insurrection of the gangster underworld. Not surprisingly, many of these observers were prone to dismiss Mussolini as a clown and a windbag, and to portray Hitler as a Chaplinesque comic figure.

Even judicious observers who rejected such simple-minded accounts had trouble making heads or tails out of fascism. For Marxists, the rise of fascism was especially problematic. It seemed to violate their most basic historical anticipations. Marxist theory had led them to believe that when the great economic crash came—as it did in 1929—the impoverished middle classes would swell the ranks of the proletariat and fuel the fires of revolution. The contradictions of capitalism would finally reach their breaking point, and the tiny ruling and owning class would be toppled by the great mass of exploited humanity. But it did not happen that way. Instead of joining the proletariat, the threatened middle classes stampeded after an outlandish band of reactionary political adventurers with an ideological platform that was all **irrationalism** and hatred.

Liberals did not have it any easier. Perhaps the central axiom of the liberal world-view was the progressive self-betterment of humanity through the application of reason. Superstition and prejudice, they insisted, would retreat before the advance of analysis and experiment. Narrow clannish identities would give way to cosmopolitan outlooks just as unthinking conformity would be replaced by enlightened, self-directed individuals. Imagine liberal bewilderment when in Germany and Italy—the heartland of European culture—a macabre cult of unreason and violence arouse. Its leaders seemed bent on mystifying the world. They sought to shroud political life in impenetrable clouds of irrationality and to base social relations on primal blood ties. How to explain the cult-like worship of the leader, the atavistic symbols, the torch-lit parades, the crowd hysteria, and the lock-step conformity?

For traditional conservatives, the fascists posed a unique enigma. In some regards, the fascists appeared to share the conservative outlook. Both had an aversion for left-wing revolutionaries and secular, liberal reformers. Both abhorred the modern tendency to base society on individualist, rationalist, progressive, and utilitarian principles. But here the affinities ended. Fascists had no respect for the traditional elites, whether they belonged to the wealthy, the highborn, the church, or the army. Fascists tended to be lower-middle-class upstarts, uneducated drifters, and vulgar adventurers. One writer describes the early Nazis as "vulgar, heavily male and beer drinking, chauvinist, xenophobe, authoritarian, anti-semitic, anti-intellectual, anti-emancipatory, anti-modernist."[1] Fascist politics centered on appeals of the most common kind directed to uncouth masses. Their social element was the mob, and their propaganda was at the level of the gutter. Moreover, their taste for street violence and pointless hooliganism was frightening. Perhaps most serious of all, they talked the language of revolution and seemed to mean it.

Fascism as a widespread phenomenon

Beyond the initial difficulties that confronted ideologically committed observers, fascism posed a number of unique challenges with which scholars have been grappling ever since. First of all, fascism was not a sharply defined phenomenon. While public memory has understandably fastened onto the two fascist movements that actually came to power—in Germany and Italy—virtually every European country had its own home-grown variety of fascism. Fascism thrived from Finland to Spain, from Belgium to Croatia—even the United States was not immune.

Each was unique: some were viciously racist, others only marginally so; some were reactions to the Bolshevik threat, in other cases the Bolsheviks were hardly a factor at all; some were related to the acute dislocations caused by rapid industrialization, others were basically peasant movements; some promised great spiritual revolutions, while others were difficult to distinguish from a simple gang of thugs. Characterizations of fascism that fit the German case, for example, will in many important regards fail to apply to the fascist movements of Rumania, Norway, or France.

Who were the fascists?

Even their social and class composition is the subject of acute controversy. There is substantial evidence that the middle class (especially the lower middle class) was disproportionately represented in the fascist ranks. But significant support at critical moments also came from some powerful industrial and financial magnates. There was also a sizeable minority of working class support. Civil servants were over-represented. In some countries fascist movements grew out of student organizations. In others, they were on an intimate footing with artistic, literary, and intellectual circles. In the less-developed countries (particularly in Eastern Europe), peasant support figured prominently. Finally, there was the critical role played by those at the margins of society: the vagrants, the ex-combatants of World War I who could not find their way back into civilian life, the rootless bohemians, the alienated students. Who then were the fascists? Lower-middle-class hooligans, economically desperate victims, idealistic youth searching for a brave new world, or obsessively conformist civil servants?

1. Alan Bullock, *Hitler and Stalin: Parallel Lives* (New York: HarperCollins, 1991) 88.

An opportunistic
ideology

Analysis is further complicated because, once in power, fascism underwent significant changes. Much of what had been central to fascism prior to assuming power—its restless dynamism, its spiritual pretensions, and especially, its egalitarian, anti-capitalist themes—was often discarded. In an important sense, the fascists stirred up a political whirlwind and then, upon assuming power, pragmatically subdued it.[2] Which fascism, then, are we pursuing: an ideology that raged and stormed about "the poetry of struggle," or the calculated mass terrorism of a power-hungry regime?

Nor can it be overlooked that fascism as an ideology is notoriously haphazard and erratic. It possesses nothing comparable to the left's great body of authoritative writings—from Marx to Marcuse. Compared with Marxist theory, fascism is a hodgepodge of confused ideas. The writings that do exist, with a few exceptions, are intellectually inferior, if not patently crackpot.

Studying fascist ideology is especially difficult because elaborate idea systems were precisely what the fascists scorned. Theirs was a revolution of the spirit, a poetic revival that sought to liberate the vital life-forces smothered by bourgeois rationality and professorial bookishness. For the fascists, reasoned arguments were timid and anemic compared with primitive instincts. They called for action, not words or ideology. In the strikingly enigmatic phrase of Oswald Mosley, the leading English fascist during the 1930s: "no man goes very far who knows where he is going."[3] This tendency toward improvisation and anti-intellectualism gives fascist thought a predictably elusive quality. Above all, fascist ideology was often exploited in the most opportunistic ways, blending into whatever political objectives were uppermost at a given historical moment. Indeed, some would dismiss the study of fascist ideology as a basically futile enterprise. It was, they argue, no more than an intellectual fig leaf to cover up the naked pursuit of power. Although this is surely exaggerated, it is difficult to deny that at times fascist pronouncements are like a roller-coaster experience: full of twists, turns, and unexpected dives.

Fascism's
incompatible
traits

All this makes the study of fascism especially challenging. Understanding fascist ideology requires opening our minds to some unconventional thinking, to combinations of political elements that seem unlikely, if not actually bizarre. For starters, consider the following curious combinations: (1) a reactionary, hierarchy-advocating political movement based on popular mass mobilization and pseudo-democratic propaganda; (2) an irrationalist politics wedded to a highly systematic and rationalized bureaucracy of total control; (3) revolutionary, quasi-messianic rhetoric that supports a substantially conservative practice; (4) a movement that sets itself against both Wall Street and the Reds; (5) a self-styled revolution of the spirit

---

2. See George Mosse, "The Genesis of Fascism," in *International Fascism: 1920–1945*, ed. Walter Laqueur and George Mosse (New York: Harper and Row, 1966) 15.

3. Cited in Zeev Sternhell, "Fascist Ideology," *Fascism: A Reader's Guide*, ed. Walter Laqueur (Berkeley: University of California Press, 1976) 342.

with a fatal attraction for thugs and assassins; (6) a movement that declares itself socialist and anti-capitalist, yet has the fiercest enmity for parties of the left; (7) a movement that rebukes everything bourgeois, yet recruits the bulk of its support from this group. What kind of ideological movement could contain all these seemingly incompatible traits?

Fascism: The Contours of an Unprecedented Phenomenon

Fascism as a Reactionary Mass Mobilizing Movement

Fascism is not merely dictatorship, not even dictatorship with a particularly sadistic streak. Western dictatorships of recent memory—Pinochet in Chile, Salazar in Portugal, Franco in Spain, and the Colonels in Greece—are regimes of control and intimidation, not movements that seek to mobilize the masses. In fact, it is precisely the passions of mass politics that dictators of this kind fear most. Dictatorships tend to protect vested economic and social interests. They represent the heavy-handed rule of the army, the wealthy, the well-born, the church, and the bureaucracy—especially when these groups feel themselves threatened by hostile forces.

Dictatorship v. totalitarianism — Neither are dictatorial regimes **totalitarian**. They do not seek to penetrate every aspect of public and private life. They are not bent on shaping the innermost consciousness of each individual's mind. They have no interest in radically restructuring human life. Dictators are quite content with a docile and passive populace. Those who do not rock the boat can expect to continue their lives much as before. They will not be constantly called upon to display unswerving allegiance to the dictatorial cause. Despite their potential for repressive brutality then, dictatorships tend to be reactive, conserving, defensive regimes of the few rather than initiating, tumultuous, revolutionizing movements whose strength derives from the many.

Fascism and mass mobilization — As opposed to ordinary dictatorships, fascism is a radical mobilizing ideology. Its free-wheeling style does not tolerate popular passivity or bureaucratic conservatism. In this, fascism is unique. All earlier ideologies that spoke of a "radical restructuring of human reality" tied to a "revolutionary mobilization of the masses" were left-wing in character; fascism has clear affinities to the right. As a dynamic mass movement of the radical right, fascism is without precedent.

Fascism as reactionary — Although fascists like to speak of their objective as a conservative revolution, fascism is not conservative in any familiar sense of the term. If anything, the term **reactionary** is appropriate. Conservatives seek to preserve important elements in an existing political reality. They fear rapid change and social upheaval—even if it is change inspired by images of past glory or archaic social forms. While they are sometimes unhappy with the forms that technologically-centered contemporary society has taken, conservatives accept, more or less grudgingly, the basic forms of modern social and economic life. They have no interest in resuscitating medieval-ism or reinstating the Inquisition or encouraging pre-scientific thinking. It is here that they part company with reactionaries.

"Reaction" in the modern Western context means rejecting the form that civilization has taken at least since the Enlightenment and the French Revolution. And since virtually all contemporary ideologies—from conservatism to Marxism—derive in some way from these epochal events, fascism has to be understood as a grand revolt against modernity. It seeks to revive values and practices that have long since become historical museum pieces.

Focus on a mythical past

Although fascists like to speak of a glorious future (as in Hitler's vision of a thousand-year Reich), their ideas tend to center on a pristine, legendary, heroic past. This mythical Eden flourished long before the decadence of modernity spoiled all that was wholesome and vital. The exaltation of "blood and soil," the fetishistic attachment to the "forest primeval," the return to the Teutonic gods, the praise of tribal instincts, all belong to this revolt against modernity. Mussolini's choice of the fasces—a bundle of rods tied about an ax, which had represented authority in Classical Rome—to symbolize Italian power is also a throwback of this kind.

Reactionary nostalgia is generally limited to marginal bands of eccentrics. It attracts those who have lost in the historical convulsions brought on by industrial expansion, democratic change, and the advance of secularization. The ranks of reactionary politics are filled by emigre royalty, down-at-the-heels aristocrats, clerical die-hards, landowners who lost out to urban financial interests, assorted theorists and hangers-on of the **ancien regime**, and of course, the more than occasional lunatic. It appeals to those who nurse their historically inflicted wounds through impotent dreaming about a return to the good old days when crown, altar, and sword were still sovereign. Reaction is, in other words, the home of those history has defeated. It is hardly the stuff of which mass movements are made.

Even if fascist ideology is not reactionary in this standard sense—fascists have little respect for monarchs, clerics, or high-born army officers—it nevertheless shares with reaction a profound distaste for almost everything that modern society has produced. Fascism is more a collection of grievances against modernity, more an anti-ideology, than a program for reconstruction. Fascists reject rationalism, liberalism, democracy, Christianity, capitalism, humanism, internationalism, individualism, egalitarianism, conservatism, intellectualism, communism, cosmopolitanism—to name only a few of their enemies. Fascist racism, anti-semitism, and xenophobia, its glorification of war, struggle, and conquest, are also essentially oppositional in character. If we understand the term establishment as referring broadly to all those forces that have transformed the modern world into what it is, then fascism can be accurately described as a full-scale revolt against the modern establishment.

What is new
in fascism?

To be sure, fascism had its precursors.[4] Critics such as Mosca, Pareto, and Michels had derided democracy's claims to represent the popular will. Enlightenment rationalism too had its powerful detractors in writers like Dostoevsky, Nietzsche, Freud, and Sorel. Nor were racism, xenophobia, and anti-semitism inventions of the fascists. The fascist revolt, however, involved at least two strikingly new elements. First of all, most of the major critics of democracy and rationalism were genuinely alarmed by the illiberal world they had revealed. But even if reason was a frail guide compared with primal instincts, and even if democracy was less than it pretended to be, this should not be taken as a signal for an orgy of brutality. The fascists, by contrast, revelled in their irrationalist and anti-democratic credo. They extolled irrationalism and violence as thrilling, positively emancipating forces.

Second, prior to the early 1920s these illiberal and irrationalist currents had been largely confined to theorists and generally marginal political groups. The fascists succeeded in harnessing these heretofore eccentric ideas to a mass-movement. This is doubly remarkable given the fact that fascism does not have a natural popular constituency comparable to the working-class tendency to support the socialists or the middle-class affinity for the liberals. And yet, psychic intoxication and lock-step conformity appear to have satisfied the deep-seated needs of many who streamed into the fascist movement. Our next question must therefore be: How did a movement lacking a natural constituency succeed in creating such an unlikely tidal wave of support for its outlandish ideas?

Fascism and the Crisis of the Middle Class

Would fascism, with its macabre ideas and its lack of a natural constituency, have made any political headway were it not for the very special crisis-ridden reality that prevailed between the two world wars? The numbing war experience and the humiliation in defeat, the inflation and depression, the dislocations related to World War I and industrialization, the threat of communism all created fertile ground for unconventional political appeals. In a desperate world such as this, political programs previously dismissed as lunatic-fringe assumed a certain plausibility and attractiveness.

Why the lower
middle-class?

At first glance, this crisis does not appear to have singled out any one group in particular. Why then was the middle class, and especially the lower middle class, so vulnerable to the fascist message? Why did so many ordinary and normally respectable people—civil servants, shopkeepers, artisans, white collar workers, those who are typically drawn to a politics of stability and compromise — feel so powerfully moved by the fascist program? Why did they forsake the parties of the liberal center to which they had traditionally given their support and join a reactionary movement that preached a total reconstruction of society?

---

4. See George Mosse, *The Crisis of German Ideology* (New York: Grosset and Dunlap, 1964) and Fritz Stern, *The Politics of Cultural Despair* (Garden City, N.Y.: Anchor Books, 1965).

No socio-economic class in turn-of-the-century Europe had as much to be satisfied with as the rising middle class, which from the French Revolution onward had progressively fashioned public life in accord with its own liberal image. Optimistic and progressive, the European bourgeoisie extended civil and human rights, enacted different forms of social legislation, and broadened the basis of the vote. Their parliamentary, free-market creed appeared to be the inevitable wave of the future.

But the tide seemed to be turning. Most ominously, a communist revolution toppled the Russian Czar, and the revolutionary rhetoric of the European left raised fears that this egalitarian and atheistic creed would spread to Western Europe. Indeed, in some Western countries such as Germany and Italy, the left was in striking distance of a peaceful revolution by means of the ballot box.

Middle-class panic   The calamitous inflation of the early 1920s dealt a severe blow to more than pocketbooks and saving accounts: it was another alarming indication that the seemingly secure basis of middle-class European civilization was eroding. When the Great Depression sent markets tumbling in 1929, this retreat from confidence turned into a rout. Liberal economic and political systems were clearly not working. The communists were gaining ground, and the ranks of the destitute—potential supporters of the left—were swelling as more businesses failed and more employees lost their jobs. Demoralized and desperate, the middle class panicked. In their retreat from liberalism, they turned to the reactionary solutions offered by the fanatical right.

Another radical alternative was open to them; they could have added their voices to those of the left-wing revolutionaries who were also calling for a basic social reconstruction. For most of them, however, this alternative was profoundly distasteful. They had always based their middle-class respectability on just those differences that distinguished them from the lowly blue-collar laborers. Even when differences in income between them and the more well-off workers were small, they jealously preserved the identifying marks of gentility and class status. They could not bear to accept a diminished social status, to say nothing of embracing it warmly. They clung to class differences most fiercely just when they were most endangered.

None were more frightened by the prospect of proletarianization than the lower middle class. The most tenuous recipients of middle-class respectability, they were its most zealous defenders as well. In addition, many of them had recently risen out of the proletarian ranks and through hard work and thrift established themselves as small shopkeepers and petty civil servants; they felt entitled to disdain those who remained behind and reminded them of their origins. The thought of returning to the working class induced in them a full-scale status panic. While the more established elements of the middle and upper middle classes had financial reserves and educational resources upon which they could draw in times of crisis, the lower middle class was separated from the working class by the flimsiest of divides. There was nothing to cushion their fall.[5]

Fascist appeals

To these confused and disgruntled social elements the fascists directed their most powerful appeals.

Identifying the villains

1. They identified the culprits allegedly responsible for the crisis. It was the Jews, communists, Wall Street tycoons, Freemasons, and other shadowy international groups who had shrewdly manipulated the world economic market to profit from the misfortunes of others. Decent citizens who labored diligently and lived frugally, but who did not bother their heads about the workings of the world economic order, were being victimized by diabolical conspiracies.

Nursing wounded pride

2. Those who felt themselves cheated out of their social status were offered an alluring compensation: they were a superior race of Aryans or the inheritors of Classical Rome. They were chosen to lead all the others. Compared with their Slavic neighbors, for example, they were princes of humanity. What they had lost in economic status, fascism offered them in national standing. While the proletarian parties asked them to accept their misfortune and throw in their lot with the underclass, the fascists flattered their wounded pride and, what is more, promised revenge.

Restoring order

3. The fascists promised to restore order, discipline, and a clear social hierarchy. The intolerable ambiguities of a cultural system that had run amok would be resolutely tidied up. Moral mavericks, sexual deviants, and intellectual non-conformists would be severely disciplined. Moreover, the fascist parties offered an avenue of upward mobility for many of the newly impoverished. They were assured that in a hierarchical society, many would be fixed in positions below theirs. "A hierarchy above them," as one writer puts it, "was a guarantee of a hierarchy below."[6] Social status would be clear; there would be no mistaking the line that divided the working from the middle class.

Fascist socialism

4. For all of their animosity toward the left—the rabble-rousers, they pledged, would be dealt with once and for all—the fascists sought to steal the socialist's fire by formulating a pseudo-socialist creed of their own. Recognizing how effective slogans such as "bread, jobs, and justice" could be, the fascists liked to cast themselves as the true guardians of the dispossessed. They pledged to protect the weak against the greed of big-business. They undertook to defend wage levels, support social benefits, and encourage workers organizations. A single, morally unified, national community would take the place of warring classes. Fascists insisted that these policies offered a third

5. See H. R. Trevor-Roper, "The Phenomenon of Fascism," in *Fascism in Europe*, ed. S. J. Woolf (London: Methuen, 1981) 21–28.
6. Trevor-Roper, "The Phenomenon of Fascism," 28.

way, belonging to neither right nor left. As the shallow contemporary formula had it: nationalism + socialism = fascism.

The epic state of mind

5. Perhaps most basically, the fascists sought to create a mythical realm of liberation and glory that would spellbind the senses and intoxicate the mind. They offered "circuses for a society without enough bread."[7] Through great torch-lit parades resonant with dramatic grandeur, through cultic practices that recall the revivalist tent, through the worship of the omniscient leader and the cathartic damning of the enemy, the fascists induced an epic state of mind that compensated for real hardships and restored lost dignity. Tens of thousands of uniformed stalwarts marching in unison imparted a sense of power and a heightened feeling of belonging. The fact that one marched shoulder to shoulder with the boss and the manager conferred a sense of borrowed honor. We can well imagine the effect on the dazed, the weak, and the desperate.

Fascist Ethical Idealism and the Middle Class

This mystique of solidarity and grandeur is bound up with one of fascism's least appreciated yet most central elements: its ethical idealism. Admittedly, ethics and idealism are strange adjectives for fascism. And yet much of what was contagious about fascist ideology had to do with its anti-materialist ethics and its anti-bourgeois idealism. Particularly in the early stages, fascist ranks were filled with middle-class youths who were moved by the promise of moral renewal, spiritual beauty, heroism, and passion.

Something was rotten in Western culture, fascists proclaimed. It knew all about pragmatism and material interests, but nothing about valor and virility. It was mediocre and complacent, an old impotent civilization that sought nothing beyond its petty comforts. Western democracy was timidly rational because, having lost its youthful poetry and abandon, it feared whatever was fresh and exciting. In its small-minded pursuit of profit, liberal economics has reduced precious life to bartering and trade. Bourgeois materialist civilization was rotting, and the fascists vowed to sweep away its remains and create a brash, young, and fearless world in its place.

The "new fascist man"

Even the briefest review of fascist writings gives a vivid sense of this romanticized ethical thrust. The fascist, Mussolini asserted, disdains the comfortable life. Happiness is not mere material comfort and ease. In the genuine fascist life, human will is subject to no desire for petty gain or profit. A safe, passionless, calculating life is not worth living. Life is a perpetual struggle, a great spiritual and mystical crusade embarked upon with enthusiasm, self-denial, and love of danger. "Inactivity is death." Fascism is, therefore, a call to sacrifice, a total life commitment. It is "total" in that it effects a "revolution of the soul" and creates a "new fascist man."

---

7. Gilbert Allardyce, "The Place of Fascism in European History," in *The Place of Fascism in European History*, ed. Gilbert Allardyce (Englewood Cliffs, N.J.: Prentice Hall, 1971) 8.

To live truly, in fascist rhetoric, is to seek the liberation of our most primal instincts. Life has nothing to do with dusty theories or scholarly doctrines. It is a hazardous adventure in which speed, power, and activism are paramount. For inspired individuals, violence directed against decadence is no crime; it is a noble, esthetically liberating activity. Indeed, bomb-throwing, dagger-wielding youth incarnate the "springtime of beauty." Fascism is a movement of artists and warriors, not merely a political party.[8]

Despite this self-intoxicated anti-bourgeois rhetoric, fascism made a great many converts among idealistic middle-class youth. It seemed to promise what no conventional ideology could: an inspired moral crusade that, beyond the emotional catharsis it offered, defended their socio-economic interests and expressed the distress they were experiencing. It assured them that they were not alone in their desperation. Their suffering was the work of evil forces that conspired to destroy national vitality. Hence, the great national fraternity was willing to do battle on their behalf. In fact, the very bourgeois idea that each person was alone in a world of cutthroat capitalist competition was part of the decadent civilization that was about to be swept away. In place of "individualist abstractions," the fascists advanced the view that society, the nation, and the state formed an organic and indissoluble moral unit.

Fascist Totalitarianism: Organic Society, Nation, and State

The shallowness of individualism

In the fascist view, individuals can realize their true human vocation only within the national political community. Like detached limbs, individuals have no life apart from the political organism they serve. Outside the organic social whole, none of our freedoms and rights have any meaning. The liberal attempt to protect us against the incursions of society and the state, therefore, is misdirected; it fails to understand the social nature of human existence. Giovanni Gentile, probably the most sophisticated theorist of fascism, claims that "man is, in an absolute sense, a political animal."[9] It is both laughably shallow and morally despicable, fascists claim, to conceive of human beings as egocentric atoms each calculating his or her own individual interests. Society is no mechanistic aggregation of separate individuals. The human "I," in the end, is always rooted in the human "we"; to perform the simplest of human actions is inevitably to draw upon a wealth of socially acquired learning. To this point, fascist arguments have much in common with those of many nationalists, socialists, and communitarian democrats.

The all-embracing state

Fascism departs from accepted Western moral discourse in the radical consequences it derives from these very familiar views. If human achievement depends on the organized socio-political community, fascists reason that the state must be the alpha and omega of our moral concerns. We are free and ethically significant only as citizens of a national political association; hence, our

---

8. Sternhell, *Fascism: A Reader's Guide*, ed. Laqueur, 337–44.
9. Cited in A. James Gregor, *Contemporary Radical Ideologies* (New York: Random House, 1968) 139.

debt to it—rather than its duties to us—is virtually without limit. Against the united will of the political community as represented in the state, the will of particular individuals or groups is inconsequential. Moral claims upon the individual person, such as loyalty to friends and family, must be set aside when they are inconsistent with our loyalty to the state. The sovereign state is both exclusive and total, the single legitimate focus to which all partial objectives must be subordinate.

It follows that labor unions defending the interests of a particular class are affronts to the total communal will. In fact, the political left is doubly illegitimate: it sets one class against another while simultaneously replacing loyalty to the state with broadly internationalist sympathies. Interest groups, regional associations, cultural leagues, indeed all independent, voluntary socio-political organizations—what we have referred to as **civil society**—are similarly disqualified in fascist eyes. Nor can religious affiliations be considered matters of private conscience; they too must be subordinated to the will of the all-embracing state.

In transcending particular interests, the state liberates individuals from their enslavement to selfish concerns. Individual existence finds its highest moral realization in the state because the state expresses the true essence of the individual. Fascists insist that there can be no real difference between individual and collective interests because the will of the individual—when it is healthy and sound—is identical with that of the collective. To be genuinely free, therefore, is to willingly set aside personal interests when they do not serve those of the community. In accepting the will of the collective as my own, I declare my freedom from weak-willed self indulgence and egoism. What is more, I achieve my highest moral goal: I am both totally free and totally submerged in the collective.

Consequently, the state in fascist ideology is more than a neutral instrument that allocates resources, regulates conflict, and provides social services. Rather than arbitrating between conflicting interests, the state itself is the incarnation of our true interests. Rather than guarding the rules of the game so that we can all effectively pursue our own life plans, the state plans our lives for the higher collective good. Indeed, nothing of value, nothing human or spiritual, can exist beyond the confines of the state. Mussolini's stark epigram is as radical as it is simple: "Everything in the State, everything for the State, nothing outside the state, nothing against the state." Fascism, in the words of a leading French advocate, is dedicated to "the total man in the total society, with no clashes, no prostration, no anarchy."[10]

Nation as soul   But why are the objectives of the state so surpassingly important? Because, the fascists contend, they represent the living will of the nation. The state incarnates the will of the nation, and the nation is *the* decisive category in human history. National belonging, in the fascist understanding, is not just one human attribute among

10. The phrase belongs to Marcel Deat; cited by Zeev Sternhell, *Fascism: A Reader's Guide*, ed. Laqueur, 347. See also Sternhell's *Neither Right nor Left* (Berkeley: University of California Press, 1986) Ch. 5.

many, but the cardinal creator of our identities which lends significance to all other aspects of our lives.

For fascists, nations are quasi-mystical entities possessing a collective living soul. Nations are often spoken of as conscious moral beings pursuing grand historical missions. In representing the national will, the state embodies a purpose that is imbued with high moral content. As the guarantor of national existence and the instrument of national self-realization, the state is the physical instrument of national survival. In a sense, the nation is to the state what the soul is to the body. Fascist nationalism and fascist statism are, therefore, two sides of the same coin.

Subordinating individual will to the purposes of the state is only another way of saying that individuals must be subservient to the will of the national community. The nation state is after all a union of national will and of political sovereignty. Hence, the terms "organic society," "nation," and "state" are often used interchangeably in the language of fascism. Society is an organic unit because it incarnates a cohesive national will. The state, as the sovereign embodiment of the national will, is the physical representation of the organic social totality.

Given the importance of the nation, Fascism preaches a form of uninhibited national narcissism. It proclaims collective egoism to be a sacred duty. National duties are our primary duties. Fascist literature is full of praise for atrocities committed in the name of high-minded, nationally-inspired purposes. Without appreciating this perverse synthesis between unparalleled cruelty and ethical idealism, we are unlikely to penetrate into the twisted dynamism that animated the fascist consciousness.

National narcissism

If the national political community is the sovereign focus of all human obligations, then the nation's goals necessarily come before the rights and needs of other peoples. The nation is not merely one constituent element in the international community of nations. For fascists, there is no sense in speaking of a chorus of nations in which each unique national voice enriches the human total. Fascists cast themselves as imperious soloists for whom all others are underlings. Other nations exist only to serve the fascists' national purposes.

The idea of a communist "International" is entirely consistent with Marxist thinking, but an international union of fascists is a contradiction in terms. (Notably, those fascists who toyed with such ideas got nowhere.) Even fascist states that fight against a common enemy can form only tactical, short-term alliances; in the end, fascist nationalism is radically exclusive and essentially intolerant.

Fascist totalitarianism

The fascist state is, therefore, totalitarian in multiple senses. On the level of judgment and opinion, it demands the total subjection of all our moral and cognitive faculties to the purposes of the state. At the level of practice, it is bent upon the total coordination and control of all aspects of human life. The totalitarianism of the fascist state extends even beyond its own borders. Other political communities—

their rights and welfare—are entirely subsumed under the goals that the national political community sets for itself. Hence, the fascist state is totalitarian both inwardly in regard to its own community and outwardly in regard to all other peoples. It forms the single all-embracing criterion for thought and action, a complete law unto itself.

Fascism and Racism

Although most forms of fascism have significant racist elements, it is difficult to point to a binding logical connection between the two. In practice, the various fascist movements related to **racism** in strikingly different ways. In Germany, racial hatred was overwhelming and obsessive. In other fascist states, it was secondary to nationalist and statist motifs. In others still—the Italian case is the outstanding example— racism was not an integral part of the original fascist doctrine. Only under pressure from its Nazi allies were racial laws introduced into Italian fascist practice, and even then they were not fully implemented. Despite this very mixed record, it is racism and the heinous atrocities committed in its name that are probably more firmly identified with fascism than any of its other unsavory characteristics.

The origins of modern racism

Racism, in the simple sense of discrimination on the basis of racial characteristics, is one of the oldest and most prevalent of human vices. As a systematic worldview and political ideology, however, it is of relatively recent origin. It emerged in the nineteenth century as a mixture of half-baked Darwinist ideas, German romantic mythology, traditional religious anti-semitism, and simple political and economic opportunism. As a systematic ideology, racism is fundamentally different from the kind of run-of-the-mill bigotry with which we are all familiar. Racist ideology ascribes momentous consequences to racial belonging. Human history, it claims, is essentially the history of the struggle between races.

Racism as an ideology

For ideological racists, the concept "humanity" has little meaning; the difference between races, they claim, is far more significant than what binds them together. The various races not only possess different intellectual capacities, they are also differently endowed morally and culturally. This is not a matter of sociological accident; it is a genetically irrevocable fate. Some races are destined to be creative and dynamic; others are ordained to be barren and parasitical. Some are by nature upright and honorable; others are congenitally devious and unreliable. These distinctions are usually followed by clear programmatic recommendations: the master races are entitled to rule; the menial races are fated to serve.

Racist ideology also has a taste for grand conspiratorial theories. Crisis and misfortune—which form the typical background for racist ideologies—are often explained as part of a sinister master plan of a lowly racial group to achieve their goal: world domination. (Invariably, small, vulnerable groups are named as the potential world-dominators.) In the most demented of these conspiratorial scenarios, the means by which domination is to be achieved is through polluting the racial purity of the most noble race. The physical annihilation of the offenders—every last one; any survivors will only begin the devilish work again—is, therefore, the highest human good.

Rather than recite the formal elements that went into racist ideology, far more will be conveyed by quoting one of its most notorious practitioners, Heinrich Himmler, head of the SS, who tells his men:

> *We must be honest, decent, loyal and comradely to members of our own race—and to no one else. How the Russians fare, how the Czechs fare is a matter of complete indifference to me . . . Whether other peoples live well or die of hunger interests me only insofar as we need them as slaves for our culture; apart from that I couldn't care less.*

Of course, there is no point in being cruel for its own sake. After all, Himmler continues, we are "the only ones in the world to treat animals decently" and we will be decent to these "human animals" as well. The "sacred law of the future," Himmler concludes, is that we have a duty to care only for our own race; "Everything else is a matter of indifference to us."

The Nazi program of exterminating the Jews, Himmler declared on another occasion, will be carried out to its final conclusion. In the pursuit of this great goal, Aryan morality requires repressing any instinct born of weakness to shield Jews from their deserved fate. And Himmler observes:

> *Most of you know what it's like when 100 corpses lie side by side, or 500 corpses or a 1000 corpses. To have seen this [job] through and to have remained decent human beings (apart from a few instances of human weakness), that is what has made us tough. It is a glorious page in our history.*[11]

Nazi racism

Although the racial campaign against the Jews was incomparably the most demonic and lethal, the Nazi vision of a homogeneous racial state was far from exhausted by anti-semitism. Racism was all-pervasive and fanatical. Apart from the Jews, other ethnic communities, such as the Gypsies, suffered bitterly at Nazis hands. Blacks were portrayed as low-grade biological creatures who were unable to rise above primitive infantility. Nazi propaganda proclaimed that blacks were being manipulated by the Jews to do their dirty work, that is, to pollute the racial excellence of the German stock by infecting it with inferior "mongrel" blood.

11. "Heinrich Himmler on SS Morality and SS Achievement," in *Fascism: Three Major Regimes*, ed. Heinz Lubasz (New York: Wiley, 1973) 121–22.

The mentally ill and the congenitally handicapped were also declared to be threats to the racial hygiene of the German **volk**. Homosexuals were treated as deformed creatures that a healthy racial community could not tolerate. "Asocial" types such as the chronically unemployed, vagrants, and non-conformists of various kinds were also said to pose serious threats to racial health. As many as 350,000 Germans were forcibly sterilized or compelled to undergo abortions in order to preserve the purity of the Aryan race. Euthanasia was also widely practiced.

Racial themes intermingle with totalitarian policies in the Nazi treatment of male homosexuals, who by their perverse practices, Himmler declared, endangered the procreative capacity of the German people. What takes place in the sexual sphere is not a private matter. It is the key to the biological survival of the volk. Hence, as part of the state's mission to cultivate the best and most homogeneous racial stock possible, it was imperative to severely punish those who refused to shoulder their racial responsibilities. Given these assumptions, is it surprising that the Nazis viewed women as "reproduction machines" whose sole concerns ought to be "children, kitchen, and church" ("Kinder, Kuche, und Kirche")?[12]

Aryan vs. Jew The image of the Aryan—blond, blue-eyed, tall, athletic, disciplined, and loyal—became the central totem of Nazi propaganda. Racial features were physically measured and categorized in all manner of scales and graphs. High levels of racial purity were necessary conditions for acceptance into elite units such as the SS. In contrast stood the Jew: short, bow-legged, hunched, hairy, beady-eyed, and hook-nosed. He represented racial degeneration in its purest and most dangerous form. Jewish culture and thought could not help but reflect Jewish biological degeneracy. Jewish art was displayed as a model of the grotesque. Jewish music was prohibited. Jewish science (Einsteinian relativity, Freudian psychoanalysis, etc.) was banned from German universities.

But it was Jewish political thinking and activity that represented the greatest threat to the Aryan race, for here they revealed their most sinister and cunning designs. The Jews constituted the dynamic force behind Bolshevism. From Marx to Trotsky, the drive to social justice, egalitarianism, and internationalism was their doing. What stood behind these diabolical ideas, Nazi racial theorists contended, had nothing to do with social conscience or moral sensitivity. These Jews propagated egalitarian-universalist ideas in order to undermine Aryan racial superiority. By reducing all peoples to the same mediocre level, they only sought to blur the patent superiority of the higher races. Furthermore, by instigating class conflict, they hoped to weaken Aryan racial solidarity. Their ultimate object was clear: to subvert the natural racial hierarchy of humanity so as to establish themselves as its undisputed masters.

---

12. For an exhaustive study of Nazi racism see Michael Burleigh and Wolfgang Wippermann, *The Racial State: Germany 1933–1945* (Cambridge: Cambridge University Press, 1991).

But the Jewish conspiracy was far too crafty to associate itself only with the left wing. In a shrewd ploy, the Jews also conspired to control the capitalist market, Wall Street finances, and industrial production. When the stalwart German worker suffered from the ravages of the depression, it was Jewish speculators who were lining their pockets. The Jews were both capitalists and communists. On the one hand they despoiled the "small man" by manipulating economic forces; on the other they exploited the unrest their manipulations caused by fomenting class conflict. It was a devilish conspiracy and it was everywhere.

To protect themselves against the omnipresent Jewish enemy, the Nazis took a number of radical steps. The Nuremburg Laws (1935) prohibited Germans working for Jews, serving Jews, conducting social relations with Jews, and of course, cohabiting with or marrying Jews. Anyone with a Jewish grandparent was deprived of German citizenship. More racial legislation followed. Jews could not teach or study in the university. They could not work in any government-related job such as the civil service or the legal profession. They were prohibited from attending concerts or from walking on certain streets. The areas in which they were permitted to live were severely restricted. Jewish businesses were closed. Distinctive yellow badges and arm bands reading "Jew" had to be worn at all times. All of this, however, was only a relatively mild prelude to the **final solution**.

The final solution
With the outbreak of World War II, the bestial machinery of mass extermination was set into place. Concentration camps were established both in Germany and in the East, and different methods of assembly-line murder were experimented with and perfected. Crammed into sealed trains, Europe's Jews were shipped eastward. Those who survived the harrowing trip and were physically fit were put to work in ghastly labor brigades. Most perished from malnutrition and exposure. Those who were less than physically fit were gassed to death and their bodies burned in crematoria. The smell of charred flesh carried for miles around. Among the six million murdered were one and half million children.

The Fuhrer (Leader) Principle

Whether it was Hitler as Fuhrer or Mussolini as Duce, the "leader" was the linchpin of the entire fascist system. His very person was understood to be the essential embodiment of the communal will. Hence, there were no limits to the reverence and adulation due him. "Mussolini is never wrong," read a mass-produced Italian poster. The sheer magnitude of the Hitler mania that swept Germany in the 1930s defies any simple characterization. This cult of the personality—carefully orchestrated from above—attributed to the leader superhuman qualities of infallible wisdom, saintliness, and heroic determination. It was an extraordinary and unprecedented form of what Max Weber had called **charismatic leadership**.

Although the leader's voice was said to be the authentic articulation of the communal will, this of course is not to be taken in the democratic sense. The leader represented what the popular will would be were it flawless and ideal, certainly not what the popular will happened to be at any given moment. As the incarnation of the national will, the leader was in no way accountable to the people for his actions. It was the leader's role to decide and the people's role to applaud and follow. The people and the leader were said to act as one, but it was the kind of unity that marks the relationship between a horse and its rider.

The leader did more than lead. No less important was the canny ability of Mussolini and especially Hitler to bridge the psychic distance between the leader and the led. Many Germans testify to having felt themselves spiritually elevated by the proximity of the Fuhrer. They sensed that he was addressing them directly, personally, and immediately. Many lost and desperate souls were convinced that he cared for them individually. The Fuhrer overcame the anonymity and alienation of mass society as well as mitigating the pain of economic hardship—all this without any real change in concrete circumstances. The exhilarating Fuhrer experience galvanized communal unity much as racial solidarity plastered over the deep cleavages of a class-ridden society. Just as individuals in a theater riveted by the same overpowering dramatic experience become a psychic community, so many Germans became part of an imagined spiritual fellowship in the light of the Fuhrer's personality and guidance.

Fascist Corporatism

Neither right nor left
Mussolini is only the most prominent of the many key figures who came to fascism by way of socialism and anarcho-syndicalism. The Nazis also had their anti-capitalist, national-socialist wing. What united these "left-wingers of the right" was their rejection of both liberal capitalism and Marxist communism. Instead they advocated a third way that claimed to overcome the defects of both.

Rejection of capitalism and Marxism
Liberal capitalism was unacceptable on a number of grounds: (1) it exploited the "small man" in favor of financiers, magnates, and speculators; (2) its individualism and cutthroat competition fomented class hatred rather than reconciling the various economic strata of the national community; (3) it was a haphazard and inefficient system by which to mobilize national economic resources.

The failures of Marxism were, if anything, more serious: (1) it focused on the working class rather than on the national community; (2) it incited class hatred rather than encouraging the collaboration of the various economic strata in the national interest; (3) it rejected nationalism in favor of a commitment to universalist goals; (4) it advocated egalitarianism rather than social hierarchy.

Liberal capitalism's advantages were its easy compatibility with nationalism, the hierarchical structure it created, the initiative it encouraged, and its avoidance of revolutionary rhetoric. By contrast, the strong points of socialism were its concern with the dispossessed and its ability to mobilize communal resources toward specified goals. What was necessary, the fascists argued, was a new synthesis, one that was neither right nor left. It would unite the protection of the workers and the mobilization of communal resources with nationalism, hierarchy, and class collaboration. It would be a socialism befitting the organic national community, not the socialism of a single class. "Workers of all classes unite," the fascists might have paraphrased the Marxist slogan, "you have only national glory to gain."

Corporatism

In Italy this revamped "socialism under the national aegis" went by the name **corporatism**. (Corporatism did not have any significant influence on the Nazi economy in Germany. Although capitalist structures were made to serve the cause of national power, corporatism as a specific system of economic organization was not adopted.) While the term is considerably older than modern fascism, having been a favorite theme of the reactionary right in the nineteenth century, corporatism was revived and reinterpreted by the theorists of Italian fascism. In its original sense, corporatism described the medieval economic system in which all those involved in a particular trade, whether workers or employers, were organized in a single corporation. Corporations acted to enforce rules of trade and to preserve

Thousands of helmeted German soldiers listen as Hitler speaks at the Nuremburg Rally of 1936.

peace between different interests within the profession. Many Catholic clerics were sympathetic to these arrangements because they seemed to hold out the promise of a cooperative, harmonized social system undisturbed either by liberal competition or by socialist class conflict. Corporatism was, in fact, the official economic policy of the Vatican during much of the nineteenth century.

Fascists were drawn to corporatism because it refused to recognize the existence of incompatible economic interests within the nation. It recognized only the social whole and, consequently, understood all sectarian interests as subordinate and partial. In the fascist version of corporatism, the totalitarian state acts as the final arbiter between the various elements that comprise the national community. Embodying the organic national will, the state manages and resolves social conflict. It coordinates class interests and oversees peaceful collaboration between all economic sectors for the general welfare. A "higher social justice," Mussolini proclaimed, would result from this socialism in the national interest.

Corporatism in practice   In practice, corporatism turned out to be something quite different. Rather than cultivating a nationalized socialism, corporatism retained most capitalist structures intact while subordinating them to what the fascists declared to be the national interest. It was a working compromise between free-enterprise capitalism and the requirements of a totalitarian state. Although the fascist state intervened directly in the economy, it neither coordinated a planned economy in the style of the communists nor acted to insure social justice and raise standards of living in the manner of the moderate socialists. If workers' interests were protected, it was to expedite efficient production. In the end, fascist socialism meant little more than class collaboration under state auspices.

Corporatism put an end to all independent labor-union activity. Strikes and all other forms of working-class insubordination were strictly prohibited. Economic organization was by industry, that is, workers and employers within a single collaborative framework. Although plant owners and workers conferred together on production schedules, the hierarchical lines of command were not altered. The conduct of business remained in the hands of the owners. Beyond being lectured about their national duties, workers were permitted to do little more than contribute their know-how toward the solution of production-related problems.

But corporatism did not allow the wealthy to pursue their profits unhindered. The fascist state controlled all classes, the wealthy included. Industrialists and financiers who had supported the fascists in the hope that they would be subservient to the will of the propertied right were sorely disappointed. The fascist state forced even the most powerful capitalists to bow to its dictates. If, for example, the capitalists collaborated with the workers or accepted government production directives, it was often against their will. In the end, fascist objectives were different from those of the capitalists. While the latter were concerned with profits, the former were set on increasing national productive capacity. In essence then, corporatism was the fascist strategy for directing both capitalist wealth and working-class labor toward the end of national power.

Theories of Fascism

Identifying fascism with the enemy

Fascism is so contentious a subject that it divides analysts into distinct ideological camps. It would involve only little exaggeration to say: "Tell me what your interpretation of fascism is and I'll tell you what your politics are." Because fascism has become associated with loathsome politics, many have tended to identify it with the ideological position they most detest. Marxists understand fascism as a predictable outgrowth of liberal capitalism; many liberals like to classify fascism together with communism as a variant of totalitarianism; conservatives assure us that fascism is a typical product of modern mass society.

Some refuse to attribute broad historical significance to the fascist phenomenon. For them (as we noted above), it is a freakish parenthesis in European history. Others relate it narrowly to the peculiar and atypical development of certain European states. Still others claim that it grew out of the authoritarian streak in Teutonic character or the hot-blooded excesses of the Latin temperament. But these views have lost much of their appeal over the years. Fascism has come to be recognized as a phenomenon with deep significance for Western history, one that cannot be accounted for by restricted ad hoc explanations.

Although interpretations of fascism come in too many varieties to be neatly pigeonholed, they can be broadly categorized under two easily remembered headings: class and mass. Some theorists, most often Marxists to some degree or other, understand Fascism as a consequence of capitalist class conflict. Theorists of a conservative and liberal disposition, by contrast, tend to see fascism as symptomatic of a general cultural crisis afflicting modern mass society. Let us take them up by turn.

Class-Based Theories

For Marxists, fascism is a direct consequence of the failure of liberalism. As long as capitalism enjoys periods of relative stability and prosperity, it is able to camouflage its essentially exploitative and repressive character. It can afford to keep up the pretense of pluralism, democratic competition, and civil rights because the privileged position of the monied and propertied is not essentially threatened. But when crisis hits and liberal capitalism can no longer rule by consensual, democratic means, it is forced to reveal its true face.

When the economic crash comes, as it must, liberals are forced to drop their deceptively humane mask. In place of non-violent domination via ideological indoctrination, information-control, and veiled threats of punishment, capitalism is now forced to make its repressive character brutally explicit. It is compelled to remove its silk gloves and revert to its (ever-ready) iron fist. Fascism is, therefore, not an essentially new form of rule; it is only capitalist dictatorship in its most exposed form. Fascism is capitalism when its conventional machinery of repression has failed—capitalism by other and more violent means. As defined by a communist theorist in the early 1930s: "Fascism is the open terrorist dictatorship of the most reactionary, most chauvinist and most imperialist elements in finance capital."[13]

A fascist-capitalist alliance

As evidence, defenders of this theory point to the largely middle-class nature of fascist support. Those who were threatened by the economic crisis—fearing that it would bring the working class to power—abandoned their erstwhile liberalism in favor of the fascists, who promised to ensure their continued dominance. Moreover, at decisive moments in fascist development, influential sections of the economic patriciate both contributed heavily to fascist coffers and lent it crucial political support. Most significantly of all, fascism in practice, despite all its pseudo-socialist rhetoric, defended capitalism and retained its major structures and privileges intact. One contemporary Marxist put it this way: "Fascism and big business thus had essentially identical interests. The fascists consolidated and increased their power. Industry extracted additional profits. One hand washed the other."[14]

Critiques of class theories

The radical clarity of this theory is marred by a number of major difficulties. First, why would a group of down-at-the-heels upstarts act to support the interests of finance capital? Casting Hitler and Mussolini as crusaders whose true object was to save capitalism strains the imagination no less than it strains the evidence. Second, accepting this theory would involve us in quite a questionable hypothesis; it would make all of fascist ideology—its irrationalism, ethical idealism, nationalist mystique, racism, and anti-semitism—into an elaborate diversionary tactic the purpose of which was really to save capitalism. Neither is the role of the financial magnates nearly as clear as Marxist theorists like to make it. According to the best evidence available, the bulk of the wealthy did not support the fascists. Finally, if it must be admitted that fascism did not dismantle the main supports of capitalism, neither can it be said that it acted as the unmitigated champion of capitalist interests. As we noted above, the fascist state was hardly a capitalist heaven. Capitalism marched to the tune of fascism, not vice versa.

Psycho-social forces

One important variant on the class theory adds psycho-social motives to the purely economic ones described above. According to this view, those who abandoned the liberal center for the fascist right did so out of a complex set of motives that went considerably beyond calculation of economic interest. Emotions such as resentment, envy, fear, alienation, loss of control, status panic, and moral indignation were actively at work. The lower middle classes were drawn to the fascist banner because of the psychological distress they suffered rather than as a matter of the objective dialectics of capitalist development.[15]

---

13. G. Dimitrov to the Third Communist International. See Renzo De Felice, *Interpretations of Fascism* (Cambridge, Mass.: Harvard University Press, 1977) 30 ff.

14. Martin Kitchen, *Fascism* (London: Macmillan, 1976) 47. For a more sophisticated Marxist analysis that recognizes the extraordinary nature of the fascist state and its relative independence from the capitalist class see Nicos Poulantzas, *Fascism and Dictatorship* (London: Verso, 1979).

15. Best known among analyses of this kind are Eric Fromm, *Escape From Freedom* (New York: Holt, 1941), and Theodor Adorno et al., *The Authoritarian Personality* (New York: Harper, 1950).

Mass-Based Theories

The fascist-com-
munist parallel

Liberals tend to reject such class-based theories. Fascism, they claim, needs to be understood in broader cultural terms. At the height of the Cold War in the 1950s and 1960s, when communism was perceived as the great threat to Western liberal civilization, many tended to assimilate communism and fascism into a single political category: totalitarianism. From this perspective, fascism and communism are siblings—more alike than they are different. Both are examples of modern mass politics with its typically levelling, lock-step, and violent character. Among the many unmistakably common elements are: (1) an elaborate ideology that rejects the existing world and projects forward to a perfect future; (2) a single mass party hierarchically organized and directed by a single leader; (3) a system of mass terror that liquidates enemies and intimidates others into silent conformism; (4) total control of all information, communication, and education; (5) central control of the entire economy through state-directed bureaucratic coordination.[16]

Critiques
of the parallel

Critics on the left complained that totalitarianism was more a partisan-political than an academic-analytic category. Theorists of totalitarianism, they charged, were so carried away with cold-warrior zeal to tarnish communism by associating it with fascism that they failed to see the glaring differences between them. At the most basic level, they belonged to wholly different moral categories. While fascism was totally and irremediably evil in both conception and execution, communism, whatever its unforgivable sins, was nevertheless noble in intention. Critics were also unhappy with the sweeping and ambiguous totalitarian label that, in their view, failed to appreciate the differences in historical context, social composition, political objectives, etc., that distinguished fascists from communists.[17]

Fascism and
modernization

But the concept "totalitarianism" is not an interpretation of fascism's significance and character. At best, it is a political category or typological niche in which to fit the fascist phenomenon. For interpretations, most liberal democrats are partial to theories that understand fascism as an outgrowth of modern mass society. Fascism is bound up with the upheavals of modernization in general rather than with the dynamics of capitalist economics in particular. The transition from traditional to modern society occasions painful dislocations economically, socially, and psychologically. Old familiar social forms and beliefs disintegrate before the new and highly aggressive forces of urbanization, industrialization, and secularization. In quick succession, family links weaken, religious authority wanes, face-to-face communal life is replaced by competitive, atomized city life, custom and tradition are

16. Carl J. Friedrich and Zbigniew K. Brzezinski, *Totalitarian Dictatorship and Autocracy* (Cambridge, Mass.: Harvard University Press, 1965). See also Hannah Arendt, *The Origins of Totalitarianism* (New York: Harcourt, Brace and World, 1968).

17. For a survey of these criticisms see A. James Gregor, *Interpretations of Fascism* (Morristown, N.J.: General Learning Press, 1974) 213–37.

supplanted by the cold rationality of the market place. In a dozen decades, Europe experienced more profound transformations and discontinuities than in the thousand years before.

Enormous bureaucratic structures developed in order to service and regulate the mass of individuals who crowded into the cities. Housing, transportation, and education were standardized and "massified," as were consumption and leisure activities. Many felt themselves lost in a vast social apparatus whose workings they could not understand and against whose power they felt distressingly helpless. It was all impersonal, lonely, and meaningless. Not surprisingly, these masses of rootless, docile individuals were putty in the hands of the modern state. Tragically, enlightenment and modernity that were to bring personal autonomy and self-reliance brought instead conformity and powerlessness.

This disoriented mass of humanity was, simultaneously, thrust into the political arena. In the name of democratization and national self-expression, they were called upon to exercise their sovereign will. To succeed electorally, political parties now had to appeal to typical mass frustrations and anxieties. Alienated and confused, the masses were the raw material out of which demagogues could construct political movements that promised all manner of pie-in-the-sky. Because their world was confusing and insecure, many of these mass individuals were willing to surrender whatever freedom they possessed in return for a sense of belonging and self-confidence. All the more so when their ordinary insecurities were aggravated by a sufficiently acute crisis. Autonomy and self-direction were then bartered away for order, authority, and certainty.[18]

Ortega's view

For theorists like Ortega y Gasset (see Chapter 2), it was less the psychological dislocations of modernization that accounted for the fascist phenomenon than the coarseness and vulgarity of the modern mass individual. The masses, he argued, were not insecure; they were dangerously self-confident. When representatives of the masses rose to positions of political leadership, they unashamedly brought with them all the ideological and behavioral baggage that is so typical of their kind. Ortega draws a damning composite of this mass character; it includes the tendency to half-baked ideas, the impatient preference for once-and-for-all solutions, arbitrariness and inconsistency, anti-intellectualism, a resentment toward all they do not understand, a vengeful, authoritarian style, enmity toward superior human beings, the inability to tolerate moral ambiguity, and the racial and ethnic prejudices of the gutter. Fascism is then a "mass" movement in the simplest sense of the word: it reflects and caters to the crude tastes of the mass individual.

Critiques of mass theories

Mass-centered theories of fascism confront their own characteristic problems. First of all, they fail to account for the undeniably greater appeal of fascism to the middle classes. Were fascism an outgrowth of the amorphous masses, we would expect support for it to be more evenly distributed among the various classes. Sec-

---

18. One very respected work exploring these themes is William Kornhauser, *The Politics of Mass Society* (New York: Free Press, 1959).

ond, mass theories tend to pitch their arguments at such broad levels of generalization that it is often difficult to pin them down to specific causal connections of the "this caused that" variety. To speak, as they do, of the "character of the mass individual" or of "the moral crisis of modern civilization" is to float weightlessly above the tangible historical facts that surrounded the fascist takeovers. By disengaging from the actual interests that moved specific groups in the struggle for power, mass theories have a way of undermining their concrete explanatory power.[19]

Fascism: Dead or Alive?

Why fascism
threatens
Those who expect a clear answer to the question posed in the above subheading will be disappointed. Beyond the difficulty that predicting the future inevitably poses, responding to this question would mean giving definitive answers to all the questions we raised in the course of this discussion, and deliberately left open. We would have to choose one interpretation of fascism out of the many contenders, because without a clear idea of what fascism is, we could hardly assess its chances of resurgence. Nevertheless, just asking the question is highly significant. Communism is barely cold in its historical grave, yet few fear that it will spring to life again. Fascism, by contrast, although dead and buried for a half century, continues to raise its fearful specter. Why should this be so?

As a systematic ideology and practice, communism can be judged by relatively simple standards of success and failure. In an odd way, its own ideological proclamations served as a powerful self-critique. It spoke of the great achievements of socialism while everyone knew better. It spoke of freedom and equality when the Gulag was an open secret. It promised to liberate humanity from need, repression, and alienation. And clearly it failed.

Fascism, by contrast, is difficult to judge by commonly available criteria of success and failure. Its macabre fascination has to do precisely with its unfathomable qualities: its irrationalism, its appeal to primordial tribal bonds, its exploitation of mass anxieties. That it crashed to a flaming defeat rather than collapsing out of its own inner contradictions only adds to the perverse mystique that fascism continues to hold for some notorious and marginal groups.

Fascist
flash points
Fascism, in the form we know it, is inseparable from the experience of the inter-war generation. Obviously, when we deliberate about its current viability, we are not concerned with a coming to life of the fascism of 1935. Clearly, were it to flourish again, fascism would be something quite different—something new but with sufficient points of similarity to inter-war fascism to be recognizable as a mutant. Where in our contemporary world are the flash points out of which such a reconstituted fascism might develop?

---

19. For fuller surveys of these and other theories of fascism see Gregor's *Interpretations of Fascism*, and Renzo De Felice, *Interpretations of Fascism* (Cambridge, Mass.: Harvard University Press, 1977).

Although generally conceded that no full-dress fascist movements of major significance exist currently, elements of fascism are alarmingly prevalent. Indeed, many believe that they are more prevalent in the Europe of the 1990s than at any time since 1945. This is particularly dismaying because those who flirt with fascism today are no longer the aging remnants of the pre-war fascist generation. This is a new generation speaking the idiom of fascism in the contemporary style.

Its adherents are for the most part young, unskilled, only partially employed, and usually poorly educated. Typically, they are lower middle class or working class in economic background. They can be found in the larger cities of most of the West European democracies. Whether as skinheads, football hooligans, motorcycle gangs, or partisans of a violent rock music culture, their element is exhibitionist bravado, machismo, and intolerance. Although their self-identification with fascism is frequently quite explicit, there tends to be a somewhat farcical and buffoon-like quality to their pronouncements. Like the vagrant ex-combatants of World War I, these groups would appear to form the hard core (the shock troops) of a potential fascist comeback. The typical axis about which these fascist-like groups center is xenophobia—hatred of and violence toward foreigners, whether North Africans, Turks, Pakistanis, Jews, or East Europeans.

The more respectable side of contemporary neo-fascism are the parties of the radical right, and they have gained substantial electoral footholds in some major West European states. Although it is generally thought they lack the full complement of fascist attributes, sufficient points of contact exist to justify the comparison. Their scare tactics are aimed at popular fears—again the lower middle class is very much in evidence—of an invasion of uncouth foreigners who carry sexual diseases, monopolize scarce jobs, and corrupt the national character. This compound of racism, chauvinism, strong-arm tactics, and anti-democratic authoritarianism cannot help but jar the historical memory.

Another potential flash point for a fascist revival is in the disintegrated remains of the ex-Soviet empire. The collapse of communism as an ideology and practice created a political vacuum into which many grotesque ideological eccentrics are being drawn. For some, the dizzyingly rapid fall from great-power status to charity case has kindled intense feelings of humiliation and resentment. Moreover, the angry reaction against whatever is tainted with communism has given the radical right a powerful boost. Long-repressed nationalist feelings that often included reactionary nostalgia, anti-semitism, and general xenophobia have resurfaced and won many converts. The proliferation of national rivalries only aggravates the tendency to insularity and authoritarianism. Destitution and personal insecurity have created an acute vulnerability to demagogic leadership and to conspiratorial tales of hidden culprits and sinister plots. Add to all this the weakness of the democratic tradition and it becomes clear that a healthy dose of concern is in order.

That fascism flickers in the embers is a safe bet; whether it will burst into flames is beyond anyone's ability to say.

Suggestions for Further Reading

Adorno, Theodore et al. *The Authoritarian Personality.* New York: Norton, 1969.

Allardyce, Gilbert, ed. *The Place of Fascism in European History.* Englewood Cliffs, N.J.: Prentice Hall, 1971.

Arendt, Hannah. *The Origins of Totalitarianism.* New York: Harcourt, Brace and World, 1968.

Bullock, Alan. *Hitler: A Study in Tyranny.* New York: Harper Torchbooks, 1964.

———. *Hitler and Stalin: Parallel Lives.* New York: HarperCollins, 1991.

Burleigh, Michael, and Wolfgang Wippermann. *The Racial State: Germany 1933–1945.* Cambridge: Cambridge University Press, 1991.

De Felice, Renzo. *Interpretations of Fascism.* Cambridge, Mass.: Harvard University Press, 1977.

Friedrich, Carl J., and Zbigniew Brzezinski. *Totalitarian Dictatorship and Autocracy.* Cambridge, Mass.: Harvard University Press, 1965.

Fromm, Erich. *Escape From Freedom.* 1941. Reprint, New York: Avon Books, 1965.

Gregor, A. James. *Interpretations of Fascism.* (Morristown, N.J.: General Learning Press, 1974.

———. *Young Mussolini and the Intellectual Origins of Fascism.* Berkeley: University of California Press, 1979.

Kitchen, Martin. *Fascism.* London: Macmillan, 1976.

Laqueur, Walter. *Fascism: A Reader's Guide.* Berkeley: University of California Press, 1976.

Laqueur, Walter, and George Mosse, eds. *International Fascism: 1920–1945.* New York: Harper and Row, 1966.

Lubasz, Heinz, ed. *Fascism: Three Major Regimes.* New York: Wiley, 1973.

Mosse, George. *The Crisis of German Ideology.* 1964. Reprint, New York: Howard Fertig, 1978.

———. *Nazi Culture: Intellectual, Social and Cultural Life in the Third Reich.* New York: Grosset and Dunlap, 1966.

Nolte, Ernst. *Three Faces of Fascism.* New York: Holt, Rinehart and Winston, 1966.

Poulantzas, Nicos. *Fascism and Dictatorship.* London: Verso, 1979.

Stern, Fritz. *The Politics of Cultural Despair.* Garden City, N.Y.: Anchor Books, 1965.

Sternhell, Zeev. *Neither Right nor Left.* Berkeley: University of California Press, 1986.

Sternhell, Zeev, with Mario Sznajder and Maia Asherl. *The Birth of Fascist Ideology: From Cultural Rebellion to Political Revolution.* Princeton: Princeton University Press, 1993.

Talmon, J. L. *The Origins of Totalitarian Democracy.* New York: Norton, 1970.

Woolf, S. J., ed. *Fascism in Europe.* London: Methuen, 1981.

Chapter *8*

Nationalism: Very Much Alive

Nationalism as an Ideology: Some Initial Considerations

The vitality of nationalism

Many progressive-cosmopolitan thinkers have anxiously awaited the demise of nationalism. Like alchemy and astrology, it was a backward phenomenon soon to be replaced by more enlightened creeds. A good piece of advice to these progressives would be not to hold their breaths. Of all the socio-political doctrines that emerged in the eighteenth and nineteenth centuries, nationalism remains in many ways the most vital and dynamic at the end of the twentieth. The irony is obvious: doctrines like communism that confidently predicted the obsolescence of nationalism have themselves become obsolete. Even the Enlightenment belief in a single reason and a single humanity has been seriously challenged by the persistence of intense primordial national loyalties.

Nationalism is probably the most resilient, popular, and tenacious form of ideological commitment in the contemporary world. At first glance, this may appear quite curious. After all, nations have become increasingly interdependent and technology is shrinking the modern world into a global village. Is it not odd that the power of nationalism continues to be immense despite the growing homogenization of world culture? From Katmandu to Guadalajara the same jeans and running shoes are available, the same world-wide media networks operate, great multi-national banks and corporations thrive, the same sports heroes, film stars and musical idols are plastered on countless bedroom walls. Japanese VCRs are transported in American trucks, using Saudi Arabian fuel, over German-built roads, to be sold in British-owned department stores in Sao Paulo. The very book you are reading is a complex international effort. And yet, the primordial self-identification with a specific national community continues to have few competitors for depth, intensity, and endurance.

This chapter will attempt to unravel the paradox. First, however, we have to make a number of important preliminary stops to equip ourselves for handling this intriguing puzzle. At the outset, we must explore nationalism's relationship to ideology in general. Is nationalism an ideology comparable to anarchism, conservatism, or liberalism? It cannot be denied, on the one hand, that nationalism does many of the same things that other ideologies do: it legitimizes authority, fosters social cohesion, mobilizes mass support, guides political action, contributes to personal identity. And yet, nationalism is different.

Nationalism and World-View Ideologies

The uniqueness of nationalism

The most important differences between nationalism and general world-view ideologies are as follows:

1. Nationalism does not normally possess a broad and systematic world-view comparable to those that figure in liberalism or Marxism.
2. Nationalism does not usually relate to the critical issue of human nature in politics. Neither is it normally concerned with the general interpretations of history that form so large a part of other ideological systems.
3. Questions regarding the best form of government or the most desirable economic system do not normally form an integral part of nationalist thinking. (Insofar as these issues do enter the nationalist debate, they often become the source of national dissension rather than unity.)
4. Other staples of ideological discourse, such as the nature of social justice or the proper pace of political change, do not figure essentially in nationalist doctrines.

Lacking these core elements of political judgment, nationalism fails to provide clear ideological direction. It is neither right- nor left-wing, neither capitalist nor socialist, neither democratic nor dictatorial. Nationalism is compatible with almost all ideological positions. In fact, it is rare for a nationalist movement not to have its conservative, liberal, and radical wings. Nationalism has had its strident fascist versions, just as it has been wedded to egalitarian socialist programs. It has (as in the Chinese Communist case) been associated with revolutionary Marxist doctrines. It has supported xenophobic reactionary causes, messianic and romantic visions of human renewal, liberal democratic regimes, and a spate of garden-variety dictatorships. Like Proteus, the figure of classical mythology who readily took on different shapes and forms, nationalism is ideologically versatile.

Nationalism as a partial ideology

Nationalism may be described as a partial ideology. Its core propositions taken by themselves are insufficient to provide either a satisfactory account of the human political condition or a broad-based guide to political action. By itself nationalism offers inspiring symbols, a highly emotional rallying point for action, and some political objectives such as national independence. But it has considerably less to say in regard to the ways in which these goals should be pursued—via terrorism or via moral education, for example. Neither does the basic nationalist urge specify what concrete form the national community is to take when independence is finally achieved. Is it to be religious, militarist, or radically egalitarian? Lacking a socio-economic theory and a general philosophy of history, it has to supplement its national message with a political doctrine that comes to it from the fund of available ideological world-views.

This does not mean that the link between nationalism and ideological commitment is a casual one. On the contrary, the ideological world-view that shapes a particular nationalist movement is decisive for the character of its nationalist program. The concept of the nation that emerges from a humanist, secular, democratic nationalism is radically different from that which derives from a racist, mystical, reactionary nationalism. Questions such as who belongs to the nation, how open will the nation be to those who seek entry, what is the nation's historical mission, how will the nation relate to other nations cannot be fully answered without referring to the general ideological perspective that lends a distinctive character to nationalist sentiments.

Relatives of a fifteen-year-old Muslim combatant with the Bosnian army grieve over his body (July 1992).

Universal vs. particular

Nationalism differs from general world-view ideologies in yet another important way. Although it is hardly a secret that different socio-economic groups are attracted to different ideological positions—for example, the contemporary middle class to liberalism—ideological advocates are not particularly interested in presenting their ideas as those of a specific group. Liberals prefer to present their world-view as worthy of universal acceptance. Liberalism, its advocates contend, is humane and just, promising a fair deal to everyone, whatever their economic standing.

Even classical Marxists who speak expressly in the name of the proletariat make it clear that it is not the narrow interests of the proletariat as a class they are out to defend. Proletarian interests deserve to be defended because these interests are, in fact, the interests of humanity at large (see Chapter 5). The liberation of the proletariat, they argue, is the condition for universal human liberation.

Nationalists, by contrast, have no reason to obscure the ties that connect their ideas to a specific group. They speak quite obviously in the name of a certain people. Neither are they concerned with presenting their national program as valid for all regardless of race, creed or ethnic origin. Nationalist movements are particularist in their very essence. To be sure, some nationalist movements have understood their goals in grand historical terms—for example, many of the early American settlers saw the Colonies as a "New Jerusalem" possessing religious and political significance for all of civilization—but even in these cases their advocates will usually turn only to members of the national community for support. They have few illusions that the alleged national mission will carry much appeal for those outside the national fold. The quality of nationalist discourse is therefore unique among ideologies: it is only mildly concerned with justifications drawing upon universal criteria of validity.

Nationalism can't be argued

This leads to a third important distinction. While world-view ideologies are prone to present their doctrines in a relatively systematic and reasoned manner, nationalism is based, almost by definition, on an inexpressible sense of communality. At its core, nationalism describes attachments, identity, ancestry, and breeding more than it makes an argument. For most of us, national identity is a personal given, a birthright. It is, in other words, an issue about which it is difficult to reason. Clearly, there is no point in trying to convince a Canadian to become an Italian in the way that one might try convincing a liberal to become a conservative.

There is, therefore, a decisive difference between nationalism, the core of which is an incommunicable sense of belonging, and world-view ideologies whose axis is critical judgment and evaluation. While world-view ideologies such as liberalism and Marxism debate the logic of history and the laws of economics, nationalist discourse evokes highly charged personal images such as the fatherland and the mother tongue. Appropriately, some of the most effective presentations of nationalism are in the form of poetry, myths, and epics. When reasoned, systematic discourse does appear in nationalist literature, it is often debate over which ideological direction the nationalist movement should be following. Because of nationalism's non-reasoned, primordial quality, our normal practice of confronting the ideology under review with challenging intellectual dilemmas must be revised for the present chapter.

Summary

Let us briefly summarize the discussion to this point. Nationalism differs from world view ideologies on at least three important levels:

1. Nationalism in itself does not present a full-scale ideological analysis or program. In fact, most nationalisms are compatible with most ideological positions. Nationalist movements therefore blend two distinct elements: nationalist sentiment and a general world-view ideology.
2. Nationalism does not usually argue its case in universalist terms as do general world-view ideologies. The nationalist appeal is almost invariably particularist in character.
3. Nationalism normally rests on the evocation of a primordial sense of belonging as opposed to a systematically reasoned creed. Hence, basic nationalist loyalties tend to discourage the kinds of analytic discussions that are characteristic of general world-view ideologies.

Modern Nationalism as a Historical Novelty

National identity is unavoidable

Nationalism differs from general world-view ideologies in another way as well: its sheer prevalence and unavoidability. In our time, the sense of belonging to a national community has become a virtually universal phenomenon. It has become quite impossible to think of who we are without referring to our national identity. Few human groupings around the world have escaped the driving force that transforms tribes, villages, provinces, clans, ethnic and language groups into peoples with a developed national consciousness. Starting at the end of the eighteenth century, gaining momentum in the nineteenth, and reaching mass proportions in the twentieth, national consciousness has become an indispensable element in both the personal identity of individuals and the political identity of states. The nationalist revolution has changed how we think about our identity in ways that can be matched by few other historical transformations. In this important sense, the nationalist revolution is more appropriately compared to such overwhelming shifts in consciousness as the Renaissance or the Enlightenment than to the rise of specific ideologies such as socialism or conservatism.

Nationalism has become so pervasive a political force that it is the obligatory prism through which modern individuals view the world—whatever their ideological loyalties may be. The division of peoples into nations appears so familiar and natural that we can hardly imagine a world constructed around other organizing principles. The national idea is not (as ideological commitments are) a fundamentally controversial matter. While there is understandable repugnance toward nationalist movements that are egocentric, repressive, or violent, there is little serious opposition to distinguishing individuals and states in terms of their national identity.

Self-determination

To this point we have been using the term nationalism in the familiar sense of a communal, particularist ideology advanced by a specific nation in order to justify a claim for its own place in the sun. But nationalism has had a different face as well, one that was especially prominent at the time of the idea's birth and infancy in the late eighteenth and early nineteenth centuries. The doctrine of nationalism was then associated with a systematic and reasoned argument for the right of all nations to **self-determination**. Nationalism was a universal principle; it declared that all nations had the right to be sovereign over their own affairs.

When Woodrow Wilson in his celebrated Fourteen Points (enunciated at the end of World War I) proclaimed that self-determination is an essential right of all nations, he was expressing the century-old view that nations, like individuals, have rights—national rights. Peoples with sufficient socio-cultural cohesion, who possess a common will and feel themselves part of a common destiny, are entitled to conduct their communal lives as they see fit. To deny them this right is to repress a legitimate need of all peoples.

Nationalism as a doctrine justifying universal self-determination does not emerge out of an intense personal sense of national belonging. It is unlikely to inspire poetry or mass movements. Notably, no political parties in today's world dedicate themselves to achieving self-determination for all peoples. Compared with particularist, communal nationalism, self-determination is therefore a somewhat bloodless doctrine. In fact, nationalism in this abstract sense probably does not qualify as an ideology at all.

Ideology or not, the idea that nations are entitled to self-determination appears, in our contemporary world, familiar to the point of cliche. It is difficult for us to reconstruct how frightening and novel the idea must have been when it appeared. (The first use of the term "nationalism" was in 1798—coinciding almost exactly with the origins of the term "ideology.") For the greater part of human history, the idea of nationhood as the critical focus of self-identity and political belonging did not exist. Neither did the claim that national identity entitled a community to self-determination and political sovereignty. Insofar as nations can be said to have existed, they were shadowy, abstract presences that had little bearing on the form or legitimacy of political authority.

The Pre-Nationalist Era

Non-national
political
arrangements

But if nationalism is so modern, what were the forms that political authority took prior to its emergence? The most prevalent types of political organizations were local in character: villages, clans, tribes, regional leagues, and provincial feudal authority. There were also city-states, as in Classical Greece, where each sovereign unit wielded political authority over only a small part of the Greek-speaking people. Classical Greece lacked any over-arching national unity. At the other extreme were the great empires such as that created by the Romans: vast mosaics of many different units organized into a single empire and held together by legal and military coercion.

There were also dynastic states such as those that prevailed in Europe prior to the French Revolution. These were patch-quilts of local allegiances unified (often only weakly) into a single administrative unit by a central dynastic monarch. Notably, the monarch's claim to legitimacy was rooted in divine will; it had little to do with the national will. Even the medieval church, whose spiritual authority often became overtly political, was a form of public power that, like all the others we have mentioned, was unrelated to the sovereign national community.

If peasants in sixteenth-century France had been asked about who they were, the answer would have been in terms of their village, region, vocation, or family. They might have said that they were from Burgundy, they were carpenters, and they were part of the Bonhomme clan. National identity would not have been a part of their answer.

Conditions for
nationalism

But why? What accounts for the absence of national identity in the pre-modern era? First of all, nationalism is based on certain levels of communication, transportation, and education. Without these distance-conquering developments there is little chance that the local peasants' horizon would extend beyond their provincial allegiances. Lacking mobility and literacy, their outlook would be determined by the immediate social groups to which they belonged. Those who were from a different region or province, even if they spoke the same language, practiced the same religion, and derived from the same ethno-racial stock, would have been considered strangers.

The Dawning of Nationalist Consciousness

Shared identity

Only when intellectual horizons widened beyond the local was it possible to recognize the broader linguistic and cultural identities that distinguish peoples from each other. When other ethno-national units are recognized not merely as exotic fables and curiosities but as real cultures with sharply different characters, the idea of the nation begins to emerge. Nationalism is an integrating sensibility; it creates a single imagined community out of many individuals who, although they have no personal knowledge of each other, feel a sense of camaraderie based on loyalty to the idea of common cultural identity. Nationalism is the triumph of the abstract over the concrete and immediate. It focuses on an intangible national community that is beyond the actual experience of any single person. It is not surprising, therefore, that educated elites have normally been the first to grasp the national idea and spearhead nationalist movements.

Nationalism arose together with the first wave of European industrialization. Understanding the relationship between these two major transformations will give us an additional clue as to why nationalism is so peculiarly modern a phenomenon. Industrialization dealt a jolting blow to the traditional, face-to-face, rural settlements that were once the mainstay of European civilization. Agrarian, tight-knit, church-dominated communities were progressively undermined by the growth of industry that drew work-seekers to rapidly expanding cities. These bustling urban centers dissolved old traditions, loyalties, and beliefs just as they undermined traditional family life and eroded religious practice.

This process of transition is commonly known as **modernization**. Because it weakened the traditional focus of individual identity, modernization was a necessary condition for the rise of an alternate kind of personal loyalty: the national community. In this light, nationalism was a reaction to the personal and social dislocations initiated by the decline of traditional society. It created a national community in place of the traditional communities that were disintegrating. In an important sense, therefore, nationalism was a community-*re*creating movement, a psychological and political answer to the vacuum created by modernization. It provided a new framework of meaning and belonging that previously had been afforded by tradition, clan, church, or village.

Summary   Recapping the historical dimension of nationalism that has been presented above:

1. Nationalism differs from general world-view ideologies in its having become the virtually universal form of political allegiance. It is not so much a controversial ideology as the inescapable context of modern politics.
2. The doctrine of nationalism, particularly in its early stages, entailed a principled belief in the right of all nations to self-determination. This is quite distinct from the particularist loyalties that give rise to specific nationalist movements.
3. Nationalism is a historical novelty—not much more than two centuries old. Prior to nationalism, different bases of political loyalty and organization were common: city-states, empires, dynastic states, and assorted local forms of authority such as the tribal, the feudal, etc.
4. The lack of communication media, transportation, and literacy kept political horizons local in character. The creation of a national community—a single imagined community that binds individuals with no personal knowledge of each other—could not be accomplished without mobility and education.
5. Nationalism was a response to the dislocations initiated by modernization. It provided a surrogate community to replace the traditional local community that had been undermined by industrialization, secularization, and urbanization.

The Affinity Between Nationalism and Democracy

The process of modernization helps us understand the rise of the national community. But nationalism, as we noted above, has another face as well: the moral-political doctrine that all nations as a matter of principle have the right to self-determination. What are the origins of this unprecedented idea? And how does the doctrine of national self-determination relate to the rise of liberal democratic ideologies that were, simultaneously, making their mark on Western traditions of political thinking?

Kant's view   Perhaps the core idea of the post-Enlightenment democratic revolution was that individuals, as rational, moral, and interest-pursuing agents, had the right to decide for themselves what kind of life plan they would adopt. They were not mere wards of the church or the monarchy—minors who needed supervision or custody. Enlightenment, the great German philosopher Immanuel Kant had said, is the freedom to rely on one's own intelligence and moral discernment in the determination of personal and public affairs. All persons are uniquely endowed and inalienably entitled to realize the potential they possessed. Those who are subjected to superior force and are unable to translate their unique personal attributes into a concrete life plan are tragically stunted in their humanity.

Personal and national self-determination

Were we to substitute the word nation for individual in the preceding paragraph, we would have the essential idea of national self-determination. Nations, like individuals, have unique characters. Each has its own irreplaceable voice in the chorus of humanity. For a nation to be authentically creative, it must be free to express this, its innermost sensibility, in its own language and through its own cultural instruments. Its destiny (perhaps we could say its collective life plan) must be in its own hands.

"In its own hands" means political sovereignty. A fully realized national existence requires independent political institutions to translate its unique national will into concrete action. It is insufficient for the nation to be committed to abstract ideals that it is powerless to realize. Just as the human spirit requires a body, so the national spirit requires a body politic to express its will. The national moral character must be incarnated in day-to-day human relations shaped by national institutions. Nations prevented from embodying their wills in sovereign political institutions are crippled collectives.[1]

Nationalism and the Activation of the Masses

Although it seems odd from our contemporary perspectives, modern nationalism is an extension of liberal democratic ideas to the national community. The democratic slogan "liberty, equality, fraternity" can be applied without great contrivance to the national idea as well. If liberal democracy centers on the rights of individuals to have their voices freely heard within the political community, nationalism demands that the nation's voice be heard in the community of nations. If liberal democracy insists that all citizens are equal in rights and duties, nationalism recognizes the rights of all nations to self-determination as equally valid. The fraternity of nations so created, like a rich chorus in which every voice contributes its indispensable part, would be marked by mutual respect and harmony. In its initial context nationalism was a universalist idea promising self-determination and international concord.[2]

Nationalism and self-government

But if nationalism represented an extension of the liberal democratic idea to the nation, it should be added immediately that liberal democracy was fostered by the nationalist impulse as well. Indeed, to be fully appreciated, each of the two must be understood as a complementary part of a larger historical phenomenon. They are the twin portals leading to the modern activation of the common people. Royalists and reactionaries certainly understood the two as being part of an integrated revolutionary threat; they condemned them both with equal ferocity. After

---

1. Elie Kedouri, *Nationalism* (London: Hutchinson, 1966).
2. Benjamin Akzin, *State and Nation* (London: Hutchinson, 1964) 51–52.

all, nationalism shatters the monopoly on power that was traditionally held by the high-born and blue-blooded. In its simplest meaning, nationalism entails the sovereignty of the national will—not the will of a divine monarch or a hereditary aristocracy. In whatever form it takes, nationalism involves some form of self-government.

Nationalism
politicizes the
masses

Nationalism politicizes the masses by making wider and wider circles of individuals relevant to the political process. It disqualifies the pretensions of the privileged few to act in place of a passive and subject people. Of course, this does not necessarily lead to genuine democracy, but it does necessitate a constant appeal to the popular will. Even in those states (perhaps especially in those states) in which nationalism has inspired brutal dictatorial political systems, it is still the masses and their genuine will that the autocratic elite claims to represent. After the advent of nationalism, it has become extremely difficult to justify political power without at least alleging that it derives from a popular national mandate.

What constitutes
a people?

But the tie between the nationalist impulse and the democratic liberal movement goes deeper still. When the revolutionaries in France proclaimed that the source of all legitimate political power lay in the people, they were simultaneously making a democratic and a nationalist statement. To base political authority on the will of the people inevitably raises the obvious question: What constitutes a people? Is every motley throng of individuals deserving of that title? When does a group of separate persons become that morally charged entity, a people?

One very celebrated answer to this problem was provided by Jean Jacques Rousseau. Not every popular will, he declared, was morally deserving. For the will of the people to be sovereign, it had to incarnate the essential will of a united community—its "general will." A miscellany of individuals—one thrown together, for example, by geographic proximity but lacking any essential unity—even if it should happen to find itself in unanimous agreement on questions of public policy, would not be expressing the "general will" and, consequently, would lack legitimacy or moral weight. It would merely be expressing what Rousseau called the "will of all," that is, the wills of many self-interested individuals that, by chance, happen to coincide—a morally irrelevant category in Rousseau's teaching.

The people becomes a deserving moral-political entity only when it incorporates an essentially united will that transcends the many wills of separate individuals. This united will sets this people off from other peoples. Political communities directed by such a general will are, in Rousseau's teaching, legitimate, that is, their pronouncements are endowed with binding moral authority. Moreover, sovereign political institutions are required in order to realize this will in practice. What is it then that transforms atomistic individuals into a united people with the right to a sovereign political community? Rousseau's reply has been widely understood to be: an emotional and moral bonding whose source is a national language, culture, and history. It is this national cohesiveness and distinctness that confers moral significance upon a community's decisions and authorizes its sovereign institutions. Clearly, the democratic and the nationalist impulses are here virtually inextricable.

National/popular will

During the French Revolution, this blending of democratic and nationalist themes is everywhere in evidence. In the famed *Declaration of the Rights of Man*, the revolutionaries formulated one of the cardinal elements of their democratic faith as follows: "The source of all sovereignty resides essentially in the nation; no group or individual may exercise authority not emanating expressly therefrom." The rights of man and the national right to sovereign self-determination are here fused into a single whole. When in the same year (1789) the American colonists began the Preamble to the American Constitution with the words "We the people," they too were presenting a compound idea, a national *and* a democratic idea. The newly formed nation that had just broken away from the mother country was now drafting a constitution that would institutionalize the concrete manner in which the national/popular will would be expressed.

In the middle of the nineteenth century, John Stuart Mill, perhaps the most distinguished of all modern liberal theorists, described the relationship between nationalism and democracy in the following way:

A portion of mankind may be said to constitute a nationality, if they are united among themselves by common sympathies, which do not exist between them and any others—which make them cooperate with each other more willingly than with other people, desire to be under the same government and desire that it be a government by themselves, or a portion of themselves, exclusively.

Mill proceeds to the conclusion that has already become familiar to us:

Where the sentiment of nationality exists in any force, there is a prima facie case for uniting all members of the nationality under the same government, and a government to themselves apart. This is merely saying that the question of government ought to be decided by the governed.[3]

Once again, self-government and national self-determination appear to be indissociable.

In 1989, exactly two centuries after the French Revolution, when the states of Eastern Europe broke away from Soviet control, followed by the dismantling of the Soviet Union itself, the democratic and the nationalist ideas were once again inextricably bound up with each other. It is often impossible to distinguish between the part played in this remarkable drama by democratic ideas and by nationalist impulses. The appeals to human rights and to national rights are so interlaced in the

---

3. John Stuart Mill, *Considerations on Representative Government* (Chicago: Henry Regnery Co., 1962) 307–309. (The book originally appeared in 1861.)

rhetoric of liberation that one hardly knows where the one begins and the other ends. The call for an authentic expression of the national will clearly has a democratic dimension, just as the enthusiasm for popular elections must be understood in terms of the drive to national self-determination.

Summary   Summarizing the main points of this section:

1. The moral autonomy of individuals and of nations entails that both require sovereignty to implement their wills and realize their uniqueness. Individuals and nations whose distinct self-expression are obstructed by external force are tragically stunted.
2. Nationalism fosters the idea that legitimate government rests on the will of the national public. Hence, it activates the masses.
3. Nationalism demarcates the community whose will democratic institutions seek to express. When, for example, Rousseau argued that the only legitimate sovereign is the "general will," he was simultaneously expressing democratic and nationalist sentiments.

Nationalist Discourse: Rhetoric and Substance

The Idea of the Nation-State

To this point, we have avoided using the most critical of all terms associated with modern nationalism: the **nation-state**. The hyphenated unity, nation-state, signifies a fusion of two distinct ideas. Although they are hardly identical, modern nationalism welds the nation and the state into a compound entity. Indeed, the compound term implies that without the other, each is somehow deficient. States that do not represent nations lack legitimacy; nations that are not embodied in states are defective and incomplete.

This modern nationalist doctrine has no historical precedent. It is, in fact, no more than roughly two centuries old. Modern nationalism differs from all previous forms of ethno-national loyalty in that it legitimizes and energizes the pursuit of statehood by nationally inspired peoples. Each national soul—so the modern nationalist doctrine insists—requires a separate and sovereign political body, a nation-state, in order to be complete.

Nations as the Building Blocks of Humanity

Classical formulations of modern nationalism (for example those of the German Romantics such as Johann Gottfried von Herder, the philosopher and humanist who defended national self-expression as a universal right, and Johann Gottlieb Fichte, the Kantian philosopher with a more stridently national viewpoint) typically begin with the proposition that nations represent the natural building blocks of humanity. Divisions between nations, rather than between races, religions, or classes, are *the* fundamental human divisions—analogous to the distinction between species in the animal kingdom.[4] Whatever may be its accuracy, this view implies that each national community's form of life makes a unique and irreplaceable contribution to the family of nations. The right of nations to live and flourish is, therefore, fundamental.

Nations form individuals

Beyond contributing to humanity in general, the national community also fundamentally forms the individuals that comprise it. National culture and sensibility percolate down to the roots of each individual's consciousness. It is not merely a question of the language we speak or the holidays we celebrate: national character is a pervasive quality that affects us down to our most intimate perceptions and attitudes. Individual creativity, for example, depends upon the national culture for inspiration. Without a common cultural reservoir in which to immerse ourselves and upon which to draw, the sources of our creativity would rapidly dry up. Individuals who have been exiled from their homeland and who live among unfamiliar landscapes and alien cultures are rootless and barren. Understandably, the individual's debt to the nation is incomparably great.

The classical theorists of nationalism were emphatic about the naturalness of nations. "The first, original and truly natural frontiers of states are undoubtedly their inner frontiers," wrote Fichte.

> *This inner frontier, drawn by the spiritual nature of man, gives rise to outward frontiers of territories as a direct consequence; and from a natural point of view men who live within certain mountains and rivers are in no way a people merely on this account but, on the contrary, men live together protected by mountains and rivers if fortune has so arranged it for them, because they were a people beforehand as a result of a far higher law of nature.*[5]

If the nation is no artificial contrivance, the state that arises to embody its will is, similarly, an organic growth. In a metaphor that was commonly used among the early theorists of nationalism, the rise to statehood represents a slumbering nation's awakening into self-conscious activity.

Nations are history's prime-movers

If nations constitute the building blocks of humanity, it further stands to reason that they are the prime movers of human history. Each nation is the natural repository of a specific form of human genius seeking its fortune in the world. The interplay, balance, variety, and conflict among these various national aptitudes are the underlying sources of historical change and advancement. Humankind is not represented in a single universal essence. Like a prism that refracts the source of light, nations refract human genius into countless shades and hues. Only in the

---

4. See Eugene Kamenka, "Political Nationalism: The Evolution of an Idea," in *Nationalism: The Nature and Evolution of an Idea*, ed. Eugene Kamenka (London: Edward Arnold, 1976) 11.

5. J. G. Fichte, *Addresses to the German Nation*, ed. George A. Kelly (New York: Harper, 1968) 190–91.

"peculiarities of nations," writes Fichte, "can we find the guarantee of present and future dignity, virtue and the merit of nations."[6] The welfare of each individual nation is, therefore, vital to human history and, as such, a critical concern of all humankind.

Nations as Organic Entities

More than a half dozen times in the last few pages alone we have had occasion to use terms related to organic growth, natural development, living bodies, and conscious minds in order to describe the character of the national community. This reflects the tendency of nationalist discourse to speak of the nation as more than the sum of the individuals that constitute it. The nation, nationalist writers are prone to say, is a living and vital organism that precedes and outlives any single national individual. It will elude empirical investigation because the national essence is not a quantity that can be measured or defined. National belonging represents a primordial sense that, although naturally available to even the simplest and least sophisticated of national members, is impenetrable by the outside observer. It involves such elusive qualities as the ability to communicate effortlessly with a co-national. References to an ineffable national soul that animates the national organism are a commonplace in nationalist literature.

This organic metaphor is more than a literary device. For the more zealous among the classical nationalists, what often follows the attribution of organic life to national existence is the contention that each individual must serve the welfare of the national whole. The nation's collective needs are the primary concern of each of its supporting limbs. In its most extreme formulations this turns into a narcissistic self-worship of the national community. National loyalty is the highest form of human loyalty because the nation is the very meaning of and condition for our individual existences.

Nationalism as Collective Egoism

Nationalism's darker side

As it emerges from the pens of its more cosmopolitan early theorists, nationalism appears to be a largely humane and tolerant doctrine with deep ties to democracy and a basic liberationist character. It requires little argument to demonstrate, however, that nationalism's more strident advocates have, more often than not, gotten the upper hand. Although nationalists will often pose as supporters of the universal right to national self-determination, in practice they usually exploit the doctrine for their own selfish ends. Historically, few real nationalist movements have expended significant energy in defending the rights of other national groups to self-determination.

This will come as no surprise. After all, nationalism is a form of collective egoism rather than of universal altruism. As a compelling ideological force, nationalism involves being moved by one's own national concerns rather than being com-

---

6. Fichte, *Addresses*, 198.

mitted to abstract pieties about universal self-determination. In fact, intense emotional identification with one's own nation has often meant the total obliteration of the universalist message that nationalism initially contained. From the perspective of a nation struggling for independence and power, nationalism is usually a celebration of one's own rights against those of others. Nationalism has a way of justifying aggression and domination when they serve the alleged national interest. One contemporary observer expressed horror at the solemnity of nationalist rituals that so easily lead to intolerance. He deplored

> *the flag waving, the sententious oratory, the endless reminders of the country's greatness, the pious incantations of the oath of allegiance, and the hushed pseudo-religious atmosphere of national ceremony. Hence, the self-righteous intolerance toward those who decline to share in these various ritualistic enactments.*[7]

Nationalism overwhelms democracy

The intense passions associated with nationalism have a way of overwhelming the liberal democratic principles with which the doctrine was originally associated. If the national good is the highest good, then subordinating the rights of individuals to it would seem to be entirely justified. Assuming that identity, creativity, and destiny depend on the nation, what are individual rights by comparison? Historically, the national call to arms has been the occasion for the most illiberal and undemocratic excesses. Nationalism has, therefore, justly earned the reputation of being the most two-sided of all ideologies: humane and universal in one face, brutal and intolerant in another.[8]

Nationalism's potential for brutality and intolerance has been hair-raisingly demonstrated in the civil war between Serbs, Croats, and Muslims in the former Yugoslavia. What atrocity has not been committed? Former neighbors and friends have set about slaughtering and torturing each other with a blind passion that is as primitive as it is repelling. Ethnic cleansing, mass rape as a means of demoralizing the enemy, the shelling of civilians, the mindless murder of innocent children, all this in the name of national differences that seem positively trivial to the outsider.

Summary

The core propositions of classical nationalist discourse can be summarized as follows:

1. Each nation requires a sovereign state to be healthy and complete. The nation-state is therefore the natural form of political organization and the most basic objective of modern national communities.
2. Nations constitute the most essential building blocks of humankind. Each nation is the repository of a unique genius, and as such, nations are the prime movers of history.

---

7. George F. Kennan, *Around the Cragged Hill: A Personal and Political Philosophy* (New York: Norton, 1992). Cited by Arthur Schlesinger, Jr., in *New York Review of Books*, 12 February 1993, 4.
8. Akzin, *State and Nation*, 52–53.

3. Individuals are pervasively formed by their national origins. Without a national culture upon which to draw, individual creativity would wither. The individual's debt to the national community is, therefore, exceedingly great.

4. Nations are organic, living entities in which individuals take part. Individuals are beholden to serve the welfare of the national collective.

5. Notwithstanding its theoretical commitment to universal self-determination, nationalism in practice is overwhelmingly particularist in character. One's own national rights tend to take priority over the national rights of others. In fact, the appeal to the national good often serves to justify bigotry and oppression.

What Constitutes a Nation?

Objective or Subjective Criteria?

We have been referring to nations and their rights as if national units are tangible entities with unmistakable attributes that are clearly visible to the naked eye. A few simple questions will quickly set this naive view to rest. Do American blacks constitute a nation? Was the Soviet Union or Yugoslavia ever a nation? Can we speak of the Basques, Kurds, Corsicans, Muslims in India, French-Canadians, Puerto Ricans, Eskimos, Druze, Afrikaners, Walloons and Flamands, or the Gypsies as nations? Are the Jews a single nation? Do the Arabs as a group constitute a nation, or are the national boundaries properly drawn between Egyptians, Syrians, Moroccans, and Palestinians? Finally, is the United States really a single nation, or a state that blends many nations?

The linguistic criterion   The unstated question in all of these cases is obviously: What constitutes a nation? If the answer is that nations are peoples that speak a distinct language of their own, then American blacks and citizens of the Soviet Union are not nations, while French Canadians and Afrikaners are. The Arabs as a group would qualify as a nation, but the Saudis, Druze, and Syrians, who speak virtually the same language, would not. By this criterion, oddly, the former Yugoslavia's Serbs, Croats, and Muslims, who speak much the same language, would not be separate nations either.

Historical and territorial criteria   If our criteria, on the other hand, were a common history and sense of destiny, the division lines would be drawn quite differently. American blacks might arguably be considered a distinct nation. So would Basques, Gypsies, and Jews. If a condition for nationhood is the existence of a geographic territory perceived as the homeland, then Kurds are a nation while Gypsies are not. If a long history—say of at least two or three centuries—is required for real nationhood, then the Druze are a nation but the Palestinians are not. And what of religious or racial criteria? What is the relationship between ethnic origin and nationhood?

These questions are of more than academic interest. If self-determination is a right to which we are seriously committed, clarifying which groups do and do not constitute nations is of critical importance. When nationalists attempt to justify the authentically national character of their people, they normally refer to a long string of characteristics that bind them into a single unit. A common language, culture, history, religion, ethnic stock, dress, institutions, landscape, laws, and music are among the many such traits that typically find their way into the arguments of national advocates. But multiplying criteria often complicates rather than simplifies the question. At what precise point does a group of common attributes rise above the casual similarities shared by many peoples and justify speaking of an "authentic national distinctness"? For example, how much religious communality is required to offset the existence of linguistic or racial diversity? Will a long history balance the absence of a unifying language?

Subjective criteria   The force that binds a nation together is as strong as it is elusive. Although many recognizable factors regularly go into the making of a nation, there are still inscrutable elements of empathy and identity that defy systematic empirical analysis. Probably the wisest strategy is, therefore, to regretfully abandon the quest for definitive objective criteria. This has, in fact, been the strategy adopted by a great many historians. In place of relying on a checklist of criteria, the subjective question is posed: Does this people believe they constitute a nation and has this conviction inspired them to struggle for their national rights?

Using subjective criteria is probably the only way to deal with cases in which the determination of national status and rights is the subject of intense controversy. To take a particularly explosive example: Israeli Jews and Palestinians clash violently in regard to their respective rights in contemporary Israel/Palestine. They also are in the habit of dismissing each other's claims to genuine nationhood. Many Palestinians reject Jewish national claims on the ground that the Jews are really a religious and not a national group. Moreover, Jewish historical ties to Israel are too remote and spiritual to carry any weight against a people that has actually been living in the land for generations. On the other hand, many Jews reject Palestinian claims on the grounds that Palestinian nationalism is quite a recent phenomenon—no more than a few decades old. Besides, they argue, how can one compare the rights of a battered people emerging from the nightmare of the Holocaust, having no other land to call its own, with a people who can easily resettle (as many have) in any one of the twenty or so other Arab states? Attempting to assess the relative value of these tangled claims with sharply objective criteria of nationhood is a thankless task. Besides, it might well lead to the bizarre conclusion that one of these peoples was not actually a bona fide nation despite the fact that it was fighting and dying for its national existence. No one would doubt, however, that both Israeli Jews and Palestinian Arabs believe themselves to be nations and act accordingly. In the absence of convincing objective criteria, this must remain our basic standard of judgment.

Are Nations the Source of Nationalism?

Underlying all that has been said to this point is the unstated assumption that nations—whatever criteria we use to distinguish them—are the source of nationalism. Or in other words, nationalism is the expression of a nation's inner sense of identity and communality. This would seem to be true almost as a matter of definition. But what appears to be obvious runs into serious difficulties when the question is examined more carefully. The seemingly undeniable derivation of nationalism from national solidarity is, in fact, a highly controversial matter—both as a historical hypothesis and as a description of the modern world.

African nationalism

To take a striking contemporary example, the boundaries of many modern African states came to be drawn as they are because of the way territories were apportioned among the various colonial European powers. These accidental boundaries often fragmented a single tribe into many different states. Within each colonially created state was a scramble of distinct peoples with different tribal, religious, linguistic, and cultural identities living side by side. Not infrequently they were intensely hostile to one another. Perhaps the only concerns that united them were their common animosity for the colonial rulers and their fierce determination to be rid of them as quickly as possible. Clearly, it was not nationalism that created the contemporary map of African states, but rather the colonial empires of the Belgians, Portuguese, English, and French.

Nation-building

When these new states received their independence, the task that stood before the leadership was monumental: they had to forge a single nation out of the mosaic of peoples that had been randomly included within the state's borders. This process of **nation-building** (as it is often called) entailed utilizing the instruments of centralized state power to foster the novel idea of a single national community. This very often meant fabricating a national culture, a national identity, at times even a national past. It was then necessary to propagate these ideas among a diverse and discordant population. Great parts of this population were beyond the reach of the media and, moreover, culturally unprepared for modern conceptions such as the nation or the state—to say nothing of their fusion into a nation-state. Nation-building involved deliberately weakening the traditional bonds to tribe and locality. This was an artificial nationalizing revolution imposed from above; by no stretch of the imagination was it the awakening into consciousness of a slumbering national will. It was a case in which the state created the nation and not vice versa.

The experience of the third world differs from the classical account of nationalism in another dramatic way. As opposed to eighteenth-century Europe when nationalism was an unprecedented form of socio-political allegiance, third-world nationalism bases itself directly on the already existing Western pattern. Nationalism came to Africa and Asia largely via Westernizing elites whose model was the dominant Western conception of national self-determination. Consequently, what took many generations to gestate and mature in the West has, in the third world, often been accomplished in the space of a few decades. Third-world nationalism appears, therefore, to be less a natural surge of communal sentiment arising from below, and more an idea imported from abroad and deliberately imposed by a political elite.

But the obvious objection will be quickly raised: the African/third-world experience, although it does raise some unsettling considerations, is surely too unique to be generalized. Isn't it clear that in the West nationalism originated out of the will of the various national communities? Here, at least, it appears certain that the nation was responsible for creating the state. Doubtless, this is the way in which the classical theorists of nationalism would have wanted us to understand the rise of the modern nation-state. But a great many modern historians and political scientists have raised serious doubts about this conventional picture. It is worth entering into the animated discussion on this point—if only briefly and glancingly—because of the provocative challenge it poses to the older and long-standard version of the nation-state's pedigree.

Nations are inventions

Nations, from this point of view, are not the elemental units that naturally constitute humankind. They do not spontaneously generate out of linguistic and ethnic communities. Neither are they slumbering essences that await the kiss of some historical prince to bring them to life. Nations are inventions. They are designed and nurtured to promote specific historical interests.

As in the African process of nation-building from above, European elites were interested in creating imagined national communities in place of local, feudal loyalties so as to consolidate their central control. It was important for them to foster a single focus of allegiance and identity that would be concentrated, not surprisingly, on themselves. To this end, they used whatever educational, bureaucratic, and communicative instruments they had at their disposal. They attempted to foster an obedience-inspiring vision of a united people, devoted to its leaders, its culture, and its homeland. The state was the emblematic crux of this national unity, and hence the welfare of the state was essentially indissociable from the welfare of the nation. If the linguistic-ethnic sense of community that the national leadership wished to encourage already existed in latent form, so much the better.

Inculcating attachment to the novel ideas of flag and country often involved inventing traditions[9] that had never before existed. Sentimentalized and self-serving versions of the national history were written, myths and heroic figures were devised, unsung precursors and prophets of the national revival were discovered, and a newly identified national literature became the focus of a newly created national education. Not surprisingly, the emergence of the nation-state is cast as the triumphant conclusion toward which the entire historical drama has been developing all along. As the nineteenth-century French writer Ernst Renan put it: "Getting its history wrong is part of being a nation."[10] In this view, nationalism appears to owe its origins more to a deliberate exercise in ideological engineering than to a spontaneous surge of communitarian feeling.[11]

Creating a national identity

Extending this position to its logical conclusion yields some perturbing consequences. Rather than a common language instinctively seeking a national home in which to be freely spoken, the common language was often created, or at least standardized, by the drive of the state to unification. A land divided by mutually incomprehensible dialects is, after all, a difficult place to govern. National educa-

---

9. See E. J. Hobsbawm and T. Ranger, eds., *The Invention of Tradition* (Cambridge: Cambridge University Press, 1983).

10. Cited by E. J. Hobsbawm in *Nations and Nationalism Since 1780* (Oxford: Basil Blackwell, 1990) 12.

11. Hobsbawm, *Nations and Nationalism*, 92.

tion did not instruct the young in a widely recognized, pre-existing national curriculum; the new national education was the instrument through which the national culture was created, defined, and disseminated. The first generation of national pupils were, therefore, also the first generation to confront the newly proclaimed national legacy.

Similarly, the growth of a national economy did not result from the natural bonding of merchants and industrialists into a single national marketplace. Rather, the growth of industrialization and finance created the need for a rational and uniform context in which to do business. And what better way to homogenize a people—the products it consumes, the clothing it wears, the holidays it observes, the guilds it authorizes—than to nationalize them into a coherent community? What better way to settle the chaos of competing currencies than to nationalize the financial market and create a single national currency? Finally, what more effective way for the central government to generate revenue for itself than for it to justify the taxes it levies in the name of the higher interests of the national community?

State creates the nation

To reiterate this challenging thesis: national consciousness did not crystalize spontaneously out of an antecedent national existence. To the contrary, the interests of various political and economic elites led them to foster national unity and to encourage a state-centered conception of the national community. The state created the nation rather than vice versa. The need for a cohesive political unit underlay the modern discovery of the nation.[12]

Whatever nationalism's specific historical origins, it has certainly outgrown them. Once the national genie escaped from the historical bottle, it soon overwhelmed the narrow purposes of those who sought to control it for their ends. In fact, it was not unusual for those who sought to ride the nationalist tiger to be devoured by it. Even if initially orchestrated from above for political reasons, national attachments subsequently took on a thriving life of their own.

More than two centuries later, national attachments are among the most powerful forces in the contemporary world. Indeed, from where we stand today in the waning years of the twentieth century, it would be foolhardy to predict whether the twenty-first will witness a gradual blurring of national identifications or, just as likely, an unprecedented burst of nationalist activity and passion.

Summary

Let us briefly review our argument in this section.

1. The question "What constitutes a nation?" turns out to be quite formidable. Constructing a definitive checklist of objective criteria to answer the question is difficult, if not impossible. The subjective sense of nationhood is probably the only practical standard of judgment.

---

12. This alternate view of the rise of nationalism has been formulated somewhat starkly in order to dramatize the point. Most of this position's defenders are more subtle and complex in their views. For some interesting discussions see works of the following writers listed at the end of this chapter: Benedict Anderson, John A. Armstrong, Ernst Gellner, E. J. Hobsbawm, Anthony D. Smith, and Charles Tilly.

2. Our second question, "Are nations the source of nationalism and of the nation-state?" is also daunting. Historically, it may well be that both nations and nationalism are ideologically engineered creations fostered by political elites in order to cultivate a single focus of political control.

Pluralism Undermines the Classical Nation-State Idea

Nationalism excludes

If nationalism's anti-democratic potential has become a commonplace, it is rarely perceived that the opposite is true as well; it has become increasingly difficult for pluralist democracy to accommodate the classical idea of the nation-state. In its simplest sense, nationalism is a limiting concept. Nations are defined by their ethno-cultural boundaries; they are communities closed to non-members. However humane and tolerant a particular form of nationalism may be, it necessarily excludes the alien. Mazzini's formulation of this basic nationalist creed cannot be improved upon. The great Italian nationalist wrote: "Every nation a state, only one state for the entire nation."[13]

Pluralism includes

By contrast to this sharp identification of the state with one homogeneous nation,[14] democratic pluralism applauds heterogeneity in virtually all regards: culturally, ethnically, racially, linguistically, etc. Rather than embodying the aspirations of a single clearly defined national community, the liberal pluralist state represents all those within its territorial borders. It expressly rejects the idea that the state ought to represent a distinct ethnic, religious, or racial community.

Rather than represent specific ethno-national communities, the pluralist state acts as a neutral mediator between them. It is required to be nationality blind. It arbitrates conflicts between ethnic communities and services their respective needs without (ideally at least) being partial to any one of them. In this sense, liberal pluralism is subversive of the nation-state. In liberal pluralist regimes, national origin becomes a basically private concern, almost a matter of conscience.

The nation-state undermined

Pluralism's most sacred and oft-repeated principle is that discrimination between citizens on the basis of color, creed, religion, or national origin is strictly prohibited. What was once the undisputed basis of the nation-state—that a state represents the will of a single culturally, racially, and ethnically homogeneous nation—has become a distasteful idea. The suggestion that the state and its institutions ought to be the possession of a particular ethno-national community is seen by pluralists as a reactionary proposition. Indeed, pluralists would probably describe

---

13. Hobsbawm, *Nations and Nationalism*, 101.

14. Mazzini's ideal of a single state representing a single nation is a rarity in the modern world. Only about 10% of contemporary states have a single homogeneous national community within their borders. The great majority contain nationally mixed populations. See Walker Connor, "Nation-building or Nation-destroying," *World Politics* 24 (1972).

A summit meeting of the European Community leadership (December 1990).

discrimination against citizens on the basis of national or cultural background as racist.

Ideological pluralism—the coexistence of many different political world-views within a single political community—belongs to the very definition of democracy. It is the most basic trait of all Western liberal states and, in itself, does not necessarily undermine the sense of national community. But ideological pluralism possesses a dynamic quality that makes it difficult to isolate or contain. Over time, ideological pluralism tends to drive on toward broader and more radical pluralist conceptions. The underlying argument goes as follows: If the right to ideological expression, however unpopular, must be protected, why should the right to cultural peculiarity be denied? If the kinds of lives individuals choose to pursue are a matter of inalienable personal choice, how can the same individual's right to ethnic particularity be rejected? The idea of a pluralism limited solely to ideological matters appears to be a difficult one to sustain in practice.

In the competition between pluralism and the classical conception of the nation-state, pluralism seems to be the choice of most Western political elites. When the narrow conception of the state as a vehicle for ethno-national expression and the open conception of the state as a loose weave of many cultural and ethnic communities have collided, Western democracies have generally opted for the latter. The idea of a uni-cultural-racial-ethnic England, France, or Germany has gradually lost ground to the rival pluralist self-understanding. (With the large influx of immigrants from the former Soviet Block, Pakistan, India, Turkey, and North Africa, this was perhaps not an unforeseeable outcome.)

It has been suggested that the powerful movement toward European unity that we are currently witnessing resulted from the erosion of the historical idea of the nation-state and its replacement by a looser understanding of national sovereignty. Without the weakening of the classic idea of the nation-state, it is hard to conceive of the European nations voluntarily relinquishing sovereignty in favor of a larger, more comprehensive union. Ironically, what was once the classic and authoritative understanding of the nation-state—that the state embodies the will of a distinct nation—has become the ideological province of the extreme right and of the neo-fascists.

The Melting Pot vs. Multi-Culturalism

Pluralism in the U.S.

If the tendency toward a pluralist rather than nationalist understanding of the state has been steadily gaining ground in Europe, pluralism long ago carried the day in the United States. Probably nowhere else in the world has the dissociation between a distinct nation and the sovereign state become so radical. For well-known reasons related to the far-flung immigrant past of all but Native Americans, the pluralist image of society struck root with particular force and tenacity. In the absence of any sharply delimited sense of national identity, pluralism has had few rivals in American political discourse. The idea of a deliberately preserved national homogeneity (as in the prevalent American perception of Japan) has become deeply suspect.

Not so very long ago the image of the United States as a **melting pot** was proudly and regularly evoked. Of late it is heard with considerably less frequency. The melting pot apparently is leaving substantial undissolved residues. Although pluralists would be understandably reluctant to formulate it in these terms, durable islands of "non-national" Americans (citizens who by even the least exacting linguistic or cultural criteria resist Americanization) are prevalent and thriving. Multi-lingual education, media, and public documents such as ballots and tax forms are only the visible tip of a large iceberg.

Multi-culturalism

In place of a melting pot, the current preferred term is **multi-culturalism**—and the two are quite distinct. The image of a melting pot involves the anticipation that the cultural peculiarities of the different immigrant communities would eventually be dissolved in the great cauldron of American life. In the end, a reasonably uniform American culture would remain dominant. This vision of an America growing stronger and more richly varied as it incorporated and assimilated additional cultural traditions was at the heart of the American dream that prevailed for the better part of the twentieth century.

Multi-culturalism, by contrast, rejects the idea that a uniform American national culture either exists or ought to exist. The United States is not a melting pot that dissolves the hard lumps of cultural peculiarity into a smooth, even-textured porridge. It is rather (to play with the culinary metaphor) a rich minestrone in which pieces of self-contained uniqueness exist side by side.

The U.S. creates Americans

When, as in the United States, the pluralist understanding of political life triumphs, the focus of loyalty in the public sphere, the glue that holds the political community together, clearly cannot be the ethno-national community. What tends to take its place is the legal-institutional apparatus of the state. As the provider of services, economic benefits, public order, and social welfare, the state often generates patriotic allegiances only loosely related to national identity. One may feel deeply committed to the state and to the public life it supports while remaining only marginally attached to the dominant national culture. Many Americans fit this description: culturally and ethnically separate and yet committed deeply to the quality of American public life, its consumer ethic, and its tolerant accommodation of many national communities.

In this light it is interesting to go back once again to the classic idea that the nation-state embodies the will of the national public, or in starker terms, that the nation creates the state. In the American experience, this does not appear to be the case. The American nation—insofar as such a unitary body exists—is that group of individuals included within the borders of the United States and defined by law as American citizens. In this case, the state creates the nation: the United States creates the American nation.

Challenges to the Denationalized State

The persistence of nationalism

One could easily surmise from the above argument that nationalism in the Western democracies is in radical decline. With the weakening of the classical idea of the nation-state, national loyalties, so it might seem, have every likelihood of suffering a silent death. This, however, would be an unwarranted conclusion. Despite the incongruity between the historical idea of the nation-state and the liberal pluralist program, nationalism per se is not necessarily weakened. National sentiments clearly flourish even in highly pluralist states that have rejected the classical idea of the nation-state. Indeed, the triumph of liberal pluralism over the traditional conception of the nation-state seems to be taking place despite the persistent strength of national commitments.

When vigorous nationalism confronts the denationalized state, deep frustrations are soon expressed. The resurgence of an alarmingly belligerent neo-fascist right in European politics is, doubtless, related to these frustrations. When French neo-fascists harangue their public with cries of "France for the French," they are demanding a realignment of nationality with citizenship, of the nation with the state. They demand that the nation-state be returned to the possession of the national public, that the classical conception of the nation-state be re-adopted. They proclaim that whatever the law may stipulate, North African Arabs are not French—any more, so say kindred spirits in neighboring lands, than Pakistanis are English or Turks are German. Paradoxically, then, nationalism—at least in some circles—appears to be intensified and energized by the gradual weakening of the nation-state.

Summary

To recapitulate the highlights of our argument:

1. A substantial discrepancy exists between the underlying logic of the nation-state and that of pluralist democracy.
2. In the pluralist outlook, the state does not represent any specific ethno-

national community; rather it is meant to service all the communities within its borders impartially and equally.

3. Ideological pluralism is the heart of democracy. Its logic, however, appears to be difficult to dissociate from the pluralism of the cultural-ethnic variety.

4. The erosion of the nation-state in its classical sense has long been the norm in the United States. In fact, multi-culturalism—the belief that uniform American national culture neither does nor should exist—is challenging the older idea of a melting pot that assimilates newcomers into a single American culture.

5. Although the classical idea of the nation-state appears to be giving way to liberal pluralism in the outlook of most Western political elites, this does not necessarily mean that nationalism is waning. In fact, the denationalization of the state is giving rise to an alarmingly belligerent neo-fascist backlash.

Nationalism: For and Against— A Historical Balance Sheet

Two centuries after nationalism transformed the Western understanding of political life, the historical verdict on its consequences for good and ill still remains to be decided. The balance sheet is heavy with both debits and credits. Nationalism was and is the source of an incalculable amount of conflict, at times of the most horrific kind; on the other hand, nationalism was indispensable for the activation of the masses, for the liberation of countless peoples from colonial rule, and for the creation of some of the greatest cultural monuments of the modern era.

The Case for the Prosecution

Nationalism
intensifies
conflict

Nationalism has had its spirited defenders alongside its relentless critics. Because the case for the prosecution seems more straightforward to make, let us begin with the critics. Nationalism, its detractors contend, has a way of transforming simple differences of interest between communities into matters of high principle and national pride. Once roused, national feeling is difficult to placate without the kinds of catharses found in hatred and violence, or at least in self-righteous flag-waving and cries of "my country right or wrong." While differences of interest can be negotiated with civility, conflicts inflamed with the rhetoric of nationalism soon take on a murderous logic of their own. Nationally inspired conflicts tend to escalate into battles that are fought to the bitter and fatal end. Even when armed conflict proves to be inevitable, nationalism, by sanctifying the cause and demonizing the enemy, tragically converts short and simple conflicts into interminable and full-scale ones.[15]

Not only does nationalism convert clashes between national communities into all-out struggles, it also tends to seriously aggravate conflicts within the nation itself. Nationalism, its critics argue, injects a dramatic ethical quality into the political union it creates. The nationally constituted community is not a temporary or tactical union of individuals who merely seek services, profit, or personal advancement. To be part of the nation involves a moral commitment, an essential human bonding based upon shared concerns, mutuality, even sacrifice. Inevitably, nationalist discourse draws on the passionate vocabulary of duty, mission, vision, dedication, and communality.

Within this kind of vocabulary, cool-headed, businesslike discussion is difficult to sustain. Given the ethically charged quality of national belonging, political debate tends to take on an intense and explosive character. After all, nothing less than the welfare of the motherland is at stake. When the national community finds itself divided on an important issue of policy, differences between the contending points of view have a way of becoming vicious and uncompromising—as conflicts over grand moral causes generally tend to become. Rather than treat political adversaries as honorable individuals with different and legitimate points of view, those defending rival policies are often condemned as traitors, enemies of the people, back-stabbers, quislings, and fifth-columnists.

Nationalism is parochial

Nor can we forget the basically parochial character of nationalism. Rather than judge each individual according to personal merit, nationalism introduces a fundamentally narrow-minded criterion: are you one of us or not? Indeed, hostility toward the alien is frequently more important to nationalism than the sense of belonging. Rather than emphasize what binds us into a common human family, nationalism regularly chooses to emphasize the divisive, the exclusive, and the sectarian. As open and inviting as national communities can be to their own, so are they closed and unreceptive to the stranger. Is it surprising that many historians understand modern racism as a particularly poisonous offshoot of nationalist provincialism?

Summary

Nor can the case for the prosecution fail to consider the well-proven potential of nationalism for anti-democratic politics and its tendency to mistreat national minorities. Or the tendency of nationalism to appeal to the most irrational and primitive of our faculties. Finally, a large measure of guilt for the evils of colonialism and imperialism must be laid at nationalism's door. For its foes, therefore, the legacy of nationalism is a dismal one: (1) it aggravates conflict between and within national communities; (2) it raises collective egoism to the level of a high civic virtue; (3) it emphasizes the provincial and divisive in human relations; (4) it often serves to justify violations of democratic procedure; (5) it is given to irrational

---

15. See Lord Acton, "Nationality," in *Essays in the Liberal Interpretation of History*, ed. William H. McNeill (Chicago: University of Chicago Press, 1967) 131–59. See also Elie Kedouri, *Nationalism* (London: Hutchinson University Library, 1960).

forms of self-justification; (6) it is frequently guilty of the mistreatment of minorities—and the list could be greatly extended.

The Case for the Defense

Defenders of nationalism concede that nationalism is capable of excesses but, they
retort, which ideological position is not? Can we truthfully say that the period prior to
the rise of nationalism, with its inquisitions, religious wars, crusades, and pogroms,
lacked fanaticism or violence? Violence and intolerance have not changed, only the
content of the principles used to justify them.[16] Even enlightened ideologies inspired
by unimpeachable ideals like liberty, equality, and fraternity have had their bloody
reign of terror and their militaristic, totalitarian regimes. Indeed, the crimes committed in the twentieth century in the name of anti-nationalist universalism may be comparable, both in number and in repulsiveness, to those inspired by nationalism.

Diversity   More important still, defenders contend, nationalism has a great many positive
qualities to its credit. Can it be doubted that much of what is authentically great in
our modern Western culture—in architecture, music, theater, art, cinema, and literature—is traceable to national inspiration? Besides, none of us would be happy with
a world that was culturally uniform, one that offered the visitor or reader or viewer
nothing but a flat and unvarying cultural landscape. The very common cliche must
be repeated: cultural and national variety is the spice of our common humanity.
That the streets of New York differ from those of Marrakech, Shanghai, and Cara-
cas in food, dress, language, music, rhythms of life, etc., only enriches our collective human wealth. Would we want it otherwise? And it is difficult to see how this
cultural diversity could flourish and survive without each national community acting resolutely to preserve its own heritage by fostering national education and cultivating a sense of attachment to the national ways.

Internationalism   Ironically, many of those who are most enthusiastic in their internationalist
sympathies are Western intellectuals with a comfortable and stable national identity.
Just as children from warm and secure homes can more easily strike out on their
own and forge healthy ties outside the family, so is it with those who can take their
own national individuality for granted. Secure in the knowledge of who they are,
they are able to meet, respect, and befriend other nationals. Cosmopolitanism is the
ideology of those whose national needs have already been successfully met. Hence,
the solution to the problem that national loyalties pose is not the rejection of nationalism per se; it is rather the need to have all peoples feel a deep sense of stability
and ease about their national identity.

Community   Consider the alternative to nationalism. "Cosmopolitan internationalism"
jumps directly from the lone individual to an indiscriminate humanity in general.
Clearly this is a hollow and unsatisfying idea. Humanity at large is far too shadowy
a notion to inspire loyalty or underwrite real obligations. A commitment to an
abstract humanity that leaves no room for the more palpable and immediate nation-

---

16. Anthony D. Smith, *Theories of Nationalism* (London: Duckworth, 1971) 12 ff.

al community is a highly suspect idea. Moral commitments must commence with the specific individuals and cultural communities that form the natural context of human life. Ironically, as we just noted, a strong national identity may be a necessary condition for successful experiments in internationalism. Far from being the enemy of human community, nationalism may well be a vital (if problematic) stage on the road to more inclusive forms of human association.

Finally, can we forget that without nationalism, many peoples suffering under foreign domination would not have risen to claim the liberty that is legitimately theirs. Although it was partly responsible for imperialism and its evils, it must not be forgotten that nationalism was also the source of those often heroic movements that opposed and finally overcame it. Nationalism has been the driving force behind noble efforts at constitutional reform, sweeping social change, and high-minded programs for tending to the disadvantaged. In developing countries, the nationalist ideal has been the galvanizing force that consolidated fragmented and warring peoples into larger, more stable political unions.

Nationalism is mandatory

In any event, talk of cosmopolitan internationalism is largely academic. At present, the influence of internationalism as a political ideal is quite limited. For every move toward the consolidation of supra-national entities like the European Community, there are a dozen counter-moves toward national self-assertion. It has become clear, besides, that multi-national states that bring many nationalities under a single sovereign roof are likely to be beset by grievous difficulties. The former Yugoslavia is one tragic example. The dismemberment of the former Soviet Union—the last surviving multi-national empire—is another. Nationalism remains for us, despite a number of cracks in the facade, the mandatory basis for contemporary political identity and organization.

Summary

In defense of nationalism it may be said that (1) its sins are no more blameworthy than the excesses of many other ideologies; (2) it has served as the inspiration for much that is great in modern culture; (3) it sustains a rich mosaic of human experiences without which we would be much poorer; (4) it fosters concrete human relations that are the necessary condition for any internationalism—humanity in general being a weightless abstraction; (5) it is inextricable from the activation of the masses in modern politics; (6) it has been the driving force in the liberation of many peoples from subjection and colonialism; (7) it has fostered modernization, nation-building, and progress in the developing world; (8) there are at present no alternatives to it.

When Nationalism Becomes Pathological

Two forms of nationalism

The debits and credits accumulated by nationalism in the two centuries of its existence are so complex and ambiguous that no attempt at balancing them will be made. But if we cannot make a single blanket judgment on so varied a phenomenon as nationalism, we can nevertheless morally distinguish between the two general forms in which it has tended to crystalize: the one humane and healthy, the other egocentric and aggressive.

Nationalism's egocentric, aggressive side is more dramatically visible than its virtuous aspect. Most of us, if asked to chart the history of nationalism in our century, would talk of strife, hatred, and war. But this may be something of an optical illusion. After all, there are no headlines every time Canadians and Americans settle disputes amicably. Nor does the absence of significant hostility between Spain and Portugal or Denmark and Sweden seem to be worthy of any special notice. Nationalism, in other words, is usually judged by its worst representatives. This tends to skew our sense of balance as well as our perception of the historical record. If the full historical record were considered, the balance might easily swing in the opposite direction. Many, perhaps even most forms of nationalism would be found to be reasonably peaceful and not particularly chauvinistic.

Why nationalism turns ugly

What accounts for those cases in which the nationalist urge turns malicious and ugly? Why have some nationalisms maintained a generally humane face while others have deteriorated into strident self-worship? The distinguished British political philosopher Sir Isaiah Berlin suggests the metaphor of a "bent twig."[17] When a tree grows naturally and undisturbed, its leaves and branches enjoy healthy development. When this same tree is prevented, for whatever reason, from growing straight and tall, its form and functioning become distorted. Unable to grow straight, it will twist and contort to assure for itself the room it needs to survive. Consider a further nuance of Berlin's image: a twig that is unnaturally bent back will lash out violently when released.

Nationalism can develop spontaneously, encountering few obstacles in the realization of its goals. In these cases, Berlin believes, there is a high probability that non-virulent forms of nationalism will develop. But there are those cases in which the will to flourish is forcefully arrested by powerful external constraints. For example, the drive to national self-determination may be obstructed by dominating foreign powers. It can be thwarted by conquest, defeat in war, economic disaster, or religious strife. A proud but weak people may find itself preyed upon by its more powerful neighbors. Wounded national pride of this kind, Berlin claims, is very often the prelude to violent self-assertion.

Nationally contented states

Those nations that can be described as contented and fulfilled—nations that either have had the good fortune of not being nationally wounded or have already healed from such traumas—are those that comprise the affluent, democratic Western world. In North America, Western Europe, Australia, and Japan, the need for national self-expression and communal well-being has generally been amply fulfilled. So much so in fact that in some of these fortunate countries at least, the old jealous guarding of national sovereignty and the insistence on an ethnically uniform nation-state appears to be undergoing a process of weakening.

The price of Westernization

By contrast, in those nations that feel themselves eclipsed by Western dominance, national identity is too threatened to be taken for granted. They find themselves in a difficult bind. On the one hand, it is impossible to deny that Western medicine, transportation and communications networks, industrial techniques, and

---

17. See for example the interview with Berlin entitled "Two Concepts of Nationalism," *New York Review of Books*, 21 November 1991, 19–23.

of course military hardware have their substantial advantages. Yet, on the other, for most non-Westerners, modernization is a profoundly unsettling experience. It means abandoning the traditions of generations, often virtually overnight. This cannot help but leave deep wounds on the national psyche.

Westernization's very success intensifies the pressures that mount against it. As the global village shrinks and becomes more uniform, national groups—especially those most vulnerable to Western influences—feel themselves increasingly threatened. Paradoxically, national jealousies and the tendency toward ethnic separateness seem to grow simultaneously with the spread of an international culture. It may well be, therefore, that the answer to the question that opened this chapter is deeply ironic: the greater the pressures toward Western-style internationalism, the more ardent the return to national particularism.

Westerners are prone to understand modernization as the spread of a universal rational civilization. This is surely not the way it appears to those on the receiving end. For them, modernization is not always a benign force disseminating enlightenment. For non-Westerners, internationalism means the triumph of the West over their own national ways. Modern technology and its attendant lifestyles are therefore frequently denounced as culturally alien, spiritually twisted, shallow, soulless, and insolent. Might it be that Westernization's victories are bending many twigs back dangerously?

Suggestions for Further Reading

Akzin, Benjamin. *State and Nation*. London: Hutchinson, 1964.

Anderson, Benedict. *Imagined Communities: Reflections on the Origin and Spread of Nationalism*. London: Verso, 1983.

Armstrong, John A. *Nations Before Nationalism*. Chapel Hill, N.C.: University of North Carolina Press, 1982.

Breuilly, J. *Nationalism and the State*. Manchester: Manchester University Press, 1985.

Esman, M., ed. *Ethnic Conflict in the Western World*. Ithaca: Cornell University Press, 1977.

Gellner, Ernest. *Nations and Nationalism*. Oxford: Basil Blackwell, 1983.

Hobsbawm, E. J. *Nations and Nationalism Since 1780*. Cambridge: Cambridge University Press, 1990.

Hobsbawm, E. J., and T. Ranger, eds. *The Invention of Tradition*. Cambridge: Cambridge University Press, 1983.

Kamenka, Eugene, ed. *Nationalism: The Nature and Evolution of an Idea*. London: Edward Arnold, 1976.

Kedouri, Elie. *Nationalism*. London: Hutchinson, 1966.

Kohn, Hans. *The Idea of Nationalism: A Study in Its Origins and Background*. New York: Collier-Macmillan, 1944.

Smith, Anthony D. *The Ethnic Origin of Nations*. Oxford: Basil Blackwell, 1986.

———. *Theories of Nationalism*. London: Duckworth, 1971.

Tilly, Charles, ed. *The Formation of National States in Western Europe*. Princeton: Princeton University Press, 1975.

Chapter 9

Contemporary Ideological Currents: Feminism, Environmentalism, and the Storm over the University

The Legacy of the Sixties

Even thirty years later, the turbulent decade of the 1960s ignites controversy. No other period in recent history has been so differently appraised, so mythologized, and so maligned as those years of civil-rights marches, anti-war demonstrations, flower power, bell bottoms, and the Beatles. Some picture the Sixties as a period of moral awakening characterized by high-mindedness, intellectual earnestness, and emancipation from conventional pieties. Others see the period as a destructive episode marked by self-indulgent, self-congratulatory posturing, dangerously half-baked adolescent thinking, and moral decadence. Whatever their differences, both sides would fully agree that those tumultuous years were the incubation period for many of our present ideological concerns.

The ideological agenda of the Sixties was carried forward by a generation then on the threshold of adulthood. Most of those who are entering positions of political and economic leadership in the Nineties underwent their formative experiences during the Sixties. (It has been said that knowing how people relate to the Sixties is a reliable indication of how they relate to political issues in general.) In the course of the three intervening decades, however, the ideological program of the Sixties has undergone some major transformations. As the youthful revolutionaries of those turbulent years became dentists, accountants, and corporate executives, their inflammatory rhetoric usually cooled into pragmatic liberal positions that are not far from the general consensus. Moreover, many of the most sensational issues raised during the Sixties fizzled out quite rapidly. Its anti-war fervor cooled with the end of the Vietnam war. Its civil-rights activism was dealt a painful blow when black radicals declared their independence from white direction and under the banner of Black Power insisted on fighting their own battles in their own way. Similarly, the revolutionary slogans and socialist visions so popular in those years were very much out of fashion a decade later—today, they sound jarringly anachronistic.

Oddly enough, the more lasting political products of the Sixties came from its margins rather than from its ideological center. Of the many liberationist ideas that are with us today—from black liberation, to women's liberation, to gay liberation, to **liberation theology**, to **animal liberation**—only the black liberation movement stood at the center of the Sixties' ferment. Feminism, one of the most influential ideological positions to emerge from the Sixties, was at the time a relatively secondary phenomenon, a by-product of the general emphasis on human equality and sexual liberation. Like civil rights for blacks and other oppressed groups, it was one more form of revolt against establishment values—although surely not the most pressing.[1]

Feminism

Ironically, feminism received its greatest shot of energy from the frustration that women radicals experienced when they were not taken seriously by their male counterparts. Expected to conform to the traditional passive female role—and this by young men who spoke so eloquently of emancipation and human equality—convinced many women that the staying power of male domination was far more powerful than they had ever imagined. It would require all the efforts of a determined and well-organized **sisterhood** to overcome.

Environmentalism

The ecological movement was even more of an intellectual step-child to the politics of the Sixties, even though it is easy to pick out many of environmentalism's typical themes in the rhetoric of the flower children. The obsession with technology and consumerism, they proclaimed, was alienating and perverted. Returning to simple, natural lifestyles would restore genuine harmony with others and with our natural surroundings. The **counter-culture** of love, inner peace, anti-materialism, and anti-militarism recoiled from the prevalent attitude that nature was there to be exploited for its raw materials. Instead, they celebrated the virtues of living *with* nature rather than overwhelming it. Although feminism was off and running in the late Sixties, environmentalism had to wait a decade and more before making its systematic and articulate appearance on the stage of Western politics.

The canon wars

The academic battle over **political correctness**, relativism, and the "canon" of great Western literature—often epitomized sarcastically as "Why is everything we read written by white, dead, European males?"—had to wait even longer.

---

1. Typically, a review of radical student politics (mainly focused on Britain) published in 1969 contained only a few lines in passing on "woman's liberation." See *Student Power: Problems, Diagnoses, Action*, ed. Alexander Cockburn and Robin Blackburn (Harmondsworth: Penguin, 1969).

Even though here too the seeds of controversy had already been planted in the Sixties, the full-blown battle developed only two decades later. Many of the academic/ideological canon wars presently being fought are in fact the unfinished business of an earlier agenda, a critical stock-taking of what the Sixties had wrought.

For those on one side of the academic barricades, the universities have betrayed their lofty objectives; they have been seduced by a stylish form of intellectual **nihilism**. Quality, standards, and objectivity are mindlessly sacrificed to fleeting, narrowly political interests. Academia, no longer the preserver of civilization's finest achievements, has become just another arena for political skirmishing. Every self-pitying minority claiming to have been victimized by some diabolical Western depravity appoints itself the new arbiter of what is and what is not intellectually valuable in our cultural tradition. By rejecting as reactionary the uncompromising standards of excellence that have always been academia's guiding light, the new Nineties radicals are the harbingers of our civilization's decline.

For others, by contrast, the full import of the Sixties' political program still needs elaboration and implementation. If racism, **sexism**, **ethno-centrism** (and a host of other Western cultural maladies) are to be genuinely rooted out, must we not radically reevaluate the educational curriculum that for so long represented white, male, Western supremacy? Isn't it mandatory that we open the highly selective and profoundly unrepresentative list of "great works" (i.e., the canon) to include new voices and different concerns?

Let us take up each of these contemporary ideological currents by turn.

Feminism

The History of Feminism

More than a century before its reawakening in the Sixties, a woman's movement battled the male establishment. The movement had its origins prior to the Civil War, continued intermittently through the Victorian era, and reached its peak in the suffragette struggle for the vote in the early years of the twentieth century. When in 1920 the Nineteenth Amendment to the Constitution gave women the right to vote, it was the culmination of nearly a century of feminist activity.

But the right to vote did not realize the deeper objectives of women activists. Although women were now formally a part of the political system, women's interests were still mostly ignored. Indeed, the fear, expressed by many of the suffragettes' opponents, that women would vote as a block for their own interests, proved unfounded; their vote was distributed much in the same way as that of their husbands, fathers, and brothers. Even more seriously, having succeeded in getting the vote, many lost interest in the cause. The Great Depression and World War II pushed women's concerns even further into the shadows. With the post-war return of millions of battle-weary soldiers from the front—each dreaming of a cozy home, a dutiful wife, and adoring children—women's causes once again had little chance of making headway.

But a number of more basic transformations were simultaneously undermining the traditional role of women in society.

1. Growing educational opportunities made traditional home-bound female roles less and less attractive to many articulate and vocal women.
2. Labor-saving appliances rendered the traditional role of dawn-to-dusk housewife increasingly anachronistic. Women, after all, no longer had to sew the family's clothing, churn butter, or bake bread.
3. Leisure time, particularly for many educated middle-class women, created a new challenge: how to find suitable avenues for self-realization. Many entered the labor market only to have their hopes dashed. They were paid less than men for the same work, they were not considered seriously for promotions, and they were the last hired and first fired.
4. Vastly improved medical techniques and hygiene meant that children would, for the very most part, live into adulthood. There was no longer any need to give birth to ten children in order to insure that at least a few would survive. A two-child family became the norm in the Western world and the heavy weight of motherhood—previously a more than full-time occupation—lightened considerably.
5. Add to this the unprecedented revolution in birth-control technologies that allowed women to be the masters of their own reproductive cycles and to plan their families so that career needs could be accommodated. For the first time in human history, easily available birth-control techniques permitted women to enjoy their sexual capacities without fearing the responsibilities of pregnancy. Being able to give themselves over as full partners to the "joy of sex," rather than being preoccupied with its burdens, women were in a position to declare their sexual independence.

The revival of feminism

When the turbulence of the Sixties erupted, many women felt that the call for liberation spoke to their own needs perfectly. As the overused cliche of those years went: It was an idea whose time had come. Despite the frustration that many women felt when feminist issues were given only token attention by men radicals, it is difficult to convey the euphoria that many nevertheless experienced at the prospect of rethinking and reconstructing the role of women in modern society. In the early heady days of the movement, it seemed that stereotypes were crumbling, that change was everywhere, and that genuine equality for women was near.

Three decades later the picture is of course far more complex. But before evaluating the accomplishments of the feminist movement, we should first elaborate on

National Organization for Women rally outside the Supreme Court (March 1993).

the central ideas that unify all feminists, and then distinguish between a variety of opposing schools that divide the feminist movement.

Simone de Beauvoir

When the movement was taking its first steps, a number of pioneering works on the "woman's question" served early feminists as authoritative texts. Preeminent among them was Simone de Beauvoir's ground-breaking *The Second Sex*, which appeared in English in 1953 (it had appeared in French in 1949). More than a decade before the rise of feminism, she had denounced the subservient position of women. "Female," she wrote, was a biological category, but "woman" was man-made, a social creation of male-dominated society. In fact, "woman" was created in order to play a role secondary to that of man. "Humanity is male," de Beauvoir asserted, "and man defines woman not in herself but as relative to him; she is not regarded as an autonomous being."[2]

Betty Friedan

But if contemporary feminism had a launching literary event, it was the publi-

2. Simone de Beauvoir, *The Second Sex* (Harmondsworth: Penguin, 1972) 18–19.

cation in 1963 of Betty Friedan's manifesto *The Feminine Mystique*.[3] Friedan struck at the heart of the American dream: the suburban middle-class housewife. There was profound unhappiness here, Friedan charged, and it was only made worse by the universal expectation that with a comfortable home, a husband who brought home a good salary, and children in the Little League, all must be well. Lived day by day, however, the role of the "happy housewife" was often a misery. Stifling and painfully shallow, it provided no sense of autonomy or personal identity, and it offered little opportunity for personal growth. Worst of all, many such women, believing that they *should* be happy with all they had, were driven to the conclusion that they were somehow to blame for their own discontent. The results, as Friedan documents them, were high incidences of alcoholism, depression, compulsive housework to fill the time, overuse of tranquilizers, and uncontrollable sexual fantasies.

Popular response to the book was stunning. Friedan became a public personality almost overnight. She was inundated with letters from women who recognized themselves in her portrait. Many of them claimed to understand for the first time that their problems were not peculiar to them, that they were part of a large group of women who were questioning the role that society had assigned to them. If books can start revolutions (which is doubtful) then here we have a book that was instrumental in catalyzing feminist sentiment by expressing a deep pain shared by many women.

Sexism and sisterhood

What unites de Beauvoir, Friedan, and all other feminists is opposition to sexism, i.e., the prevalent practice of treating women as unequal without reference to their specific talents or abilities. Men who relate to women as inferior, who need to dominate them simply because it is the man's place to command and woman's place to follow, are contemptuously described by feminists as male chauvinists. The chauvinist not only recognizes the brute fact that our world is visibly divided into nurses and surgeons, secretaries and bosses, cheerleaders and quarterbacks; he believes that this is the way things ought to be. Because many feminists are convinced that sexism and male chauvinism are the rule rather than the exception, "sisterhood" (the solidarity of women) is a critical counterweight to "patriarchy" (male domination). Sisterhood equips individual women with the strength to overcome their sense of isolation and, hence, provides the morale and esprit de corps that fuel the feminist movement.

Feminism's Unique Revolutionary Challenge

Feminism's uniqueness

After the initial rush of exhilaration in the Sixties, serious feminists conceded that the task they were undertaking was monumental. The feminist revolution entailed challenges more daunting than those faced by other more conventional political revolutions. Ordinary political revolutions entail dislodging a small, privileged elite from power. A mass of the disgruntled and disentitled rises up

---

3. New York: Dell Publishing, 1963.

against easily identifiable enemies and displaces them. When the enemy is visible and the objective clear, a revolution is a reasonably straightforward operation. For a number of overlapping reasons, women find themselves in a very different position.

1. Men do not constitute a small minority that can be dislodged. No storming of the Bastille or of the Winter Palace will dismantle patriarchy. No historical revolutionary strategy seems appropriate to feminist objectives.

2. Men's privileges are rarely upheld by overt wielding of power. No police force or army keeps women in their place. For the most part (as with Friedan's suburban homemakers), women take an active part in choosing the social roles they play. Patriarchy is above all a matter of complex attitude patterns, stereotypes, and reciprocal expectations that prevail between men and women. It is less a fortress of overt privileges and more a set of implicit assumptions that are as tenacious as they are subtle and pervasive.

3. The battle lines of gender conflict cut through every family, rich and poor, urban and rural, elite and mass, liberal and conservative. **Sexual politics** are reenacted in every relationship between men and women; they are even present in the earliest interactions between boys and girls. Organizing women is unusually difficult. Collaborating with the enemy is virtually inevitable. To unify women and revolutionize men's attitudes is therefore a herculean task: it requires penetrating into the inner emotional world of both women and men and changing our conceptions of ourselves in a fundamental way.

4. Even zealous and optimistic versions of feminism concede that ground will be gained only inch by inch. Liberation is no overnight wonder. Only the most radical feminists (to be discussed below) make the case for a revolutionary strategy that would move at a faster pace.

If the importance of revolutions could be measured by the extent of their day-to-day impact on the actual lives of real people, a successful feminist revolution would be perhaps the most important revolution in history. It would involve a dramatic transformation of roles and attitudes that reached down to the most basic levels of our cultural assumptions. Beyond eliminating male-dominated institutions, the liberation of women would require undoing millennia of entrenched mental habits.

Controversies within feminism   Faced with such an elusive yet powerful enemy, it is not surprising that feminists differed sharply among themselves as to the underlying sources and remarkable staying power of patriarchy. Nor did they see eye to eye in regard to more practical concerns; they debated both short-term tactics and long-term strategies. They even disputed the essential objectives that feminists were pursuing. Controversy centered on the following issues:

1. What is the source of women's oppression? Is it rooted in a complex of his-

torical causes that evolved naturally out of the biological division of labor between the sexes and the differences in their physical attributes? Or is women's inequality to be ascribed to a more or less conscious strategy employed universally by men to justify, maintain, and protect their privileges? Clearly, the answer given to this question will determine which strategies are to be adopted in combating sexist practices in the present. For example: are men to be trusted as partners in the struggle for liberation?

2. Is the subordination of women a unique case unto itself or is it inseparable from other forms of exploitation such as those suffered by the poor, by third-world populations, by racial minorities? Hence the fundamental question: should women make common cause with other victims of oppression? Is it possible for women to succeed in liberating themselves from oppression without at the same time striking at the deeper causes that underlie human oppression in general?

3. What is to be done? How are women seeking liberation to proceed? Should it be via legal and legislative battles to remove inequalities in law, in status, in income, and in hiring practices? Or are the kinds of changes available through legislative/legal means only superficial and cosmetic? Is raising consciousness the answer? Or perhaps real change would involve even more radical means such as feminist separatism or violent revolutionary tactics.

4. Should feminists accept the basic form of liberal capitalist democracy and pursue their objectives within its framework? Or is the liberal capitalist regime itself one of the principal causes of women's oppression?

Women's responses to these questions fall into three broad (and necessarily oversimplified) categories: (1) moderate/liberal feminism, (2) socialist feminism, and (3) radical feminism.

The Varieties of Feminist Thought

Moderate/Liberal Feminism

Moderate/liberal feminists make up far and away the largest and most influential branch of the women's movement. Through the National Organization for Women (NOW), they have been active in issues like credit discrimination against women, sex bias in education, abortion rights, job discrimination against pregnant women, comparable pay for comparable work, pension equity, and the (failed) Equal Rights Amendment (ERA).[4] Their accomplishments, while quite impressive, fall far short

---

4. See Joyce Gelb and Marian Lief Paley, *Women and Public Policies* (Princeton: Princeton University Press, 1987).

of what they consider even a minimal program for women's equality.

Moderate feminism's program

Liberal feminists reject one-dimensional conspiratorial accounts of women's subordination. Although many men are guilty of oppressing women, the victim/villain dichotomy that portrays the relationship between the sexes as a fight to the finish is neither accurate nor constructive. After making all the justified critiques of sexism and chauvinism, women and men must live with each other and accommodate each other's needs. There is no other future. As inheritors of the Enlightenment tradition, liberal feminists are convinced that both men and women can be reeducated. The feminist struggle must avoid demonizing men as irremediably oppressive. Instead it must concentrate on emancipating women from outdated subordinate roles and on impressing upon men that their own true interests lie with autonomous, self-possessed women who can serve as equal partners, rather than submissive underlings. Men who are sympathetic to the women's cause are, therefore, important assets that should be cultivated. (About 10% of NOW members are men.)

Suggestions that the respective interests of women and men are irreconcilable, that men are the enemy, or that women should seek their fortunes apart from men only serve to weaken the movement. Unrealistic radical fantasies alienate the very women who most need emancipation. Moreover, they stiffen male resolve to resist feminism at all costs. Nor should it be forgotten that the majority of women perceive of motherhood and a loving relationship with a man as a central part of their lives. Woman as mother and spouse must therefore remain central to any viable feminist program. Mocking these roles as reactionary and unworthy of free women transforms feminism from a serious political force into a side-show that attracts ridicule and has no real effect.[5]

Unlearning sexism

Liberal feminists are relatively optimistic about changing the gender patterns that have prevailed for centuries. Sex roles have been learned, they argue, and can be unlearned as well. They have been embedded in institutions and laws, and here too they can be reformed and redrafted. Moreover, institutional and legal reforms are not merely formal and cosmetic. Changes in the institutional/legal reality of sexism necessarily make for changes in the assumptions of those who act within these institutional/legal structures. If the law mandates that men and women have equal access to medical and legal training, soon the stereotype of the man as doctor and lawyer and woman as nurse and secretary will disappear for lack of a supporting reality. Even dyed-in-the-wool supporters of patriarchy will be hard pressed to sustain a myth that is visibly contradicted by reality.

By identifying the sources of role stereotypes in the major socializing institutions of our society—the family, the educational system, and the mass media—liberal feminists believe that they can be effectively rooted out. Since environmental factors socialize us to fit into our ascribed gender roles, a different kind of socialization pattern would create different kinds of women and men. It is quite clear that

---

5. A critique of radical feminism along these lines can be found in Betty Friedan's *The Second Stage* (New York: Summit Books, 1981).

boys are not inherently competitive, aggressive, and outward-seeking any more than girls are essentially submissive, emotional, and inward. Replacing older school books that portray boys as intrusive and adventurous and girls as sensitive and nurturing with more progressive ones in which both genders are simultaneously bold and vulnerable will slowly bring about the desired change. Presenting women in the media as reporters, athletes, professionals, and intellectuals will gradually make its mark on the consciousness of the malleable younger generation. Inevitably, changes in the public status, incomes, and images of women will create changes in their private lives as well.

Reform, not
revolution

Above all, liberal feminists see their struggle as taking place within the existing political system. They have no principled argument with pluralist liberal democracy in its familiar contemporary form. On the contrary: they contend that the existence of free, democratic institutions is a necessary condition for the success of the movement. Violent, radical change, they warn, even it were feasible, would in the end lessen, not increase, the prospect of freedom for both men and women. The ultimate aim of liberal feminists is, therefore, integrationist; they seek to integrate women into the ongoing political system, providing them with a fair share of the rewards and advantages it distributes.

Liberal feminists have few reservations about capitalist competition. The world is a place of winners and losers, but until now women were not given a fair chance to compete. There is nothing essentially wrong with the liberal capitalist world that cannot be remedied by allowing women to participate as equal partners. What needs to be done then is to ensure that women participate fully in what was in the past a man's world. This may mean, under certain circumstances, providing women with a compensatory head start or with special incentives and benefits (such as **affirmative action** programs), but these are only temporary corrective devices that ought to disappear as soon as women can compete on an equal footing. Once women have taken their equal place alongside men, feminism will have become superfluous.

Critiques of
moderate
feminism

Women from the more radical schools of feminist thought find the liberals both timid in their analysis and naively misguided in their practical program. The following two critiques are regularly heard:

A. Much like the suffragettes, liberal feminists exaggerate their victories. They tend to equate liberation with winning legal battles in male-dominated institutions. But just as the vote did not bring equality for women, neither will formal victories in the congress or the courtroom overcome patriarchy. Chauvinism will easily survive such inessential skirmishes. What these measures really accomplish is to dupe the middle-class women who benefit by them. They become convinced that women's problems are being satisfactorily worked out while in fact there is no real change in the underlying causes or the basic reality of patriarchy.

B. The liberals' program aims not so much at liberating women as it does at co-opting them into the world that men have created. All they want is for women to be more like men. Women are to compete as men by assuming masculine character traits. They are to be predatory, upwardly mobile, self-interested individualists who can do anything men can do. This is not liberation but an undignified aping of precisely those traits that have long been responsible for the subjection of women. What will feminism have gained if successful women join men in exploiting their less successful sisters?

Socialist Feminism

Engels

More than a century ago Friedrich Engels, the life-long intellectual partner of Karl Marx, wrote in *The Origins of the Family, Private Property and the State* (1884) that bourgeois marriage reproduces, on a small scale, the oppression and exploitation of capitalism. The family, he argued, is a microcosm of the relationships prevailing in society at large. Wives constitute a household proletariat, while husbands assume the role of owners and bosses. Thus, sexual exploitation and class oppression are the combined results of the capitalist system. To liberate women, therefore, it is necessary to liberate both women and men from capitalism, the true source of human enslavement.

Sex-class oppression

Although socialist (or Marxist) feminists generally accept the fundamentals of Engels's analysis, they nevertheless insist that the oppression of women is not simply another instance of capitalist oppression. Patriarchy, even if it derives from the dynamics of capitalism, is not reducible to it. Because the effects of sexual subjugation aggravate those deriving from class subjugation, socialist feminists contend, women are doubly oppressed. They are part of a sex-class whose subjection combines household drudgery and cheap labor with sexual submission and reproductive services. Both as producers and as reproducers, women are instruments serving male objectives.

Witness even the socialist movement itself: the old patterns of male domination continue to prevail. Even among radical socialists, sexism is a secondary concern. Hence, socialist feminists emphasize the importance of maintaining separate women's political organizations. Women require their own political structures and their own ideological self-understanding in order to successfully confront the compound abuse they suffer as laborers and as homemakers.

Socialist feminists differ from their liberal opponents most profoundly in regard to the sources of women's oppression. For liberals, women are discriminated against because of unfortunate defects in the liberal capitalist system. Hence, liberals invest their best energies into reforming the offending elements in an otherwise acceptable reality. Socialists, by contrast, assert that the exploitation of women is an integral part of capitalism itself. It cannot be corrected without dismantling the entire system. The best liberals can do is to improve the lot of privileged middle-class women in a superficial way. Socialists seek to cut away to the root of the problem. Hence, they concentrate on the agony of destitute women, working women, and women members of minority groups. In the plight of these disentitled masses, the failures of capitalism are radically revealed. Poor, afflicted women personify the injuries of capitalism in their most condensed form: the union of class oppression and sex exploitation.[6]

Capitalist exploitation

According to socialist feminists, capitalism exploits women in a number of related ways:

1. Women form an expendable, back-up labor force to be utilized when market needs expand. Their wages are low, their prospects for advancement slight, their job security minimal.
2. Women perform a host of critical but unpaid household chores that free men for more lucrative work. Woman's menial labor within the family is thus the indispensable but unrewarded foundation of capitalist production.
3. Capitalism exploits women as consumers by appealing to the most debilitating of feminine stereotypes. It preserves the image of woman as mindless, petty, narcissistic, and temperamental.
4. Consistent with capitalism's tendency to reduce the living and human to the instrumental and profitable, advertising reduces women to the status of sex objects.

Self-enslavement

Why do women put up with all this? What accounts for the compliance with which generations of women have accepted male domination? Many socialist feminists argue that the special power of sex-class oppression lies in the effective control of ideas by the male establishment. The feminine mystique, they charge, is a powerful ideology of self-enslavement that women have been manipulated into accepting. It acts as a narcotic that numbs the critical senses and conditions women for the subordinate role that capitalist society expects them to play. The feminine mystique is so much part of everyday thought, it so thoroughly organizes the very categories through which we perceive the world, that women who do just what men expect them to do will often insist that they are acting freely. Thus, menial domestic labor, child-rearing, and sex to satisfy men's needs are accepted as part of the natural order of things. In the feminine mystique, "the home" takes on mythic qualities; it is fetishistically made over into a shrine to which women are expected to sacrifice their entire selfhood. Most women, taken in by the ideology of traditional femininity, make this sacrifice willingly.

Born-to-shop consumerism is another element in the enslaving mystique of femininity. It promises momentary escape from domestic isolation and personal emptiness, but only by indenturing women to an endless consumerist cycle that is as much a bonanza for capitalism as it is a crippling compulsion for women. Moreover, the mystique of being truly feminine demands that women torment themselves with wildly impractical wardrobes—from three-inch stiletto heels, to labor-

---

6. See Sheila Rowbotham, *Women's Consciousness Man's World* (London: Penguin, 1973) 116–26.

intensive hair styles, to tight, skimpy, and uncomfortable dress. All these restrict women's freedom of movement (in all senses) and identify them immediately as available sex objects. Needless to say, those who dissent from the mystique of the happy housewife are dismissed as pathetic misfits.

Consciousness raising

Exposing the everyday dynamics of this enslaving ideology is for socialist feminists the major theoretical task of the women's movement. Recognizing that "the personal is political," that the suffering of individual women is the concrete embodiment of an organized system of oppression, provides the key to unmasking and discrediting the feminine mystique. Hence, "consciousness raising" as a means of combating the feminine mystique became a socialist staple, and later a staple of the women's movement generally. By sharing with each other their individual experiences of domesticity, child-raising, sexual harassment, women's work, and male-chauvinist behavior, women became aware of how often their own private sense of desperation was only a single instance of a common form of emotional distress. Realizing that they all suffered at the hands of capitalist patriarchy was the first step toward defeating it.

Critiques of socialist feminism

Socialist feminists have suffered from the crisis that radical left-wing ideology has undergone since the fall of the Soviet Union. But beyond such practical difficulties, socialist feminists also face a number of difficult substantial problems in justifying their position.

A. Sexism is hardly a creation of capitalism. It has flourished for thousands of years in every climate and in virtually all cultures. Even if we concede that capitalism creates its own variant of women's oppression, the tie between the two appears to be circumstantial rather than essential.

B. If patriarchy and capitalism are integrally related to each other, why has sexism so dramatically gone on the defensive in much of the Western world while capitalism continues to thrive?

C. The fusion of class and sex, proletarian and housewife, production and reproduction, is strained and implausible. It overlooks the clear identification of different women with different economic classes; it ascribes false-consciousness (or delusions about one's real interests) to the greater part of the female sex; it claims, against the evidence of our common sense, that the market economy and male dominance are really much the same thing. Confusing economic and gender oppression will only mean that neither of them receives its due.

D. Linking women's liberation with radical revolutionary programs ignores the manifest historical evidence: radical revolutionary regimes are no friend of liberation—neither for men nor for women.

Radical Feminism

Many radical feminists are sympathetic to socialism, just as many socialist feminists have a basic affinity to radical feminist ideas. Where radicals and socialists differ from each other, and where both of them differ from the liberals, is once again in regard to the sources of women's oppression. Liberals ascribe women's inferior status to gender roles that have been learned and must be unlearned. Socialists insist that sexual oppression and class oppression are inextricable from one another; that liberating women entails ending capitalist exploitation. Radical feminists reject both these claims. Neither unlearning sex roles nor eliminating capitalism will eliminate patriarchy. Both of these are incidental to the true source of women's subordination: deliberate male repression. Man is the enemy because "*all men have oppressed woman.*"[7]

Women's oppression is the source of all others

Women's oppression by males, the radicals contend, is the most basic and essential of all forms of oppression. Class and racial oppression derive from it and not vice versa. Hence, the elimination of oppression begins with the liberation of women from male domination. Radicals remind us of the unconscionable atrocities that male-controlled cultures have committed against women: foot-bindings, clitoridectomies and other genital mutilations, witch-burnings, suttee (burning a widow on her husband's funeral pyre), prostitution, and pornography. These practices are not unfortunate exceptions to male benevolence; they incarnate the vicious, often overtly murderous repression of women by men. Some radical feminists speak of a women's "holocaust."[8]

Patriarchy, violence, and rape

As opposed to the liberals and socialists who believe that male dominance is maintained through the control of ideas, radicals assert that patriarchy preserves itself by violence. Rape provides a dramatic case in point. It reveals in purest form the truth of male-female relationships. In rape, the facade falls, the conventional adornments of civility and romance are dispensed with. (It is often argued that pornography does the public relations for rape; pornography is the theory and rape is the practice.) In rape, brute physical domination and the total violation of woman's selfhood—the real agenda of male supremacy—come out of hiding. As rapist, man unmasks his genuine collective face. Although not all women have been raped and not all men have raped, the rapist acts for all men and intends to intimidate all women. Just as the firing squad preserves a political system by threatening the would-be insurrectionist with lethal violence, so rape is both male supremacy's underlying reality and its ultimate weapon.[9]

Female separatism

Whereas liberal feminists aim at "liberating the man in every woman and the woman in every man," radicals spurn the thought of an androgynous humanity in which men and women blend into some neuter status. For the most extreme radicals, female separatism is the only sufficient response to patriarchy. Often associat-

7. *Redstockings Manifesto* (New York: Redstockings, 1979). Cited in David Bouchier, *The Feminist Challenge* (New York: Shocken Books, 1984) 75.
8. See Mary Daly, *Gyn/Ecology: The Metaethics of Radical Feminism* (Boston: Beacon Press, 1978) 384, cited by Hester Eisenstein, *Contemporary Feminist Thought* (London: Unwin, 1984) 109.
9. See Susan Brownmiller, *Against Our Will: Men Women and Rape* (New York: Simon and Schuster, 1975).

ed with lesbian activists, separatism is based on the axiom that chauvinistic qualities are inherent in the male psyche. No re-education or economic reform can touch
the heart of man's patriarchal nature. Dignified coexistence with men, to say nothing of equality, is impossible.[10]

A women-centered perspective

For radical feminists, lesbians are in an especially advantageous position to
attain female autonomy. They not only suffer women's oppression in its most highly concentrated form, they have also put behind them the constraints of ordinary,
male-centered definitions of femininity. Women—whether lesbian or not—must
thoroughly identify themselves with women's concerns and, in so doing, rid themselves entirely of male-implanted ideas and expectations. Women who authentically
wish to be autonomous must disengage themselves from "mankind" and its inexorably repressive character.[11]

For separatists, men are unnecessary—even sexually. The male-sponsored
myth that only vaginal (that is male-aided) orgasm represents the fully mature
female sexual experience is, in fact, a part of the ideology of male domination. Its
objective is to sustain women in a passive, beholden-to-men role. Based on the
research of Masters and Johnson, they claim that clitoral orgasm is no less satisfying and mature. With vaginal orgasm discredited, the man's role in sexual satisfaction is eliminated. A woman no more needs a man than "a fish needs a bicycle."
Women are capable of being sexually independent.[12]

Female superiority

Other radical feminists argue the superiority of females over males. They point
to a number of biological facts: women have longer lifespans, resist disease better,
are more adaptable to extreme physical conditions, and have a higher birth survival
rate than men. More important, woman are morally superior. They are less aggressive and violent, more given to compassion and tenderness. A world made over in
woman's image would be more peaceful, humane, spiritual, and nurturing. This
view is rejected by most feminists as being only an unacceptable mirror image of
the male supremacist ideology.

Rejecting marriage and motherhood

Although many, perhaps most, radical feminists reject both complete separatism and female supremacism, they nevertheless harbor the deepest suspicion
for traditional gender-related institutions such as marriage, motherhood, and the
family. These institutions, radicals charge, are the preeminent sources of
women's oppression; until they are abolished, women will not be free.[13] Marriage and the family are for the radicals what capitalism is for the socialists and
conditioned sexual roles are for the liberals. They perpetuate economic depen-

10. Perhaps the most interesting and influential of radical feminist essays is Shulamith Firestone's *The
Dialectic of Sex* (London: Paladin, 1972).

11. Eisenstein, *Contemporary Feminist Thought* 48–57.

12. Ann Koedt, "The Myth of the Vaginal Orgasm," in *Notes from the Third Year: Women's Liberation*,
ed. Ann Koedt and Shulamith Firestone (New York: Notes from the Third Year, 1971).

13. See Eva Figes, *Patriarchal Attitudes: The Case for Women in Revolt* (Greenwich, Conn.: Fawcet,
1970) 181; also Adrienne Rich, *Of Woman Born: Motherhood as Experience and Institution* (New York:
Norton, 1976) 276.

dence, demand a lifetime of unpaid menial labor with no social benefits, force women into domestic solitary confinement, impose motherhood as the natural female destiny, and compel women to enter men's chauvinist world, with very foreseeable results.

Male-propagated ideologies of romance and love beguile women into entering such manifestly repressive institutions. Disseminated and inculcated by every available source of communication and socialization, the "boy meets girl" fairy tale has achieved an almost sacred status in our popular perceptions. The mystification of the bridal ceremony, the honeymoon, and living happily ever after shroud the onset of male-dominated marriage in an alluring glow. These myths of courtship are the bait that lures women into the trap of patriarchal power.

Even those radical feminists who in the 1980s and 1990s had second thoughts about motherhood were unambiguous in their rejection of the monogamous, nuclear family. They envisioned motherhood in a drastically altered context. It would be a freely chosen option unrelated to sexual politics or the suffocating conventions of marriage. Freedom from sexism, collective child-rearing, and the minimal presence of men would transform its character from the coercive institution that it has been into a gratifying and emancipated way of life.

Critiques of radical feminism
Radicals feminists deny that men are in a position to criticize their ideas. Male critique is only a predictable form of self-defense. Nevertheless, other feminists have directed serious critiques in the radical's direction, and to these we turn briefly.

A. Radicals undermine the foundation of feminism by identifying it with positions that the vast majority of women find unacceptable. If radical feminism focuses on lesbianism, separatism, female supremacism, and the rejection of the family, it will remain eccentric and ineffective. Whatever intrinsic intellectual interest radical critiques of sexism may have, radical feminism as a political force will never be more than a historical curiosity.

B. Demonizing men is more a cry of pain than a constructive policy. Neither does the portrayal of woman as the eternal victim advance the cause of liberation. Demonizing and victimizing are little more than fail-safe methods for relieving women of concrete responsibility for their own lives. They are part of the naive escapism (how else can female separatism and schemes for collective child-rearing be understood?) in which radicals like to indulge. How much easier it is to reject the world than to present a viable alternative to it.

C. Human life is far too complex to be exhausted by one-dimensional explanations. Hence, single-perspective accounts of history and society—especially conspiracy theories—have very poor track records. Whether the all-powerful villains are capitalists, Jews, Western imperialists, or men, theories of this kind inevitably suffer from grotesque exaggerations. At times they even reflect genuine emotional pathology.

D. Unless one is willing to dismiss the dramatic progress in gender relations over the past decades as a male-induced mirage, the radical position appears to be indefensible. The relationship between men and women is clearly not a zero-sum game in which one side wins only by having the other side lose. It is a series of evolving adaptations and accommodations. In fact, the liberation of women may well turn out to be a critical condition for the liberation and happiness of men. In any case, there can be no human future but one in which women and men act in concert.

Three decades after its origin, the movement for women's liberation has some major accomplishments to its credit, even though they still fall short of the goals it set for itself.

The impact of feminism   Comparing gender relations as they stood in 1960 with those that prevail today reveals some remarkable transformations. Feminist ideas have made deep inroads into our daily lives. Sexist language (terms like mankind, chairman, fireman, etc.) is slowly being phased out; the identification of certain professions with men almost exclusively has become increasingly anachronistic; the absence of women from visible public positions has been, at least partially, corrected. Even in regard to domestic duties, men are considerably more likely to take an active part in household and child-rearing activities. In educated circles, basic feminist ideas have already become the prevailing (if not always practiced) consensus.

Women's studies programs are available on most campuses. Affirmative action is slowly changing the sexual makeup of student bodies and faculty. School textbooks have begun to reflect more gender equity. Legislation over a broad front of issues has made discrimination against women more difficult to sustain. Although women still cluster in certain traditionally female professions such as teaching and nursing, here too change is in the air—a generation ago a "male nurse" was a puzzling contradiction in terms; today women can be pilots and plumbers, and men can be caregivers. Does all this add up to feminist success? It depends on whether one concentrates on the half of the glass that is full or on the half that is still empty.

Environmentalism, Ecology, and Green Politics

Environmentalism as an Ideology

At first consideration, environmentalism does not seem to qualify as an ideology. It appears to have more in common with benevolent civic causes such as the crusade against drug abuse or the campaign for safe driving than it does with comprehensive world-views like Marxism or classical liberalism. Beyond being narrow in focus, environmentalism also lacks the highly controversial qualities that we have come to expect of ideology. Who, after all, is for unbreathable air and polluted rivers?

A challenge to traditional ideologies

First impressions notwithstanding, environmentalism (or the ecological movement or green politics) not only qualifies as an ideology, it is probably the single genuinely new Western ideological creation of the last 150 years. Indeed, the environmentalist ethic and its vision of the human future run against the grain of three centuries of Western political thinking. Responding to unprecedented challenges, it proposes answers that are still quite dismaying to many conventional liberals, conservatives, and radicals. First of all, it challenges key assumptions about the desirability of growth, progress, and higher standards of living that are common to most modern ideological systems; second, it denies that subduing nature through the use of human reason and technology is always a morally worthy or practically viable objective; third, it breaks the standard mold according to which ideologies belong either to the left, right, or center; and fourth, it proposes fresh moral standards by which to assess our public and private activities.

Planetary Crisis

We will describe the substance of environmentalist ideology presently, but it should be clear that such dramatic reorientations in thought did not materialize without major changes "on the ground." Alarming reports of changes in the Earth's natural environment began to appear in the late 1960s and early 1970s. The planet's health, many believed, was in deep trouble. Aside from the visible smog clouds and contaminated rivers, scientists detected other far more alarming dangers. These were no longer isolated local problems with local solutions; at stake was a complex of interrelated threats to the natural system of the planet itself. Ordinary human activities were assaulting the very foundations of life on Earth.

1. *The greenhouse effect and global warming.* Because of the burning of fossil fuels such as gasoline—mainly in internal combustion engines like the automobile—the amount of carbon dioxide in the atmosphere has increased rapidly. Concentrations of atmospheric carbon dioxide trap radiation that would otherwise escape into space and, much like a greenhouse, elevate temperatures close to the planet's surface. The quickening rate of deforestation, especially the destruction of the tropical rain forests, has compounded the problem because plants and trees absorb substantial amounts of carbon dioxide from the atmosphere.

   It has been predicted that raising global temperatures even a few degrees could have Armageddon-like effects on the Earth and its inhabitants. The polar ice caps would melt, raising ocean levels and flooding coastlines and low-lying areas. Oceans would flow inland through rivers, salinating the water and killing marine life. Rising temperatures would parch the land, and green farmlands would turn into desert. The extinction of certain critical links in the food chain would wreak ecological havoc with all forms of Earth life.

2. *Depletion of the ozone layer.* The planet's protective cover of ozone—an inert gas in the atmosphere—prevents ultraviolet light from reaching the Earth's surface. Unimpeded, ultraviolet light would cause skin cancer, diminish crop yields, and kill micro-organisms that are critical for the ocean food chain. Distressing predictions made by scientists in the early 1970s that atmospheric ozone was being depleted were confirmed in 1985 when a gaping hole in the ozone layer was found over a huge area of Antarctica. Among the culprits for ozone depletion, the best known are fluorocarbons, commonly used in spray cans and air conditioners.

3. *Deforestation.* The reduction of tropical rain forests to about half their original size means the extinction of tens, perhaps hundreds, of thousands of species that lived in these teeming biological hothouses. Whether through land development, logging, or acid rain—another consequence of air pollution—these forests have been disappearing at the rate of about 1% a year. Food chains upon which all living things depend for sustenance have been severely disturbed. Moreover, since many medical breakthroughs have relied heavily on studying the biological processes that take place in these species, their extinction represents an irreversible loss for knowledge and for human well-being.

4. The more familiar, though by no means less alarming, environmental hazards can be listed together: overpopulation, with its increasing pressures on the Earth's ecosystems; air and water pollution; the erosion of topsoil critical for farming; nuclear contamination; the depletion of natural resources; oil, chemical, and radioactive spills that befoul beaches and oceans; the exponentially growing quantity of waste, much of it toxic, created by humans.

The Rise of an Ecological Consciousness

The combined impact of these unprecedented crises has compelled growing numbers of people to rethink humanity's relationship with its natural surroundings. At stake, they insist, is far more than having pretty vacation spots where we can get away from it all; the planet is in danger. Earth's ability to recover from the ravages of human exploitation can no longer be taken for granted. It has become clear that the carrying capacities of spaceship Earth are not limitless. The age-old vision of Earth as a bottomless cornucopia of plenty, resistant to human designs and infinitely renewable, is in need of revision.

The result of this sober recognition is a new moral vision specifying the proper relationship between human life, other forms of life, and our earthly home. It is a humbler vision than what is commanded in the biblical narrative:

> *Be fruitful and multiply, fill the earth and subdue it. Be masters of the fish of the sea, the birds of heaven and all the living creatures that move on earth.*[14]

Ecological humility

Multiplying, subduing, and mastering have given way in ecological sensibilities to sharing, concern, and humility.

For much of human history, human beings "lived their ecological role." They were part of the food chain—both preying on others and being preyed upon in turn. The changes they effected in their immediate ecosystems were no greater than those made by rabbits or beetles. Needless to say, they had no effect on the biosphere as a whole.[15] The melting permafrost of pre-industrial era glaciers, for example, gives no sign of human pollution. Indeed, prior to industrialization, the impact of humans on the Earth's plant and animal life, its seas, land, and atmosphere, was probably negligible.

The end of nature

Two and a half centuries later, some wonder whether we are the last generation on Earth that will be able to save the planet. Others declare that human intervention into nature has been so massive and omnipresent that nature—understood as that which is independent of human designs—no longer exists. Everything on earth is now artificial; in one way or another, all things betray signs of human intervention.[16]

Subduing nature

Human intervention relates not only to the transformative powers of technology; it derives no less from a mind-set, an implicit belief that humans are the center of creation and, as such, free to utilize all they survey for their own purposes. Note the language we employ to describe our relationship to nature: Nature in itself is inhuman, wild, and menacing. It must be subdued, mastered, overcome, humanized, dominated, and conquered. Science, the prototypical Western mode of knowledge, forces nature to relinquish its secrets, to subordinate its powers to human purposes. Our planet is a great quarry of natural resources that we mine, log, farm, fish, and hunt; the Earth, and all it contains, exists to serve human material advancement. In short, our relationship to nature is instrumental, parasitic, and totally human centered. Even the sky becomes airspace.

Virtually all the major contemporary ideologies share this fundamental vision of humanity mastering nature for its own purposes. (The one significant exception is the romantic or reactionary right with its profoundly anti-modernist bias.) Marx praised the bourgeoisie for "subjecting nature's forces to man" and liberating the peasant from "rural idiocy." Liberals and socialists are full of praise for advances that put nature to work for us. Bolsheviks and classical liberals, whatever their profound differences, are in full accord that growth, expansion, progress, rising stan-

---

14. Genesis 1:28.

15. R. O. Slater, "Man's Use of the Environment—the Need for Ecological Guidelines," *Omega*, ed. Paul K. Anderson (Dubuque, Iowa: Wm. C. Brown, 1971) 19.

16. Bill McKibben, *The End of Nature* (New York: Random House, 1989).

dards of living—the increasing power of humanity over nature—are among the very highest of all objectives. Whether this is done via five-year plans or through free-market competition, whether for the glory of the party or for the benefit of the individual, the criteria of success are productivity and technological prowess. Little wonder then that similar ecological disasters face both North America and the former Soviet Union.

The Challenge to Anthropocentric Humanism

Interdependency

Environmentalists challenge the anthropocentric (human-centered) premise that is common to both the left and right. It is, they charge, a form of species arrogance or **speciesism**. Understanding nature as a force to be aggressively mastered in order to enhance human wealth fails to appreciate how much a part of nature we are. Nature is a great web of interdependencies, not a service station at which we tank-up and leave. Each species is linked to all others in a dynamic and highly sensitive system of balances. We can no more pursue our own human aims without regard for the environment than we can drill a hole in our own cabin on board a ship. What we do here has effects there; ecologically we are all our brother's keeper.

Intrusions into delicately poised ecosystems can have devastating effects. Removing one micro-organic link from the food chain (by the use of pesticides, for example) can cause the extinction of those species dependent upon it. In widening circles of devastation, larger species will come under pressure. The balance of plant life, also dependent on certain animal feeding patterns and on the existence of rodents, worms, and insects in the soil, may be severely disrupted as well. What began as a simple attempt of the farmer to rid himself of an agricultural pest, can become an ecological nightmare. Drought, famine, soil erosion, deforestation, the creation of deserts, and disturbances in the atmosphere may well be the results of such inadvertent intrusions into nature.

Toxic waste

Similarly, the casual use of non-biodegradable materials (styrofoam, many forms of plastic) passes on to our children and their children's children an abhorrent legacy of waste and toxicity. These monuments to our momentary convenience will continue to wreak havoc long after our tombstones are worn and our bodies have mixed with the soil. The long-term destructive effects of these massive quantities of non-recyclable materials on ground water, air quality, and soil fertility can only be imagined. What began as a marginally easier way to carry groceries home may well end up as mountains of festering and indestructible refuse. Well might the ecologist paraphrase the biblical prophet's demand: walk humbly with nature.

This call for ecological humility takes its place in a long line of ideas that have systematically undermined the contention that humanity is the center of creation. Copernicus and Galileo revealed our heliocentric (sun-centered) planetary system, reducing the earth to only one of many planets revolving around the sun and denying the physical centrality of human beings in the universe. Darwin's evolutionary ideas decentered humanity even further by recognizing homo sapiens as a natural species with a biological history reaching back to the protozoa. Ecologists wish to take this process a critical step forward: humanity is not only related to all other species, it must begin to respect them as well. It must recognize itself as an inhabitant of the planet along with many other forms of life and develop a reverence—even an awe—for life in its variety, and for the Earth itself. No longer can we lord it over creation. Human rapaciousness is not only ethically indefensible; it has become a peril to the life of the planet.

An Earth-centered ethic

Clearly, however, we cannot go back to live with the bears. What then do the ecologists propose? We can, they believe, as part of a new Earth-centered ethic, accept the connectedness of all life—not merely as a brute biological fact but as a morally demanding responsibility. Henceforth, all of life, from the tiniest single-celled organism floating in the sea, to plants, insects, mammals, reptiles, birds, even to the inanimate rocks, rivers, and clouds, must be seen as our natural partners in creation. They must not be treated simply as our property or our resources. We are not the Earth's masters, only part of its universal dust-to-dust cycle. We have no intrinsic authority over other species.

Nature needs to be preserved for its own sake, not only for ours. Other forms of life (perhaps even rivers and mountains), have their rights as well. We must desist from the supercilious habit of reducing all things to their human use value. **Humanism**, the belief in the special destiny and unique prerogatives of humanity—once a badge of honor in Western thought—becomes for the ecologist the very source of our present predicament.

Much of our venerated historical folklore takes on a very different spirit when viewed from the ecologist's perspective. Consider for example the well-known story recounting how European settlers bought the Island of Manhattan from the Indians for $24 worth of trinkets. The civics-textbook version of the tale emphasizes that it was the greatest bargain of all time; the Indians, who naively believed that the sky, air, and land could not be bought and sold, were convinced to accept a pittance for a choice piece of real estate. Perhaps, the ecologists would say, we have only now reached the point where we realize that there is something very important to be learned from the Indians' wisdom. More significantly still, we may finally understand there is much that we need to unlearn in the tradition of Western thought.

Light Green, Middle Green, Dark Green

For a movement barely two decades old, green politics has splintered in a throng of competing groups and positions. As is so common in ideological discourse, radical ecologists (often spoken of as deep ecologists or dark green ecologists) present more challenging, intellectually stimulating ideas than their moderate confederates. The moderates, however, seem to have the upper hand in actual accomplishments. The often harsh quarrel between these two positions extends from essential questions of substance and purpose to practical issues of strategy and tactics.

Moderate environmentalists

Moderate environmentalists (such as those represented by the Sierra Club, Nature Conservancy, and Audubon Society) approach the ecological crisis with a measured, pragmatic attitude. They are reformers in approach, lobbying groups by organization, and disposed to flexibility in strategy. A partial list of their objectives would include making large-scale recycling mandatory, insisting on the broad use of bio-degradable substances, tightening automobile emission standards, careful monitoring of pesticides, developing clean sources of energy, and fighting environmentally destructive practices such as strip mining and indiscriminate land development. Not a few of these objectives have, at least partially, been achieved.

Although the Earth-centered ethic and ecological humility are deeply embedded in their program, moderates have little sympathy for the anti-technological rages of their more radical associates. Neither do they accept the radicals' claim that human beings are in no way privileged creatures and that all species have precisely the same rights. Ecology, they might say, is an equation in which human beings figure prominently. For them, ecological issues virtually always involve delicate balances and difficult choices between human welfare and environmental obligations. To claim, as some radicals do, that the pristine forest's right to remain in its undisturbed state has an unconditional veto over human actions is, for them, an irresponsible caricature of green politics.

Radical ecologists are divided among themselves in a number of profound ways. Some—generally gentle in disposition, reflective in temperament, and given to rustic, occasionally reclusive lifestyles—are moved by a quest for the spiritual values they find lacking in modern life. Their awe of nature seems imbued with pantheism, the view that God is everything and everything is God; in other words, that God and the universe are one. To experience the rhythms and textures of nature is, they sense, to confront the sacred and the infinite. As one such writer put it:

> *Most of the glimpses of immortality, design and benevolence that I see come from the natural world—from the seasons, from the beauty, from the intermeshed fabric of decay and life.*[17]

Gaia

At times these spiritual tendencies come close to animism (the belief that inanimate objects are spiritually alive), even outright paganism. The earth, for some of these deep ecologists, is possessed of an immanent life-force that, like a living organism, corrects its own imbalances and preserves its global welfare. Over eons of time Gaia, goddess of the earth, sets things aright. To be sure, this gives scant comfort to contemporary ecologists who face the urgent threat of global warming or the rapid disappearance of the rain forests. After all, there is no assurance that Gaia, even if she succeeds in preserving planetary life, prefers human life to beetles.

17. McKibben, *The End of Nature*, 71.

Earth First! demonstrators at the Lincoln Memorial (September 1987).

Earth First!   Not all ecologists are so gentle or spiritual. Some, like the Earth First! group, are unyielding in their ideas and fierce in their tactics. Anthropomorphic conceits, they declare, must give way to biocentric conceptions of nature, i.e., to the recognition that humans are co-equal with all other species. A mountain lion's right to life does not, in essence, differ from our own. Nor is our right to live and develop intrinsically different from the rights of rivers to flow where they will and of trees to grow and die in peace. Those who violate these elemental imperatives have set themselves on an apocalyptic collision course with nature. The greenhouse effect and ozone depletion are only the first of nature's retaliations for human arrogance. Earth First! enthusiasts add their own immediate punishments to those of nature that may be slower in coming. They indulge in ecological sabotage, or ecotage. Most notoriously, they have spiked trees—driven long spikes into tree trunks. The trees are not harmed, but chain-saw wielding lumberjacks are placed in mortal danger. Some of the leaders of Earth First! have already been sentenced to prison terms for activities of this kind.

Social ecology   Even among radical environmentalists, however, consistent biocentric doctrines are not the rule. Far more common is a synthesis of ecological concerns with other human-centered agendas such as socialism and feminism. Social ecologists[18]

---

18. See Murray Bookchin, *The Modern Crisis* (Philadelphia: New Society Publisher, 1986).

argue that the pattern of human domination over nature underlies the ubiquitous tendency of human beings to dominate one another and to reduce the beautiful, even the human, to the status of merchandisable objects. Eco-feminists as well believe that male subjection of women is essentially related to the time-honored tradition of human beings lording it over nature. In fact, most green political parties of Europe—parties dedicated to what is often called the "new politics"— mix environmental themes with feminism, social egalitarianism, participatory/decentralized democracy, sympathy for Third World problems, and disarmament.[19]

Tactics   Tactically, ecologists span the spectrum from buttoned-down legislative lobbyists to tree spikers and splashers of paint on fur coats. Some have chosen conventional political means such as forming political parties. Green parties have sprung up all over Europe and have enjoyed substantial support from young, urban, well-educated, middle-class voters. Ecologists with more anarchist sympathies reject the established political process on principle, favoring instead voluntary local cooperative associations. More dramatic and less conventional are the tactics of organizations like Greenpeace. Recognizing that media attention is the secret of success, Greenpeace activists have resorted to sensational ploys like navigating their ship, the *Rainbow Warrior*, into waters where nuclear testing is about to take place. (French secret agents blew up the ship in reprisal, but the *Rainbow Warrior II* now takes its place.) They have fought whalers about to harvest whale populations and have sailed their ship, a kind of floating public relations exhibition, to ports from Tunisia to Israel, warning that toxic-waste dumping is making the Mediterranean Sea the most polluted of all the Earth's major bodies of water.

Vision   Whatever their differences, ecologists share a basic vision of humanity living in harmony with nature. Something is deeply wrong, they argue, with a civilization that creates anxious, compulsively consumerist, gadget-intoxicated, convenience-addicted individuals. We have forsaken the rigorous life that would put us in touch with the natural world and other human beings. Hence, we are tense and restless at day's end when we should be weary with the day's labor. Having lost touch with nature, we have lost touch with ourselves. Instead of responding to the sun, wind, and earth, we breathe air-conditioned air in fluorescent-lighted offices, eat processed food, travel in speeding cars, and spend motionless hours glazed and benumbed in front of the TV.

We need to change our priorities, to return to basics. We must go back to the "elemental pleasures of eating and drinking and resting, of being dry while it is raining, of getting dry after getting wet, of getting warm after getting cold, of cooling off after getting hot." Of being tired at sundown, and at life's end feeling a

---

19. See Albrecht Rothacher, "The Green Party in German Politics," *West European Politics* 7, no. 3 (July 1984): 109–16, and Thomas Poguntke, "New Politics and the Party System: The Emergence of a New Type of Party," *West European Politics* 10, no. 1 (January 1987): 76–87.

Critiques of
environmentalism

"great weariness, . . . like the lesser weariness that comes at day's end—a weariness that has been earned and can therefore be accepted."[20]

Not everyone shares this vision. For some it is a self-indulgent fantasy that appeals typically to urban middle-class malcontents but is laughed at by those who really live on the land. Besides, critics argue, environmentalism is flawed in a number of basic ways:

A. Purveyors of doom have been with us as long as human beings have walked the Earth. Ecologists are only the latest in a long line of self-styled prophets of fire and brimstone. Like the others, we will long outlive their oracular declarations. (Doomsday ecologists in the early 1970s did not think we would even make it this far!) We should take their predictions with a large grain of salt for at least two reasons: first, they exaggerate wildly with the clear intention of panicking us into accepting their dubious programs, and second, they do not take into account the virtually limitless capacity of human ingenuity to respond to those problems that authentically exist. As has always happened in the past, new technologies will be found to compensate for resource depletion and to correct environmental damage. Green gloom is nothing but a call for despair and resignation. Had we as a species halted our forward progress because of the fear that we would not be able to handle what we created, we would still be cave-dwelling Neanderthals.

The ecologist's counsel of returning to the simple life brings to mind Jonathan Swift's quip about strategies of this kind: they propose supplying our wants by lopping off our desires, cutting off our feet when we need shoes.

B. Human beings are not just another species. Perhaps we are not the exclusive lords of creation, but we are surely the one and only self-conscious, rational, knowledge-seeking creature on the planet. This entails certain responsibilities but grants major prerogatives. The right of a river to flow cannot be equated with the human right to divert the river's waters for agriculture or to construct an energy-creating dam.

C. What real responsibility do we have towards human beings who will live three centuries from now? Are we obliged to set aside our own well-being and that of our immediate descendants because of the possibly destructive consequences our actions may have for individuals who will live in a civilization we might hardly recognize? Beyond the abstract moral issue, there is also the unavoidable empirical question: Do we care enough about our remote posterity to make painful sacrifices today? Would we, for example, give up the automobile if their welfare depended on it? If, as I suspect, the honest answer is a regretful no, the ecologists'

---

20. Bill McKibben citing and paraphrasing from Wendell Berry, *What Are People For?* (San Francisco: North Point Press, 1990) *New York Review of Books*, 14 June 1990, 34.

tirades against contemporary waste and pollution lose much of their sting.

D. Ecological consciousness is mostly a Western phenomenon that appeared after our civilization achieved high levels of affluence. At least part of this success is attributable to our unrestrained exploitation of the Earth's natural resources and our simultaneous befouling of the environment. (Wealthy nations have less than a quarter of the world's population but consume about 80% of its energy and mineral resources.) Now that we have made it, do we have the right to demand that the billions of people living in deep poverty all over the third world restrain their industrial development to improve the planet's air quality? Do we have a moral right to refuse them Western-style development? And if we don't, what are the real prospects for Green politics?

The Storm Over the University

The Challenge to Academia

The image of the university as an island of serene learning sheltered from the bustle and interests of workaday life—an ivory tower—was always a myth. Those familiar with the character of the real academic world would greet such romanticized idylls with a knowing smile. But if the university is no enclave of pure contemplation, until quite recently it was the accepted premise of the entire academic enterprise that universities are, nevertheless, the repository of our civilization's most precious intellectual possessions and the guardians of its highest standards of excellence. Here, in an ambience of intellectual freedom, talented and learned individuals could pursue truth with a minimum of distractions.

The classical idea of a liberal education

Few disagreed over the methods by which these high standards of excellence were to be taught. Human excellence would be spread through exposure to the best that our civilization has created. By entering the inspired worlds of Plato, Shakespeare, Dante, Kant, and Freud, the as yet unformed minds of young adults would be made to confront a lofty standard that would move them to reach beyond the common and easily accessible. They would be challenged by a horizon of human achievement more noble than anything they had known before. Students would take away from their studies life-long standards of true quality and high-mindedness. Habits of critical thinking would replace the conventional pieties of the marketplace. This, in a nutshell, is the classical conception of a liberal education.

The canon

Which works qualify as our civilization's most treasured possessions? Which authors appear on the reading list of everyone aspiring to be liberally educated? These questions have come to be known as the issue of the "canon." By a canon we mean those texts that have received at least semi-official acceptance as privileged and necessary elements in a cultural tradition. In this sense, Mozart is part of our Western musical canon but Heavy Metal is not; Goethe, Racine, and Milton are entrenched in the Western literary pantheon while Pogo, Dear Abby, and Roseanne are not. Who makes these very important determinations? Until recently, the unchallenged answer would have been: those in the best position to do so. An informal consensus of poets, writers, and expert readers selects our literary canon; those with the finest musical sensitivities and training control the musical canon, and so on. Across the centuries, these canonical works become even more deeply entrenched as successive generations are again and again awed by their unique greatness.

Once this was clear; today, however, it provokes a storm of controversy. A vocal opposition now attacks all these ideas as both reactionary and false. They object to the content of the canon, to the idea that the canon is somehow privileged, to the underlying premises of liberal education, to the notion of the university as a repository of our cultural treasures, indeed to the very ideal of a dispassionate academic pursuit of truth. What happened to the seemingly unassailable ideal of a liberal education? Why this sharp departure from what was, the virtually unanimous presupposition of academic life?

1. The changing demographic complexion of the university community has begun to be felt. Once mostly white, male, and middle and upper class, it now includes a rainbow of racial hues, more equal numbers of women, the lower end of the economic spectrum, and the openly gay. These dramatic changes have transformed not only the student body but the faculty as well.

2. The coming of age of Sixties radicals has had its inevitable impact. Those who persevered in radical Sixties' politics and entered academic life are today the mid-life backbone of many university faculties. The storm over the university may be understood at least partially as the belated ideological challenge of Sixties radicals to the intellectual assumptions of the liberal establishment.

3. Add to these demographic and generational changes a host of unsettling relativist ideas that have been gaining ground for quite some time, such as post-modernism, deconstruction, and the new historicism. These new ideas assault conventional perceptions of value, objectivity, and truth at their most basic level. They call into question not merely the truth of this or that theory, but they undermine the very idea of a truth that is independent of particular historical contexts.

Knowledge and power

What is considered true and worthy and excellent, they argue, is always related to the interests of those who declare them to be true, worthy, and excellent. Knowledge is not an otherworldly spiritual essence. Determining what is true cannot be dissociated from the power relations of a given society or from the authority of specific individuals to enforce certain standards and reject others. These preferred standards inevitably reflect and serve the racial, sexual, and class interests of the dominant establishment. In the hands of minorities, feminists, and radicals, such ideas become potent weapons with which to puncture what they see as mainstream academia's pretensions to be the exclusive guardians of the canon.

One cannot deny, as a matter of simple fact, that our canon over-represents DWEMs—dead, white, European males. (For example, all of the greats listed above, as well as the majority of thinkers considered in this book, fall into this category.) The concerns of women, gays, non-whites, like the experience of the third world, find only token representation on our cultural honor roll. Nor can we doubt that the canon prefers authors of middle- and upper-class backgrounds; the world of the poor and downtrodden—although encompassing incomparably greater numbers of individuals than the aristocracy—is hardly documented at all.

For radical critics, the connection between the canon and its official guardians is all too obvious. Isn't it perfectly clear that the white, male, Euro-centric establishment seeks to perpetuate its domination through a partisan, self-serving canon? A hegemonic "old boys club" spanning the centuries has systematically glorified its own world while ignoring the experience of others. The classical canon reflects a political reality in which non-WEM concerns were invisible and voiceless. It has sexist, racist, repressive, and imperialist traits because these were the dominant traits of the civilization that gave rise to it. In a world where most people are non-white, half are women, and the majority working class or poor, the old canon is simply an anachronism. It is high time for it to go!

A new canon? No wonder then that radicals concentrate their heaviest fire on university course curricula. Curricula are not technical matters to be left to professorial determination. (Besides, professors are, more often than not, WEMs themselves.) The right to determine the canon is the right to determine the content of our minds. The canon is politics by other means. If knowledge is power, then the power to decide what is and what is not knowledge must be doubly powerful. The voices of non-whites, women, and the poor must therefore be heard in deciding on our standards of relevance and excellence. We need to create a canon that represents the variety of human experience, rather than one that draws exclusively on the world of a small and privileged minority. A new representative canon would be the logical and democratic implication of the demographic transformations that society and the universities have undergone.

In addition to readings from the Bible, texts from the Koran and Confucius need to be added. Native American, Hispanic, and African myths need to be read alongside Greek mythology and the Homeric epics. Together with the poetry of Keats and Shelly, the raging lyrics of urban rappers should be heard. Women writers who recount the struggle of females against male domination should be preferred over writers who portray women as empty-headed, conniving, or hysterical. The sufferings of gay men and women in a **homophobic** world should be included no less than conventional love stories like *Romeo and Juliet*. Malcolm X was no less a gadfly than Socrates and hence his life and ideas deserve no less attention. Philosophies of liberation should be emphasized in preference to the conventional philosophies of hierarchy, authority, and privilege.

Abandon the canon? As far-reaching as these revisions to the canon may be, for many in the radical camp they do not go far enough. For some, Western civilization and particularly American culture are so riddled with repressive (patriarchal, racist, hierarchical, imperialistic) traits that its canon is simply beyond remedy. It can only be abandoned.

For others of an even more radical bent, the really charged issue is neither the canon's unrepresentative character nor even its essentially tainted nature. The problem lies with the idea of a canon itself, for the very notion of a canon assumes an elitist and hierarchical view of culture. Its central criterion is the self-standing excellence of a cultural creation rather than its representativeness or its humanly liberating qualities. It dissociates literature, philosophy, art, and music from their social impact and judges them by autonomous esthetic or intellectual criteria. Culture becomes a series of sanctified, largely inaccessible monuments that perpetuates the stratification of society by excluding the less knowledgeable from higher cultural pursuits.

Realizing that the masses will not be inducted into the rarified worlds of Mozart and Milton, radicals choose to rethink the entire concept of culture so as to include the whole of society. Only by democratizing culture, by deflating the pompous claims to superiority of an elite culture, can an egalitarian society come into being. Indeed, they argue, societies that divide their cultures into high and low do so because their social relations are already stratified into similar hierarchies.

Moreover, the entire standard of excellence begs the question of excellent for whom. Beethoven's string quartets are no more excellent for the inner city than the earthy rhythms of reggae music are excellent for the philharmonic. Appealing to radically relativist doctrines that understand "excellence" and "truth" as social constructions deriving from specific power relations, the anti-canon camp denies that there can be a self-sufficient standard of excellence. The canon reflects not so much excellence as it does political dominance. If it has any value at all, it is as a case study of the way that political control translates into the control over ideas. Studying the canon is an excellent way of honing one's skills at unmasking and demythologizing the hegemony of a ruling elite. The traditional idea of a liberal education has here been turned entirely on its head.

Politicizing the university

Some have been quick to derive explosive conclusions from these arguments. If excellence and truth are partisan terms in the political struggle for advantage, the politicization of the classroom would seem to be entirely justified. For if the content of what we read is already political, why should its treatment not be overtly so? And if overtly so, why not in the service of race, gender, and class issues that have for so long been unrepresented? Why shouldn't the lecture hall be used as a place to recruit support for the victims of oppression if, across the corridor, other professors continue to teach the old canon which is no less political in character? If the university is a political battleground and not an ivory tower, why not silence speakers and harass professors who are unsympathetic to minority needs? Why not insist on speech codes that are sensitive to the grievances of women, or on **politically correct** attitudes to the sufferings of people of color, or on censoring views that are offensive to gays? Why not turn the entire university system—from admissions, to faculty recruitment and promotion, to curricula, to student government, etc.—into a lever for social transformation?

Critiques of
the radical
canon-bashers

Why not indeed! retort the outraged opponents. Among the many indignant responses, the following are particularly prevalent.

A. Radicals misunderstand what education is about. It has nothing to do with representativeness. Education is not intended to provide an indiscriminate sampling of what our civilization has produced. By its very nature education is elitist because it involves exposure to selected works of high quality. Its aim is not catering to popular demand but rather developing the kind of critical thought that discriminates between popular demand and the genuinely valuable. The educational process seeks to transcend the merely average by encouraging students to distinguish between kitsch and culture, beauty and tinsel, truth and sophistry. Were education to become nothing more than a reflection of popular tastes and political pressures, it would be indistinguishable from propaganda.

B. Our intellectual tradition bestows the highest praise on those thinkers who have broken ranks with the crowd and set off in new directions. The intellectual rebels and non-conformists, from Socrates to Galileo to Freud, hold far more honored positions in our canon than most orthodox establishment figures. The idea of the canon as smug and uncritical is absurd.

   Moreover, because the tradition is so highly diverse and full of disagreements, we do not read the canon complacently. Unless we apply discriminating judgment, it is a baffling hodgepodge of contradictions. Immersion in the canon provides the finest available training in developing just the critical bent of mind that the radicals wish to cultivate. Indeed, reading Sophocles, Moliere, and Marx was, for many generations, the stuff of which liberation from bourgeois orthodoxies was made. One cannot help but wonder whether a homogeneous, politically correct education based on an ideologically tailored canon could produce anything but conformism and cliches.

C. Why should we apologize for the fact that we are a Western people with a Western culture? No more than speaking English implies a belief that English is superior to other languages does emphasis on Western civilization involve an arrogant dismissal of the others. There is nothing wrong with each ethnic or cultural group wishing to educate its members in its own cultural traditions. But our common glue is undeniably Western, and this ought to serve as the basis for our common culture.

D. Many defenders of the canon are willing to accept the validity of the radicals' complaints. The canon should be expanded to include deserving works of non-DWEMs. The operative word here is deserving. Writers do not enter the canon as an act of charity. Even if we accept the need for affirmative action to redress race and gender imbalances in the university community, the idea of an affirmative-action canon is preposterous. Here there is a single standard: excellence. The view of some radicals that standards of excellence unfairly prejudice non-DWEM writers, that they somehow violate their basic rights, must be respectfully rejected.

It is truly lamentable that women, the poor, and non-whites were excluded from cultural activity. This exclusion was, unfortunately, terribly effective; only the extraordinary escaped its impact. There are few works of canonical quality authored by non-DWEMs. But the past cannot be undone, certainly not by attributing to inferior cultural creations qualities they do not have. All the mea culpas of the white male establishment will not create an alternative canon of quality. (It is, besides, odd to claim that this repression was frightful and at the same time to find a canon of high-quality works authored by the repressed.)

Moreover, devaluing the canon by filling it with undeserving creations is self-defeating. When undeserving works are introduced into the canon, the inevitable consequence is to discredit the entire idea of the canon rather than to glorify the newly introduced work. Violating the canon's inherent standards of excellence will only sink the entire canonical ship. The only solution to the problem the exclusively DWEM canon presents is to transform the reality that fostered it. We must give women, non-whites, etc., an equal opportunity to create works deserving of inclusion.

E. Every reasonable person knows that ideas have contexts and that these contexts affect the way our ideas are conceived and organized. We all know that different cultures and eras have different standards and values. Nor are we so naive as to discount the effect of political dominance on the marketplace of ideas. But to leap to the reckless conclusion that because ideas are contextual they cannot be subjected to any independent standards of validity, that truth is a partisan term, that excellence means no more than whatever I happen to like, signifies only that academia is at present in a silly season that will hopefully pass quickly.

This fashionable form of nihilism affronts every standard of fair-mindedness and reason. First, if one is to be consistently relativist, then even the doctrine of radical relativism is only contextual and not true. Second, if there are ultimately no better or worse standards, why is the struggle for the rights of the oppressed any more worthy than the counter-struggle in favor of the privileges of the WEMs? Third, and most essentially, these doctrines violate what decent, rational people know to be true. Philosophy and nuclear physics are higher human pursuits than mud wrestling and cock fighting. Tolstoy and Dostoyevsky are incomparably greater writers than the authors of the throwaway schlock available at supermarket check-out counters. Holocaust denial is not just another historical interpretation; it is false and vicious. A taste for necrophilia is not just a case of different strokes for different folks; it is pathological. When elementary moral and intellectual standards such as these become problematic, a civilization is in deep trouble.

Suggestions for Further Reading

Feminism

Daly, Mary. *Gyn/Ecology: The Metaethics of Radical Feminism*. Boston: Beacon Press, 1979.

De Beauvoir, Simone. *The Second Sex*. Harmondsworth: Penguin, 1972.

Eisenstein, Hester. *Contemporary Feminist Thought*. London: Unwin, 1984.

Elshtain, J. B. *Public Man, Private Woman*. Princeton: Princeton University Press, 1981.

Firestone, Shulamith. *The Dialectic of Sex*. London: Paladin, 1972.

Friedan, Betty. *The Feminine Mystique*. New York: Dell, 1963.

Gelb, J. *Feminism and Politics*. Berkeley: University of California Press, 1989.

Janeway, Elizabeth. *Man's World, Woman's Place*. New York: Delta Books, 1971.

Millet, Kate. *Sexual Politics*. Garden City, N.J., Doubleday, 1970.

Mitchell, Juliette. *Woman's Estate*. New York: Vintage Books, 1973.

Rowbotham, Shiela. *Woman's Consciousness*. London: Penguin, 1973.

Environmentalism

Berry, Wendell. *The Gift of Good Land*. San Francisco: North Point Press, 1981.

Bookchin, Murray. *The Modern Crisis*. Philadelphia: New Society Publisher, 1986.

Dobson, Andrew, and Paul Lacardie, eds. *The Politics of Nature: Explorations in Green Political Theory*. London: Routledge, 1993.

Leopold, Aldo. *A Sand County Almanac*. Oxford: Oxford University Press, 1981.

McKibben, Bill. *The End of Nature*. New York, Random House, 1989.

Pepper, David. *Eco-socialism: From Deep Ecology to Social Justice*. London: Routledge, 1993.

The Storm Over the University

Bloom, Alan. *The Closing of the American Mind: How Higher Education Has Failed Democracy and Impoverished the Souls of Today's Students*. New York: Simon and Schuster, 1987.

D'Souza, Dinesh. *Illiberal Education: The Politics of Race and Sex on Campus*. New York: Free Press, 1990.

Foucault, Michel. *The Foucault Reader*. Ed. Paul Rabinow. Harmondsworth: Penguin, 1986.

Gless, Darryl J., and Barbara Herrnstein Smith, eds. *The Politics of Liberal Education*. Durham: Duke University Press, 1992.

Kimball, Roger. *Tenured Radicals: How Politics Has Corrupted Our Higher Education*. New York: Harper and Row, 1990.

Pickering, Andrew, ed. *Science As Practice and Culture*. Chicago: University of Chicago Press, 1992.

Rorty, Richard. *Contingency, Irony and Solidarity*. Cambridge: Cambridge University Press, 1989.

$$Chapter \quad 10$$

Epilogue:
Toward the Third Millennium

The approach of the third millennium has the natural effect of encouraging historical stock takings. And so we close our survey with a very tentative and interim ideological balance sheet. No prophecies will be forthcoming. These are usually as wrong as they are arrogant. No more is intended than an analysis of some major trends in contemporary ideological debate. Where these are heading—what lies over the historical horizon—can only be touched upon in the most provisional way.

Civil Society vs. Grand Mobilizing Ideologies

Radicalism of left and right discredited

Unquestionably the most dramatic ideological development of the recent past is the dissolution of communism as a practice and as an ideology. This came roughly forty-five years after the disintegration in defeat and ignominy of the radical fascist right. The sensational failure of the two modern attempts to create mass mobilizing, totalitarian societies with uncompromisingly radical political aims has rendered grand ideological systems highly suspect in Western eyes. Ideologies that promise a brave new world, a leap into freedom, a Reich of a thousand years, are likely to trigger allergic reactions in those with any kind of historical memory.

The decline of mass-mobilizing ideologies

Communism's collapse represents a compound success for the West: a victory of the free-market economy over collectivist, planned economies, and perhaps even more important, a triumph of pragmatic, low-key, individual-centered ideologies over grand, mass-mobilizing ideologies. Most people, most of the time, clearly prefer to live their own lives and attend to their own goals rather than serve grand historical purposes. Moreover, turbulent revolutionary upheavals, even when they come, can be sustained for only relatively short periods. These concentrated bursts of historical energy inevitably diminish as everyday imperatives overwhelm the revolutionary epic state of mind. In other words, the forces that create and inspire revolutions are very different from the forces necessary to sustain and routinize them. The true victor in the saga of communism's collapse is the widespread and powerful desire to live a satisfying everyday life following one's own freely chosen life plan.

The centrality of civil society

This form of non-public, voluntary activity overlaps with an analytic concept that has become very popular in recent studies of the transition to democracy: **civil society**. It is an old term, going back to Hegel, Locke, and Hobbes, and it broadly connotes that area of human activity that lies between the intimately familial on the one side, and the state directed on the other. Some of the states emerging from Soviet control have virtually no history of a flourishing civil society. For them, there have only been two planes of human life: the family, where biological and emotional nurturing took place, and the state, where everything else took place. State control extended from the economy, to the world of ideas, to the local soccer league. The individual confronted the state as an isolated atom facing an all-powerful institution.

Civil society, as it has developed in the West, comprises a rich mosaic of voluntary associations that come into being and are sustained by individuals in their private capacity as citizens. These range from economic corporations, to charitable institutions, to farmers' granges and cooperatives, to student and faculty organizations, to churches, to the neighborhood book club. Although they may sometimes petition the government, they are independent of governmental direction. By dispersing power among many voluntary social organizations, civil society limits political control. It mediates between the individual and the state by forming a natural social buffer that cushions the impact of the political.

Mass-mobilizing ideologies, with their crusading single-mindedness, stand in sharp contrast to the diffuse pluralism of civil society. No wonder then that one of the express purposes of mobilizing ideologies is to overwhelm the diverse sectorial and private interests of civil society in the name of a grand historical goal. They seek to homogenize the variety of voluntary civil associations and subject them to central control. A rich civil society may well be the most effective deterrent against the advance of mass-mobilizing ideologies.

A Contemporary Ideological Balance Sheet

Our present ideological calm

Civil society's contemporary attractiveness is a measure of our misgivings about grand ideological agendas. Not surprisingly, these revolutionary, mobilizing ideologies seem, at least for the present, to be at ebb tide. Although they have hardly disappeared, militantly radical ideologies demanding vast political upheavals have tended to recede to the margins of most Western ideological discourse. The Western ideological heartland, which ranges from a modified classical liberalism to a moderate democratic socialism, does not seem to be imminently threatened by serious challenges. Even if we reject as premature the claim that the triumph of the liberal/social democratic center means a final resolution to the ideological debate of the past 250 years, it is difficult to deny that we have arrived at a certain relative calm in our Western ideological odyssey. Whether this is a calm that foreshadows greater, more permanent calm or a short lull between unending storms is precisely the kind of prophecy that will not be forthcoming.

There are, nevertheless, some telling signs that we have indeed turned a corner. The integration of the European Community highlights unprecedented levels of inter-state cooperation. It even reflects a gradual erosion in the exclusive sovereignty of the nation-state. The GATT and NAFTA trade agreements (with the Pacific Rim countries and with Canada and Mexico respectively) promise to promote a world-wide openness in trade. It has, in fact, become a commonplace to claim that contemporary competition between Western states no longer centers on the political front. Today's rivalries increasingly focus on technological innovation, trade deficits, and shares of the world market.

The processes of democratization and conflict resolution also have some substantial gains to display. Spain and Portugal, not long ago rigid autocracies, have clearly entered the family of democratic nations. Germany, Italy, and Japan seem to have largely overcome their turbulent pasts and today qualify as reasonably stable democracies. There are also reasons for cautious optimism in regard to a number of South American states. Conflicts that for years seemed intractable—like those in South Africa, the Middle East, and Ireland—give some hope of compromise and accommodation. Moreover, it has been more than a half-century since the last democratic state abandoned its democratic character. One especially hopeful indicator is best formulated as a question: When was the last time that two authentically liberal democratic states went to war with each other? Taken together, these advances in democracy and conflict resolution give some credence to the view that modern ideological discourse has become gentler and more humane.

Ethnic antagonisms

Still, we cannot ignore the empty half of the glass. The decline of the grand ideological systems was offset by the rise of narrow ethnic antagonisms and long-buried national rivalries. Tribalized politics, as it has been called, is only peripherally concerned with systematic ideological doctrines and cannot be mapped on any familiar left-right continuum. Its concerns are more rudimentary: are you friend or foe, kinsman or alien? What one happens to believe about free-market economics or democratic government is less important in these conflicts than what one eats, how one dresses, and which dialect one speaks.

The collapse of communism

This return to ethnic politics is, of course, directly related to the collapse of communism. The severe hardships accompanying the transition of the republics of the former Soviet Union to a market economy have provided hothouse conditions for macabre ideological mutants to develop. Demagogic and unscrupulous political leaders play on the dark fears and felt needs of a hungry and humiliated people. Xenophobic, racist, anti-semitic, quasi-fascist voices out of the past are a serious concern for all those who saw in the breakdown of the Soviet Empire a potentially liberating, progressive event.

In communism's favor it may at least be said that it imposed external order and plastered over the many natural fissures that broke the surface of its multi-national empire. Communist internationalism, however sporadic and inconsistent it was, effectively set itself against expressions of chauvinism and racism. With the removal of Soviet control, all manner of latent, long-forgotten conflicts burst out with a fury that has stunned even the most hardened observers of East European politics. The conflicts in the former Yugoslavia, in the former Soviet Georgia, in Azerbaijan and Armenia, in the Muslim former Soviet republics of Central Asia (and too many others to mention) seem a throwback to an earlier age. Not only in the obvious sense that their bloodiness recalls primitive butchery, but in the specific historical sense that the Yugoslavian war, for example, is an eerie reenactment of the Balkan conflicts that led to the outbreak of World War I.

The Right-Left Continuum: How Relevant Is It?

Fundamentalism vs. modernization

The inapplicability of our conventional ideological categories of left and right is even more dramatically manifest in the confrontation between the liberal democratic West and the rising tide of Muslim fundamentalism. Although here—as opposed to the primordial ethnic conflicts in the post-Soviet world—great world-views are clearly in collision, they are not what Western ideological debate has prepared us for. The differences between the two positions are so basic that it becomes difficult to identify in the opponent's discourse any issues or even a vocabulary with which we are familiar. Western conservatives and radicals have considerably more in common with each other than either has with the religiously inspired ideology of the Ayatollahs. Western ideological conflict takes place against the background of at least some commonly shared cultural values. Hence, the confrontation between the democratic West and Muslim fundamentalism is not easily dealt with in conventional ideological terms. Perhaps it is best characterized as a collision between basically incongruous civilizations.

This potentially explosive dispute between civilizations is, nevertheless, quite relevant to our tradition of ideological discourse. It dramatically refutes an assumption held by most of the West's ideological mainstream. It has been widely assumed since the Enlightenment that Western civilization's progress toward modernization followed a natural and inevitable dynamic that was destined to be copied by all modernizing societies. The growth of science and technology, it seemed clear, would bring with it rationality, democracy, tolerance, and the relegation of religious belief and practice to the realm of the private. The world, in Max Weber's famous phrase, would gradually become "disenchanted" or demystified as the mental habits associated with scientific rationality took root.

We can now say that this hypothesis is false. No smooth, natural, or universal transition takes humanity from the pre-modern, via scientific rationality, to the triumph of human rights, pluralism, and parliamentarianism. Technological advance does not necessarily bring democratic values with it. Scientific sophistication can co-exist with virtually any kind of political regime. Modernization can transform some forms of behavior, while leaving traditional ideas substantially intact in others. What is more, the specter of modernization at times can trigger an intense backlash. Defenders of traditional orthodoxies, panicked by the penetration of

Western values, have been prone to launch full-scale attacks against the intruding foreign bodies. These very different routes to modernization lie at the heart of much contemporary ideological conflict—especially the looming confrontation between the West and fundamentalist Islam.

Categories falter

Even within the confines of Western ideological discourse itself, the old left-right categorization seems to be faltering somewhat. This is particularly true of the most fashionable ideological currents that have emerged in recent decades. The ecological political ethic, for example, cuts across all ideological camps and is unclassifiable in left-right terms. Neither does feminist theory neatly conform to left-wing expectations. The struggle to revise the canon, if it can be classified as left-wing in inspiration, belongs to a novel kind of cultural left rather than to the more familiar economic and political left. Black radicalism, and especially the more militant forms of black separatism, appear to have more in common with ethnic nationalism than they do with the accepted logic of leftist theories.

Post-materialism

Nor are the sociological bases of the left-right split what they once were. The lower classes, long the standard bearers of left-wing political programs, have moved rightward toward more hard-line positions on security, foreign affairs, and law and order. The upper classes, especially if they are well-educated, have shown a marked tendency to move away from pocketbook voting in support of their economic interests, toward a principled concern with cosmopolitan, liberationist, anti-authoritarian, ecological values—what one writer calls a post-materialist ideological agenda.[1] All of this is enough to raise at least initial queries about how relevant the left-right classificatory scheme remains. Although these conventional categories have plenty of fight left in them, there may perhaps be another, as yet shrouded, organizational principle (or principles) making its way onto the ideological stage.

Ideology in the Global Village

The communications revolution

Even on a very short list of contemporary developments in ideological discourse, we cannot omit the profound effects of the revolution in communications that has transformed our world into a global village. The technology of communication seems to make headway with the speed of a geometric progression. In the early years of the twentieth century, ideas could be communicated in print or by word of mouth. Then came the radio, followed by the television, and in quick succession, satellite communications, cables, the fax machine, electronic mail, vast networks of computer hookups, and the cellular telephone. No corner of the earth is left uncovered by the global news networks. No esoteric information or exotic culture or remote vista is further away than the computer terminal or the television screen. Inevitably, the nature of ideological discourse has been affected.

---

1. See Ronald Ingelhart, *The Silent Revolution* (Princeton: Princeton University Press, 1977), and his more recent study *Culture Shift in Advanced Industrial Society* (Princeton: Princeton University Press, 1990). Ingelhart summarizes his position in "Value Change in Industrial Societies," *American Political Science Review* 81, no. 4 (1987): 1289–1303.

The pluralism
of the airwaves

With the penetration of multiple communications networks and the easy accessibility of information, ideologies are faced with new opportunities and with serious new problems. On the one hand, their message can be brought home with an immediacy and reach never before possible. On the other hand, it becomes increasingly difficult to avoid the pluralism of the airwaves. The routine exposure of the modern individual to various messages and differing points of view renders mass mobilizing ideologies, with their single-minded enthusiasms, more difficult to sustain. If ideological messages can target their audiences more effectively, it also becomes unlikely that theirs will be the only message received. Barring massive efforts at self-isolation (such as those practiced by traditional communities who wish to keep the world out), or outright governmental jamming of the avenues of communication, the likelihood that a modern person will be exclusively exposed to a single political ideology grows increasingly remote.

Moreover, the variety of messages and the multiplicity of available communication channels means that the listening/viewing/on-line audience is highly fragmented. No longer does a unified audience react to the identical stimuli as when, for example, Franklin D. Roosevelt addressed the nation in his radio-transmitted fireside chats. It requires a truly extraordinary event to tear scattered attentions away from their diverse interests and focus national attention on a single concern.

How will the civic virtues, those shared communal values that bond a national character and create political solidarity, be affected by this novel dispersal of concerns? Can serious ideological commitments survive the loss of a single public center? Or should the point be put in the opposite way? Perhaps the approaching era of total media immersion portends greater imposed unity, greater vulnerability to ideological domination, and easier manipulation of docile audiences. Or might it be that the ready availability of information will raise the critical threshold of an increasingly sophisticated audience and render demagogic tirades and empty sloganeering less effective than ever before? It is impossible, of course, to foretell which of these trends (or which blend of them) will eventually dominate. Nonetheless, it is certain that ideological discourse will evolve dramatically as it adapts to the possibilities and constraints of an age of communication.

Ideology in a Relativist Age

Even more problematic for sustaining ideological commitments is the growing ascendance of value relativism in Western culture. Although relativist doctrines have had a following since the days of the Sophists, they have never been anything near as popular as they presently are. Relativist doctrines have not only become commonplace to point of cliche, they have become increasingly radical as well. They go far beyond the kind of wide-eyed relativist speculations most adolescents indulge in. ("Were I born a Hindu in India, I'd believe what Hindus in India believe. What I believe because I was born a Protestant in America is, therefore, wholly arbitrary.") Modern relativism argues that human knowledge, far from constituting a pure mental achievement, is shaped decisively by economic needs, by the will to power, by psychological compulsions, even by the professional interests of the academic community. Social truths always conceal hidden agendas; they are in fact the product of these hidden agendas. Even science, long the holdout of certainty, has not remained immune from relativist unmaskings.

Undermining ideology

Ideological certainties are relativism's most vulnerable target. In no form of thought are interests more patently obvious than in political ideology. Whether the interests are economic or power-related, it is relatively easy work to unmask lurking agendas and deconstruct pretensions to objectivity. But having become accustomed to unmask the interests underlying ideological principles, how are we any longer to believe without attacks of self-consciousness and doubt? (An old Persian tale tells of a centipede who, having been asked to reveal how it managed to move its many legs in unison, thought hard and gave a detailed explanation. Afterwards, however, it could no longer walk.) This is not merely a psychological problem. Where value relativism makes serious inroads, recruitment to ideological banners becomes that much more difficult.

The paradox of ideology

And yet, ideological belief is a political necessity. To return full-circle to our opening chapter, ideology provides the indispensable justifications for a particular allocation of resources, for a certain meting out of punishments and privileges, and for a determinate set of political rules of the game. Without ideological justification, all of these would be little more than nakedly coercive practices with little chance of long-term survival. Hence, whether it is easy for us to justify their ultimate validity or not, our ideological guidelines must be solidly entrenched in order for organized political life, as we know it, to function satisfactorily. The paradox of contemporary ideological thinking turns out to be particularly frustrating: although our ideological certainties have been undermined by the modern relativist style of thought, our need for ideological certainty continues to be as strong as ever.

We have traversed an exceptionally large and elaborate body of modern ideological thought. Inevitably, each reader will be drawn, whether by argument or by temperament, to one or another of the many doctrines we have discussed. It is unlikely though that this book will have made any converts. The complexity and many-sidedness of the issues involved in intelligent ideological discourse has, after all, been an underlying theme in all that has been said. The author will count his efforts successful if the reader comes away from his analyses, expositions, and critiques at least confused at a higher level.

Glossary

affirmative action The attempt to encourage the success of minorities and hitherto under-represented groups by favoring them in hiring and admissions policies.

alienation A central term in Hegelian and Marxist thought. Marx intends by it a profound loss of self in which human needs, aspirations, and powers are thwarted by exploitation and by hostile material conditions. In **capitalism**, Marx believes that the **proletariat** is alienated from their own human essence, their labor, and their fellow human beings.

ancien regime Refers specifically to the socio-political realities of pre-revolutionary France. More broadly it connotes the pre-modern, pre-democratic socio-political order that reactionaries tend to admire.

animal liberation A philosophical/ideological position that argues against **speciesism** or the doctrine that only human beings are endowed with rights.

bourgeoisie In Marxist terminology, the owners of the means of production in a capitalist society. Often used as a synonym for the ruling class.

bourgeois revolution Revolution of a rising commercial middle class against the **ancien regime**'s aristocracy, monarchy, and church. Such revolutions normally demand civil rights, free trade, and the rule of law. The French Revolution of 1789 is its classic instance.

capitalism An economic system based on private ownership of the means of production and free trade.

centrist In contemporary politics, centrists are usually supporters of a middle-of-the-road position and opposed to both **left** and **right**.

charismatic leadership A type of leadership distinguished by the sociologist Max Weber. Its central characteristic is devotion to the leader because of the virtually super-human qualities she or he is said to possess. In recent times the term has been devalued to mean a leader with a crowd-pleasing manner.

civil society That area of social life that is neither familial and intimate on the one hand, nor state-directed on the other. It includes voluntary organizations of various kinds, ranging from private economic enterprises, to farmers granges, to the Little Leagues.

class In Marxist thought, classes are the fundamental units of **capitalist** society. Class membership determines one's interests, perspective, and consciousness. The class that owns the **means of production** (the ruling class or **bourgeoisie**) is set against the exploited class (the **proletariat**).

classical liberalism The initial form of liberalism (which has been revived in our time) that believes in minimal government, absolute property rights, and **laissez-faire** economics.

communism A form of social organization that prohibits private property and insists on the state control of all industry. It is controlled by a single all-powerful party and has usually tended toward a **totalitarian** political system.

conservatives Those who prefer preserving the traditions of the past into the present. They typically oppose rapid or radical changes.

corporatism The Italian fascist economic system in which private ownership was retained but made part of a nationally controlled command economy. Its object was to overcome class conflict, coordinate productive forces, and strengthen national power.

counter-culture The anti-establishment lifestyles developed by Sixties radicals.

cult of the personality Relating to a political leader as if he possessed an almost god-like status. The leader's personality and achievements become synonymous with the ideology and the cause itself. Often used in regard to Hitler, Stalin, and Mao.

deficit spending An economic policy proposed by the British economist John Maynard Keynes. Keynes predicted that by borrowing money and investing it in the economy, governments could stimulate economic growth.

democratic centralism The Leninist doctrine that prohibits factionalism within the Communist Party and demands complete compliance with decisions that have already been reached.

determinism In the context of Marxist discourse, the view that changes in objective material realities necessarily bring changes in political realities. Determinists deny that changes can be made by acts of revolutionary will. (Contrast with **voluntarism**.)

dialectic A method of reasoning based on the collision of opposites. Whether in the give and take of discussion (Plato), the clash of opposing ideas (Hegel), or the struggle between rival economic classes (Marx), what emerges from the dialectical confrontation is a synthesis, a higher level of understanding or existence.

dictatorship of the proletariat After assuming power, the **proletariat**, in order to resist bourgeois counter-revolutionary intrigue, must act decisively and turn the instruments of coercion against their class enemies. In Marxist thought this is the intermediary stage between revolution and the **withering of the state**.

direct action The direct and violent destruction of institutions and authority advocated by those anarchists who disdained all parliamentary political activity.

end of ideology A movement of the mid 1950s and early 1960s arguing that ideology was in decline. Its supporters believed that both the **left** and the **right** had given up their extreme positions and a new open bargaining style of politics was emerging.

end-state theories of justice The view, criticized by Nozick, that the morally just distribution of social resources can be decided upon in principle, not left up to the free and voluntary contracts, exchanges, inheritances, etc., made between individuals.

Enlightenment A deeply influential intellectual movement centered in eighteenth-century France that emphasized the importance of rationalism, science, and progress. Its enemies were religious orthodoxies, monarchical autocracy, as well as superstition and blind adherence to custom.

ethno-centrism The tendency to be so centered on the concerns of one's own ethnic group that the needs and perspectives of others are ignored, even rejected.

Fabian socialism A pragmatic, gradualist democratic socialist movement in which many of England's leading intellectuals were involved. Flourished at the end of the nineteenth and beginning of the twentieth centuries.

false consciousness In Marxist terminology, false consciousness occurs when one's own thoughts are dominated and distorted by ideas that serve the interests of others; for example, when the **proletariat**'s outlook is dominated by the interests of the **bourgeoisie**.

final solution The Nazi policy of totally exterminating the Jewish people. A third of the world's Jews, roughly six million men, women, and children, were killed in the Nazi Holocaust.

first principles Those premises and axioms that underlie philosophical or political theory.

forces of production See **means of production**.

general strike The anarcho-syndicalist doctrine that the collapse of the capitalist state will come when all the workers defy the **bourgeoisie** and cease working en masse.

general will In Rousseau's teaching, the authentic will of the entire political community. It is expressed when individuals disregard their own private interests and consider only the common good.

great chain of being The medieval view that all of creation is part of a single hierarchy with God at its pinnacle and the lowliest of inanimate objects at its base.

Great Cultural Revolution Between 1966 and 1969, incited by Mao's call for renewed revolutionary enthusiasm, masses of youths challenged the hegemony of the Chinese Communist Party, undermined authority, humiliated experts, and disrupted economic production—as well as indulging in less ideologically motivated activity like pillaging and murder.

Greens (Green politics) Supporters of various ecological causes who use a multiplicity of political strategies—from the parliamentary to the violent—to achieve their end of preserving the natural environment.

guerrilla warfare A style of warfare that emphasizes attacking a larger and better equipped enemy at its vulnerable points, living off the land (usually rugged, inaccessible terrain), cultivating the support of the native population, creating a highly mobile fighting force, and attempting to wear down the enemy rather than engage in open battle. Associated with **Maoism**.

gulag The system of labor camps in the Soviet Union to which dissidents were sent, especially at the height of **Stalinism**. A former inmate, Alexander Solzhenitsyn, documented the enormity of the atrocities in his book *The Gulag Archipelago*.

homophobia An antipathy for homosexuals, often linked with attempts to disqualify their sexual preferences either legally or morally.

humanism Until recently, the optimistic belief in the unique capacities of human reason, morality, and creativity. For many green ideologues, it has come to mean an arrogant belief in the human superiority over the rest of nature.

idealism A philosophical position that holds ideas to be pre-eminent. Hegel, for example, believed that the development of our material civilization reflects a prior and more basic development in our ideas. (Contrast to **materialism**.)

imperialism The domination and exploitation, both economically and politically, of developing third-world countries by the wealthy capitalist states. For Lenin, it was the most advanced and final stage of capitalism.

individualism The political doctrine that the individual ought to be the ultimate repository of political power and that the state exists to serve and protect the individual's needs and rights.

infrastructure The basic material forces that prevail in a particular community. They include the form of ownership, the kinds of productive processes, and the available resources. (Contrast with **superstructure**.)

instrumentalism A view of the state and society as means serving the ends set by specific individuals. It denies that the state or society are more than the sum of its individual parts. (Contrast with **organicism**.)

invisible hand Adam Smith (and other free-market liberals) argues that unregulated trade is systematically controlled by the invisible hand of prices, supply, and demand. Its overall effect is the benefit of all.

irrationalism The belief, associated with fascism and a number of earlier critics of democracy, that primal instincts and emotions are the true sources of human action.

Keynesian economics   John Maynard Keynes argued that via government **deficit spending**, economies could shake off the effects of recession and depression. (Contrast with **laissez faire**.)

kibbutz   A communal cooperative village in contemporary Israel based on socialist principles.

laissez faire   The economic doctrine that a free market system without government intervention best serves the cause of general wealth and welfare.

left-wing   Those who tend toward radical solutions to political problems. Left-wingers are prone to socialist, egalitarian, and cosmopolitan policies. (Contrast **right-wing** and **centrist**.)

legitimacy   The sense in a political community that political power is justly held and fairly administered. Legitimacy is necessary for transforming brute power into rightful authority.

Leninism   Lenin's interpretation of Marxism stressing **voluntarism**, **democratic centralism**, the party as **vanguard**, and the centrality of the **dictatorship of the proletariat**.

liberals   Those who support an individualist, rights-based, property-centered social structure. They range from **classical** to **welfare** liberals.

liberation theology   A movement, most developed in the third world, especially Latin America, that emphasizes Christianity's message of social justice. It ministers to the poor and in a variety of ways, including the overtly political, attempts to improve their lot.

libertarianism   Neo-classical liberals often refer to themselves by this name. It also is used by right-wing anarchists who believe that government per se is illegitimate.

Maoism   The revolutionary doctrine of Chinese Communism that stresses guerrilla warfare, the centrality of the peasantry in the revolutionary process, the importance of Chinese nationalism, and the priority of ideological commitment to technical expertise.

march on Rome   The theatrical demonstration of strength through which Mussolini came to power in October 1922. Threatened by the mass march, King Victor Emmanuel appointed Mussolini Prime Minister.

mass society   Post-traditional, industrial society tends to create a large, undifferentiated, and volatile mass of common people who are wooed by opportunistic politicians, advertisers, and demagogues. It often entails the absence of voluntary organizations that mediate between the state and the individual. (Compare with **civil society**.)

materialism   A philosophical position that holds material conditions to be pre-eminent. Marx, for example, believed that the development of our ideas reflects prior and more basic developments in our material conditions. (Contrast to **idealism**.)

means (or forces) of production   The actual physical means by which a society creates its sustenance. For some, sophisticated technology is central, for others, subsistence agriculture is dominant. In Marxist thought, those who own or control the means of productions are a society's ruling class. (Contrast with **relations of production**.)

melting pot   The long-prevalent idea that the successive waves of immigration to the United States were to be made over into a reasonably homogeneous American People. (Contrast with **multi-culturalism**.)

minimal state   A position supported by neo-classical liberals like Nozick. Any state action that goes beyond protection against violence by others and perhaps certain very limited administrative functions is illegitimate.

modernization   The process by which traditional cultures lose their ancestral beliefs, institutions, etc., and enter the modern world. It includes urbanization, industrialization, secularization, bureaucratization, the growth of nationalism, and mass society.

multi-culturalism   The conception of the United States as a mix of different ethnic, religious, and racial groups that ought to retain their cultural and even linguistic peculiarities rather than melt into a homogeneous American culture. (Contrast with the **melting pot**.)

nation building   The process by which national identity is created. Often refers to the transition within new nations in the third world from tribal clannish identities to national ones.

nation-state   The typical form of the modern state in which nations express their uniqueness through sovereign political institutions.

natural rights   Those rights that are inherent in the very idea of a human being. Natural rights are not granted by the state and, hence, they may not be violated by the state.

negative freedom   The view that liberty consists in being free from external constraints in the pursuit of one's objectives. (Contrast to **positive freedom**.)

New Deal   An economic program put into practice by President Franklin D. Roosevelt during the 1930s to deal with the devastation caused by the Depression. It created large public works projects to put the unemployed to work and relied heavily on **deficit spending**.

nihilism   Denying that there exists any real basis for what we consider knowledge, truth, and morality.

non-restrictive view of ideology   A view that holds all political positions to be ideological in character. (Opposed to the **restrictive view**.)

operational codes   The translation, by political leaders, of abstract ideological principles into practical standards for behavior and policy-making.

organicism (organic society)   The view that society is more than a sum of the individuals comprising it. Society has a moral standing and moral obligations of its own. Society is the whole of which the individuals are constituent parts. (Contrast with **instrumentalism**.)

original position   In Rawls's system, a kind of **state of nature** preceding the establishment of the state. From this position, individuals operating from behind a **veil of ignorance** would have to decide on the nature of the institutions and economic system they will adopt.

original sin   The view in Christian theology that Adam and Eve's violation of God's command not to eat from the Tree of Knowledge in the Garden of Eden has tainted all of humanity.

particular conception of ideology   In Mannheim's terminology, a view that unmasks the interests of ideological adversaries. It seeks to discredit a particular enemy. (Opposed to the **total conception of ideology**.)

patriarchy   Systematic male domination of women, which feminists view as subtle and all-pervasive.

pluralism   That form of political organization—normally associated with liberal democracies— which believes that a multiplicity of ideologies, ethnic groups, religions, etc., within a state is beneficial to its health and democratic character.

political correctness   Refers to a contemporary vocabulary of political discourse that is acutely sensitive to minority concerns, homosexuals, women, etc. Often said by its detractors to be coercive, conformist, and caricatured.

positive freedom   The view that liberty involves being true to one's higher self, i.e., acting so as to realize one's truly human capacities. (Contrast to **negative freedom**.)

prejudice   In Burke's teachings, those judgments and evaluations that derive naturally from a rich and dynamic tradition of political life. Opposed to theory and reason.

pre-modern ideology   The form of political discourse characterizing the traditional societies that existed until about the middle of the eighteenth century. It was based on a single mandatory world-view. (See **traditional societies**.)

prescription   In Burke's teachings, the compelling weight of historical precedent and tradition.

proletariat   The working class, which has nothing to sell but its labor. In Marx's view, it embodies the true aspirations of human liberation.

racism   The belief in the superiority and inferiority of different races, often entailing differential treatment for higher and lower racial groups.

radicals   Those for whom the present reality is so defective as to requires a major and rapid overhaul.

reactionary   A political position that rejects the form that modern history has taken and wishes to return to some idyllic past. Often associated with those who wish to revive the monarchical, clerical, traditional society of the Middle Ages.

relations of production   In Marxist thought, the human relations that underlie production, or the ways in which people organize in order to produce. In this category Marx places a society's typical divisions of labor, systems of authority, and patterns of ownership. (Contrast with **means of production.**)

relativism   The view that judgments in regard to knowledge and morality inevitably reflect different human and historical contexts. Radical relativists believe that there are no universal criteria by which to judge ideas or ethics.

restrictive view of ideology   A view that derogatorily describes only some political positions as ideological. (Opposed to the **non-restrictive view.**)

right-wing   Those who tend to favor conservative, property-based, nationalist policies. They support slow change, stable authority, and traditional values.

Romantic reaction   A movement, opposed to **Enlightenment** rationalism, that emphasized the sentiments, passions, and enduring quality of tradition. It was often (although not always) **reactionary** in character.

self-determination   The doctrine that each nation has the right to an autonomous political authority by which to rule itself.

sexism   The belief that one sex is pre-ordained to dominate while the other must follow. Used most often in feminist discourse to describe male arrogance and repression of women.

sexual politics   The relations of power and domination that prevail between the sexes. They manifest themselves, feminists argue, in subtle but pervasive ways.

sisterhood   The feminist belief that solidarity between women is necessary in order to fight **patriarchy.**

social contract   An explanatory device utilized by thinkers like Hobbes, Locke, and Rousseau to explain the origins and nature of political authority. Individuals enter into an agreement or contract whose purpose is to create a state and determine its legitimate powers.

Social Darwinists   Employing Darwin's ideas on the survival of the fittest in natural evolution, these **classical liberals** of the late nineteenth and early twentieth century argued that government intervention on behalf of the weak would disturb the natural and desirable struggle for survival.

social democracy   The fusion of socialist and democratic commitments into a single doctrine. Social democrats argue that without this fusion, each element fails individually.

socialism   An economic system based on equality, government ownership and direction of heavy industry, and only limited private property.

socialism in one country   Stalin's doctrine that socialism could and ought to be consolidated in the Soviet Union before being exported to other countries.

sociology of knowledge   Mannheim's attempt at a science that would specify the relationship between the context of ideas and their character.

speciesism   The anthropocentric view that nature is to be aggressively mastered by humans. (Contrast with **animal liberation.**)

stagflation An economic situation in which inflation and stagnation co-exist. Keynesian economics seems unable to deal with this problem.

Stalinism The theory and practice of Soviet Communism as dictated by Stalin. It stresses **socialism in one country**, a **totalitarian** state, the destruction of all dissident activity, and the **cult of the personality**.

state apparatus Marx uses this term to refer to the physical force of the state embodied in the police, army, prison system, and bureaucracy.

state of nature The hypothetical period that precedes the state. From its character, thinkers like Hobbes, Locke, and Nozick derive the legitimate boundaries of state power.

superstructure Those cultural, religious, moral, legal, intellectual, political, and esthetic creations that derive from the basic material forces that prevail in a given society. (Contrast with **infrastructure**.)

total conception of ideology In Mannheim's terminology, a view that understands all ideas as normally and regularly shaped by the context in which they arise. (Opposed to the **particular conception of ideology**.)

totalitarianism A political system whose aim is to control all aspects of human life. It is usually marked by a single party, a secret police, a charismatic leader, and devotion to an all- encompassing, messianic ideology.

trade-union consciousness In Leninist doctrine, the proletariat, left to its own devices, will not truly perceive its revolutionary role. At best, it will be interested in trade-union issues such as the piecemeal improvement of its living and working conditions.

traditional societies Societies in which a single mandatory world-view and behavior pattern prevails. Alternative, competing position are not given serious consideration. (Contrast with **modernization**.)

united front A communist strategy of opposing the right wing by unifying under a single leadership all the progressive parties. The underlying objective is to vanquish the right and become the dominating force within the progressive coalition.

Utilitarianism An influential philosophical and political movement led by Jeremy Bentham and later by John Stuart Mill. It contended that the basic moral criterion for action ought to be whether it promotes the greatest good of the greatest number.

utopia An image of the perfect society without conflict, malice, greed, or crime. The term derives from the Greek for "no place." First used by Thomas More in the sixteenth century.

utopian socialists A group of early socialist thinkers —Fourier, Owen, and Saint-Simon—derided by Marx as being out of touch with the real economic realities of developing capitalism.

vanguard party For Lenin, the party was not the conduit through which mass interests or opinions were expressed. The party set the revolutionary agenda. It led the masses and educated them as to their true revolutionary role.

veil of ignorance Those in Rawls's **original position** will have to deliberate in complete ignorance of what their individual interests are.

volk A German term combining the sense of nation, folk unit, and blood community. It was often used by Nazis and their predecessors to indicate the essential bond of all Germans.

voluntarism A view, usually associated with Leninism, that revolutionaries can dictate the pace of political and social change even in advance of developing economic conditions. (Contrast with **determinism**.)

welfare liberalism The view that only by government intervening in the marketplace can the initial aims of liberalism —individual autonomy, liberty, human dignity — be preserved.

welfare state A state committed to providing its people with a wide range of social services — health care, unemployment insurance, social security, old age benefits.

withering of the state In Marxist doctrine, the coercive state will disappear after the advent of communism. The state, reflecting the dictatorship of one class over another, will no longer be necessary in an age of plenty and harmony.

I n d e x

Academia, challenge to, 239,
    263–68
Affirmative action, 98–99, 246
    definition of, 277
Airwaves, pluralism of, 274–75
Alienation, 129–31
    definition of, 277
Altruism, 101
    in libertarianism, 84
    in Rawlsian theory, 101
American Revolution, 35
Anarchism
    critique of regimentation,
        167–68
    critiques of, 172
    image of, 167
    and New Left, 170
    Tolstoyan spiritual, 168
    violent, 169
Anarcho-syndicalism, 169–70
Anarchy, State and Utopia (Robert
    Nozick), 82–87
Ancien regime, 32, 184
    definition of, 277
Animal liberation, 238
    definition of, 277
Anti-semitism, 185, 194–95
Aryan, versus Jew, in Naziism, 194
Association, forms of, 124
Augustine, St., 47
Authority, 8
Autonomy, in liberalism, 73

Bakunin, Mikhail, 169
Benevolence, in libertarianism, 84
Bentham, Jeremy, 67
Berlin, Sir Isaiah, 234
Bernstein, Eduard
    Evolutionary Socialism, 108–09
    versus Marx, 108

Bolsheviks(ism), 147
    Nazi view of, 194
Bourgeoisie, 131–32
    control of ideas by, 129
    definition of, 11, 277
    dictatorship of, 128–29
    fascist appeal to, 185–87
Bourgeois revolution(s), 146
    definition of, 277
    in Russia, 148–50
Burke, Edmund, 33–40
    critique of social metaphysics, 36
    critiques of, 38–40
    defense of tradition, 41
    versus Leo Strauss, 44
    *Reflections on the Revolution in
        France*, 34–37
    versus Voltaire and Rousseau, 33

Canon, 238–39, 263–64
    abolition of, 265–66
    critiques of, 264–65
    modification of, 265
        critiques of, 267–68
Capitalism, 63, 91, 108, 248
    alienation in, 130–31
    consequences of, 64–65
    contradictions of, 133–34
    crises of, 135–36
    definition of, 277
    dismantling, 136
    effects of, 130–31
    efficiency of, 63
    in fascism, 200
    fatal flaw of, 132
    and imperialism, 153
    Nazi view of, 197–98
    nineteenth-century, 118–20
    Rawlsian view of, 97–98
    revolutionary role of, 131–32

socialist feminist critique of,
    248
    virtues of, 63
Centralization, 115
Centrist
    definition of, 277
    origin of, 16
Charismatic leadership, 195
    definition of, 277
Charity, 90
Chiang Kai-shek, 162–63
China
    communism in, 162
        future of, 166–67
        victory of, 164
    nationalism in, rise of, 162
Chinese Revolution, 160–67
    history of, 160–64
    peasant base of, 163–64
Choice, consequences of, 6
Civil society
    centrality of, 271
    definition of, 190, 271, 277
    versus grand mobilizing ideolo-
        gies, 270–73
Class(es), 127–28
    definition of, 277
Classical liberalism, 59–64, 71, 92
    comeback of, 88
    contemporary, 78–88
    critiques of, 64–65, 88–95
    definition of, 277
    and democracy, 92–93
    versus Rawlsian liberalism, 104
    revision of, 64–73
Collectivism
    dangers of, 112
    flaws of, 85
Communications revolution,
    274-75

Communism, 106
  Chinese. *See* China, communism in
  collapse of, 270, 272-73
  dawn of, 137
  definition of, 277
  fall of, 117–25, 159
    left-wing reactions to, 117–18
  future society of, 137–38
  ideology of, discrediting of, 117
  parallels to fascism, 201
  critiques of, 201
Community, 112, 232–33
Competition, 98
Confucianism, 160
Consciousness-raising, 249
Conservatism, 28–55
  American, as classical liberalism,
    57–58
  Augustinian, 47
  versus fascism, 180–81
  Freudian, 47–48
  Hobbesian, 47
  meaning of, contextual nature of,
    28
  origins of, 30–31
  pessimism of, 47–48
  themes of, 32–55
  and traditionalism, 29–33
  as universal reason, 40–41
Conservatives
  definition of, 277
  understanding of ideology, 10
Conviction, and ideology, 6–7
Cooperation, natural, 168
Coordination, versus political con-
    trol, 170
Corporatism
  definition of, 197, 278
  fascist, 197–200
  in practice, 198
Cosmopolitanism, 232-33
Counter-culture, 238
  definition of, 278
Counter-discourse, 4
Cult of personality, 158
  definition of, 278

de Beauvoir, Simone, *The Second
  Sex,* 241

Declaration of the Rights of Man,
    219
Deficit spending, 71–72
  definition of, 278
Deforestation, 255
Democracy, 92
  egalitarian, Plato's view of, 50
  fusion with socialism, 107
  and nationalism, 213–17, 220
  and solidarity, 92
Democratic centralism, 146
  definition of, 278
Deng Xiaping, 166
Determinism, definition of, 278
de Tracy, Antoine Destutt, 16–17
Deutsch, Karl, 7–8
Dewey, John, 65–66
Dialectic
  definition of, 278
  Hegelian, 123
Dictatorship of bourgeoisie,
    128–29
Dictatorship of proletariat, 136–37
  definition of, 278
  in Leninism, 155–56
Dictatorships, 128
  versus fascism, 183
Direct action, 53
  definition of, 278
Distribution, determining justice in,
    99–103
Diversity, 232

Earth-centered ethic, 258
Earth First!, 260
Eco-feminism, 261
Ecological consciousness, rise of,
    255–57
Ecological humility, 256
Ecological movement. *See* Environ-
    mentalism
Economies, successful, 94–95
Education, liberal, 263
Egalitarianism, in liberalism, 73–74
End of ideology, 23
  definition of, 278
End-state theories of justice, 85
  definition of, 278
  problems with, 86

Engels, Friedrich, T*he Origins of
  the Family, Private Property
  and the State,* 247
Engels, Friedrich and Karl Marx,
  Communist Manifesto, 145
Enlightenment
  definition of, 278
  ideas of, 32–33
  optimism of, 46–47
  Romantic reaction against, 33
Environmentalism, 238, 253–63
  critiques of, 262–63
  as ideology, 253-54
  moderate, 259
  radical, 259
  tactics of, 261
  vision of, 261–62
Equality, Rawlsian view of,
    99–101
Ethnic politics, 272
Ethno-centrism, 239
  definition of, 278
Evolutionary Socialism (Eduard
  Bernstein), 108–09

Fabian socialism, 107–08
  definition of, 278
False consciousness, 129, 140
  definition of, 18–19, 278
Fanaticism
  ideology as, 22–23
  and rationalism, 37
Fascism, 174–205
  appeals to middle-class, 186–88
  characteristics of, 180–81
  class-based theories of, 199–200
    critiques of, 200
  corporatism in, 197–98
  and crisis of middle class,
    185–88
  versus dictatorships, 183
  ethical idealism in, 188–89
  flash points for, 203–04
  focus on mythical past in, 184
  historical context of, 175
  incompatible traits of, 182
  liberal view of, 201–02
  Marxist view of, 199–200
  mass-based theories of, 201–02

critiques of, 202–03
and modernization, 201–02
national narcissism in, 191
parallels to communism, 201
  critiques of, 201
and racism, 192–95
as reactionary mass mobilizing
  movement, 183–84
reactions to, 180–81
rise of, parallels to rise of Naziism in Germany, 175–79
shock of, 180, 272–73
socialism in, 187
theories of, 199–203
totalitarianism in, 189–92
as widespread phenomenon, 181
Fascist man, new, 188
Female separatism, 250–51
Feminism, 238–53
  controversies within, 243–44
  history of, 239–42
  impact of, 253
  moderate/liberal, 244–47
    critiques of, 246–47
    program of, 245
  radical, 249–53
    critiques of, 252–53
  reform in, 246
  revolutionary challenge of,
    242–44
  socialist, 247–49
    critiques of, 249
  unique aspects of, 242–43
Feminine Mystique, The (Betty
  Friedan), 242
Fichte, Johann Gottlieb, 217–18
Final solution, 195
  definition of, 278
First principles, 3
  definition of, 278
Forces of production, 132–33. *See
  also* Means of production
Fourier, Charles, 120–21
Free competition, virtues of, 80–81
Freedom. *See also* Liberty; Nega-
  tive freedom; Positive freedom
  in Hegelian theory, 125
Free market, 78–81, 100
French Revolution

Burke's critique of, 34–35
democratic and nationalist themes
  in, 216
in development of ideology,
  15–16, 32
and modernity, 32
Freud, Sigmund, 47–48
Friedan, Betty, *The Feminine Mystique*, 242
Fuhrer principle, 180, 195–96
Fundamentalism, versus modernization, 273–74

Gaia, 259
General strike, 170
  definition of, 279
General will, 33, 61
  definition of, 279
Gentile, Giovanni, 189
Germany, rise of Naziism in,
  175–79
Global warming, 255–55
Glorious Revolution, 59
Good, in liberalism, 74–75
Government, positive, 68–69
Great chain of being, 2
  definition of, 279
Great Cultural Revolution, 165
  definition of, 279
Greenhouse effect, 254–55
Greenpeace, 261
Green politics. *See also* Environ-
  mentalism
  definition of, 279
  shades of, 258–61
Greens, 109
  definition of, 279
Groupthink, 53
Guerrilla warfare, 163–65
  definition of, 279
Gulag, 118
  definition of, 279

Hayek, Friedrich A., 77–82
  responses to, 78–79
  The Road to Serfdom, 77–82
Hegel, Georg Friedrich, 122–25
  influence on Marx, 126–27
Hierarchy, 31

necessity of, 50–55
Himmler, Heinrich, 193.
History, Hegel's philosophy of,
  122–23
Hitler, Adolf, 179–80, 195–96
Hobbes, Thomas, 31, 47
  Leviathan, 13
Homophobia, 265
  definition of, 279
Homosexuals
  in canon, 265
  Nazi treatment of, 194
Human imperfectability, 46–50, 141
  critiques of, 49–50
Humanism, 258
  anthropocentric, 257–58. *See also*
    Speciesism
  definition of, 279
Humankind, wisdom of, 36
Human limitations, 31

Idealism, 124
  definition of, 279
Ideological discourse
  levels of, 12
  nature of, 1–26
Ideological positions, coherence of,
  16
Ideology
  certainty in, 13–14
  conservative understanding of, 10
  contemporary balance sheet of,
    271–73
  and conviction, 6–7
  definitions of, 9–15
    ideological nature of, 11–12
  development of, and Marxism,
    17–19
  end of. *See* End of ideology
  erosion of, 108
  as false consciousness, 19
  as fanaticism, 22–23
  functions of, 24–25
  in global village, 274–75
  history of, 15–26
  individual interests in, 18–19
  justification of, 6–7
  liberal understanding of, 10–11
  Marxist understanding of, 11, 17

Ideology (*continued*)
  negative connotations of, 10, 17
  non-restrictive view of. *See*
      Non-restrictive view of
      ideology
  origin of, 17
  paradox of, 276
  particular conception of. *See* Particular conception of ideology
  versus political theory, 13–14
  and power, 6–9
  pre-modern. *See* Pre-modern ideology
  radical understanding of, 11
  and relativism, 275–76
  restrictive view of. *See* Restrictive view of ideology
  total conception of. *See* Total conception of ideology
  as true knowledge, 17
Ideology and Utopia (Karl
    Mannheim), 19–21
Imperialism
  capitalist, 153
  definition of, 279
Incentives for excellence, in Rawlsian theory, 98
Individual interests
  in capitalism, 62
  in ideology, 18–19
Individualism, 57, 64, 111
  definition of, 279
  fascist critique of, 189
  radical, flaws of, 88–90
  in Rawlsian theory, 103–04
  redefinition of, 69
  Smith's view of, 64
  in welfare liberalism, 65–67
Individuals
  versus bureaucrats, 78–79
  separateness of, 83–84
Industrial Revolution, 119
Industry, worker control of, 170
Inequality(ies), 99–100
  economic, 91–92
Infrastructure, 128
  definition of, 279
Instrumentalism, 74–75
  definition of, 279

Intellectuals, in ideological discourse, 21–22
Interdependency, 257
Internationalism, 232–33
Invisible hand, 63
  definition of, 279
Irrationalism, 180
  definition of, 279
Italy, rise of Fascism in, 175–79

Jews
  versus Aryans, in fascism, 194
  Nazi treatment of, 194–95
Justice
  in distribution, determining, 99–106
  end-state theories of, 85
    definition of, 278
    problems with, 86
  Theory of Justice, A (John Rawls), 95–96
Justification, of ideology, 6–7

Kant, Immanuel, 213–14
Kerensky, Alexander, 154
Keynes, John Maynard, 71
Keynesian economics, 71–72
  definition of, 280
Kibbutz, 110
  definition of, 280
Knowledge, power and, 264–65
Kropotkin, Peter, 168
Kuomintang, 160–63

Labor unions, 190, 198
Laissez faire, definition of, 280
Laissez faire capitalism, 107
Laissez faire economics, 91–93
Learned ignoramuses, 52–53
Left-right continuum, 16, 273–74
Left-wing
  definition of, 280
  origin of, 15–16
Legitimacy, 8
  definition of, 280
Lenin, Vladimir Ilyich Ulyanov, 145–54
  versus Marx, 148

and origins of Russian Marxism, 145–49
Leninism
  definition of, 280
  and Marxism, 155–56
  versus Stalinism, 156
Leviathan (Thomas Hobbes), 13
Liberal education, 263
Liberalism, 57–116. *See also* Classical liberalism; Welfare liberalism
  American versus European, 58–59
  contemporary, 76–87
  critique of fascism, 180
  early, program of, 59
  egalitarianism in, 73–74
  history of, 59–64
  modern, 57–59
  pre-Rawlsian, 95
  themes of, 73–76
  varieties of, 72–73
Liberals
  definition of, 280
  understanding of ideology, 10–11
Liberation, dialectics of, 134–36
Liberation theology, 238
  definition of, 280
Libertarianism, 83
  definition of, 280
Liberty. *See also* Freedom
  and free market, 81
  Nozick's defense of, 83
  two senses of, 58
  in Utilitarianism, 69–70
Locke, John, 59, 60–62
  Second Treatise on Civil Government, 60–62

MacDonald, Ramsay, 113
Mannheim, Karl, *Ideology and Utopia*, 19–21
Maoism, 162
  definition of, 280
Mao Zedong, 161–66
  as military tactician, 163–65
March on Rome, 175
  definition of, 280
Marriage, radical feminist view of, 251–52

Marx, Karl, 111, 125–43
  Hegelian influence on, 126–27
Marx, Karl and Friedrich Engels,
    Communist Manifesto, 145
Marxism
  adaptation to Russian conditions,
    156
  Bernstein's view of, 108–09
  critique of fascism, 182
  critiques of, 139–43
  in development of ideology,
    17–19
  after fall of communism, 117
  and Leninism, 155–56
  Mao's view of, 162
  Nazi view of, 196
  view of ideology of, 11
  view of nature of, 256–57
Masses
  character of, 51
  versus elite, 50
  guidance by communist leader-
    ship, 148–49
  and nationalism, 210–11
  Strauss's view of, 42
Mass man, 51–52
Mass-mobilizing ideologies, decline
    of, 270–71
Mass society, 51–52
  definition of, 280
  modern, and relativism, 43
Materialism. *See also* Post-material-
    ism
  definition of, 280
  Marxist, 127–28
Mazzini, Giuseppe, 226
Means of production, 127
  definition of, 280
Medieval thought, 1–3, 40
Melting pot
  definition of, 280
  versus multi-culturalism,
    228–29
Mensheviks, 145–46
Middle-class. *See also* Bourgeoisie
  fascist appeal to, 185–87
Mill, James, 67
Mill, John Stuart, 59, 67, 107, 216
  On Liberty, 69–70

Minimal state, 83
  definition of, 280
Mirabeau, Honoré-Gabriel Riqueti,
    Comte de, 8
Modern ideology, 1–9
  clash of world-views in, 3
  and conventionality of social
    arrangements, 4
  origins of, 15–16
Modernity, French Revolution and,
    32
Modernization
  definition of, 280
  in fascism, 201–02
  versus fundamentalism, 273–74
  and nationalism, 213–14
More, Thomas, *Utopia*, 120
Mosley, Oswald, 182
Multi-culturalism
  definition of, 281
  versus melting pot, 228–29
Mussolini, Benito, 175, 180,
    188–90, 195–98

Nation(s)
  as building blocks of humanity,
    217–18
  constitution of, 221–30
    criteria for, 221–22
  fascist view of, 191
  formation of individuals in, 218
  as inventions, 224–25
  as organic entities, 219
  as source of nationalism,
    223–26
National identity, creation of,
    224–25
Nationalism, 206–36
  African, 223–24
  as collective egoism, 219–21
  conditions for, 212
  critiques of, 230–32
  defense of, 232–33
  and democracy, 213–17, 220
  as ideology, 206–10
  modern, as historical novelty,
    210–11
  and nations, 223–25
  particularity of, 209

  pathological, 233–34
  persistence of, 206, 229
  pre-nationalist era, 211–12
  and self-government, 214–15
  unarguability of, 209
  versus world-view ideologies,
    207–10
Nationalist consciousness, dawning
    of, 212–13
Nationalization, 113–14
  and activation of masses,
    214–17
  definition of, 113
National narcissism, in fascism, 191
National Organization for Women,
    244–45
National will, 216–17
Nation building, 223
  definition of, 281
Nation-state, 191
  definition of, 217, 281
  effects of pluralism on, 226–28
Natural rights, 73
  definition of, 281
Nature
  end of, 256
  ideological approaches to,
    256–57
Naziism
  characteristics of, 180–81
  Freudian view of, 48
  racism in, 193
  rise of, parallels to rise of Fas-
    cism in Italy, 175–79
Negative freedom, 59
  definition of, 281
  in liberalism, 75–76
NEP. *See* New Economic Policy
New Deal, 71
  definition of, 281
New Economic Policy, 154–55
New Left, 170–71
  anarchism and, 171
Nihilism, 42, 239
  in canon-revision, 271
  definition of, 281
  and relativism, 43–44
Nonrestrictive view of ideology,
    23–26

definition of, 281
Nozick, Robert, *Anarchy, State and Utopia*, 82–87
Nuremburg Laws, 197

October Revolution. *See* Russian Revolution
On Liberty (John Stuart Mill), 69–70
Operational codes, 12
  definition of, 281
Order, unplanned
  versus design, 77–78
  and prices, 79–80
Organicism, definition of, 281
Organic society, 114, 191
  definition of, 281
Original position, 96–97, 103
  definition of, 281
Original sin, 31
  definition of, 281
Origins of the Family, Private Property and the State, The (Friedrich Engels), 247
Ortega y Gasset, José, 50–55
  critique of, 54–55
  The Revolt of the Masses, 50–51, 55
  view of fascism, 202
Owen, Robert, 121
Ozone layer, depletion of, 255

Particular conception of ideology, 20
  definition of, 281
Patriarchy, 242, 250
  definition of, 281
People, constitution of, 215–16
Permeation, 107–08
Perspective
  generic human, 97
  of least favored, 99
Piecemeal reform, in liberalism, 76
Planetary crisis, 254–55
Planning
  coercion and conflict in, 80
  consequences of, 77–79
Plato, *The Republic,* 13, 50
Plekhanov, George, 145

Pluralism, 57
  of airwaves, 275
  definition of, 281
  effects on nation-state, 226–28
  in liberalism, 75
Political correctness, 238–39, 266–67
  definition of, 282
Political theory(ies)
  versus ideology, 13–14
  limitations of, 35
Political traditions, variety of, 40
Positive freedom, 75
  definition of, 282
Post-materialism, 274
Poverty, 90
  effects on democracy, 112
Power, 7–8
  and ideology, 7–9
  and knowledge, 264–65
  monetary analogy for, 6–7
Pragmatism, in liberalism, 76
Precedent, 31
Prejudice, definition of, 37, 282
Pre-modern ideology, 3, 31
  definition of, 282
Prescription, 31, 37
  definition of, 282
  versus rationalism, 37
Prices, 79–80
  and unplanned order, 79–80
Production. *See* Forces of production; Means of production; Relations of production
Products of work, alienation from, 130
Profit motive, failure of, 93–94
Proletariat, 129, 141
  definition of, 282
  dictatorship of. *See* Dictatorship of proletariat
  as universal, 133
  victory by, 135–36
Property, as social product, 89–90
Property rights, 61
  and unpropertied, 66
  in welfare liberalism, 65–67
Proudhon, Pierre-Joseph, 89–90

Psycho-social forces, in fascism, 200

Racism, 39
  definition of, 282
  in fascism, 185–86, 193–95
  as ideology, 192–93
  modern, origins of, 192
  in Naziism, 193–94
Radicalism, discreditation of, 270
Radicals
  definition of, 282
  understanding of ideology, 11
Rationalism
  Burke's critique of, 36–37
  and fanaticism, 36–37
  versus prescription, 37
Rawls, John, 95–106, 111
  critiques of, 103–06
  A Theory of Justice, 95–96
  thought experiment, 96
Reactionary, 183
  definition of, 282
Reason
  Straussian, 42
  universal, 74
    conservatism as, 40–41
Redistribution, problems of, 84–85
Reflections on the Revolution in France (Edmund Burke), 34–37
Regimentation, 166
Relations of production, 132–33
  definition of, 282
Relativism, 42–43
  and contemporary ideology, 275–76
  definition of, 282
  Mannheim's struggle with, 21
  modern, effects of, 43
  and modern mass society, 43
  and nihilism, 43
Renan, Ernst, 224
Republic, The (Plato), 13, 50
Restrictive view of ideology, 22–23
  criticism of, 24
  definition of, 282
Revisionist liberalism. *See* Welfare liberalism

Revolt of the Masses, The (Ortega y Gasset), 50–52, 55
Revolutionary consciousness, 147
  emergence of, 135
Rewards, 98–99
Right, in liberalism, 73
Right-left continuum, 16, 273–74
Rights
  individual, 62
  to life and liberty, 60–61
  to property. *See* Property rights
Right-wing
  definition of, 282
  origin of, 16
Road to Serfdom, The (Friedrich A. Hayek), 77–82
Romantic reaction, 33
  definition of, 282
  view of nature, 256
Rome, march on, 175
  definition of, 280
Roosevelt, Franklin Delano, 71
Rousseau, Jean Jacques, 33, 36, 75, 215
  The Social Contract, 33
Russia
  communism in. See Communism
  post-Revolutionary, 154–59
  pre-Revolutionary, 144–54
Russian Civil War, 154
Russian Marxist party, founding of, 145–47
Russian Revolution, 154–59
  beginning of, 151–53

Saint Simon, Claude Henri de, 121–122
Second Sex, The (Simone de Beauvoir), 244
Second Treatise on Civil Government (John Locke), 60–62
Self-determination, 211, 213–214
  definition of, 282
Self-enslavement, 248–49
Sexism, 239, 242
  definition of, 282
  unlearning, 245
Sexual politics, 243

definition of, 282
Sisterhood, 238, 242
  definition of, 282
Sixties, legacy of, 237–39
Skepticism, in liberalism, 75
Slavery, 39
Smith, Adam, 62–64
  and individualism, 64
  The Wealth of Nations, 62–63
Social contract
  Burke's view of, 37–38
  definition of, 282
  Rousseau's view of, 33
Social Contract, The (Jean Jacques Rousseau), 33
Social Darwinists, 73
  definition of, 282
Social democracy, 106–115
  in America, 112–113
  contemporary, problems of, 113–15
  critiques of, 115
  definition of, 283
  varieties of, 109–10
  versus welfare liberalism, 111–13
Social democrats, 106–07
Social ecology, 260–61
Socialism, 106. *See also* Fabian socialism
  continental European, 108–10
  critique of, 81
  definition of, 283
  evolutionary, 109
  fusion with democracy, 107
  Hayek's view of, 81
  modern, origins of, 118–20
  in one country, 159
    definition of, 283
Social metaphysics, 36
Social relations, alienation from, 130
Social solidarity, 101
Sociology of knowledge, 19–22
  definition of, 283
Sorel, George, 170
Soviet Union. *See* Russia
Species, wisdom of, 35
Speciesism, 257

definition of, 283
Stagflation, 72
  definition of, 283
Stalin, Iosif Djugashvili, 157–59, 161
  as ideologue, 159
Stalinism, 156–59
  definition of, 283
  versus Leninism, 156
State
  denationalized, challenges to, 229–30
  fascist view of, 189–92
  minimal, 83
  moral status of, 124
  power of, limits of, 61
  role of, 61, 66
    liberal prescription for, 74
State apparatus, 128
  definition of, 283
State of nature, 60
  definition of, 283
Strauss, Leo, 40–46
  critiques of, 45–46
  versus Edmund Burke, 44–45
Sun Yat-sen, 160–61
Superstructure, 128
  definition of, 283
Surplus value, definition of, 134

Taxes, 83
Theory of Justice, A (John Rawls), 95–96
Tienanmen Square, 166
Tolerance, self-contradiction of, 44
Tolstoy, Leo, 168
Total conception of ideology, 20–21
  definition of, 283
Totalitarianism, 120, 186
  in communism, 203
  definition of, 286
  fascist, 192–194, 203
  Stalinist, 159–162
Toxic waste, 260
Trade-union consciousness, 147
  definition of, 283
Tradition(s)
  critique of, 41
  in ideological debate, 30

political, variety of, 40
revolt against, 32
Traditionalism
  and conservatism, 28–32
  themes of, 31
Traditional society(ies), 3
  definition of, 283
  in modern ideological debate, 30
  and pre-modern style, 30–31
  response to challenges, 30–31
Trotsky, Leon, 151–52, 154, 156–58
Truth, absolute, 31

United front, 161
  definition of, 283
University, politicizatio[n]
  See also Academia,
Utilitarianism, 67–69
  versus classical libera[l]
  definition of, 283
Utopia, 76
  definition of, 283
Utopian socialists(ism),

definition of, 283
legacy of, 122

Vanguard party, 147
  definition of, 283
  peasant, in Chinese Revolution, 162–63
Veil of ignorance, 96–97
  definition of, 283
Volk, definition of, 194, 283
Voltaire, 32
Voluntarism

consequences of, 72
definition of, 283
origin of, 64–65
practical program of, 71–73
in practice, 102–03
setbacks for, 104–06
versus social democracy, 111–13
theoretical basis for, 95–106
Welfare state, 110
  definition of, 283
Westernization, 235
[Wi]lson, Woodrow, 211
[wit]hering of the state, 137
[d]efinition of, 283
[Wo]men. *See also* Feminism
[in] canon, 265
[c]apitalist exploitation of, 248
[N]azi treatment of, 194
[ro]le of, transformation of, 240
[wor]k, alienation from, 129–30
[wor]ld, alienation from, 129–30

[Xen]ophobia, 204
fascism, 185–86

DATE DUE

HIGHSMITH #45230

Printed
in USA